THE USES OF POWER

7 Cases in American Politics

EDITED BY

ALAN F. WESTIN

THE USES OF POWER

7 Cases in
American Politics

Harcourt, Brace
& World, Inc.

NEW YORK
BURLINGAME

HUGH DOUGLAS PRICE
COLUMBIA UNIVERSITY

LOUIS W. KOENIG
NEW YORK UNIVERSITY

ALAN F. WESTIN
COLUMBIA UNIVERSITY

VICTOR G. ROSENBLUM
NORTHWESTERN UNIVERSITY

ALLAN P. SINDLER
DUKE UNIVERSITY

JOHN P. MALLAN
SMITH COLLEGE

& GEORGE BLACKWOOD
BOSTON UNIVERSITY

ANDREW HACKER
CORNELL UNIVERSITY

PRINTED IN THE UNITED STATES OF AMERICA

Library of Congress Catalog Card Number: 61–17826

CONTENTS

Viewing American Government by Case Studies

THESE seven cases are about the power to govern in America—who has it, who can veto it, who uses it, and what happens when the powerful collide with each other. In place of traditional exposition and descriptive analysis, we have chosen to paint a broad landscape of American politics through a series of narratives that tries to capture the perspective, the emotional involvement, and the rhythms of American politics.

To begin with, we have concentrated on the seven major seats of power in the American political system—Congress, the Presidency, state and federal courts, regulatory agencies, political parties, local and state government, and private interest groups.

We have examined these centers of power with the assumption that most of our readers have some basic knowledge about American government. We have tried, therefore, to keep these cases informal in tone and colorful in detail. To emphasize the central issues of American government today, we have picked cases involving such aspects of our government as federal grants-in-aid, foreign economic assistance, judicial review of police practices, federal regulation of industry, struggles for party control, state taxing and spending policies, and lobbying by economic groups. No seven cases, of course, can fully capture the broad spectrum of problems facing American society in these complicated times. The seven glimpses of American politics presented here, however, nicely illustrate the central problems that mark our society.

Each case considers some conflict of the past decade—some conflict representative of issues that remain vital and alive today. Sometimes with microscope and sometimes with telescope, we have examined the uses of power in politics: the congressional response to President John Kennedy's aid-to-education bills in 1961; President Harry Truman's management of foreign aid to Spain and Yugoslavia in 1950; recent state court and Supreme Court responses to police search-and-seizure methods; the "loyalty fight" over ideology and party primacy between Southerners and non-Southerners in the Democratic Party; the Federal Communications Commission's ruling on Channel 10 in Miami, Florida, and the uproar that followed it in the 1950's; Massachusetts Governor Foster Furcolo's campaign for a sales tax to finance state social welfare programs and his resulting defeat at the polls in 1960; and the lobbying contest between the railroads and the trucking industry that came to a head in the setting of truck weights on Pennsylvania highways between 1949 and 1952.

These cases offer evidence of our belief that comprehensive and documentary accounts of concrete struggles for political power can provide the best testing ground for theories about what our governmental system really is and how it functions.

Finally, we have focused not merely on institutions but on men—the men who use power, those who pursue it, and those who seek to referee the power struggles: Presidents, influence peddlers, governors, Chamber of Commerce leaders, congressmen, judges, party convention delegates, labor union officials, church and school spokesmen, police chiefs, regulatory agency commissioners, public relations men, state legislators, and Cabinet members. Here, then, is the infinitely varied, multidimensional corps that makes up the American political Establishment. Here, in brief, are the purpose and ambition, talent and luck, courage and compromise, leadership and responsiveness, that inescapably make American politics a matter of one-nosed, two-eared human beings, not simply ideological clashes and public opinion polls.

If, in sum, we have suggested the fascination, the complexity, and the invigorating seriousness of American government and politics, we will have fulfilled our purpose.

ALAN F. WESTIN

1 THE CONGRESS

Race, Religion, and the Rules Committee:

The Kennedy Aid-to-Education Bills

Hugh Douglas Price

COLUMBIA UNIVERSITY

"The bill landed at noon on the Speaker's desk, and by 4 o'clock it was all mixed up in an argument, not only about education, but about integration, segregation, stabilization, inflation, taxation, and religious freedom."
—JAMES RESTON in the New York *Times*

"The New Frontier is having trouble with its first round-up."
—MINORITY LEADER CHARLES HALLECK

${A}$MERICANS over the age of ten widely regard education as "a good thing." Aside from its intangible values it increases the earning power of the individual, promotes the economic growth of the community, and strengthens the defense potential of the nation. In a democratic country a certain level of popular education is necessary. It is no surprise that American politicians are as agreed on the virtues of education as they are on those of motherhood.

The question of whether federal aid for schools is a "good thing" is, however, quite another matter. The Constitution makes no direct mention of education, and the traditional pattern has been one of local support and jealously guarded local control of public schools. Supporters of federal aid have sought to convince a majority of Congress, and of the public, that federal aid is necessary and that federal control can be avoided. This has not been easy, even with the assistance of the postwar baby boom, burgeoning enrollments, and Soviet sputniks.

Proponents of federal school aid have failed to create, especially in the House of Representatives, the sort of solid, committed majority that can carry a controversial bill to victory even in the face of determined and skillful opposition. Politics is not a matter of simple majorities and minorities. There are always many major issues at stake and it is often the *intensity* with which a particular view is held that may be of crucial importance. The really determined majority will usually carry the day over an equally determined minority. But the nominal majority—including many half-hearted supporters and wavering adherents—is much more vulnerable.

It was the weakness of the nominal majority (and not just the Senate filibuster) that for years was the stumbling block for civil rights legislation. During the 1950's this weakness was again one of the key problems facing supporters of federal aid to education. As one school-aid supporter put it in 1958 (in the *Education Digest*):

Every possible legislative maneuver has been used to strangle, emasculate, garotte, boobytrap, stab in the back, bleed to death, or blow to pieces Federal aid bills. They have been bludgeoned, trampled, gored, torn to shreds, and kissed to death. Both political parties have been guilty of this legislative mayhem and very often the *coup de grace* has been administered by the White House.

Such a tale of legislative woe is typical of the controversial measure supported by a nominal majority, but opposed by a determined minority. "Legislative mayhem" has not been the only difficulty faced by school-aid bills; often, the measures have been "politically accident-prone." Where a really cohesive majority exists, however, such misfortunes seldom occur.

Congress and the three "R's": Race, Religion, and the Rules Committee

The political graveyard of most school-aid bills has been the House of Representatives. Education bills calling for massive federal aid for construction and teacher salaries have regularly sailed through the Senate—even in the 80th Congress dominated by the late Senator Robert A. Taft (sponsor of one major school-aid measure). It is the House of Representatives that has repeatedly defeated or bottled-up even those bills limited to aid for classroom construction. The reasons for this are both political, in the broad sense, and parliamentary; both types of factors were in evidence in the 1961 school-aid fight.

In the 1960 Presidential campaign John F. Kennedy strongly endorsed federal aid for school construction and teacher salaries. In his bid to become the nation's first Catholic President he clearly emphasized his opposition to granting public funds for church schools. His subsequent school bill reflected this stand, and thus aroused sharp criticism from the hierarchy of the Roman Catholic church. The hierarchy's reaction served, in turn, especially in the House, to arouse bitter controversy over whether there should be a public school program without some form of assistance for the nonpublic schools, which enroll about 15 per cent of the nation's children. The opponents of any aid at all were able to capitalize on this schism in an effort to defeat all of the President's major education aid proposals.

Major proposals for substantial federal aid to public schools were seriously advanced by Senator Robert A. Taft (in 1947 and 1948), strongly backed by President Truman (in 1948 and 1949), and requested—somewhat reluctantly—by President Eisenhower (in 1955, 1956, and 1957). Finally, in 1960, both the Senate and the House passed school-aid bills, although in different form. The House Rules Committee, however, prevented the bill from going to a conference committee to adjust the differences, and the legislation died. Could President Kennedy and his new administration break the jinx? By September 1961 the new Administration's proposals for aid to public schools had joined the long list of previous legislative casualties. This was in sharp contrast to the President's record of legislative victories on other domestic legislation. This case study seeks to present "the reason why."

Emergence of an Issue: From Horace Mann to the New Frontier

To understand the controversy over federal aid to schools it is necessary to look briefly at the background of the controversy. What has been the pattern of American education and the source of the much debated "crisis" in education? It is dangerously easy to slip into a stereotyped view of American schools all being part of a single system, enjoying overwhelming public support, explicit constitutional endorsement, and extending back to George Washington and the other founding fathers. Such, of course, is not the case. Neither Washington nor any of the other signers of the Constitution attended public school for the very good reason that public schools did not exist at the time. Today about 15 per cent of the school-age population attend various nonpublic schools.

Universal education, like universal manhood suffrage, was largely a nineteenth century innovation—and it was hardly less controversial. In 1800 such schools as existed were usually private institutions operated by the dominant local religious group: Congregational in some areas, Episcopalian in others. But the demand for education grew rapidly, as did the number of religions. Free school societies were founded to provide for pauper children and others who could not afford private schools. In the era of Jacksonian democracy interest in free public elementary education became a major political issue, especially in the Northeast. Under the leadership of reformers such as Horace Mann (in Massachusetts), the common school ceased to be a second-class institution for "common" people and began to emerge as the school intended to be common to all the people.

With the continued proliferation of Protestant sects and the post-1840 influx of large numbers of Catholics, it became ever more difficult to provide nonsectarian religious teaching in the public schools. The most frequent compromise was to rely on Bible reading (King James Bible, both Old and New Testaments). This satisfied some, but by no means all of the Protestant groups. However, it made such schools unattractive for most Catholics, who regarded them as definitely sectarian. As a result the common schools came under fire for their "secularism," their "sectarianism," and their "Godless" teaching (this was in the 1850's, not just the 1950's). In New York, Catholic leaders unsuccessfully sought public funds for the operation of Catholic schools.

The Catholic church was not the only one interested in developing a parochial school system. For several decades some Presbyterians struggled to maintain such a system, but eventually gave it up. A more vigorous effort was made by the Evangelical Lutheran Church (the Missouri Synod), which continues to emphasize denominational schooling even today. Lutheran schools drew largely on the rural and small-town German-Lutheran population of the Midwest. More recently, orthodox Jewish communities have stressed the importance of separate day schools for Jewish children.

By 1860 public elementary education was widely available in New England—which continued to have a significant number of private schools—and in the Midwest. In the latter, public secondary schools and state universities also were emerging (the Northwest Ordinance of 1787 had required that certain lands be set aside for use of education). Except in North Carolina, there was little progress in the South.

In the period from 1870 to 1890 serious efforts were made in Congress to adopt some program of federal aid for the public schools. Senator Henry W. Blair of New Hampshire was the leader of this unsuccessful attempt. The measure was not popular in the South, which feared federal intervention, nor with many Catholics. The Catholic parochial school system continued to grow, with a great number of local variations. Catholic church leaders of the period held differing viewpoints as to the role of their church in America. The conservative view stressed the seeming hostility of some American institutions (such as the public schools), as well as the open hostility of such groups as the American Protective Association (a late nineteenth-century group strongly critical of Catholicism and of immigration). The more conservative Catholic bishops tended to regard parochial schools as an absolute necessity. The more liberal viewpoint drew a distinction between the American ethos and the anticlerical liberalism of Europe. Bishops holding this view were more interested in establishing a Catholic university, and indicated that the public schools were quite useful as far as they went. At the Third Plenary Council of the American hierarchy, in Baltimore in 1884, the bishops determined to make it obligatory for each Catholic parish to establish its own school and for each Catholic to send his children to a parochial school. This goal has never been completely met, but the proportion of elementary school children in nonpublic schools increased from 7.6 per cent in 1900 to 14.8 in 1959.

By the end of the nineteenth century there were two major and a number of lesser educational systems. The public school system accounted for over 90 per cent of all students, but it was divided in the South and border states into separate systems for white and Negro students (with the latter receiving very little attention until the 1940's). The public schools were financed by local school districts, with the trend in recent decades toward larger, consolidated districts and schools. There has also been a marked increase in reliance on state aid, with many states adopting "minimum foundation" programs to provide at least a specified minimum of funds per pupil. The pluralism of America is indicated in the resulting differences in state education programs. State aid accounts for almost 80 per cent of school expenditures in Delaware, but less than 5 per cent in Nebraska; expenditures per pupil vary from $726 annually in New York to $244 in Alabama; average classroom teacher salaries range from $3,415 in Mississippi to $6,700 in California; pupil/teacher ratios vary from 18.1 students per teacher in South Dakota to 33.7 in Mississippi. The percentage of adults unable to read or write varied in 1950 from less than 1 per cent in Iowa to almost 10 per cent in Louisiana.

The Catholic parochial system constituted the second major system. The percentage of nonpublic school enrollment (mostly Catholic) today ranges from less than 1 per cent in North and South Carolina to 27.5 per cent in Rhode Island (and is also over 20 per cent in New York, Pennsylvania, Massachusetts, New Jersey, Illinois, Wisconsin, and New Hampshire—a key bloc of states). Each Catholic parish generally raises its own school funds by regular Sunday offerings, tuition charges, or supplementary activities. (Such offerings may be deducted from gross income for tax purposes, but tuition charges may not.) In recent years many dioceses have developed central funds for financing new classroom construction. The bishop usually delegates supervision of the parochial schools in his diocese to a specially trained school superintendent. The parents' right to send their children to parochial or other nonpublic school was upheld by the Supreme Court in two cases decided in 1925. Such nonpublic schools are, however, subject to state standards in regard to compulsory attendance, number of days annual instruction, requirements for graduation, and other administrative details.

As a result of this particular pattern of historic development it is by no means easy to draft a politically acceptable school-aid bill. On the one hand such a bill must not seem to threaten the continued operation of substantially segregated public schools in the South, but neither can it endorse the existing system. On the other hand a successful school-aid bill must not seem to threaten the continued vitality of Catholic parochial schools, but neither can it treat them on the same basis as the public schools. In domestic politics just as in international politics many issues are "negotiable," although some are not. For the current generation of congressmen, segregation and parochial schools are politically nonnegotiable. A bill that becomes substantially entangled in either of these two high-tension issues will find itself short-circuited.

Issues and Interest Groups: Pro and Con of Federal Aid / Serious congressional interest in the possible need for federal aid developed during World War II. The Depression had slowed the rate of classroom construction in much of the country, and with the war, construction came to a near halt. Teacher salaries had held up relatively well during the Depression, but the combined effect of the draft, wartime full employment, and inflation sharply reduced the number of available teachers and the financial attractiveness of teaching as a career. All of this might have had only a limited effect but for one crucial factor: the baby boom.

The war years saw a dramatic reversal of the previously declining American birth rate. The baby boom of the early 1940's has continued throughout the postwar period. This development was of interest not only to demographers but to educators. There is a vast difference between operating an existing school system with a relatively stable population and providing vastly expanded facilities for rapidly growing enrollments. Because there is a five- or six-year "lead time" from birth to enrollment, local school districts were on notice that difficult times lay ahead. Public school enrollments shot up from 23.3 million in 1945–46 to 33.5 million by 1957–58. For the decade of the 1950's, enrollments increased about 11 million, and a further rise of over 8 million is projected for the 1960's. Can local governments, even with state aid, be counted on to handle the job?

At this point analysis becomes more controversial. Enrollment figures are accepted by everyone, but figures on the "classroom shortage" are debatable. Precisely because of the strong tradition of local control there are no uniform national standards even for settling basic factual questions such as this. Hence it may be useful to summarize—briefly—the arguments and some of the figures advanced by supporters and by opponents of federal aid. Then we shall look at the organizations most directly involved in the struggle, and at the pattern of congressional response up through 1960.

The case *for* federal aid rests on the following:

First, there is an "education crisis." This crisis is evidenced both by the sheer quantitative shortage of classrooms and by the low quality of much teaching. There is serious overcrowding, reliance on double shifts, and continued use of obsolete facilities. In most states teacher salaries are so inadequate that the profession fails to attract, and keep, enough first-rate men and women.

Second, local school districts, and most state governments, have been strained to the very limit already. In raising money for education and other local services they have had to rely largely on antiquated nineteenth-century taxes, especially the property tax, to try to meet twentieth-century problems. These taxes are relatively inefficient as fund raisers, are politically sensitive to an extreme degree, and are often regressive or otherwise inequitable. The federal government, by contrast, has in the income tax an unmatched source of revenue that is both efficient and equitable. The money may indeed all come from the same pockets, but federal funds come more easily.

Third, federal aid is desirable because there is now a clear national responsibility for education. Given the high internal mobility of our population and the importance of sound education for science and defense, the state of our schools is no longer a matter of mere local concern. Many low-income states are making a greater relative effort than some of the high-income states; if these efforts are still insufficient there should be some equalization through the medium of federal grants-in-aid.

Fourth, federal aid does not mean "federal control" of local schools by Potomac bureaucrats. National assistance for education (in the form of land grants) dates back to the Northwest Ordinances of 1785 and 1787. Federal aid for land-grant colleges dates back to 1862, for vocational education to 1917, for the school lunch program to 1945, for assisting federally "impacted areas" to 1950 (and before), for loans to construct college dormitories to 1950, and for the popular GI Bill of Rights to the end of World War II. Most of these programs have involved certain minimum standards and administrative procedures for obtaining aid, but there have been no real complaints of federal interference with curriculum or teachers. (Local administrators do complain often, but almost invariably about the degree of *state* control and supervision, which they erroneously identify with *federal* control.) Actually, then, "federal control" is a bogeyman invented by fiscal conservatives who oppose government spending in general.

The case *against* federal aid, aside from the problems of the South and of parochial schools, has been made with equal vigor.

First, the "education crisis" has been vastly overrated. Enormous progress has been made—the "classroom shortage" has been reduced from 340,000 in 1954 to 142,000 in 1960–61. Almost half the public school students are now attending schools constructed since the end of the war. Meanwhile, teacher salaries have been going up at the rate of about $250 per year.

Second, federal aid would, in the end, mean substantial federal control. This might begin with testing and guidance programs, but would eventually affect teacher certification and curriculum content. He who pays the piper always helps call the tune. State education officials would be reduced to the dependent status of state highway officials (most of whose funds now come from Washington).

Third, expectations of possible federal aid have a stultifying effect on state and local governments. These bodies tend to postpone bond issues and other expenditures in the hope of federal assistance in the near future. Thus expectations of federal aid are, to some extent, creating an artificial crisis.

Fourth, the federal government's fiscal situation is infinitely worse than that of any state or school district. Federal tax rates are already prohibitively high, but the costs of necessary defense and foreign aid force the government to ever greater expenditures. Even if a federal aid program were begun as a temporary measure, pressures would develop to expand it and to make it permanent. Senator Barry Goldwater and other opponents have repeatedly cited the old proverb: "If the camel once gets his nose in the tent, his body will soon follow."

The drive for federal aid has been sparked by the National Education Association, and assisted by a wide variety of other groups. The NEA, with a membership of around 700,000 teachers, has a particular concern for improved teacher salaries. The NEA itself is a rather loose collection of related agencies and commissions representing not only classroom teachers but also school administrators. It is organized on a "federal" basis, with some state branches concentrating largely on state and local activity, and others giving more support to the national level. Its political "muscle" is thus both limited in extent and diffused. In most of the big cities teachers are more likely to belong to the American Federation of Teachers, an affiliate of the AFL-CIO. Further, there is a separate National Catholic Education Association, as well as a major separate teachers' organization in California. In general, the NEA receives strongest state support from the mountain states of the West and from certain southern states. Since teaching is largely a woman's profession, and often a short-term one for the young single woman, it does not furnish the ideal basis for a powerful national professional organization (such as the American Medical Association or American Bar Association).

Other major groups supporting federal aid have included: the AFL-CIO and its American Federation of Teachers, Americans for Democratic Action, National Congress of Parent-Teachers Association, American Association of University Women, Council of Chief State School Officers, American Association of University Professors, American Parents' Committee, United Mine Workers, and National Farmers' Union. The National Association for the Advancement of Colored People has supported federal aid provided that it goes only to nonsegregated schools.

Opposition to federal aid has been a special concern of the United States Chamber of Commerce. The Chamber has vigorously opposed school-aid bills in testimony before Congress, and has helped to organize effective state and local opposition. Like the NEA the Chamber devotes considerable time, money, and staff to preparing research material on education, distributing such materials as well as its regular publications, and "briefing" witnesses who will testify before congressional committees.

Other major groups opposing federal aid have included: the National Association of Manufacturers, Council of State Chambers of Commerce, the Farm Bureau, American Legion, Daughters of the American Revolution, Investment Bankers Association of America, and the Southern States Industrial Council.

During the 1950's the National Catholic Welfare Conference affirmed its "traditional opposition to outright continuing Federal support for education" and to "the use of Federal funds for teachers' salaries." In the 1959 Senate hearings the Conference also emphasized that if there were to be federal assistance it "should be granted on a temporary basis for specific purposes and to areas of proven need." It also urged that the claim of nonpublic schools "to that measure of justice permitted by law and suggested by legislative precedent" be recognized.

The groups that can most effectively generate substantial local pressure for federal aid are the local school boards. From time to time individual boards have submitted resolutions for or against aid, but there has been no substantial attempt to develop a national policy. The National School Boards Association is a very loose confederation of state associations, but only in 1961 did it vote to become an "action" group and take national policy stands. The group then expressed opposition to federal aid "until the school boards of America express the need for such funds." Members of school boards are, it should be noted, usually businessmen, lawyers, or— in rural and small-town areas—farmers. Individually they are much more likely to sympathize with the Chamber of Commerce than with the NEA.

Congressional Response: Three Near Misses /   Since World War II there have been three brief periods in which it appeared likely that Congress would pass some form of major aid to education. The first came in 1948–49 when the Senate twice passed substantial school-aid bills. Senator Taft was one of the cosponsors. He successfully opposed amendments that touched on segregation or use of funds for auxiliary services (such as bus transportation) by parochial schools, arguing that such matters should be left up to the states. In 1948, however, the conservative-dominated House Committee on Education and Labor refused to report the measure out.

In 1949, a similar bill was passed by the Senate, but ran into new complications in the House. Congressman Graham Barden (of North Carolina) sought to bar any federal aid funds from going to nonpublic schools, even for auxiliary services. This drew a sharp reaction from Catholic leaders. Francis Cardinal Spellman denounced it as "discrimination [as] shocking as it is incomprehensible." The week after the Cardinal's speech, Mrs. Eleanor Roosevelt commented on the subject in her syndicated newspaper column. Mrs. Roosevelt did not concentrate her critical comments on the constitutional distinctions involved (that benefits go to the child, not to the parochial school as such) nor in the details of Barden's legislative maneuvers. She indicated her support for separation of church and state, and opposition to granting tax funds to parochial schools. Although this was not quite the issue, her stand served to set off an even bigger explosion.

Cardinal Spellman released to the press a letter strongly criticizing Mrs. Roosevelt, concluding that her record of "anti-Catholicism" and support for "discrimination" was "unworthy of an American mother." She responded, and recriminations overflowed into press and editorial stands. The school bill then bogged down in what many members of Congress regard as one of the ugliest and most bitter disputes to hit Capitol Hill in this century. Eventually, in 1950, the House committee voted 13 to 12 against reporting out the Senate bill. The committee majority included two promising young congressmen: John F. Kennedy and Richard M. Nixon.

From 1950 to 1953, congressional attention and national resources were concentrated on the Korean War. The Eisenhower Administration regarded education as one of many subjects to be studied and analyzed by various conferences and commissions. Then the Supreme Court's 1954 desegregation decision raised a major new complication. In 1955, Eisenhower submitted to Congress a very modest education proposal, developed by his Secretary of Health, Education and Welfare, Mrs. Oveta Culp Hobby (known among some Democrats as "Secretary of not-too-much Health, Education and Welfare"). It called for providing federal loans, plus some limited grants, to the states for school construction. The bill was denounced by Senator Robert S. Kerr (Democrat of Oklahoma) as "conceived by investment bankers and dedicated to the money lenders." The NEA complained that it was time for "fact-facing instead of fact-finding." In July 1956, a more generous Democratic-sponsored bill was defeated in the House, where a sizable block of Republicans voted to add the "Powell" antisegregation amendment and then against passage of the measure.

The second "near miss" on school aid came in 1957. The previous year the President had endorsed a more ambitious program calling for substantial federal grants for construction of classrooms, and he repeated the request early in 1957. Pro-aid Democrats had favored an even more sweeping measure, but finally worked out a compromise. This bill was narrowly defeated, due in part to lack of executive support (the President having become more alarmed over the galloping budget) and in part to timely floor action by Virginia Congressman Howard W. Smith, chairman of the Rules Committee and one of the most astute parliamentarians in the House.

The President was first reported to have "approved" the compromise, but in a letter to Republican Congressman Peter Frelinghuysen, he said he declined "to pass judgment on all the details." HEW Secretary Marion Folsom subsequently said there was "no question" that Eisenhower favored the bill and would sign it. House Republican leader Joe Martin, however, indicated that the President "was not entirely satisfied." Press Secretary James Hagerty—serving as a sort of Delphic oracle—held that both Folsom and Martin were correct, but that the President would accept the bill. After a confusing House floor battle, pro-aid Democrats sensed that the only way to pass a bill would be to support a substitute measured based on the exact provisions of Eisenhower's bill of the previous year. The way thus seemed open for a coalition that could pass the bill. As Congressman Stewart Udall put it:

> Finally, after ten years thrashing around on this thing we have reached an agreement on Ayres' amendment. We on this side have decided to go all the way with the President, cross every "t" and dot every "i" and go down the line with precisely what the President wants. We can join hands with you. . . . We can pass a school bill today.

To prevent any such thing from happening, Virginia's Howard W. Smith ("Judge" Smith to his colleagues) obtained the floor and moved to "strike the enacting clause" from the legislation under consideration. This motion would kill the bill, and take precedence over the vote on the proposed substitute. Judge Smith's motion passed, by the narrow margin of 208 to 203. At a subsequent press conference the President said that he was fed up with compromising on education bills and that the only measure he had "thoroughly" favored was the original Hobby proposal.

The sweeping gains made by the Democrats in the 1958 elections heightened the conflict between President and Congress. Those gains also illustrate the important difference between what British novelist C. P. Snow has termed "open politics" and "closed politics." Democratic gains in the House and Senate were in the arena of open politics, but were not necessarily reflected in the more crucial areas of party leadership and such inner circles as the House Rules Committee. For at the same time that the House and Senate membership in general was reflecting the liberal swing of 1958, there was a marked conservative shift in certain of these key arenas of closed politics.

There was to be new Republican leadership in both House and Senate. Senator William Knowland had returned to California to run—unsuccessfully—for governor. He was replaced by Senator Everett Dirksen of Illinois, former Senate Republican whip. In the House, Indiana Republican Charles Halleck had long been feuding with Joseph Martin, the long-standing Republican leader. Eisenhower, according to Sherman Adams (who should know), had found Martin's leadership "uninspired" and "lackadaisical." Hence there was no White House intervention to protect Martin when Halleck organized to overthrow him. For the President's new vigorous role of halting the spenders he needed a tough in-fighter who could rally the necessary "one-third plus one" to uphold a veto. Tough, gut-fighting Charles A. Halleck, whatever his other limitations, could perform this function with skill.

The change in House Republican leadership had major consequences for the political balance of the Rules Committee. Two of the four Republican members had been of moderate to liberal leanings. But both had moved on to other offices, Hugh Scott running successfully for the Senate in Pennsylvania and Henry Latham accepting a New York judgeship. Halleck moved to replace them with firm conservatives. This broke the old pattern whereby the Speaker and Richard Bolling, his key representative on Rules, could turn to Martin or one of the moderate Republicans to break a deadlock.

The Senate again passed a school-aid bill, but the Rules Committee held the gates tight against a companion House version. Finally a bill for construction only was reported out, and a drive to bring it to the floor via a petition to discharge was launched. Eventually one Republican member of Rules relented, and the measure was reported to the House by a 7 to 5 vote. The House, for the first time in history, passed the school-aid bill, even though the "Powell" amendment had been added to it. The bill could go to conference, however, only by unanimous consent in the House or if a resolution was adopted by the Rules Committee. This time Judge Smith and his cohort on Rules held firm. Thus the President was spared the necessity of signing a bill he opposed, or of vetoing it in an election year. Clearly, if Kennedy won the 1960 election, one of the first pieces of business would be deciding on a strategy to deal with the impasse in the House, and especially with the strategic Rules Committee.

The Speaker vs. Judge Smith: Expanding the Rules Committee

One of the most pressing problems facing the incoming Kennedy Administration was what to do about the conservative-dominated House Committee on Rules. In the preceding Congress courtly old Judge Smith and William Colmer (of Mississippi, the second-ranking Democrat) had repeatedly joined with the four Republican members (all staunch conservatives) to prevent, delay, or make difficult floor consideration of liberal legislation. The other six Democrats on the twelve-man committee (each of whom had gone on the committee with Speaker Sam Rayburn's approval) were powerless to vote special rules to bring controversial legislation to the floor. Before 1959 Speaker Rayburn had often been able to pry one vote from the Republican side, frequently with the cooperation of his long-time Republican counterpart, Joseph Martin. But after Charles Halleck deposed Martin and replaced the two moderate Republicans on the committee with conservatives this tactic was no longer possible. Unless something could be done to break this stranglehold, Kennedy's legislative program in general— and federal aid to education in particular—would probably never reach the House floor.

The question of what to do about the Rules Committee was largely up to Speaker Rayburn. For several years liberal Democrats in the House, many of them informally organized into the "Democratic Study Group," had been urging him to "do something" about the situation. The Speaker, however, had been unwilling to launch an all-out fight on the issue. After almost half a century of service in the House (Rayburn was elected in 1912) the Speaker had come to value compromise highly. But Rayburn was also a dyed-in-the-wool Democrat, with a strong feeling for party regularity and a deep sense of responsibility to cooperate with the President. The Rules Committee impasse was a threat both to the Democratic party and to the new President. A bare two weeks after the 1960 election, Republican leader Halleck announced that he intended to carry on business as usual with the conservative southern Democrats. By the end of November, Halleck was conferring with Smith and Colmer (pronounced "Calmer") on plans for the new session of Congress.

There were several courses of action open to the Speaker and his lieutenants. These included various moves to weaken the institutional power of the Rules Committee itself, or efforts to change the political balance of the committee without altering its power. Examples of the former strategy included adoption of the "21-day rule,"[1] reducing the number of names required for a discharge petition, or making the Speaker an ex officio member (who could break tie votes). Less drastic moves would modify the committee's own procedure (lessening the powers of the chairman), or deprive the committee of the jurisdiction to prevent House-passed bills from going to a House-Senate conference. The Speaker, however, had no real objections to a powerful Rules Committee—quite the reverse. The objection was to the control of its power by a coalition willing to flout the wishes of the President, the House majority leadership, and a majority of the total membership.

What the Speaker preferred, then, was both a powerful Rules Committee and a "responsible" majority. Even a one-man majority would suffice in facilitating the presentation of major Administration bills and in blocking consideration—as virtually everyone desired—of facetious bills or pressure-supported legislation (veterans' benefits or federal employee pay raises) that most members opposed but hated to have to take a stand on.

A working majority could be established in either of two ways. First, and most painless, the Rules Committee could be enlarged. Adding a single Democrat would upset the long-standing 2–1 ratio of majority to minority party. The ratio, however, could be maintained by expanding the committee from 12 to 15 (with 10 Democrats and 5 Republicans). Halleck could be expected to add another conservative, but Rayburn would be able to add two "dependable" Democrats. (In order to avoid upsetting existing balance in regard to civil rights legislation, one of the two would have to be

[1] The "21-day rule" had been tried in 1949–50. It permitted chairmen of standing committees to call up a bill if the Rules Committee delayed more than 21 days.

a southerner.) This would ordinarily leave an 8 to 7 majority willing to report "liberal" or other Administration-backed measures, except for civil rights. To obtain a rule for civil rights bills the northern Democrats virtually have to obtain some Republican support within the Rules Committee, although on occasion one of the more moderate southerners has helped to grant a rule then voted against the bill.

There was a tougher way of shifting the balance within the Rules Committee that appealed to many northern liberal Democrats. Mississippi's William Colmer had campaigned against the Kennedy slate of electors in Mississippi (where the "independent" electoral slate had won, and cast its votes for Senator Harry Byrd for President). On this somewhat shaky ground an effort could be made to remove Colmer from the Rules Committee on grounds of party disloyalty. He could then be replaced by a "loyal" Democrat, which would establish a 7 to 5 "liberal" majority on the committee. Even more important, from the liberals' point of view, this would be a major step toward strengthening party sanctions against bolts in the South and provide indirect assistance to hard-pressed southern moderates. Moreover, it would be a "permanent" change, at least in the sense of not being limited to the 87th Congress. By contrast, an expansion of the committee would be, since new rules are adopted at the beginning of each Congress (by the House; not, as yet, by the Senate) subject to reversal at the beginning of the 88th Congress in January 1963.

Committee assignments are recommended to the House by the party caucus and there is a precedent for depriving "disloyal" members of their assignments. The Republican leadership had done so after the 1924 election in which several Republicans campaigned for the LaFollette third party. But the Democrats had not followed this precedent in 1948 in regard to the Dixiecrat bolt. Further, such a move would vitally affect many members, including influential southern leaders favorably inclined to the Speaker. After all, if Colmer were "purged" this time, who might it be the next time? Besides, three other Mississippi congressmen had also supported the independent elector slate. The final choice of strategy would be up to the Speaker.

Battle of the Septuagenarians / Rayburn's first efforts were to attempt a compromise. He sought to win Judge Smith over to a peaceful expansion of the Committee on Rules. Not surprisingly Smith flatly refused, but countered with an offer to raise no obstacles in the committee to prevent floor consideration of the five proposals (including aid to education) that Kennedy had named as his priority items. This was unsatisfactory to the Speaker.

Shortly before the opening of the new Congress Rayburn met with leaders of the Democratic Study Group, and indicated that he would support the move to replace Colmer with a more responsible Democrat. But this approach aroused sharp resistance, and was opposed by such important patriarchs as Clarence Cannon (chairman of the Appropriations Committee) and Georgia's Carl Vinson (who runs the House Armed Services Committee as his personal fiefdom). The "disloyalty" theme was also beclouded by other examples of party irregularity that had gone unpunished. There was, for example, Adam Clayton Powell's 1956 support of President Eisenhower. As Judge Smith put it: "We will see whether whites and Negroes are treated the same around here."

There was thus some danger of winning the battle but losing the war. After all, purging Colmer from the Rules Committee was only a means to more important ends. If the fight so alienated southern Democrats that they were driven into a full-scale coalition with the Republicans on the Floor of the House, most of Kennedy's legislative proposals would then be in even worse danger. The 1960 elections had seen Democratic strength in the House depleted by 21 seats (all non-southern), and Republican strength increased accordingly. Passing the President's program would require, in addition to clearance by the Rules Committee, cooperation by southern Democratic committee chairmen and as many votes from southern Democratic "moderates" as possible.

Whether so intended or not, Rayburn's initial moves against Colmer brought not only protests but indications of support for the alternative of expanding the committee. On January 11, a week after the House had routinely adopted the rules of the previous session (including a 12-man Committee on Rules), the Speaker indicated that he now planned to press for an expansion of the Rules Committee, rather than the purge of Colmer. This tactic, however, would require not just a majority of the Democratic caucus but a majority of the whole House membership, including Republicans. This would be a real test of strength between the 79-year-old Speaker and 78-year-old Judge Smith.

Rayburn had planned initially to call a "binding" meeting of the Democratic caucus, but then decided against it. Such a move did not seem necessary and would alienate some southerners. When the caucus did meet, behind closed doors, it took only 15 minutes to endorse the Rayburn resolution for enlarging the Committee on Rules and to formally instruct Judge Smith to report it out. (Ironically, the proposal had been referred, like any change in the rules, to Judge Smith's committee!) Meanwhile jockeying for support continued in the cloakrooms and corridors. Even with the solid support of northern and western Democrats the Speaker would need about 60 votes from Republicans and southern Democrats to ensure a majority in the House.

The day after the Democratic caucus Republican leader Charles Halleck and the Republican Policy Committee of the House announced their oppo-

sition to the Rayburn proposal. Meanwhile a small band of mostly moder-
ate-to-liberal Republicans had been urging that House Republicans avoid
an open coalition with the southern Democrats. They were given no opportunity even to present their case to the Republican Policy Committee, and
on January 23 the Republican conference (Democrats hold a "caucus," but
Republicans meet in "conference") voted overwhelmingly to make support
for Judge Smith an official party stand. Because new Republican assignments to committees had not yet been made, this gave Halleck powerful
leverage to exert on some wavering Republican members.

As the day for the scheduled showdown approached, Rayburn supporters
checked and rechecked their preliminary counts. A two- or three-vote margin was the best they could hope for, and some members were still wavering. This was too close for comfort, so the vote was postponed from January
27 to January 31, the day after President Kennedy's State of the Union
message. As Republican leader Halleck quipped, "the New Frontier
is having trouble with its first round-up."

The stakes in the fight rose when Rayburn threw his personal prestige
into the struggle. Now they were to rise once more as the President moved
to backstop the Speaker's own efforts. The President, when questioned on
the matter at his first televized press conference (on January 25), handled
the issue with aplomb. The internal organization of the House was, he said,
a matter entirely under the control of the House members. But, he added—
with an obvious smile—"as an interested citizen" he was following the
fight, and felt that the members of the House "should have an opportunity
to vote themselves on the programs which we will present."

The President's words were backed up by administrative action. Cabinet
members set to work trying to cajole likely congressmen. Halleck complained that Interior Secretary Stewart Udall, a former House member and
strong supporter of aid-to-education, was applying unfair pressure to western Republicans for whom Interior Department policies on reclamation,
public lands, and water policy are vital. A White House task force, headed
by congressional liaison man Lawrence F. O'Brien (a former House administrative assistant), made one last effort to systematically contact every
member of Congress. On the morning before the vote President Kennedy
himself was reported to have phoned three key House members.

The day of reckoning was January 31. When the Speaker entered the
Chamber at noon both representatives and the gallery spectators stood up
and applauded (an unusual tribute, in violation of House rules). The galleries were packed, and were obviously pro-Rayburn. After the customary
opening prayer and a quorum call the Speaker recognized James W. Trim-
ble (an Arkansas member of the Rules Committee) who called up House
Resolution No. 127: *"Resolved,* That during the Eighty-seventh Congress
the Committee on Rules shall be composed of fifteen members." The floor

debate was limited to one hour, with 30 minutes allocated to each side. It was unlikely to change a single vote. Judge Smith and his supporters were opposed to "packing a committee"; Rayburn's supporters were opposed to "frustrating the will of a majority." The Speaker climaxed the debate by leaving the rostrum to take the floor and urge adoption of the resolution to ensure that the House would be in a position to move the President's program.

Finally the clerk began to call the roll. By the best estimates the Speaker should squeak through, but it would be close. Anxious congressmen hovered over the tally sheets that are always in evidence when a really close vote is at hand. In the early part of the alphabetical roll Judge Smith was off to a substantial lead, then Rayburn caught up, and so it went for an agonizing 30 minutes. If there were an exact tie the Speaker himself held a tie-breaking vote, otherwise he would not participate. The Rayburn forces had sought firm commitments wherever possible. They had also sought "contingent" votes from members who much preferred to be recorded for Smith, but who, if their vote would make the crucial difference, would shift to Rayburn. There were thought to be three or four such "contingent" votes available, and it was considered likely that the Speaker personally could call on another one or two members to switch if absolutely necessary.

When the final tally was in, the Speaker had won: 217 for the resolution, 212 against. Rayburn had the solid support of northern and western Democrats, most of the border-state Democrats, slightly over one-third of the southern Democrats, and a crucial 22 Republicans. Judge Smith, in addition to his general Republican support, had polled 64 Democratic votes, all from the South or the border states. The 22 Republicans supporting Rayburn were mostly from the urban Northeast, and were generally from the more liberal wing of the party (former Republican leader Joseph Martin was absent, but had recorded his stand in support of Rayburn, which was paired to cancel out one pro-Smith Republican).

The pattern of Rayburn's southern support was more complex. In general the Deep South went heavily for Judge Smith (Mississippi and South Carolina provided no Rayburn votes at all), although Rayburn did do better in Alabama and Arkansas than in such generally "moderate" states as Florida and North Carolina. The more liberal southern Representatives and those from districts with a lower percentage of Negroes were also much more likely to support the Speaker. This, for example, was the case with the Alabama delegation. The Speaker also enjoyed striking support from his home state of Texas, and from the majority of the senior committee chairmen from the South (the factor at work in Arkansas). The only chairmen of major committees who opposed Rayburn were Smith himself, and Representative Harold D. Cooley, chairman of the Agriculture Committee. Cooley, one of the members to receive a last-minute call from the President, had narrowly missed defeat in 1956 when he had refused to sign the "southern manifesto" against the Supreme Court's desegregation decision. His two other North Carolina colleagues who had refused were defeated. He apparently was unwilling to risk fate a second time.

The Administration thus had its victory. Whether it could repeat the trick on controversial legislation—such as federal aid to education—remained to be seen. It also remained to be seen whether the expansion of the Rules Committee would extend beyond the current Congress.

Changes Made and Changes Not Made /   The way was now clear for the Speaker to "reform" the unruly Rules Committee. The appointment of two "dependable" Democrats should provide a working majority, and this majority could—if it so desired—push through a variety of changes in the committee's own rules and procedure that would trim the very considerable discretion of the chairman. The two new Democratic appointees were Carl Elliott, an Alabama liberal (on economic issues but not on civil rights), and B. F. Sisk, a liberal from California. The additional Republican post went, as expected, to a conservative. This made the Rules Committee lineup, in order of seniority, as follows:

DEMOCRATS	REPUBLICANS
HOWARD W. SMITH (Va.), *Chairman*	CLARENCE J. BROWN (Ohio)
WILLIAM M. COLMER (Miss.)	B. CARROLL REECE (Tenn.) *
RAY J. MADDEN (Ind.)	KATHARINE ST. GEORGE (N.Y.)
JAMES J. DELANEY (N.Y.)	H. ALLEN SMITH (Calif.)
JAMES W. TRIMBLE (Ark.)	ELMER J. HOFFMAN (Ill.)
HOMER THORNBERRY (Tex.)	WILLIAM H. AVERY (Kans.) †
RICHARD BOLLING (Mo.)	
THOMAS P. O'NEILL JR. (Mass.)	
CARL ELLIOTT (Ala.)	* deceased
B. F. SISK (Calif.)	† replaced Reece

The two ranking Democrats plus the five Republicans would now constitute a conservative minority; the remaining Democrats—usually under the leadership of shrewd Dick Bolling—would hopefully be the new nonconservative majority.

When the expanded committee held its first meeting in Room G-12 of the Capitol Building (an ornate room on the gallery floor level of the House wing), there were only twelve swivel chairs arranged around the long conference table. For the newcomers, Judge Smith provided metal folding chairs, such as are available for spectators at the committee's open meetings. He opined that the new members would not be around long enough to justify spending money for more swivel chairs. (Carl Elliott's constituents promptly took up a collection to purchase a chair for their man!) Judge

Smith eventually relented on the chair issue, but he seemed to be taking his defeat hard. He indicated that, having received a mandate to call up legislation, he would do so—with a vengeance. Hearings were scheduled on a variety of rather weird resolutions (calling for adjournment over the hot summer months, televizing the proceedings of the House, counting the gold at Fort Knox, and so forth), most of which were opposed by the Speaker. The new majority was obviously going to be maneuvered into voting as "obstructionists" on such matters.

In the embittered atmosphere following the close floor fight there was thus serious doubt as to the wisdom of pushing through other changes within the Rules group. House committees are supposed to have a regular meeting time, but Rules had none, meeting only at the call of the chairman. In this and many other ways, Judge Smith exercised discretion and discretion can be crucial, especially in the last few weeks of a Congress. But just as the Speaker and his supporters had ultimately backed away from purging Colmer or from forcing a "binding" caucus, they decided to drop the idea of making internal changes that would further ruffle the feelings of Judge Smith. Forgiveness was to be the watchword. But this was a decision they might well regret in the closing weeks of the second session of the 87th Congress.

The President Presents His Program: Catholic Bishops Dissent

While the Rules Committee struggle was moving to a climax the President-elect was faced with the problem of developing his own Administration proposals on a great range of issues. During the campaign he had repeatedly endorsed federal aid to education, both for school construction and for teacher salaries. He had also emphasized that he favored such aid for public schools only and opposed granting funds to parochial schools. In his widely quoted speech to the Greater Houston Ministerial Association he had stated: "I believe in an America where the separation of church and state is absolute—where no church or church school is granted any public funds." This statement had not allayed the fears of all Protestants, but it had disturbed some Catholic leaders.

In politics it is often the case that a leader has to lean over backwards to avoid being accused of favoritism. As the nation's first Roman Catholic President, John F. Kennedy, despite the forebodings of some fundamentalists, was likely to be in this position. If some southern Baptists feared seeing Kennedy in the White House, the hierarchy of the Catholic church had at least equally good reason to look on his campaign with a certain lack of enthusiasm. After all, it was that eminent Baptist Harry S. Truman who had outraged Protestant spokesmen by seeking to send a full-fledged ambassador to the Vatican. And it was New York's Governor Nelson Rockefeller—also a Baptist, who was to win admiring praise from Cardinal Spellman (and stringent criticism from Protestant and Jewish leaders) for his program of state aid to private colleges and universities in New York. A Nixon in the White House, especially after defeating a Catholic, would have been under some pressure to seek to accomodate strongly held views of the Catholic hierarchy. A Kennedy in the White House, especially after being suspected of Papist biases, might well be expected to lean in the opposite direction.

The President's Task Force on Education / Shortly after the election Kennedy named a number of special advisory task forces to study certain substantive areas. Such groups can accomplish a variety of objectives. Their mere existence is a convenient excuse for postponing commitments on policy, launching trial balloon proposals, or providing favorable publicity where a decision has been made but where public support is needed.

Among the Kennedy task forces was one on education. Chairman of the six-man group was Frederick Hovde, president of Purdue University and a leading figure in the State Universities Association. The other five members were Benjamin Willis (superintendent of public schools in Chicago, and soon-to-be president of the American Association of Secondary School Superintendents); Russell Thackery (executive-secretary of the American Land Grant Colleges Association); John Gardner (president of the Carnegie Corporation, a foundation with a special concern for education); Francis Keppel (dean of the Harvard School of Education); and Alvin Eurich (a vice-president of the Ford Foundation). This was, as the saying goes, "a distinguished body." It would speak with most authority on problems of higher education. On that subject the task force might help to bring various points of view together and generate additional interest and support. It could also bring in a verdict in favor of federal aid for public schools. The basic conflicts on that issue, however, could hardly be resolved by a task force, especially one with no representatives of the conservative, southern Democratic, Catholic church, or NAACP positions.

The report of the Education Task Force was released on January 6, 1961. It recommended three major legislative proposals plus a number of administrative actions. The chief proposals were:

1. Federal support for the public school system. Here the committee recommended general aid of $30 per year for each pupil in average daily attendance in public schools (cost: $1.2 billion per year). In addition, it recommended an added $20 per child for states with personal income per student below 70 per cent of the national average (cost: $140 million); and also an added $20 per child in the public schools of those cities with over 300,000 population (cost: $120 million per year).

2. Federal support program for housing and academic facilities for the

colleges and universities. Here the committee called for expansion of the existing college housing loan program, and establishment of a new program of grants and loans for construction of academic facilities, such as classrooms. For the latter program it recommended $500 million, with $350 million in grants and the rest in loans, for the first year (a dormitory can be built on a loan paid off by room rents, but a classroom produces no direct income). Hovde, incidentally, subsequently testified that he favored $1 billion per year for academic facilities but that the committee had felt that budgetary considerations would not permit that amount. He was right— the Kennedy Administration limited its college facilities requests to $300 million, all in loans! This also avoided the ticklish question of outright grants to private and denominational colleges.

3. Federal support to strengthen the National Defense Education Act (NDEA). Here the committee proposed general extension of the NDEA, with increased loan funds for college students, elimination of the controversial non-Communist affidavit, and extension of the forgiveness feature on loans (then applicable only to public school teachers) to all teachers.

The second and third recommendations related to private and parochial institutions, as well as to public ones. But the really big item—massive federal aid for elementary and secondary schools—was to be available for public schools only.

The report received relatively little attention in the nation at large and played no direct role in shaping the Administration's proposals. But from all appearances it was closely studied by many Catholic church leaders. Their reaction was generally negative. A week after the task force report had been released another education panel, which had been appointed by Arthur Flemming (Eisenhower's last Secretary of Health, Education and Welfare), submitted recommendations relating to expansion and extension of the NDEA programs. This panel, which included among its 20 members, the Right Reverend Monsignor Frederick G. Hochwalt, Director of Education for the National Catholic Welfare Conference, had not dealt with elementary and secondary schools. In commenting on the report Monsignor Hochwalt emphasized this point, and indicated that he could not agree at that time to any increased federal support for education beyond the specific recommendations in the report submitted to Secretary Flemming.

As the day for Kennedy's inauguration approached Catholic press criticism of the Hovde recommendations mounted. On January 17, three days before the inauguration, the recommendations were the subject of a major address in which they were criticized from the standpoint of the Roman Catholic church:

> I believe and I state that these recommendations are unfair to most parents of the nation's 6,800,000 parochial and private school children. Such legis-

lation would discriminate against a multitude of America's children because their parents choose to exercise their constitutional right to educate them in accordance with their religious beliefs.

The requirements of the National defense as well as the general welfare of our country demand that, in educational opportunities, no child be treated as a second-class citizen. Hence, it is unthinkable that any American child be denied the Federal funds allotted to other children which are necessary for his mental development because his parents choose for him a God-centered education.

To me it is also unthinkable that Congress would deny a child funds to study mathematics, science, and languages simply because his parents supply additional funds for the study of religion.

I cannot believe that Congress would accept the proposals of the task force and use economic compulsion to force parents to relinquish their rights to have religion taught to their children.

I cannot believe that Congress would enact a program of financial assistance and secondary education unless all children were granted equal educational privileges, regardless of the school they attend.

By denying this measure of equality to church-related school children and their parents, the task force proposals are blatantly discriminating against them, depriving them of freedom of mind and freedom of religion.

If Congress were to comply with the task force proposals as outlined by its committee (and once again I express my faith that Congress would not do so), and compel a child to attend a State school as a condition for sharing in education funds, it would be engaging in thought control.

These were strong words, and they were from no monsignor. The speaker was Francis Cardinal Spellman of New York. The 71-year-old Cardinal, who had tangled on this subject with Mrs. Eleanor Roosevelt and Congressman Barden a decade earlier, was yielding no ground to the 43-year-old President-elect from Boston.

A "New Frontier" for Education? /   Whether the task force report had been intended as a trial balloon or not it served to indicate stormy weather for the President's aid-to-education legislation. Both Kennedy and his Secretary of HEW, Abraham A. Ribicoff, had been in the House of Representatives during the bitter parochial school dispute of 1949–50. So had several of the key congressmen who participated in working out the details of the program. But there seemed no simple alternative that could avoid even more certain political dangers. On February 20, a month after the inauguration, the President sent his special message on education to Congress. The final draft of the proposed school-assistance bill was ready a week later. Neither the message nor the bill indicated any concessions to supporters of aid for nonpublic schools.

Drawing up the measure was more a matter of choosing among the vast number of past proposals than of trying to work up new ones. The spending totals and general outlines were subject to close check by the White House, but the details—and there are a great many in a major aid-to-education bill —were worked out initially between the responsible HEW officials and the House and Senate Democrats most deeply involved in the subject.

The man who would actually administer the program—if it passed—was not yet in Washington. For commissioner of education, the President, recognizing the increased role of federal aid for higher education, had broken with the tradition of naming a secondary school administrator. After considering a great many possibilities he had decided on Dr. Sterling Mc-Murrin, a philosophy professor, a Morman, and the academic vice-president of the University of Utah. Due to his duties there Dr. McMurrin had not yet arrived in Washington.

In his message to Congress the President made recommendations in each of the three areas covered by the Hovde task force, plus vocational education. But congressional attention was concentrated on his proposals for aid to elementary and secondary schools:

> I recommend to the Congress a 3-year program of general Federal assistance for public elementary and secondary classroom construction and teachers' salaries.
>
> Based essentially on the bill which passed the Senate last year (S. 8), although beginning at a more modest level of expenditures, this program would assure every State of no less than $15 for every public school student in average daily attendance, with the total amount appropriated ($666 million being authorized in the first year, rising to $866 million over a 3-year period) distributed according to the equalization formula contained in the last year's Senate bill.
>
> This is a modest program with ambitious goals.

Then the message touched on the crucial issue of parochial schools:

> In accordance with the clear prohibition of the Constitution, no elementary or secondary school funds are allocated for constructing church schools or paying church school teachers' salaries, and thus non-public school children are rightfully not counted in determining the funds each State will receive for its public schools.

Whether this emphasis on constitutional prohibitions would head off a dangerous fight over the policy involved was rather doubtful, given the somewhat confused state of the law and the great variety of possible forms of assistance.

The message indicated most of the major choices that had shaped the Administration's bill: the spending total would be only about half that recommended by the task force. The bill would not be limited to the less controversial matter of school construction, but would include aid for teacher salaries. There would be some equalization between high- and low-income states, but rather less than the Senate would probably push for. The allocation of funds among states would be made not on the basis of school-age population, but on average daily attendance in public schools. (This attempted to meet a criticism made in the Rules Committee in 1960 that it was ridiculous to grant a state funds for its *total* school-age population when none of the funds could go to nonpublic schools.) And 10 per cent of each state's funds would be set aside by it for special education projects (in slum neighborhoods, for depressed areas, special guidance programs, and so forth). This latter program was of special relevance to big city school systems; it was of some concern to Southerners who feared that desegregation might be a special program.

The Administration's one key innovation—its 1961 secret weapon—had not been mentioned in the preliminary message. This was the tie-in of the general school assistance bill with renewal of the popular program of federal aid for "impacted areas." The latter program had developed, on a small scale, during World War II. The installation of a major military or naval base in an area often resulted in taking much of the land off the tax rolls as well as in a greatly increased school enrollment. Hence some federal funds were made available both for construction and for operating expenses of schools where there was such a federal "impact." In 1950 the programs had been given regular authorization in Public Laws 81–815 and 81–874. With the Korean War, increased defense spending, missile programs, and all the rest, the programs had mushroomed. Federal aid under "815" or "874" was now going to school districts enrolling between ¼ and ⅓ of the total national public school enrollment. From fiscal 1951 through fiscal 1961 the programs had paid out around $1 billion in school construction funds and slightly more than $1 billion for operation and maintenance.

House supporters of general school assistance had often chafed at the way many members would vociferously attack general aid bills, but push for every possible penny of "impacted areas" grants. Because so many military and naval installations are in the South, this had meant that many of the leading opponents of general school-aid bills were also among the top beneficiaries of impacted areas aid. In Georgia, for example, about 10 per cent of all education expenditures were financed by the federal government, largely through the impacted areas program. Like so much legislation, the impacted areas statutes were not made permanent, but come up every so often for renewal. This cycle guarantees both supporters and opponents a chance to reshape the measure, and gives the Congress as a whole an important political advantage in bargaining with the administration and bureaucracies. In 1958 Congressman Frank Thompson had managed the bill to renew the programs under "815" and "874." He and Lee Metcalf had shaped the renewal so that aid for children of parents both working and residing on federal property would be made permanent, but assistance under the other parts of the program would expire again, on June 30, 1961. Renewal of these politically popular programs could be a powerful lever in the effort to pass a general aid bill.

The Administration, in effect, would be holding the expiring portions of the impacted areas programs as a hostage to help force through the general public schools bill. If this "package" approach made political sense to House strategists it also made a certain amount of bureaucratic sense to HEW officials. If the Administration's bill were adopted it would funnel funds to the states, but certain school districts in the states would also be receiving funds directly under "815" and "874." It seemed rational, therefore, to cut back the "impacted areas" program to take account of the new federal aid intended for the states. At a meeting in Palm Beach, Florida, in December 1960, Kennedy accepted Thompson's plan for the "package" approach.

When finally ready for introduction the Administration bill ran to 29 double-spaced pages. It consisted of three titles. Title I established the newly proposed school assistance program. Title II extended, in reduced form, the Public Law 815 program. Title III extended, also in reduced form, the Public Law 874 program.

There was a final matter of settling on House and Senate sponsors to introduce the legislation. Since the bitter religious controversy relating to the Barden bill in 1949–50 it had been regarded as wise to have public school bills introduced, at least in the House, by a Catholic congressman. This would deter at least one form of criticism. For several years the honor had gone to Augustine Kelley, an Irish Catholic with a rich brogue who had several children serving in various Catholic orders. But Kelley had died. In the previous Congress the Murray-Metcalf bill was similarly insulated by the fact that Senator Murray was a Catholic, although Metcalf was not (Metcalf was so identified with the education cause that some school teachers thought his first name was "Murray"). Ordinarily sponsorship would go to the appropriate subcommittee chairman, but in the House this was Cleveland M. Bailey. No man had fought harder for federal aid, but "Cleve" Bailey was a West Virginia Protestant. Fortunately, the second-ranking Democrat on the House subcommittee was Frank Thompson. Thompson was a Catholic, but he was also an all-out supporter of the Administration bill and had played a key role in its drafting. It was thus Thompson who introduced the measure in the House where it became H.R. 4970.

In the Senate the situation was different. Former Senator Murray, a Catholic and the education subcommittee chairman for years, would have been the logical sponsor, but he had retired at the end of the previous Congress (and was soon to pass on). His successor was Wayne Morse. Morse was an ardent supporter of federal aid, for both construction and teacher salaries, but he was also known for his support of aid to nonpublic schools. More serious, he had the reputation—well-deserved in the eyes of many—of being one of the most individualistic—even erratic—men in a highly individualistic body. He had served in the Senate first as a liberal Republican, then as a one-man Independent party, finally as a rather partisan Democrat. No one questioned Morse's intellectual ability (except Clare Booth Luce, who in an angry moment had suggested that his problems stemmed from having been kicked in the head by a horse), but in his sixteen years in the Senate, he had never had the responsibility for managing a major Administration bill. This time, however, he was chosen to lead the Senate fight for the federal school-aid bill.

A word should be said about the difference between House and Senate in regard to sponsoring legislation. In the House a bill can have only one sponsor. Other members desiring to indicate their support in advance, or seeking to share in credit, can sponsor identical legislation. (They need only pick up a copy of the original bill, cross out the bill number and the original sponsor's name, drop it into the hopper and it will be printed with a new number and their name.) Some House members have urged that joint sponsorship of bills be permitted, supposedly to economize on printing costs. The suggestion has gotten nowhere in the House, but in the Senate, joint sponsorship is possible, and over the past three decades has become quite frequent. A senator introducing a bill can ask that it lay over on the table for a few days before being referred to committee; during this time any senator desiring to be listed as a "cosponsor" can add his name to the bill. This practice, however, is frowned upon by many of the more senior members of the Senate's "inner club." The late Alben Barkley, longtime majority leader, would have none of it, and Georgia's Richard Russell, "dean" of the southern Democrats, has denounced the practice vigorously.

When Morse introduced the Administration measure it became Senate bill S. 1021. He asked that it lay over while other senators considered whether they wanted to be listed as cosponsors. Within a week twenty-one additional Democrats (only two from the South: Fulbright of Arkansas and Yarborough of Texas) had signed on as cosponsors. Since it was an Administration bill there were no Republican cosponsors, although it was likely to receive considerable support from liberal Republicans, who are relatively more numerous in the Senate than in the House.

The Catholic Hierarchy Dissents /   When the President's message on education was delivered to Congress on February 20 the lines of conflict had pretty well been drawn. Ordinarily one of the main functions of the committee hearings in Congress is to elicit the views of various affected interests and groups. But on aid to education no one felt compelled to wait for the hearings—the issue was an old one and most views were already crystallized. On the non-Catholic side a spokesman for Protestants and Other Americans United for Separation of Church and State (POAU) greeted the message with enthusiasm: "We congratulate the President for declaring that direct Federal aid to church schools at the elementary and secondary levels is unconstitutional." On the Catholic side, the Most Reverend Lawrence J. Shehan, Bishop of Bridgeport, Connecticut (and chairman of the department of education of the National Catholic Welfare Conference), expressed "keen disappointment" that the President had excluded private and parochial schools. Granting that there were "certain constitutional problems," the Bishop asked: "Is there not ingenuity enough in the Federal Government to devise an acceptable course that would safeguard the Constitution and meet, at least to some extent, the needs of all children?"

Catholic criticism of the Kennedy proposals mounted rapidly. Some of the strongest words came from the various Catholic diocesan newspapers, such as the Boston *Pilot,* the Brooklyn *Tablet,* the Newark *Advocate,* and the *Catholic Standard* of Washington, D.C. Congressmen, especially those from urban areas in the Northeast, began to receive substantial amounts of mail on the issue. An authoritative statement of the position of the Catholic hierarchy was expected from the administrative board of the National Catholic Welfare Conference. The board, consisting of the five Cardinals of the American Catholic Church plus the ten archbishops and bishops who head departments (of which education is one) of the conference, met in Washington on March 1 in a closed session. Following the meeting Archbishop Karl J. Alter, chairman of the administrative board, released the following statement:

> Yesterday the Administrative Board met and considered in addition to the routine questions the particular problem of Federal aid to education. In the absence of the official minutes I think I can summarize the discussion fairly and briefly as follows:
> 1. The question of whether or not there ought to be Federal aid is a judgment to be based on objective economic facts connected with the schools of the country and consequently Catholics are free to take a position in accordance with the facts.
> 2. In the event that there is Federal aid to education we are deeply convinced that in justice Catholic school children should be given the right to participate.
> 3. Respecting the form of participation, we hold it to be strictly within the framework of the Constitution that long-term, low-interest loans to

private institutions could be part of the Federal aid program. It is proposed, therefore, that an effort be made to have an amendment to this effect attached to the bill.

4. In the event that a federal aid program is enacted which excludes children in private schools these children will be victims of discriminatory legislation. There will be no alternative but to oppose such discrimination.

Press reaction to the hierarchy's statement was, to say the least, mixed. Many Protestant and Jewish spokesmen expressed shock that the hierarchy seemed willing, in effect, to kill the President's public school bill unless some aid to parochial schools was included. In a widely quoted column, New York *Times* correspondent James Reston saw the move as one likely "to hurt both religion and education." But Reston went on to add:

> The claims of the Catholic Church cannot be lightly brushed aside, as President Kennedy originally tried to push them aside, by saying that aid to parochial schools was "clearly unconstitutional" and by adding that "there isn't any room for debate on that subject." This merely envenoms the debate that is now obviously in progress.
>
> The main reason for Federal aid in the first place was to see to it that the Nation develops all the brains it has, and if this reason is valid, it surely needs Catholic brains as well as Baptist or Presbyterian brains.

The President's comments on which Reston was drawing had been made at his March 1 White House press conference. At his March 8 press conference the possibility of federal loans for parochial schools took up almost a third of the time. The President repeated that he felt there was no room for debate in regard to grants for parochial schools, and that "by my reading of the constitutional judgments in the Everson Case, my judgment has been that across-the-board loans are also unconstitutional." The President admitted, however, that "there have been some kinds of loans to nonpublic schools which have been supported by the Congress and signed by the President and about which no constitutional problem has yet been raised, and the National Defense Education Act is the best example." But the President emphasized that if Congress wanted to consider some form of loan program for nonpublic schools it should be considered as a separate matter from the Administration's proposals. He added that he "was concerned that it should not be made an issue now in such a way that we end up the year with, again, no aid to secondary schools."

At two points in his press conference the President had seemed a bit irritated that any major fight over aid for parochial schools should develop just at that time. There had, he pointed out, been no great effort to provide across-the-board loans when the Eisenhower aid to education proposals were debated in Congress. He gave the impression of a man being some-

what unfairly imposed upon by unusual demands: "I also point out that
this matter was not made an issue in recent years until this time, except in
the case of the amendment offered at the end of the last session by Senator
Morse which was just offered in the Senate and was not offered in the
House of Representatives, to the best of my knowledge." On the latter
point, incidentally, the President's knowledge was incomplete. An amendment providing aid for parochial schools had been offered in the House by
Congressman Roman C. Pucinski (a Catholic Democrat from Chicago) in
the 1960 debate. Under House rules, however, an amendment must be
"germane" to the subject being considered and a point of order was raised
against the Pucinski proposal. Since the bill under consideration dealt only
with public schools, the objection had been sustained and the amendment
ruled out of order. The Administration's own bill had been carefully
drafted, and titled, to ensure that the same point could be raised again.

The sharpness of the split between the President and the Catholic hierarchy was somewhat surprising. The existence of a considerable divergence
of views, however, was not surprising. The young President was a millionaire's son, a Harvard College graduate (who had never attended parochial
schools), and a man who obviously enjoyed the companionship of assorted
Harvard intellectuals. He was not a product of expressly Catholic institutions and culture, who had gone into politics. Rather, he was a politician
who happened—probably to his advantage—to be a Catholic. His greatest
love was politics (in which he pursued success with all the passion of a man
possessed by what Max Weber termed the "Protestant ethic").

By contrast the leaders of the American Catholic church have generally
been, in the secular sense, self-made men. They have come from homes of
moderate or less-than-moderate means. As Archbishop (now Cardinal)
Richard Cushing pointed out in 1947, "in all the American hierarchy, resident in the United States, there is not known to me one Bishop, Archbishop
or Cardinal whose father or mother was a college graduate. Every one of
our Bishops and Archbishops is the son of a working man and a working
man's wife." Leadership in the Catholic church, somewhat like leadership
in Congress, generally comes only with age. Many of the top members of
the hierarchy had been more or less contemporaries of Al Smith. It would
be surprising if an influential part of the hierarchy had not regarded Kennedy as the wrong Catholic running for the wrong office at the wrong time.

A man much more in tune with the thinking of the hierarchy was Congressman John McCormack, the House majority floor leader. He had
entered Congress in 1928—the year of Al Smith's defeat—and was a de-
vout Catholic and recipient of several Catholic honorary awards. He had
been serving as Democratic majority leader before Kennedy had been first
elected to the House. There had been friction between the two while Kennedy was in the House, and later over politics in Massachusetts. Hence

there was a minimum of surprise when, in a March 5 radio interview, McCormack called for "long-term loans at reasonable rates of interest for the construction or the renovation or the repair of private schools." In the House the influence of the 69-year-old McCormack was not to be taken lightly. The President might well reflect that in regard to aid for education his problems were coming not singly but in battalions.

Committees at Work: A Month of Hearings

The first major hurdle for the school-aid bill would come in the respective House and Senate committees handling the legislation. The House bill (H.R. 4970) had been routinely referred to the Committee on Education and Labor; the Senate bill (S. 1021) had gone to the Committee on Labor and Public Welfare. These two committees, or rather their subcommittees, would arrange for public hearings on the bills, consider proposed amendments, and eventually vote on reporting the legislation out of committee.

These two committees had roughly similar formal jurisdiction although they had important differences of political "climate," style of operation, and even subcommittee structure. Back in 1946 the Legislative Reorganization Act had sought to consolidate the unwieldy number of standing committees into a limited group of major subject-matter committees. Since that time, however, most of the standing committees had proliferated into a number of specialized subject-matter subcommittees. These subcommittees have come to acquire their own professional staff, office facilities, memberships, and chairmen. The result is that the working committee structure of both houses is a *two-level* one. The full committees ordinarily serve as a sort of "holding company" for related subcommittees. It is the latter that ordinarily conduct the hearings and carry out the initial "mark-up" of a bill, which then goes to the full committee.

The Senate Labor Committee had seven subcommittees, but only one dealing with education. The chairman of the full committee, Lister Hill of Alabama, was also a member of that subcommittee. But the subcommittee chairman was Wayne Morse. The membership of the subcommittee was:

DEMOCRATS	REPUBLICANS
WAYNE MORSE (Ore.), *Chairman*	CLIFFORD P. CASE (N.J.)
LISTER HILL (Ala.)	JACOB K. JAVITS (N.Y.)
PAT MCNAMARA (Mich.)	BARRY GOLDWATER (Ariz.)
RALPH W. YARBOROUGH (Tex.)	
JOSEPH S. CLARK (Pa.)	
JENNINGS RANDOLPH (W. Va.)	

Of the subcommittee members only Goldwater was generally opposed to a substantial federal aid program. There was little doubt that the committee would vote, by a heavy majority, for something close to the Administration's recommendations.

On the House side, however, things were much more complicated. The Education and Labor Committee had something of a reputation for being "one big, unhappy family." Its members represented neither a microcosm of the full House nor an assembly of representatives with generally similar constituent interests (as on, say, agriculture). Rather, it tended to be split into sharply conflicting factions. Most of the Democrats (such as James Roosevelt) could be counted on to support organized labor; most of the Republicans (such as Clare Hoffman) would go down the line for management. House "moderates" seldom go on the committee, and those who do find it a trying experience. Only two of the thirty-one members were from the South. It was a misfortune for the bill that it had to be handled by a committee primarily concerned with the controversial subject of labor-management relations, and so polarized in its membership.

Several of the key members who had been vitally interested in education were no longer around and those remaining were divided among three subcommittees. Lee Metcalf had gone off the committee, and then had been elected to the Senate. Stewart Udall had been named Secretary of the Interior. Carl Elliott had, as noted already, gone onto the Rules Committee. Further depletions seemed possible. Edith Green of Oregon had been widely mentioned as a candidate for Secretary of HEW. The post had gone to Ribicoff, but should he receive an appointment to the Supreme Court (to which he was thought to aspire), Mrs. Green would be a likely successor. New Jersey Democrats were urging Frank Thompson, the bill's House sponsor, to accept the party's 1961 nomination for governor. (Meyner was not eligible for a third term, and if the Republicans nominated former Labor Secretary James Mitchell, a liberal and a Catholic, the Democrats would be in trouble.) They sought, therefore, to draft Thompson. Thompson, however, decided to stay on in the House—this just might be the long-awaited year for enactment of aid to education.

The House committee was also working under a very heavy load of major legislative proposals, including controversial minimum wage law changes as well as the various education proposals. To add to the turmoil, the committee had a new chairman. Graham Barden, the former chairman, had decided not to run again. Under the inexorable laws of seniority this left Adam Clayton Powell, the controversial Harlem minister-politician, in line to become chairman. Powell was moving to shake things up a bit. He had brought his top secretary in as committee clerk (promoting the newly wed Mrs. Powell, who remained in his office, from $3,074 to $12,974 a year), began to make changes in the subcommittee arrangements (including a new subcommittee on labor-management irregularities that he could use to study job discrimination), and sought to take over part of the minority party staff's office space (where the ranking Republican member barricaded himself in for a time). For the moment, however, he had indicated that not only would he withhold introducing the controversial Powell (anti-segregation) amendment, but that if someone else introduced it into the education fight he would lead the march down the aisle to vote against it. For that, many members would be willing to forgive him a few indiscretions.

The Senate Hearings: Harmony Prevails /   Most committee hearings are scheduled for mornings, with the afternoons reserved for House and Senate floor proceedings. The Senate hearings on aid to education began on the morning of March 8, the day on which the presidential press conference was to concentrate on parochial school aid. Senator Morse was presiding and most of the subcommittee members were present. The hearings were open to the public. The senators were seated, somewhat likes judges, behind a semicircular dais. There was a table for the witness who was testifying and tables for the press. Spectators could take seats or stand in the back of the room.

Much of the Senate hearings and later floor debate was to reflect the particular style of Senator Morse. As a former law school dean, Morse perceived his role of chairman as quasi-judicial. He intended to prepare a sound "record" on which senatorial judgments could be based, and regarded himself as "counsel" to the President in regard to the education bill. He also was very conscious of his role as a spokesman for the Administration; he was "a private" in the ranks of the President's supporters. He was known as something of a maverick, but he was evidently enjoying the responsibility—and the power—that goes with handling a major piece of legislation. His conduct of the hearings was extremely fair to every witness, and politically skillful.

The Administration's lead-off witness was to be Secretary Ribicoff, accompanied by the usual phalanx of departmental assistants. But before the Secretary was called, two senators, not on the committee, were to be heard in brief statements. Senator Fulbright, a long-time supporter of aid to education, made a brief statement praising the proposals in general and the equalization formula in particular. Senator Hill (who also serves on the Appropriations Committee) observed that if less funds were appropriated than the maximum authorization there might be nothing above the $15 per child grants and no equalization. Fulbright agreed that that might present a serious problem.

The other senator to testify was New Hampshire's Norris Cotton. He made a brief statement in favor of his plan to rebate to the states one-fourth of the federal taxes collected in each state on cigarettes. This was one of many schemes to provide some financial aid for education via a tax rebate rather than through the appropriations process. Cotton's proposal would have provided about $455 million per year, but there would have been no equalization between high- and low-income states—a consideration dear to the hearts of many senators. And it would have involved some regional discrimination—Utah, for example, would have received very little. (Mormon doctrine disapproves of stimulants such as liquor or tobacco.)

With these preliminaries out of the way Secretary Ribicoff made a general presentation of the Administration's position. Senator Hill returned to the problem of equalization, then Morse made a major request:

> I think you well know that there will probably be introduced an amendment to this bill which would seek to provide interest-bearing loans to private schools. . . . I would like to ask the administration, through your office, to prepare a brief for this committee setting forth the position of the administration on the constitutional questions and other legal questions raised by such an amendment.

The request was broadened to include additional views on the so-called "fringe benefits" (bus service) and the question of the constitutionality of federal aid to education per se (this was hardly a serious issue legally, but Senator Goldwater had raised it at various times). Finally, the Secretary was requested to furnish a memorandum indicating "the Federal aid which now goes to private institutions, denominational and otherwise, in this country, to hospitals, institutions of higher learning, private foundations, and the like. . . ." Work on this material was to keep lawyers of the New Frontier, both in HEW and in the Justice Department, busy for most of the following three weeks.

Before the committee adjourned for the morning there was one touch of comic relief. Morse, in a statement that was to become the basis for a humorous column by a Washington *Post* writer, said he had a request "from one group that wanted to appear as witnesses before this committee in historic costume, and I have notified them that this committee room is not a theater or a stage." The particular individuals were not identified, but apparently were opposed to any aid for parochial schools. They had planned to appear in costume as Madison and Jefferson in order, as the *Post* columnist put it, to portray how the founding fathers would roll over in their graves at the thought of aiding parochial schools. Whatever their intention it did not accord with Morse's concept of orderly committee procedure.

The second day of Senate hearings was given over to officials of the National Education Association, the executive-secretary of the Council of Chief State School Officers (a key group in carrying out any aid program), and Senator E. L. Bartlett of Alaska. The latter had a serious problem:

under the bill's equalization formula Alaska appeared as a very high-income state and hence would receive the minimum per student grants. But this failed to consider that in Alaska the price of many items is almost double that of the national average (more than double for building classrooms). The proposed cuts in the impacted areas program would hit Alaska heavily, but the new program would be of very limited help unless an exception was made to the Administration's formula. Morse indicated that he would take the matter up with HEW officials.

The witnesses appearing for NEA were old hands at the subject and received friendly questioning. The tone was indicated when Senator Javits asked if NEA did not see considerable merit in the Cooper-Javits proposals for attempting to reach a "minimum foundation" of spending per pupil. Javits then added, "I think you will find that we will be on the side of what you consider the angels no matter how this thing works out. I think everybody knows that." On the subject of state allocations Morse added a revealing "practical comment": "My situation may be a little bit different than some in that I have the responsibility of doing what I can to get that necessary one vote over 50 per cent" (to pass the bill).

The witness appearing for the Council of Chief State School Officers, Dr. Edgar Fuller, indicated that he had replies from a survey of state school superintendents (or their equivalent) and that most favored the bill. There were, however, significant suggestions and exceptions. The chief school officers had earlier voted 3 to 1 in favor of including aid to salaries in a federal aid bill, but had been 100 per cent in favor of including current operating expenses (which the Administration bill did not cover). He also pointed out that the lack of federal aid for education was complicating the problem of financing education at the state level because of the proliferation of *other* federal grant programs:

> If they want to spend a dollar for highways, they can get 9 Federal dollars. If they are willing to pull out the billboards, it will be $9 plus. If they want to extend their welfare or health services, they can get matching money from the Federal Government to help them to do it. If they want to build hospitals, they can in many instances get $3 of Federal money for each dollar of their own. And so on through the list.
>
> This gives the services which are competing for the State dollar in State legislatures a very great advantage over education. If they vote $1 for education, education gets $1. If they vote $1 for roads, roads get $10. . . . This competition has made it hard to get money at the State level for education.

This would seem to be an argument in favor of requiring state funds to match the federal, but Dr. Fuller indicated that most state officials opposed a matching requirement (as did the NEA).

In an afternoon session the committee heard several more witnesses, including spokesmen of the United States Chamber of Commerce and National Association of Manufacturers. These were the leading interest-group opponents of the bill, but they were saving their best efforts for the House. The spokesman for the manufacturers said he had "no quarrel" with seeking "educational excellence," although he had grave doubts as to the real motivations involved:

> The Hovde committee proposes to lift the schools to a higher standard. This obviously means a Federally determined standard of excellence, a national educational program to be made effective by Federal financing, Federal prescription of curriculum content, and Federal regulation of teaching, testing, and guidance procedures.

The final witnesses of the afternoon were from the Parent-Teachers Association and the AFL-CIO (both supporting the bill). The AFL-CIO witness, who was accompanied by Andrew Biemiller (AFL-CIO's legislative tactician, and a former Wisconsin congressman), argued that there was need for "safe, well-ventilated classrooms in buildings designed to provide maximum opportunity for learning."

The third day of hearings began with Senator Lee Metcalf, who was concerned over possible cuts in the impacted areas program, and concluded with the Grand Master of the Masonic Lodge for Puerto Rico, who opposed aid for parochial schools. In between the committee heard spokesmen for a wide variety of organizations including the NAACP, the Baptist Joint Committee on Public Affairs, and the American Jewish Congress. The latter two opposed aid for nonpublic schools. The strongest opposition, however, came from C. Stanley Lowell, associate director of Protestants and Other Americans United for Separation of Church and State. He presented a variation on the familiar theme of the dangers of letting the camel get his nose under the tent:

> I should like to call attention to the end result of a program of grants to church schools or loans to church schools. Once the Congress reverses our tradition and embarks upon such a course, it will find that turning back is extremely difficult. The movement tends to be the other way. From small loans to large grants—so the process unfolds—until the taxpayers are charged with the entire bill for these schools.

Lowell went on to cite an editorial from the February 1 issue of *Christian Century,* a leading Protestant publication. The editorial read:

> Cardinal Spellman has not changed his mind. His aim is still to compel Protestants, Jews, and others to support a wholly controlled function of

the Roman Catholic Church. The compulsion lies in the use of the taxing powers of the Federal Government to raise funds for Catholic schools. He has given us fair warning, so he should have our answer. American Protestants will never pay taxes to support Catholic schools. We will oppose enactment of laws which require such payments. If Congress is pressured into enacting such laws, we will contest them in the courts. If the courts reverse themselves and declare such laws constitutional, we will still refuse to pay these taxes, paying whatever price is necessary to preserve religious liberty in a pluralistic society.

Lowell agreed with Senator Morse that this was "strong language," but went on to add:

I can assure you it would be among the mildest expressions on record should the Congress initiate a program of taxing all citizens to pay for religious teaching. This program would provoke such outbreaks of inter-creedal vituperation as would hitherto have been deemed impossible among us.

The NAACP spokesman found himself in a rather difficult position. Powell had already disavowed introduction of the "Powell amendment" and Morse made his own opposition to it clear before the witness began:

I indicated the other day I am not a mathematician, but I can count Congressional noses. I do not think, contrary to your opinion, that there is any chance of passing the administration bill with the civil rights amendment added to it. I think that failure would be most unfortunate, because our real need, in my judgment, is to get the principle of Federal aid to elementary and secondary education on the statute books of this country. We can then proceed, in independent legislation, to see to it that our educational program is carried out in accordance with the constitutional rights of all citizens.

The dramatic high point of the hearings would not come until the following week when Monsignor Hochwalt would present the case for the Catholic bishops. Most of the major opponents of aid for nonpublic schools had been scheduled relatively early in the hearings, before the case for such aid had itself been presented. Morse, who was doing everything possible to avoid "intercreedal vituperation," had indicated that all witnesses would have the right to file subsequent rebuttal statements. Eventually he had to schedule an additional day of hearings for other Protestant groups who had not yet been heard.

On Monday, March 13, House hearings were to begin and the Senate hearings were to continue. Morse, in a philosophic moment, wondered "to what extent a senator presiding over a meeting really has any right to give advice." After indicating that this was "an individual judgment" he continued:

> I shall speak to the hierarchy of the Catholic Church who will be testifying
> before us later. I think the leadership of that denomination has a great
> opportunity in their testimony to say, in effect, to the American people:
> "We are willing to agree that we should start with the public school system
> and, therefore, we are going to urge the passage of this public school law
> without any amendments added to it which are likely to endanger the
> passage of any legislation at all. We also reserve our right to carry out
> what we think is our duty to press the Congress of the United States for the
> passage of a separate and independent bill which raises the question as to
> whether or not loans which yield sufficient interest to pay for the cost of
> the use of money are constitutional."

Morse added that "it is a little presumptuous for a Senator to be giving
gratuitous advice," but that he would take the risk.

At almost the same hour that Morse was offering his "advice," in New
York Cardinal Spellman was issuing an additional statement of his views.
The Cardinal was "still opposed to any program of Federal aid that would
penalize a multitude of America's children" because they attended parochial schools. President Kennedy was "to be commended for his interest in
education" and for his proposals for higher education, which were "fair
and equitable to all students." But "the administration's proposals in the
field of elementary and secondary schools are not fair and equitable." The
Cardinal concluded that "equivalent benefits to children attending private
and church-related schools" and yet benefits not violating the Constitution
"would seem to be an attainable objective." The specifics were "matters for
the discretion of Congress."

Monsignor Hochwalt's testimony supported similar conclusions. The
Monsignor began by pointing out the scope of the Catholic school system:
some 10,300 elementary schools, plus around 2,400 high schools, with a
combined staff of 102,000, and enrollments totaling over 5,000,000 students. He continued:

> These schools are established, operated, and maintained by Catholic citi-
> zens, by people of the same income group as those living about the neigh-
> boring public schools.
>   They are integrally a part of what is basically a dual system. Public and
> private schools form a necessary partnership for the fruitful service of this
> country. We are one people and it is in our national interest that both
> systems make their full contribution in the service of our children. Any
> other attitude would be extremely shortsighted and self-defeating.
>   A great many parents of parochial school children would welcome Fed-
> eral aid as a necessary help to them in a time of financial strain. They do

feel the double burden of supporting two school systems, and are apt to inquire much more pointedly now than heretofore why the proponents of Federal aid do not take into consideration their needs. They point out that the classroom shortage exists as demonstrably in the private school system as it does in the public school system.

What can be done for the private school and in particular the parochial school?

We have the courageous example of Government aid to our colleges without discrimination. My petition today points up the need to grant similar assistance to the elementary and secondary schools by way of long-term, low-interest rate loans, with the interest rate computed on an annual basis. To grant Federal assistance to only part of the American educational effort is to deny to the other parts the chance to grow. In fact, it hinders parents in that free choice of education which is essentially theirs.

The Monsignor went on to point out that in many parts of the Western world, including England, Ireland, Scotland, Belgium, Holland, and parts of Canada, church-related education was supported in whole or in large part by the government: He concluded:

> I am here today to ask the legislators to think in balanced terms of the problems before us, for if Federal aid is necessary, if it is to come and if it is to be granted to the States and to the public school system, then, in the interest of all of our citizens, I would urgently plead for a consideration of the present plight and the future needs of our private schools, especially our parochial schools.

Senator Morse commended the Monsignor on the "objectivity" and "fairness" of his statement, adding "that this committee must face up to this problem." He then made something of a surprise announcement, suggesting formation of a special legislative advisory group of senators and House members to determine the best procedural course to pursue in regard to handling of the issue of aid for nonpublic schools. Monsignor Hochwalt had some reservations about this approach:

> I have a feeling that one measure would pass in this Congress, the Federal aid as such. I have a feeling that a second measure, which would provide for our schools, wouldn't have much of a chance.
>
> Therefore, it seems to us that our welfare should be considered in tandem with the administration bill in some fashion so that that can be done.

Morse agreed that "if I were sitting in your position, I would be rather inclined to hold tenaciously to the point of view you just expressed." But, he continued, we "have some differences in responsibilities." With this the Monsignor agreed, and shortly thereafter the session adjourned for lunch.

Additional Protestant spokesmen were heard on March 20. Among those testifying were Dr. Gerald E. Knoff, representing the National Council of Churches, Dr. Robert E. Van Deusen, of the National Lutheran Council, and James DeForest Murch, of the National Association of Evangelicals. Dr. Knoff's statement was typical: "The present controversy is not of our choosing. The National Council of Churches did not raise the issue. Yet a principle is at stake. If Roman Catholic leaders raise their demand as a moral issue, Protestant leaders must reply that they oppose the proposal as a moral issue." Morse repeated his view that although grants to nonpublic schools would be a violation, "there is no constitutional violation as long as there is, in fact, no subsidy." Although a loan program would be legally acceptable, the "politics of the situation" was something else:

> I well know, and I think many in this room will agree with me, that if we have both public grant and private loan mixed in this bill, the odds are against any bill at all. I repeat again this morning; I will repeat up to the last minute of these hearings; I will repeat in executive session; and I will repeat on the floor of the Senate, that I am not going to support private schools in an attempt to add a loan amendment to this bill. I think it would defeat a public school bill.

Obviously the Administration faced a problem not only in the substance of aid for nonpublic schools but also in the procedure to be followed in considering such a program.

House Hearings: *The Perils of Partisanship* /   Hearings in the House began, rather inauspiciously, on March 13. The Labor Committee's regular hearing room is on the fourth floor of the old House Office Building, room 429 (several of the key members have their offices on the same floor). The General Education Subcommittee, however, was to begin its hearings in the spacious caucus room of the same building. Congressman Cleveland Bailey, the chairman, was presiding. He began by welcoming the three newly appointed members of the subcommittee, then reviewed some of the rules of committee procedure: witnesses should submit fifty copies of their statements, be prepared to summarize their statements orally, and expect questions from the committee members, who would be subject to the House's customary "five-minute rule," which limits each member to that amount of time. Bailey also indicated that, to "prevent repetition of testimony," public witnesses would be limited to spokesmen for national organizations. On the subject of aid for nonpublic schools, the subcommittee would hear "two witnesses each on both sides," but others could file statements for the record.

Secretary Ribicoff was to be the first House witness. Bailey prepared to turn the job of chairing the hearing over to Frank Thompson, but before he could do so Congressman Frelinghuysen (Republican of New Jersey) objected that the subcommittee had not held any previous meetings and hence could hardly have laid down ground rules for witnesses. He also complained that he and other minority members had received no list of witnesses scheduled to appear and were on so many subcommittees that he would like to know what the schedule of meetings was to be. Bailey brushed Frelinghuysen's complaints aside and turned the proceedings over to Thompson.

Frelinghuysen and Thompson represented adjoining districts in New Jersey, but were sharply different—often clashing—personalities. Frelinghuysen was a moderate-to-progressive Republican who had consistently supported aid for school construction. The bearer of one of the most famous names in New Jersey history, he had been a hard worker on the Education and Labor Committee, although his chief interest was in foreign affairs (in 1961 he had been appointed to the Foreign Affairs Committee, but retained his membership on Education and Labor, where he was now third-ranking Republican). A *magna cum laude* graduate of Princeton, Frelinghuysen sometimes seemed to approach issues more in the spirit of academic research than of down-to-earth politics. He was, for example, plainly shocked at the Administration's coupling of school aid with extension of the impacted areas program and dubious that the President's "modest program" could have a significant effect on both school construction and teacher salaries.

Frank Thompson, by contrast, was a tough-minded liberal Democrat. A former minority leader of the lower house of the New Jersey legislature, Thompson had moved ahead in the House of Representatives rapidly. Although a highly intelligent and cultured man (one of the leaders in the campaign for a Federal Advisory Council on the Arts), he was blunt-spoken and approached politics with something of the same vigor (and combativeness) for which he had been decorated at Iwo Jima. His congressional district, incidentally, included the township that had figured in the *Everson v. New Jersey* case on public aid for parochial students' bus transportation. Both he and Frelinghuysen were lawyers.

The Administration had worked out its program without taking any heed of Frelinghuysen or the other liberal Republicans in the House. (Frelinghuysen had been sitting in the audience at the Senate hearing waiting to hear Ribicoff's testimony the previous week.) The failure even to consult with Catholic educators or with the liberal Republicans in the House offered a dangerous parallel to Wilson's attitude on the Versailles Treaty. The Administration proposals might seem "moderate" by Kennedy's Senate norms, but for the House, aid for teachers' salaries was a "radical" move.

Secretary Ribicoff managed to present a general summary of the provisions of the bill before the committee members set to wrangling again. Questioning ordinarily proceeds with majority and minority members alternating in order of seniority. The subcommittee consisted of the following:

DEMOCRATS	REPUBLICANS
CLEVELAND M. BAILEY (W. Va.), *Chairman*	PETER FRELINGHUYSEN (N.J.)
FRANK THOMPSON, JR. (N.J.)	ALBERT H. QUIE (Minn.)
JOHN BRADEMAS (Ind.)	PETER A. GARLAND (Me.)
JAMES G. O'HARA (Mich.)	
RALPH J. SCOTT (N.C.)	

Frelinghuysen led off with a request for additional data, then sought to raise a parliamentary inquiry: Had thought been given to divorcing the impacted areas legislation (Titles II and III) from the general public school aid (Title I)? He added that he was asking "for guidance only" since he did not "have any expectation that I can impress on the committee the advisability of discussing the two problems quite separately." Thompson indicated that Frelinghuysen had thereby answered his own question.

Frelinghuysen pushed on to query the Secretary on his views of adding to the bill some provision for aid for nonpublic schools. Ribicoff said he was "absolutely opposed" to attempting to do so "in this bill." Frelinghuysen then inquired about the status of the HEW brief on constitutional problems that had been requested by Morse. The Secretary indicated that it was in progress. On a question about providing some form of aid for nonpublic schools in a separate bill, Ribicoff set forth what was to be the Administration's standard public position: "Should Congress undertake to prepare a bill and present it, I would make my comment when I saw the bill and what it contained." Finally Thompson called time on Frelinghuysen, who regretted that the five-minute limitation was being enforced. Thompson somewhat acidly commented that since the gentleman had consumed twelve minutes already the rule was hardly being used strictly.

Much of the questioning was repetition of what had already been heard in the Senate. There was, however, an obvious sense of partisanship and frustration that had not marked the Senate hearings, the five-minute rule—an unthinkable limitation for the Senate—was a cause of recurring dissatisfaction. Congressman Albert H. Quie of Minnesota, after a ten-minute round with Secretary Ribicoff, objected that he was still trying to pursue his first question. Thompson suggested that "practice in phrasing them would save time." Quie replied that "practice in phrasing should come from the Secretary," a sentiment often indicated but seldom expressed so directly.

The House hearings ground on for the remainder of the week, with sessions every day. By the end of the week most of the major witnesses from outside Congress had been heard. These included Paul Blanshard (for POAU), spokesmen for the National Education Association (for the bill) and the United States Chamber of Commerce (against the bill), the president of the New York City Board of Education (who asked for aid for non-public schools, thus arousing a storm of criticism in New York), Michigan's Governor Swainson (for the bill), Dr. Knoff of the National Council of Churches and Dr. Van Deusen of the National Lutheran Council (who both opposed aid for parochial schools), and Monsignor Hochwalt.

Congressman Thompson asked the Monsignor to clarify the significance for Catholic congressmen of the Catholic bishops' stand. The Monsignor indicated that supporting a federal aid bill that excluded parochial schools was a moral question which would be up to the particular congressman or Senator to answer. The bishops' position was not a matter of faith binding on all Catholics. The Monsignor also indicated that there had been a certain evolution of the hierarchy's position in regard to federal aid. At one time fear of federal control had been a major consideration, and he indicated that the hierarchy was still not enthusiastic: "The position of the bishops in general, which we agreed to, was that we are not going to do anything to bring about Federal aid, we are very reluctant to see it come, but should it come, based on the equity you are speaking of, then we think our concern should be provided for." This point, incidentally, was made in a discussion with Congressman John Brademas of Indiana (the Methodist son of a Greek Orthodox father and a Disciples of Christ mother, but who had taught at a Roman Catholic college in Indiana before his election to Congress).

The second week of hearings was devoted largely to members of Congress, most of whom made short appearances in support of full-scale payment of the "impacted area" funds. Congressman Thompson indicated that "if this bill fails with 815 and 874 in it, this subcommittee would need nothing more, having had all this testimony, than to reconvene after that tragedy, report out 815 and 874 and it will go through on the consent calendar." Later, however, when "tragedy" struck, Thompson was to express a different view.

Major appearances were made by Senator Barry Goldwater, who was questioned sharply by both Thompson and Brademas, and by former HEW Secretary Arthur S. Flemming. Although Eisenhower was subsequently to denounce the bill, Flemming generally supported it. His one major difference with the Administration was in regard to the categories of educational expenditures to be aided. He believed the federal funds "should be earmarked for servicing debts already incurred for school construction, for servicing debts that may be incurred for new construction, and for the construction of new buildings on a pay-as-you-go basis." He argued that this would make easier the introduction of a state matching requirement, would release substantial amounts of state and local funds for increasing teacher salaries, and would help allay congressional fears of "federal control." Such an approach would have been less satisfactory to the NEA than the Kennedy Administration's proposals, but might have rallied important support from liberal Republicans (of the Frelinghuysen type). In months to come the Administration might well regret that it had not taken this approach.

Final committee hearings were held on March 29, just prior to the Easter recess. Rabbi Morris Sherer, representing Agudath Israel (a national organization of orthodox Jews), testified in favor of aid for nonpublic schools. This was in contrast to the opposition voiced by reform and conservative Jewish organizations and by most Jewish lay groups. Congressman Thompson reiterated his opposition to including such a provision in the main Administration bill.

The House subcommittee had heard 79 witnesses in person, and received statements, letters, and resolutions from many others. The completed record ran to two published volumes, totally 1,052 pages (the record of the more verbose Senate subcommittee ran to 1,329 pages). The public hearings had, as usual, raised a great many problems. They had not indicated any easy solutions. If a compromise were to be reached it would take time: time for tempers to cool outside Congress, and time for the Administration and its congressional supporters to work out a second line of defense on the explosive parochial school issue.

Parochial School Issue: Search for Compromise

April was to be a hectic month for the new Kennedy Administration. Not only were Communist forces in far-off Laos continuing to advance, but the American-supported Cuban counter-revolution had failed: Both represented major setbacks for the President. And both problems flared as the President's supporters in Congress were involved in a series of maneuvers over the parochial school issue. The Administration's initial attempt to dismiss the whole question on grounds of constitutionality had obviously failed. The "wall of separation" between church and state was a popular metaphor—going back to Thomas Jefferson—but it was a very poor description of actual church-state relations. If any "wall" exists, it must be said to resemble one of the serpentine walls that Jefferson laid out for the University of Virginia, and with a number of gaping holes to boot.

Congressman John W. McCormack had followed up on his announced support for loans to nonpublic schools with an inquiry on the constitutional problems involved. He submitted his inquiry to Professor Arthur E.

Sutherland of the Harvard Law School. As a Republican and an Episcopalian, Sutherland could hardly be accused of bias in favor of the Catholic church's position (though some might doubt his enthusiasm for any federal aid to education). After a lengthy analysis of the precedents, Sutherland ended with the conclusion that "the Supreme Court of the United States has never held that a loan such as that in the statute which I outline above, would be in excess of congressional powers because of the First Amendment." During the Senate hearings Morse had sent queries on the issue to several other leading constitutional lawyers. None of those who responded were in any substantial disagreement with Sutherland's view, although some emphasized the difficulty of providing for a court test of any federal aid program (federal courts do not entertain "taxpayer's suits").

The brief that Morse had requested from Secretary Ribicoff was released on March 28, as congressmen were preparing to leave Washington for Easter recess. In general the brief supported the President's view that outright grants or across-the-board loans for nonpublic schools were unconstitutional. It went on to argue that the existing programs of aid for parochial schools (or for students at parochial schools) typically either "bear a clear-cut relationship to children's health or promote a special purpose with a clear national defense implication." The former would cover grants for textbooks or for bus transportation (both of which the Supreme Court had upheld) as well as the school hot-lunch program (which had not been litigated). The latter rationale would, the brief argued, cover programs such as the 1958 National Defense Education Act (NDEA), which "permits the U.S. Commissioner of Education to make loans to private schools to acquire science, mathematics, or foreign language equipment."

Were the existing programs the maximum that would be constitutional? On this question, the brief hedged, admitting that there "may be some other special purposes for which loans would be equally defensible, but any special proposal would have to be evaluated" in terms of the relevant criteria. The brief concluded with a section suggesting how Congress might seek to ensure a court test of any additional legislation enacted in this area.

On the following day Senators Joseph S. Clark (Democrat, of Pennsylvania) and Morse introduced a "Private School Construction Loan Act" (S. 1482). Clark, facing the prospect of a tough 1962 primary fight with either Philadelphia Congressman William Green or Governor David Lawrence (both Catholics), was an enthusiastic supporter for some form of aid for parochial schools (which enroll over 20 per cent of all Pennsylvania students). The proposal reflected Morse's view that interest-bearing loans for general construction were constitutional more closely than it did the HEW brief's emphasis upon special nonsectarian purposes. The bill would have authorized 40-year loans for nonpublic schools for construction of classroom facilities. Interest charged would be ¼ of 1 per cent above the average rate on all outstanding U.S. obligations. Schools receiving loans would be barred from practicing racial discrimination. Finally, any school applying for a loan would have to satisfy the Commissioner of Education that "the making the loan will not violate the First Amendment to the Constitution." The commissioner's findings on this question could be challenged in federal court by a taxpayer (if the loan had been approved) or by the private school (if the loan had been denied).

Senator Morse indicated that his committee intended to hold "fair and full hearings" on the proposal, with "every point of view" being heard. Hearings, which had been tentatively scheduled for April 13–14, were canceled. The separate bill approach and the possibility of a multitude of taxpayer suits did not appeal to supporters of the Catholic church position. Many Protestant groups were up in arms over the bill. Although Morse's views on loans for parochial schools might be constitutionally acceptable, they were not politically acceptable at the moment.

The Clark-Morse proposal was not the only one to receive attention during April. In his January statement Cardinal Spellman had made reference to funds "to study mathematics, science, and languages." This trinity of secular subjects had been covered in the NDEA of 1958. If the government could lend funds for the purchase of equipment in these fields why couldn't it lend—or grant—funds to build classrooms for these purposes? This would be "released time" in reverse—the otherwise church-related parochial school would have certain classrooms available only for these nonreligious subjects.

This was the gist of a bill introduced on the House side on April 18. Its sponsor was Herbert Zelenko, a Jewish congressman from a Manhattan district with a heavy Catholic population. His bill, H.R. 6439, was a "single package" proposal including both the Administration's public school program and provisions for grants (not loans) to nonpublic schools for science, mathematics, and modern foreign languages classrooms. The proposal was understood to have received favorable comment from Cardinal Spellman, whose archdiocese includes Manhattan. The Administration could not go along with grants, but the idea of aiding the construction of certain "special purpose" classrooms had a certain political—if not architectural—appeal. The possibilities for a compromise, at least between the Administration and the parochial school supporters, were improving. Common ground on the substance of the aid was, perhaps, in sight, but the question of parliamentary tactics was still to be resolved.

Amending the National Defense Education Act /   The Administration was still dead set against attempting to include public school assistance and loans for parochial schools in the same bill. Parochial school proponents saw no real hope for passing a separate bill. Was there a way out of the seeming dilemma? If the loans were to be narrowed from the general construction aid envisioned by the short-lived Clark-Morse bill to the "special purpose programs" named in the Zelenko proposal, why not incorporate them as amendments to the existing NDEA legislation? Most provisions of the NDEA were not due to expire until June 30, 1962, hence there was no necessity for congressional action until the following spring. Tying the parochial school loans in with extension of NDEA seemed the best way of keeping the hopes of parochial school champions alive, without threatening the chances of the public school bill.

On April 25 President Kennedy sent a message to Congress formally requesting extension and expansion of the NDEA. The President made no specific mention of adding loans for special purpose classrooms for parochial schools but he pointed out that the existing programs had "included measures to strengthen our elementary and secondary school system." The message continued:

> Our national strength and welfare demand a strong and balanced educational system. Many proposals have been made by both public and private organizations to achieve this strength and balance.
>
> I am transmitting herewith draft legislation to amend, improve and extend the National Defense Education Act. *Some* of the recommendations of these organizations are included in the draft legislation. It is also appropriate that the Congress consider *other* proposals contained in these and other reports.
>
> The legislation herewith proposed is an integral part of the proposals sent to the Congress for strengthening the basic elements of our educational system. It complements legislation already being considered to authorize general aid to public elementary and secondary schools.
>
> [italics added]

The New York *Times,* following the school-aid fight with particular interest, gave the story a page-one headline: "COMPROMISE ON SCHOOL AID SOUGHT UNDER DEFENSE ACT." And, three days later, Cardinal Spellman issued a statement declaring that "common ground" might exist in view of the "substantial concessions" made in the HEW legal brief (which had been published more than a month before).

By the end of April, then, the impasse seemed to be clearing. The Administration was not officially asking for anything for the parochial schools, but if Congress wanted to amend the NDEA to permit loans for "special purpose" classrooms, no objection would be made. By this tactic, the Administration seemed to have everything to gain and, since NDEA did not expire for another year anyway, nothing to lose.

The Committees Report the Administration Bill /   The Administration bill was not yet over the hump but by early May backers of the bill were quoted as being "moderately confident that victory is in sight after a fight of more than a decade." And they had reason to be optimistic. The respective House and Senate subcommittee chairmen were both strong supporters, so there would be no trouble there. The chairmen of the respective full committees—Congressman Powell and Senator Hill—would offer no obstacle so long as the segregation issue was avoided. There was a clear majority for a federal aid program in both committees. And the Senate had long since reached a consensus in favor of federal aid. Even the House Rules Committee—a perennial danger spot—had been reconstituted. The division on the House floor might be close, perhaps so close that aid for teacher salaries would have to be dropped, but there was reason for hope. As a New York *Times* correspondent noted on May 14: "Religious and racial complications have faded to such an extent that President Kennedy's school-aid program now seems to be in fairly good shape in Congress."

The chief question still dividing Administration strategists was whether the NDEA amendments (including loans for "special purpose" classrooms) should or should not be considered jointly with the public school assistance bill. Catholic spokesmen, after all, were not just interested in seeing a congressional debate on the loan program—they wanted to see the provisions enacted into law. This had been one of the basic objections to the separate bill approach. But Senator Morse and Congressman Thompson, the respective managers of the Administration bill, felt that joint consideration would only have the effect of killing all aid to education legislation. The debate between advocates of the "one-big-bill" approach and the "two-separate-bills" approach was not easily resolved, even in regard to Senate floor strategy. On the House side it was to erupt into a major new threat to the legislation.

The Senate Labor Committee went into closed session to begin final committee "mark-up" of the bill on May 10. On that afternoon committee Democrats huddled with key Administration leaders on the touchy problems of formulas for state allocations and for counting pupils. At the meeting, in addition to key committee Democrats, were Secretary Ribicoff, Lawrence F. O'Brien (White House congressional liaison chief), majority leader Mike Mansfield, majority whip Hubert Humphrey, and "Bobbie" Baker (omnipresent secretary to the Senate majority—a Lyndon Johnson protégé). As the Washington *Post* noted: "The makeup suggested the meeting was concerned with computing not only aid but votes."

On the following day the mark-up was completed. Pleas by Republican Senator Javits for his modified equalization formula were rejected. Instead the committee majority moved to drop the Administration's $15 per student minimum (which chairman Lister Hill had warned against) and apply the equalization to the entire amount appropriated, with a maximum ratio of 3 to 1 (between low- and high-income states). The basis for allocating the funds would be shifted from average daily attendance in public schools to total school-age population (which would give something of a bonus to states with large parochial enrollments). The committee voted to extend the impacted areas programs in virtually their existing form, thus refusing the cut-backs requested by the Administration. The final committee vote on reporting the revised bill to the Senate was 12 to 2, with only Dirksen and Goldwater in opposition.

The bill then went on the Senate legislative calendar as item 228. The committee report was ordered printed on May 12. It included the customary brief summary of the bill, explanation of changes made by the committee, and a minority report signed by Goldwater and Dirksen (plus individual views added by Goldwater). Meanwhile there was renewed talk of holding back on Senate floor action until the committee reported out the NDEA amendments including parochial school loans. Secretary Ribicoff, majority leader Mansfield (a Catholic himself), and White House aide Larry O'Brien were understood to favor the one-bill approach. Morse, however, remained opposed. So were a number of other northern liberals, and the National Education Association—all feared that the parochial loan issue, even in its narrowed form, might kill the public school bill. Hearings on the NDEA amendments could be rushed to completion and that bill still brought out for joint consideration with the public school bill. A final decision on this key tactical question was not reached until after Senate debate on the public school bill was formally under way. But before looking at further Senate developments it may be well to review briefly developments on the House Education and Labor Committee.

The House subcommittee mark-up of the public school bill came on May 9. The group split 4–3 on straight party lines to vote down a series of amendments proposed by Republican Frelinghuysen. The subcommittee majority, like the Senate committee, voted to continue the impacted areas programs at existing levels and to compute aid on the basis of total school-age population rather than average daily attendance. But instead of dropping the $15 per child minimum entirely it reduced it to $12 per child. Like the Senate group, it then voted to increase the authorization for Title I (so that as few states as possible would receive less under the new allocation although many would receive somewhat more). In this form the bill went to the full committee.

While the Senate floor debate dragged on, the full House committee met in several days of closed sessions to complete marking up of the bill. Republican efforts to knock out aid for teacher salaries, to add an antisegregation amendment, and to require a teacher loyalty oath were all voted down on straight party lines. The loyalty oath, incidentally, was urged by

Congressman Edgar W. Hiestand of California, a leading member of the much-discussed John Birch Society. The final vote to report the bill out, as it had been modified by the subcommittee, was 18–13. The minority consisted of the committee's twelve Republicans (including Frelinghuysen) plus one southern Democrat (Ralph Scott of North Carolina). Rather than reporting the amended version of H.R. 4970, the majority took the option of reporting the revision out as a "clean bill" (with a new bill number: H.R. 7300). This would make its handling in Committee of the Whole somewhat easier. The revised bill became item 171 on the House union calendar, and ordinarily would remain there until a "special rule" providing for floor consideration was granted by the Committee on Rules and adopted by the House.

The Senate Votes: The Ayes Have It

The Senate is a very special institution and most senators are strongly dedicated to keeping it that way. The Senate Rules, if strictly invoked by a determined minority, can bring that august body to a virtual standstill. But except on civil rights, such a breech of senatorial etiquette is unthinkable. The normal course of action is for Senate business to proceed "by unanimous consent" rather than by the normal rules. Skilled legislative leaders— such as Lyndon Johnson—can touch base with all those senators concerned on an issue and, proceeding under various unanimous consent requests, transact business at a rate that rivals the supposedly "more efficient" House of Representatives.

Contrary to popular impression, the self-styled "world's greatest deliberative body" ordinarily debates major legislation under very strict limits and with a rule of "germaneness." Such a limitation, of course, can only be imposed by adopting a "unanimous consent agreement" specifying the time limit and imposing "germaneness" (which is not—and the southerners hope never will be—part of the regular Senate Rules). Such self-imposed limitation of debate is, of course, a great convenience to the senators who can thereby plan their future activities, knowing when they must be on hand if they intend to vote on an issue.

For the 1961 school-aid bill, however, such a "unanimous consent agreement" could not be successfully negotiated. Senator Mansfield, the majority leader, propounded such an agreement—specifying two hours' debate on each amendment and ten hours' debate on the bill itself—but this suggestion was unsatisfactory. (Southern senators were concerned over "freedom riders," use of federal marshals in Alabama, and possible amendments relating to segregation in schools.) After some further wrangling, Senator Goldwater finally entered an objection to any over-all limitation on debate:

I do not believe, with respect to an important issue such as this . . . that we should decide the question in a week. It might take 2 weeks. It might take 3 weeks. I am prepared to fight this as long as it takes. I do not want to be pushed into voting on Friday, on Monday, or on Tuesday. When the vote comes naturally. I shall not obstruct the vote.

Thus Mansfield—who, unlike Lyndon Johnson, his predecessor, obviously had not been doing his homework, withdrew his request. Limited unanimous consent agreements were subsequently adopted for each major amendment, and the debate dragged out from May 16 to May 26.

Actually the term "debate" is rather misleading. The Senate seldom witnesses a direct "debate" between opposing views; rather there are successive "colloquies" in which senators express their "judgment" of an issue. On one day the supporters of a bill will have the floor, and will engage in lengthy colloquies. Ordinarily these take the form of openly leading and often "loaded" questions (for which a senator may yield) of the form: "Is it not true that . . ." or "Does not the distinguished senator believe . . ." Although the point may be most doubtful, the customary reply is: "As the distinguished senator so ably points out . . ." or "In my judgment that is certainly . . ." The emphasis on giving "judgments" rather than making flat assertions (as is common in "the other body," meaning the House) is typical of a body dominated by lawyers and acutely aware of the mixture of fact and value that enters into most important decisions. (As President, Kennedy dropped use of "colloquy"—which is carried on among equals—but retained the senatorial emphasis on "judgment.")

Finally, the difference in constituency size and term of office between House and Senate has the most profound consequences. The typical senator (like the American political party) is a living compromise, representing large and generally diverse constituencies. Except in the year or two immediately preceding re-election, most senators can afford to "be statesmen" even to the point of voting against apparent constituency wishes on at least some issues. Most House members, by contrast, represent small districts, which are often relatively homogeneous (compare a senator from the *state* of New York with a House member from Manhattan or rural, upstate New York!). Also, by the time major legislation reaches the floor of the House the next campaign is never much more than a year away. On many issues the House thus represents a variety of extremes (somewhat like a European multiparty system), with a conservative bias resulting from rural-biased state apportionment of districts. Only a few representatives, usually from districts that are both diverse and relatively "safe" (like Richard Bolling's Kansas City district: a microcosm of downtown, stockyards, and suburbia), can afford to play the "statesman" role constantly with any degree of safety.

On the explosive parochial school issue, for example, compromise was accomplished *within* most senators themselves, but would have to be negotiated *between* members in the House. In that body there were many Catholic members from overwhelmingly Catholic districts, and many Republican and southern Democratic members from districts where a priest is seldom seen. In the Senate, almost every senator (except those from some southern states plus Utah and Idaho) had a considerable Catholic minority to consider. But only Rhode Island has a clear statewide Catholic majority (Massachusetts is half and half). Hence the religious issue was approached gingerly, especially by the Catholic senators from predominantly Protestant states (like Jack Miller from Iowa) or the Protestant senators from heavily Catholic states (like Saltonstall from Massachusetts).

School-Aid Debate: Early Rounds /   Senate proceedings on May 16 began routinely. There was a brief prayer, delivered by an out-of-town Lutheran minister (both House and Senate have regular chaplains on their payroll, but visitors often like to substitute). Following the usual "morning hour" (a period reserved for brief statements, not exceeding 3 minutes) Senator Humphrey, acting for the majority leader, moved that the Senate proceed to the consideration of Calendar No. 228 (which was the school-aid bill). This was routinely agreed to, although such a motion is itself debatable (and on a civil rights bill might require weeks). In obtaining recognition, the majority leader (or, as here, his substitute) and the minority leader always receive precedence. Because of their key roles in regulating procedure, they occupy the respective front-row desks on the main aisle. Senator Richard Russell—acknowledged field marshal of the southern Democrats—sits immediately behind the Democratic majority leader, in a position to seek quick recognition from the chair as well as to keep abreast of all negotiations between majority and minority.

Senator Morse, the bill's floor manager, was then recognized. He asked for unanimous consent that both majority and minority staff members of the committee be permitted access to the Senate floor during the days of debate on the bill. This consent was routinely granted. Morse then made an opening speech on the bill, outlining the case for federal aid, inserting into the record the state-by-state enrollments and amount of aid to be received, plus the text of the HEW brief on legal issues. Senator Dirksen persuaded Morse to yield for a question as to whether the equalization formula could be understood "without a course in quadratics, least squares, a book of logarithms, and probably an engineer's slide rule?" The debate was on.

Observers often suspect that floor debate is much less important than decisions reached in conferences held just off the Senate floor. On the afternoon of May 16 this was quite literally true. In midafternoon Morse, who would ordinarily remain on the floor so long as the bill was under consideration (a grueling stint), left the chamber to join the majority leader (Mansfield), majority whip (Humphrey), and Senator Lee Metcalf in a final conference on the question of tactics: one bill or two? At the meeting were Secretary Ribicoff, Lawrence O'Brien (from the White House), and the ubiquitous "Bobbie" Baker (of the Senate staff). Mansfield, Ribicoff, and O'Brien apparently made a last plea for the one-bill approach, but failed to convince Morse and the other senators. The NDEA amendments would, it was decided, be rushed to the Senate floor soon after the public school bill passed. It would not, however, be considered jointly. Mansfield emphasized that this was a Senate decision, and the Administration officials had no voice in it. (Kennedy was on his way to Canada.)

The floor debate was unlikely to change many senatorial minds. It can serve, nevertheless, a wide variety of purposes. To the lawyers in particular it is important in the debate (as in the hearings) to "make a record." Future administrative and perhaps judicial decisions may hinge on the evidence of what the debates indicate was "legislative intent" in regard to some ambiguous provision or unforeseen contingency. A major floor speech may be made for the benefit of either home consumption (Senator Herman Talmadge of Georgia was under considerable pressure from Georgia school teachers to support the bill despite possible segregation complications) or of national publicity (which may well have been in the mind of Senator Goldwater). And there is the continual round of senatorial "mutual admiration" which makes easier the carrying on of business in a body of widely differing viewpoints.

A considerable number of proposed amendments had been drafted by various senators (or, more likely, by their administrative assistants). These proposals, by Senate rule, are submitted to the parliamentarian, printed up in chronological order, and eventually motioned up for debate. The major pending amendments could be grouped into four main categories: (1) issue of funds for segregated schools (four roll calls eventually taken); (2) modifying the state equalization formula (only two roll calls); (3) substitution of some form of tax rebate to the states in place of federal appropriations (four roll calls); and (4) various changes in the scope of the aid program —parochial schools, current operating expenses, dropping teacher salary aid.

Of these the issues touching on segregation were obviously the most explosive. The legal right of the Secretary of HEW to withhold funds from a southern state maintaining segregated schools was cloudy. Arthur Flemming, Eisenhower's last Secretary of HEW, had written the NAACP that he felt he lacked any specific authorization to do so, and Ribicoff indicated the same in a short letter to Vermont's Senator Prouty (who had inquired early in the debate). Some southerners, however, feared a sort of "one-two punch"—federal aid now, but a threatened withdrawal of such aid at some future date. At any rate, any amendment that even seemed to pose a threat to funds for southern schools would be likely to set off a full-scale southern filibuster. Conversely, any wording that even seemed to prevent withholding funds from segregated schools could be counted upon to provoke Congressman Powell into introducing his antisegregation amendment (which would kill the bill in the House). On this issue the "legislative intent" made in the course of Senate debate might indeed be of major future concern.

The other issues could be handled with relative ease so long as the Administration managed to walk the tightrope on segregation. On the second day of debate, however, that issue almost exploded. The mix-up began with Lee Metcalf, a long-time school-aid advocate who was also a former justice of the Montana Supreme Court. While serving in the House Metcalf had devoted great attention to the legal issues revolving around the position of the southern schools in relation to federal aid. In essence, he agreed with the Flemming and Ribicoff opinions. Now Senator Talmadge had drafted an amendment that would give the force of law to this view. On an issue touching segregation the Senate could hardly accept a "Talmadge amendment" as such. Apparently Metcalf was asked if he would introduce such a provision (thus removing the Southern "taint"). Then the rumors began to fly. Majority leader Mansfield indicated that he agreed with his fellow Montanan, but he failed to emphasize that this was very much a personal opinion of his own, not an opinion of the Administration. The reporters went to press with stories of an Administration "deal" with the southern Democrats.

At this point, the drama entered a crucial stage, and legal briefs had to go out the window as "politics" reasserted itself. Senators Morse and Humphrey, well-known civil rights supporters, assured the Senate that the Administration had no intention of supporting any such amendment. Secretary Ribicoff got on the phone to reassure the unpredictable Adam Clayton Powell, who had warned that if there were any such deal he would "fight them tooth and nail with the Powell amendment, and they won't get any legislation because that will be the end of it over on this side of the Capitol." The threatened crisis was averted, but it left frayed nerves, on the Senate side especially. The experience apparently had no educational effect on the majority leader, who was to set off another "rhubarb" a month later by giving a major speech expressing his own very personal views on the touchy Berlin issue.

Amendments Touching on Segregation /   Four amendments that dealt with segregation, directly or indirectly, were brought to a vote. Two were introduced by southern Democrats, the other two by northern Republicans. All four were voted down, as seemed necessary if the bill were to pass. The first proposal to come to a vote was Strom Thurmond's (S.C.) to prohibit withholding of funds under the school-aid program because of racial segregation. This proposal was defeated 70 to 25 (with 19 southern Democrats and 6 conservative Republicans, including Goldwater, in the minority). A much more sophisticated proposal, which accorded with Metcalf's controversial legal analysis, was offered by Georgia's Senator Talmadge. It made no mention of "segregation," but barred withholding of funds from any state education agency "which has complied with the provisions of this Act." This proposal was voted down, 61 to 30. The minority included all twenty-two southern Democrats (Blakely of Texas on a pair), five conservative Republicans, and four non-southern Democrats (including Mansfield and Metcalf).

On the antisegregation side Republican Senator Bush (Conn.) introduced an amendment that was as extreme—and as unlikely to pass—as the Thurmond proposal. Bush sought to require that funds should be granted only to states "proceeding toward full compliance with the constitutional requirement that racial discrimination be ended in public schools." This amendment was defeated, 61 to 25, with twenty-one Republicans and four northern Democrats in the minority. Even New York's Jacob Javits, a leader of the civil rights group, argued against the proposal as "unwise, untimely, prejudicial" to the chances of the bill. As Javits put it: "Notwithstanding our deep feelings about the Alabama violence, we still have to keep our eye on the ball. The ball is the passage of the education bill." Southern senators wisely left the debating to their non-southern colleagues.

A more sophisticated antisegregation move was drafted by Kenneth Keating, New York's other Republican senator. Like the Talmadge amendment (on the other side of the issue) Keating's proposal made no direct mention of segregation. Drawing on language in the Clark-Morse private school-loan bill (see above, p. 45) Keating sought to add a provision authorizing taxpayer's suits to prevent any "unconstitutional" expenditure of funds under the public school bill. This was an ingenious move, that put Morse in the position of having to argue against language he had drafted. It also raised a number of constitutional issues, such as the immunity of the sovereign from suit and whether taxpayer's suits could be authorized even by an act of Congress, but it was all in vain. The obvious intent was to permit suits to block funds going to segregated schools in the South, and hence it suffered from the same political disadvantage as the other proposals relating to segregation.

On the Keating amendment the Senate managed to rise above the usual friendly "colloquies" and engage in genuine, informed debate. Keating, a long-time member of the House Judiciary Committee (and a very able lawyer), gave one-time law school dean Morse some hard moments in the debate, but Morse had the votes—and knew it. The Keating amendment was defeated, 62 to 32. Supporting Keating were 30 Republicans and 2 northern Democrats (Douglas of Illinois and Hart of Michigan). This whole episode left the segregation issue legally unchanged, except for thousands of words of "legislative history."

Other Amendments and Final Passage /   In comparison to the segregation issue, the remaining areas of dispute were relatively tame. The next most controversial of these was probably the question of the equalization formula that would be adopted to distribute aid among the various states. On what should it be based, and with what ratio of equalization? The committee had written in a special provision for areas of very high cost, thus taking care of Alaska. A last-minute attempt by Senator Clark to put in a special provision to take care of a similar problem for the District of Columbia came too late for committee adoption, but was accepted on the floor on a voice vote. Senators Cooper and Javits pressed for a roll call on their alternate equalization formula (for which they had argued, without success, in the committee). It was defeated, 50 to 30.

Ohio Senator Frank Lausche (Democrat) sponsored an amendment to restore the Administration's original authorization ceiling and base the aid on public school enrollment rather than school-age population. Lausche, sometimes regarded as a bit of a moralizer, had become concerned about the "injustice" of counting all children when aid would go only for those in public schools. He had introduced an amendment on the subject in the 1960 Senate debate (on which the Senate had taken one of its rare "division votes" to avoid forcing members to go on the record). He returned to the subject again. The issue had major ramifications and had been carefully considered, pro and con, by both Morse and Thompson (as well as by Monsignor Hochwalt, in the House hearings). Lausche's proposal was rejected, 61 to 32.

The only major amendment adopted by the Senate was one proposed by Vermont Senator Winston L. Prouty, and accepted by Morse. Prouty proposed that federal funds be used to pay operating and maintenance costs (but not debt service), as well as for construction or teacher salaries. This position had been strongly urged by many state school officers, and Prouty argued that it strengthened "state's rights." Some senators disagreed on this, and others (such as Joseph Clark) felt it would tend to dissipate the aid too widely to have a major impact. After Morse obtained Prouty's consent to modify the amendment to ensure that no federal funds would go toward operating costs of parochial schools (in states providing funds for bus transportation or textbooks) the amendment was adopted by a 51 to 39 vote. Democrats supported it roughly 2 to 1; Republicans opposed it roughly 2 to 1.

There were four roll calls on amendments to substitute some form of tax rebate to the states for education in place of direct appropriations. Morse, confident of his votes to defeat the various proposals, chided his colleagues on the variety of such legislative gimmicks. As he put it: "I have fingered through all the amendments of which I have knowledge, and I have not found one which proposes that we ought to remit any part of the internal-revenue funds collected on liquor to send clerical students to divinity schools." The assorted proposals were sponsored by Senators Blakely, Cotton, Case (S.D.), and Proxmire. All were defeated by margins of better than 2 to 1.

The remaining amendments dealt with the scope of the aid program. Goldwater forced a vote on adding loan provisions for parochial schools, but with the NDEA amendments pending, this was not a serious issue. Morse's motion to table the Goldwater amendment was accepted 66 to 25. Another Goldwater motion to strike authorization for aiding teacher salaries went down on a voice vote. Another Cooper-Javits amendment to reduce the authorization to the level originally recommended was defeated on a near party-line vote. And a proposal to limit the administrative costs of the program to $1 million annually was similarly disposed of, 63 to 24.

With the stockpile of amendments exhausted, debate on final passage of the bill was carried over until May 25. The outcome was a foregone conclusion and the closing arguments were made before almost empty galleries, with only a handful of faithful wire-service men in the press galleries. Shortly after five o'clock, Mansfield huddled with Dirksen, then with Thurmond, to draft a final unanimous consent agreement. It limited the remaining debate on final passage to three hours. At about seven o'clock Goldwater created a minor stir by producing a copy of the bill, already printed and bearing the notation "Passed the Senate, May 25, 1961." For once Morse was caught off guard, but aides soon brought the word that this was perfectly normal printing procedure and the bill was not authenticated until signed by the enrollment clerk (and that would wait for the official Senate vote!).

A little before eight o'clock the bells sounded for the final quorum call, then for the vote. The *Congressional Record* prints the final result of each roll call but does not indicate the full process that goes into that result. Ordinarily many senators are not on the floor as the roll call begins, and may arrive after their name has been called. After the alphabetical roll the chair then recognizes each senator who is standing at his desk (the late arrivals). Some senator, however, may still not have made it to the floor. To handle this development, especially for senators seeking to maintain 100 per cent voting participation, the Democrats have a well-oiled process for delaying completion of the roll call for a few additional minutes. Each senator is entitled, before the result is announced, to rise and make a parliamentary inquiry as to how he is recorded. If Bobbie Baker, the majority clerk, sees that a Democrat is missing he passes the word to one of the senators who has voted. That senator pops up, is recognized, and makes a parliamentary inquiry as to how he is recorded. A chain reaction then follows (to the mystification of the gallery visitors). On final passage of the school bill, Senator Clark was detained, but after 8 or 10 "parliamentary inquiries," he arrived. The bill then passed, 49 to 34, with twelve additional senators on "pairs" (six for and six against the bill).

On final passage the bill was supported by all non-southern Democrats except Dodd of Connecticut (Connecticut fared lowest in the final equalization formula), Hickey of Wyoming, and Lausche of Ohio. The southern Democrats were split; most southern "moderates" were for passage, most southern conservatives were opposed, as indicated below:

SOUTHERNERS VOTING (OR PAIRED) *for* PASSAGE:	SOUTHERNERS VOTING (OR PAIRED) *against* PASSAGE:
HILL (Ala.)	BYRD (Va.)
SPARKMAN (Ala.)	ROBERTSON (Va.)
GORE (Tenn.)	THURMOND (S.C.)
KEFAUVER (Tenn.)	JOHNSTON (S.C.)
ERVIN (N.C.)	EASTLAND (Miss.)
JORDAN (N.C.)	STENNIS (Miss.)
FULBRIGHT (Ark.)	TALMADGE (Ga.)
YARBOROUGH (Tex.)	RUSSELL (Ga.)
SMATHERS (Fla.)	ELLENDER (La.)
	LONG (La.)
	McCLELLAN (Ark.)
	HOLLAND (Fla.)
	BLAKLEY (Tex.)

A total of ten Republicans voted, paired, or announced their support of final passage: KUCHEL (Calif.), JAVITS (N.Y.), AIKEN (Vt.), PROUTY (Vt.), WILEY (Wisc.), MRS. SMITH (Me.), CASE (N.J.) COOPER (Ky.), CARLSON (Kans.), and FONG (Hawaii).

After the vote was taken there was the usual round of congratulatory speeches for Morse, and Morse gave his thanks to the hard-working professional staff of the committee. The Senate had done its work—as it had on a variety of education bills dating back to the 80th Congress and Senator Taft. The big test would be the House. Before the vote had been taken majority leader Mansfield had noted that over the past decade "a variety of obstacles, including the threat of a Presidential veto" had prevented enactment of an aid-to-education bill. Now, however, "for the first time the prospects of accomplishment are bright." In regard to the situation in the House the distinguished majority leader could hardly have been more wrong.

Trouble in the House: The "Unholy Alliance" Gets Religion

In the Senate a major bill is thoroughly considered both in committee and on the floor. In the House there are two additional hurdles that most bills must face after committee clearance, but before final House debate. The first of these is the problem of obtaining a "rule" (technically a special resolution) from the Committee on Rules, providing for consideration of the measure and setting the conditions of debate. Without such a "rule," a bill languishes on one of the House calendars with little hope of being considered. (The exceptional means available for circumventing the Rules Committee—suspension of the rules, discharge petition, and calendar Wednesday—all involve substantial disadvantages and are seldom resorted to.)

The Rules Committee usually holds open hearings on the granting of a rule. Ordinarily the chairman of the committee involved, the ranking minority member, and perhaps the bill's sponsor will appear before the Rules Committee. Venerable committee chairmen, sitting in the witness chair in Room G-12, find themselves on the receiving end of sharp questions. The Rules Committee can delay granting a rule, or refuse outright. It can provide for several hours, or even days of debate, or for only one or two hours. It can even grant a "rule" waiving points of order (usually done only for appropriations bills containing some "legislative" material) or a "closed" or so-called "gag rule" under which no amendments are permitted that are unacceptable to the sponsoring committee chairman. (This is ordinarily reserved for complex Ways and Means bills, such as tax revisions.) For most controversial bills the resolution adopted is an "open rule" (permitting amendments subject to the "germaneness" requirement of the House), providing for several hours of debate to be equally divided between supporters and opponents of the measure. Once the "rule" is granted by the committee, adoption of the rule and consideration of the measure are routinely scheduled for House attention. Both parties send out weekly "whip notices" urging members to be present for expected roll-call votes.

Thus in 1960, after a year of trying, school-aid supporters finally obtained a "rule" (House Resolution 536) for consideration of a school construction bill. The resolution provided:

> *Resolved,* That upon the adoption of this resolution it shall be in order to move that the House resolve itself into the Committee of the Whole House on the State of the Union for the consideration of the bill (H.R. 10128) to authorize Federal financial assistance to the States to be used for constructing school facilities. After general debate, which shall be confined to the bill, and shall continue not to exceed four hours, to be equally divided and controlled by the chairman and ranking minority member of the Com-

mittee on Education and Labor, the bill shall be read for amendment under
the five minute rule. . . . At the conclusion of such consideration the
Committee shall rise and report the bill to the House with such amendments as may have been adopted, and any member may demand a separate
vote in the House on any of the amendments adopted in the Committee of
the Whole to the bill or committee substitute. The previous question shall
be considered as ordered on the bill and amendments thereto to final passage without intervening motion except one motion to recommit with or
without instructions.

The immediate problem facing Congressmen Thompson and Bolling was
to get Judge Smith to schedule hearings on granting a "rule," and then to
make sure they could count on at least eight of the fifteen Rules Committee
members to support it. Once this was done there would be a second special
hurdle, indicated in the resolution above, and that would be "Committee
of the Whole" consideration of the bill.

In the House a bill is actually considered twice, or at least under two
different sets of circumstances. First it is debated, subject to amendments
in "Committee of the Whole." Only at the completion of such consideration
is the measure then reported to the House proper. The Committee of the
Whole and the House are, in terms of membership, the same bodies. But
there are crucial differences in operating procedures. The most important
of these is not the difference in who presides or in how many members
constitute a quorum, but that in Committee of the Whole there are *no*
record votes. Votes may be by voice, or standing, or by tellers, but on none
of these is there any official record of who voted and who did not, or of how
any member voted. (In very exceptional circumstances the press may attempt to identify each member, but this is difficult.)

In Committee of the Whole a premium is placed on effective organization and on the sense of commitment that will hold members on the floor
hour after hour. Thus early in 1961, Administration supporters were caught
off guard on a controversial minimum wage vote, which was lost 186 to
185 (with a dozen or more "supporters" skulking in the cloakrooms or
House barbershop). Here supporters of aid to education have had serious
trouble, more trouble than would be expected in the regular House proceedings, or in the Senate. As Congressman Bolling frankly put it in 1957:
"If a secret vote were taken on Federal aid to education a majority of the
House would probably vote against it." Most close observers would agree
with Bolling—it only needs to be added that the Committee of the Whole
procedure comes as close to being a secret vote as one can get without
actually using unmarked ballots. Thus in Committee of the Whole an education bill may be gutted by damaging changes, have whole titles omitted,
or provisions such as the "Powell" amendment may be added. The measure
that emerges from Committee of the Whole may be one that has little

chance in regular House proceedings, even though record votes may be taken on the changes adopted in Committee of the Whole sessions.

Congressman McCormack and the Rules Committee / By early June, House aid-to-education activity was proceeding at several levels. Individual members were being deluged with mail, much of it strongly for or strongly against aid for parochial schools. House offices were humming with the noise of the "autotype" and "robotype" machines (devices similar to the old player-piano roll that automatically type a form letter on an electric typewriter, but with the secretary typing in the address and salutation by hand). On June 1 the Education and Labor subcommittees, meeting jointly, began hearings on amendments to the NDEA, including loans for special purpose classrooms for nonpublic schools. And, in the inner recesses of the Capitol Building and House offices some very delicate maneuvering was underway to test the "climate" of the Rules Committee.

The subcommittee hearings on the NDEA had gotten off to a somewhat shaky start when Dr. Sterling McMurrin, the new Commissioner of Education, had been unwilling to take an official stand on the proposals for aid to nonpublic schools. Neither the President nor Secretary Ribicoff appeared at all anxious to be committed to support of aid to parochial schools—the issue could easily be damaging both to President Kennedy's re-election chances in 1964 and to Secretary Ribicoff's "availability" for nomination to a seat on the Supreme Court, should a vacancy occur. As a result most congressional contacts with HEW tended to go to Assistant Secretary James Quigley, a former Pennsylvania congressman (and a Catholic). The proposals for parochial school aid were endorsed by a spokesman for the AFL-CIO, by Monsignor Hochwalt, and by committee chairman Adam Clayton Powell (an ordained Baptist minister, as well as a congressman). Such aid was strongly opposed by both the president and the executive-director of the Council of Chief State School Officers, and by a spokesman for Protestants and Other Americans United.

The top strategist for the parochial school supporters appeared to be none other than House majority leader John McCormack. McCormack was reported to have sought assurances that the Administration bill (for public school grants) would not be called up for House action before the NDEA amendments (suggesting parochial school loans) were also ready for floor action. Here, again, was the old tactical question: Which goes first, and one bill or two?

Administration supporters were anxious to get on with the public school bill. Judge Smith is a proven master of delay tactics, and a controversial bill's chances usually lessen as a session draws to its hectic close. But the Rules Committee ordinarily meets only at the call of the chairman, and hearings for the school-aid bill still had not been set. Judge Smith, obviously in no hurry, indicated that it was "customary" for the committee to hear testimony from the chairman of the committee seeking a rule. Congressman Powell, the chairman, was attending an International Labor Organization meeting in Geneva.

Meanwhile supporters of the parochial school loans were doing some canvassing of their own. Would the NDEA amendments be granted a "rule," and if so what sort of chance did they have in the House? With Smith, Colmer, and the five Republicans opposed it would require the support of every one of the other members of Rules to clear the measure. Could this support be counted on? It soon appeared not—the eight-man "Rayburn majority" included three Democrats from the South (all three Methodists) who were under strong pressure to oppose any aid for parochial schools. Without their support the parochial loan proposal (in NDEA) would never even reach the House floor, and it could not be proposed as a floor amendment to the public school bill because of the "germaneness" rule.

In the House, however, supporters of aid for parochial schools still had much more leverage than in the Senate. The percentage of Catholic representatives is almost double that of Catholic senators (88 out of 437, compared to 12 out of 100). More important, the eight-man "Rayburn majority" in the Rules Committee included three Catholic Democrats: Ray Madden (Ind.), James Delaney (New York), and Thomas P. O'Neill, Jr. (who represents John F. Kennedy's old Boston-Cambridge district in Massachusetts). Without their cooperation the Administration bill could not be cleared.

Amid conflicting reports of possible White House intervention to move the parochial school provisions to the floor first (Ribicoff and Lawrence O'Brien were understood to favor this, as they had in the Senate) and of a showdown between John McCormack and Speaker Sam Rayburn (the latter demanding that the public school bill be cleared), the maneuvering continued. Finally on June 15 the specific cause of the difficulty became public. Rules Committee members O'Neill and Delaney (both Catholics) served notice that they would not vote for a rule for the public school bill until the NDEA parochial school provisions were also ready for the floor. This raised the possibility that a one-bill strategy might be forced on the Administration, against its wishes, by the unusual line-up in the Rules Committee.

The President, back from his European meetings with DeGaulle and Khrushchev, got the bad news at the regular Tuesday morning meeting with congressional leaders. Informally Rayburn was reported to have told Kennedy that the education bill was "as dead as slavery." For the public, however, Rayburn would only indicate that the bill "is in trouble." Congressman Powell, back from Geneva, was equally pessimistic. "I don't think we can pass it this year unless someone blows the whistle," Powell said. But there were serious doubts that even the President was in any position to settle the dispute, or had much taste for attempting to do so.

That same afternoon, June 20, there was an unusual executive session of the Rules Committee. Richard Bolling, strategist for the Administration supporters, moved to set the following Tuesday for the beginning of hearings on the public school bill (hearings ordinarily require only thirty or forty minutes, but might be dragged on into a very extensive series). This would be the last opportunity before the week-long vacation over July 4. One of the Republican members countered with a substitute motion that no hearings be held until the parochial school proposal was also before the committee. This substitute, delaying action on the Administration proposal, was adopted 9 to 6. The line-up was one of the most unusual in the history of the committee. The majority consisted of the five Republicans, plus southern Democrats Smith and Colmer, plus Catholic Democrats O'Neill and Delaney. The coalition of Republicans and southern Democrats had often been referred to as an "unholy alliance;" now, one wit suggested, "the 'unholy alliance' has got religion."

Meanwhile the Education and Labor Committee was making slow progress on the NDEA amendments. Republican members, aware of the logjam in Rules, adopted various delaying tactics. It was June 27 before the full committee voted to report the measure, 19 to 11. Its prospects, however, appeared extremely poor. Several Republican members of the committee indicated support for the original NDEA provisions (which had been recommended to Congress by President Eisenhower), but they opposed the committee's changes. In their minority views to the committee report they particularly criticized the attempt to make the NDEA amendments the vehicle for authorizing loans to nonpublic schools. To many members of the House the committee bill (H.R. 7904) was perceived simply as "the parochial school" bill.

Although none of the three education measures (public school bill, aid to higher education, and NDEA amendments) had yet been cleared by the Rules Committee, they had been discussed from time to time on the floor of the House. Interested House members can obtain a special order granting them time to deliver a major floor speech at the conclusion of a day's business (no one guarantees them an audience). As early as March 30, Congressman Pucinski had presented the case for aid to nonpublic schools in a floor speech. On April 26 Thompson had presented the results of a professional poll of New Jersey adults on the aid issue; on June 1 Carroll Kearns (the ranking Republican of the full committee) had outlined a substitute measure; on May 2 Frelinghuysen had spoken on the education program during the first 100 days of the Kennedy administration. On June 29 Frelinghuysen was recognized for two hours to present a "Report on American Education" prepared by the House Republican Policy Committee. Thompson presented a detailed one-hour reply on July 24.

Opposition to federal aid seemed to be mounting outside Congress also. At the annual Governors' Conference in Honolulu a resolution opposing aid to teacher salaries was narrowly defeated by a 24 to 23 vote (with the majority including three territorial governors appointed by the President). The governors supported aid for school construction, 35 to 12. On the same day Republican House leader Charles Halleck read a letter from former President Eisenhower strongly opposing the Administration's aid-to-education proposal. Appearing on the weekly televized report of the Republican House and Senate leaders (dubbed the "Ev and Charlie Show" around Washington) Halleck quoted Eisenhower's warning that the proposals "would ultimately result in Federal control of education." Fears of federal control had also been fueled by the ill-timed release of a sixty-page HEW pamphlet entitled "A Federal Education Agency for the Future."

The final blow to the President's original education proposals came in the Rules Committee on July 18. Both the public school and parochial loan (NDEA amendments) measures were awaiting special rules, as was the bill for aid to higher education. But Congressman James Delaney was still not satisfied—a few days earlier he had indicated that all three bills should be killed, and a new "nondiscriminatory" measure drafted to permit federal grants to parents of children attending public or nonpublic schools. In the committee the other two Catholic Democrats (Ray Madden and Thomas P. O'Neill) disagreed, but only one vote was needed to give the old coalition a majority.

It was William Colmer who presented the motion to table all three education bills. Colmer's motion was adopted, 8 to 7, with the majority consisting of the five Republicans, southern Democrats Smith and Colmer, and Delaney. This decision could be reconsidered, but Colmer followed with an immediate motion to reconsider, which Clarence J. Brown (the ranking Republican) moved to table. This motion also was adopted, and under the committee rules no further motion to reconsider would be in order. Thus none of the three bills could be called up. Less than six months after the climactic fight to expand the Committee on Rules, Judge Smith and the old "coalition," plus one unexpected recruit (Congressman Delaney), had killed what the President had termed "probably the most important piece of domestic legislation" in his program.

The Administration Tries Again / With all three of the Administration's major education bills thus bottled up in the Rules Committee, the next move was up to the President. For the benefit of his White House press conference Kennedy indicated that he was "hopeful" that supporters of his education program "will use those procedures which are available to them under the rules of the House to bring this to a vote and that a majority of the members of Congress will support it." The original proposals (or some substitute measure) could still be brought to the House floor by resort to one of three procedures. A discharge petition was one possibility, but there seemed very little prospect of obtaining the necessary 219 signatures. Many House members are opposed to using discharge petitions, even for bills they favor, on the ground that the procedure is a threat to the integrity of the committee system. There was even less possibility that the education bill could be passed under "suspension of the rules" procedure, which requires a two-thirds majority of those voting. The bill might, however, be called up by the Education and Labor Committee chairman (Adam Clayton Powell) under the rarely used procedure of "calendar Wednesday." Passage then would require only a simple majority of those voting.

The House customarily avoids the "calendar Wednesday" proceeding, but one-third of the members is sufficient to require its use. When "calendar Wednesday" is used there is first a call of the legislative committees, in alphabetical order. The chairman of a committee that is called may, without a special rule, request the consideration of any bill previously reported out by his committee. Only a simple majority is required to approve consideration and to pass the bill. On paper, "calendar Wednesday" looks as easy as operating under a special rule granting two hours of general debate, but in practice, members often complicate it by resorting to parliamentary obstruction, repeated quorum calls, and other unusual tactics. But these informal hazards seemed less formidable than the formal complications involved in the resort to a discharge petition or suspension of the rules.

Granted that a procedural loophole was available, there was still a major political problem. What sort of measure might, despite the religious issue, win the support of a majority? Chances for the President's original public school proposals seemed virtually nil. Alternatively, school-aid supporters might seek to use the expiring provisions of the popular impacted areas program as the core of a watered-down "compromise" measure. Congressmen from districts receiving substantial impacted areas aid might be willing to go along with a bill extending that program and providing for general aid for classroom construction, but not for teacher salaries. Any measure voted by the House would have to go to a House-Senate conference committee, which might report a more substantial bill reflecting provisions of the measure passed by the Senate in May.

President Kennedy still showed little inclination for directly intervening in the education struggle. During late July and early August his attention was concentrated on winning congressional approval for his highly controversial program for long-term financing of foreign aid. Members of the House Foreign Affairs and Senate Foreign Relations Committees, rather than those involved in the education fight, were invited to the White

House. The President's pleas for national unity in the face of the Berlin crisis could be destroyed by a bruising floor fight over aid to schools. And the President's requests for increased defense spending were already being matched by Republican suggestions for domestic economy moves.

When HEW Secretary Ribicoff sounded out congressional sentiments on the possibility of a compromise bill he found little enthusiasm. Senators were opposed to settling for what Hubert Humphrey called "a patchwork that would please no one," and preferred to try for a broad bill in the next session. Speaker Sam Rayburn and most school-aid leaders in the House were dubious that any general aid bill would pass the House. But the President, reluctant to draw a complete blank in the education field, requested that one more effort be made to salvage at least part of the Administration program. Aid for teacher salaries would be dropped, but a one-year program of 325 million dollars for classroom construction in overcrowded school districts would be linked to extension of impacted areas aid and of the college student loan provisions of the NDEA. This package, introduced by Congressman Frank Thompson as H.R. 8890, would be brought to the floor via "calendar Wednesday" procedure. A second bill, H.R. 8900, embodied the Administration's proposals for 1½ billion dollars in loans and grants for higher education.

The Administration's compromise, H.R. 8890, satisfied no one. The National Education Association repudiated it. Opponents of federal aid, sensing victory, attacked it. Liberal Republicans, who had supported the move to expand the Rules Committee, criticized the resort to "calendar Wednesday." The bill was rushed through the Education and Labor Committee, with discussion limited to seventy minutes. The following day, August 30, was a Wednesday. Without attempting to obtain a rule, school-aid supporters planned to call the new proposal up under "calendar Wednesday" business.

Opponents of the bill were confident that it would be defeated. When the clerk began the call of committees no other chairman sought to use the day, thus delaying a showdown. When the Committee on Education and Labor was called, Congressman Powell called for consideration of H.R. 8890. Congressman Hébert, a Louisiana Democrat, asked for the yeas and nays on the question of consideration (which is nondebatable). The roll call, which was on whether to consider the bill rather than on whether to pass it, was a stunning defeat for the Administration. The count was 242 opposed, and only 170 in favor. Most Catholic Democrats (including Congressman Delaney) voted in favor of consideration, but there were only 21 southern Democrats and a mere 6 Republicans voting yea. The massive opposition consisted of 160 Republicans, 70 southern Democrats, and 12 non-southern Democrats.

The President was to suffer yet one more defeat on aid for education.

With rejection of the stripped-down compromise the way was clear for a straight renewal of the impacted areas program and NDEA. The Administration wanted a one-year renewal, so that a package education bill could be tried again in 1962. But the House leaders agreed to bring up, under suspension of the rules, a two-year extension. This extension sailed through the House, 378 to 32. Meanwhile Judge Smith indicated that he had no plans for granting a rule for the less controversial bill for aid to higher education. It would have to carry over to the second session, despite the President's desire that it be enacted before Congress adjourned.

On the Senate side, the President and his supporters made a final try to limit extension of impacted areas aid and NDEA to one year. But by a 45 to 40 vote the Senate refused. The President's plea was heeded by only one southern Democrat (Kefauver) and only five Republicans (Javits, Keating, Cooper, Wiley, and Case of New Jersey). The Senate-passed bill was then passed by the House, on September 18, by 342 to 18. The unwelcome measure, S. 2393, then went to the White House. It gave the President none of the major provisions he had requested, and it extended for two years those programs that he wanted extended for only one year. When the President signed the bill in late September, it was no festive occasion; no school-aid supporters would come forward to claim the ceremonial pen.

Conclusion: Some Cautionary Comments

As Congress prepared to adjourn in September a new school year was beginning. For the seventeenth straight year enrollments were setting a new record. There were the usual reports in some areas of crowded classrooms, inadequately qualified teachers, and use of temporary quarters. But from other areas there were reports of an excess of teacher applicants. Prospects for direct federal aid to elementary and secondary schools, however, no longer rested on calculations of the classroom gap. The bitterness of the 1961 legislative struggle and the difficulties of reaching a consensus on the status of nonpublic schools will not be soon forgotten. In private, many school-aid supporters admitted that federal aid of the sort proposed by President Kennedy was dead, not just for the 87th Congress, but probably for the decade of the 1960's.

What had gone wrong? To opponents of federal aid nothing had gone wrong. But among school-aid supporters there were bitter recriminations. Senator Morse, a leading supporter of aid for both public and nonpublic schools, laid the blame on the Catholic hierarchy and the failure of the House of Representatives to establish clear procedures for majority rule. Others argued that the Catholic response was inevitable, given the insistence of the National Education Association that there be aid for teacher salaries in the program. To the editorial writers of the New York *Times* (which had ardently favored aid to public schools), the outcome was "the tragic end to a chapter of legislative irresponsibility and inept executive leadership." The *Times* concluded: "The story of the school bill's debacle has been a succession of profiles in lack of courage."

The one point on which all could agree was the lack of Presidential leadership. In the speech that opened his 1960 campaign Kennedy had said that this decade "will demand that the President place himself in the very thick of the fight, that he care passionately about the fate of the people he leads, that he be willing to serve them at the risk of incurring their momentary displeasure." This was certainly not the course that the President had followed in regard to education. But in national politics there are always a number of major issues at stake. The President was simply not prepared to jeopardize his whole legislative program—and perhaps his chances for re-election—by a bitter fight to the death for aid to education. Lacking a popular ground swell in support of the program, the President's chief alternative was to press for some acceptable compromise to aid for nonpublic schools. And this was a move involving the very greatest risks for a Catholic President.

Back in January, on the eve of the Rules Committee fight, Congressman Richard Bolling had compared Judge Smith's political skill to the "way a great conductor conducts an orchestra." Bolling continued:

> But on an economic issue, or a welfare issue, if there are, let's say, five or six of them, he'll play them as carefully as he can and very skillfully to kill as many as possible, but if he has to knuckle under in order to get X by going along with A he will. It's really magnificent skill. As a legislative technician I can only admire him.

The President's legislative problem was, like that of Judge Smith, to get as many victories as possible, but to "knuckle under" when necessary. By the end of the 1961 session the President could count an impressive series of legislative victories, including aid for depressed areas, broadened minimum wage coverage, and a liberal housing bill. He had fought hard for long-term financing of foreign aid, although he had had to settle for substantially less than he asked for. The Administration had deliberately refrained from endorsing civil rights legislation in order to facilitate passage of other parts of its program. Similarly, the President apparently decided to knuckle under on aid to education. He could not hope to win every round against the conservative coalition in the House.

If politics is viewed as the art of the possible then the President's inaction does not appear so strange. But what of the role of Congress itself? Was the defeat of school aid a failure of leadership within the House (where the Speaker must make some of the same painful choices as the

President does), a result of antiquated parliamentary procedures, or the upshot of individual irresponsibility? One could hardly blame the machinery —when a new bottleneck developed in the expanded Rules Committee, a bill could always be brought to the floor by other means. If a solid majority of the House had favored federal aid it surely would have been passed. Lacking such a majority a bill still might have been enacted, depending upon the quality of leadership behind it, the degree of public controversy, and the intensity of opposition. On all three counts the education bill was in trouble.

Congress in general and the House particularly can be counted on to express strongly held local views, as well as certain institutional attitudes. Here the contrast between the Senate and the House is particularly fascinating. Senators, representing large, diverse constituencies and serving long terms, tended to take a more nearly "presidential" view: education was important, it needed increased resources, and a federal grant-in-aid program was an acceptable solution. For members of the House, however, the specifics of the program were vital, fear of "federal control" was widespread, and feeling on the parochial school question—pro and con—was intense. Moreover, many House members have had unpleasant experiences with highly organized pay increase campaigns of postal employees and civil servants; they dreaded the possibility of adding the nation's teachers, even indirectly, to their future problems.

Could the President have imposed his "national" view of the matter, even in the face of determined congressional opposition? One can never know for sure, but there is considerable reason to think he *could* have done so, but only at the cost of disaster for much of the rest of his program, sharpened religious cleavage in America, and seriously endangering his own re-election prospects. Even in this age of strong Presidential leadership there are limits on any President's political resources. Faced with many different political problems and having only limited resources, even of time and human energy, a President must choose his showdown battles with care.

Every congressional session involves hundreds of little legislative skirmishes, only a few of which develop into full scale battles. The President recognized that civil rights legislation automatically leads to an all-out legislative Donnybrook (or Gettysburg), and consequently he made no effort to push for such legislation (which is politically vital only in election years, especially Presidential election years). This circumstance made it easier for Democratic leaders in the House to court substantial southern Democratic support, with Georgia's Representative Carl Vinson as the key counterweight to the ultraconservative Judge Smith. As a result the President was able to get through most of his antirecession measures (which had top priority) and much of his domestic legislation other than education and the subjects deliberately held back for 1962, such as general tax revision and medical care for the aged.

As the dispute over education developed it became obvious that the subject was more in the class with civil rights than with such mundane matters as minimum wage, housing and urban redevelopment, or social security coverage. In regard to education there were at least three discernable levels of disagreement. On the first level there were low-temperature disputes over detailed matters of program administration, state allocation formulas, and so forth that could be adjusted by normal bureaucratic and interest group bargaining. Such disputes would exist even if there were a clear national consensus in favor of federal aid.

At an intermediate level was the more basic split over the desirability of such a program, typified by the opposing views of the National Education Association and the U.S. Chamber of Commerce. This sort of conflict can still be handled, although it becomes difficult if the issues are framed in symbolic terms ("federal aid" versus "federal control").

At a third level, such high temperature issues as segregation and the role of parochial schools are generally beyond the ability of Congress to handle. Next to being shot up by Puerto Rican nationalists (as happened in 1954), there are few less appealing prospects, especially for the House, than a floor fight combining race, religion, and control of the schools.

Despite the outcome of the 1961 struggle, congressional discussion of the wisdom and of the need for greater federal support for education will continue. House Democrats of the "pragmatic liberal" type, who prefer obtaining half a loaf to waging losing fights, plan to press for early passage in 1962 of the Administration's proposals for aid to higher education. After all, they argue, the war babies for whom Senator Taft had been concerned in the 1940's are now graduating from high school. Elementary school enrollments in 1961 were up only 1.2 per cent over 1960 figures, whereas college enrollments were up 7.5 per cent. Federal assistance for higher education would lighten the burden on states and localities—and on the Catholic education system—thus indirectly helping them meet the burdens of supporting elementary and secondary schools. Such a federal program would also be more directly geared to meeting the needs of science and defense. Whether such a measure can be enacted remains to be seen. The issues of race and religion should be less dangerous, but there always remain the normal hazards of the legislative process—such as the Rules Committee.

Sources

THE best introduction to congressional action on federal aid to education is the annual volumes of *Congressional Quarterly Almanac,* especially for 1949 and 1950, 1956 and 1957, and 1960. For the 1961 Kennedy proposals there was a wealth of material inserted from time to time in the Appendix or appearing in the body of the daily *Congressional Record.* For floor debate on the House Rules Committee see the January 31 issue; for Senate debate on the education bill see the issues from May 16 through May 25. Political maneuvers were reported quite extensively in the New York *Times,* but see also the *Wall Street Journal* and the Washington *Post.*

The hearings of both the House and Senate committees have been published. For the House see "Federal Aid to Schools," *Hearings before the General Subcommittee on Education of the Committee on Education and Labor* (87th Congress, 1st Session), Parts 1 and 2. For the Senate see "Public School Assistance Act of 1961," *Hearings before the Subcommittee on Education of the Labor and Public Welfare Committee* (87th Congress, 1st Session), Parts 1 and 2. Separate hearings were held in both House and Senate on the "National Defense Education Act" (including proposed loans for nonpublic schools), and in the House on "Aid to Higher Education." These also have been published.

For their willingness to fit interviews into busy schedules the author is indebted to John R. Miles of the U.S. Chamber of Commerce, Robert Pennington and other staff members of the National Education Association, and Representatives Richard Bolling, Peter Frelinghuysen, and Frank Thompson. The author also benefited from discussions of the bill with several of the 1961 Congressional Fellows of the American Political Science Association. Finally, an earlier draft benefited substantially from the comments of Professors David B. Truman, Frank Munger, and Nelson Polsby, Dr. Robert L. Peabody, Charles Clapp, and George Chall. Naturally, none of the above should be taxed with any responsibility for particular statements or for the over-all point of view expressed in this study.

Foreign Aid to Spain and Yugoslavia:

Harry Truman Does His Duty

Louis W. Koenig

NEW YORK UNIVERSITY

"A short time after the Germans surrendered in Trieste, Tito announced that he was going to occupy the territory. . . . I asked the Commanding General of the Armed Forces in Europe how long it would take to get three divisions to the Brenner Pass. He needed . . . a couple of days. . . . I said to Tito, 'Come over, Tito, I'll meet you at the Brenner Pass in about three days,' and he didn't come."
—HARRY S. TRUMAN

"I never had any use for Franco. . . . I never gave him any house. He wouldn't let a Baptist be buried in daylight. That's the truth. He had to be buried at night in plowed ground."
—HARRY S. TRUMAN

No One Case

 can capture all the facets of the Presidency. A President may operate one day at a Summit Conference, another day in hard bargaining with his own party leaders in Congress over a minimum wage bill, and still another day to resolve a sharp conflict within his own executive branch between his Secretaries of State and Defense.

This case focuses on the administrative style of President Harry S. Truman as mirrored in two episodes. In the first, the President took the initiative in establishing a program of aid to Communist Yugoslavia in 1950. In the second, the President faced congressional pressure in the same year to compel him to give aid to Fascist Spain, against his wishes.

Our primary interest here is not in relating a set of inside conversations or previously undisclosed bargains involved in these two incidents. Rather the case seeks to probe the view of the Presidency held by the man who sat at the executive desk in the Oval Office at 1600 Pennsylvania Avenue.

Fortunately, President Truman has provided, in his two-volume *Memoirs* and in many of his "from-the-hip" comments, a good deal of insight into his perspectives. These will be our perspectives as the case unfolds.

On the basis of his own experience, Truman has pictured what to him constitutes the elements of a "strong" President. He sees the Presidency as essentially a concentration of monumental responsibility and solitary power. He wrote in the preface to his *Memoirs* that

> The Presidency of the United States carries with it a responsibility so personal as to be without parallel. Very few are ever authorized to speak for the President. No one can make decisions for him. No one can know all the processes and stages of his thinking in making important decisions. Even those closest to him, even members of his immediate family, never know all the reasons why he does certain things and why he comes to

certain conclusions. To be President of the United States is to be lonely, very lonely at times of great decisions.

Truman would be the first to attest that quiet and repose are no part of the modern President's solitude. He is truly a fortress perpetually under siege from problems that bear on foreign affairs, domestic welfare, and national security; from administrative subordinates who press for his approval of their favorite programs and policy proposals; from legislators whose support must be won or whose opposition mollified; from some knotty problem of patronage or another related aspect of the management of his party; from the spokesmen of the group interests that abound in our society, spokesmen who insist—sometimes shrilly—in getting something from government. Truman has portrayed the President's situation even more graphically: "Being a President is like riding a tiger. A man has to keep on riding or be swallowed."

In his writings and comments, Truman has provided a recipe for Presidential self-preservation. For dealing with his department secretaries, who may both help and hamper him, Truman simply stipulates, "It is a very satisfactory arrangement if the President keeps his hands on the reins and knows exactly what goes on in each department. That he has to do if he is to be successful." For another thing, the President must have a clear idea where the tasks of his subordinates properly end and his own tasks begin. Truman sees it this way:

> There are a great many men who labor diligently behind the scenes before a policy statement can be announced. The President, of course, can neither speak nor listen to each and every one of them. But their work ends where the President's work begins, for then he has to make the decision. And when they have spent days, perhaps months, in the study of just one situation, the President faces a multitude of decisions every day.

Various commentators, including Winston Churchill have hailed Truman's skill and courage as President in making great decisions. Truman himself, it can be pointed out, concurs in this happy judgment: "I have been asked whether I have any regrets about any of the major decisions I had to make as President. I have none. . . . I do not see how I could have acted very differently."

In these reflections on the Presidency, Truman pictured himself as a strong President—a man who commands and pursues his objectives with utmost vigor. His long years as an elected political figure from Missouri and the realities of congressional and public resistance to some of his programs, however, sometimes obliged him to put rhetoric aside, to moderate his tactics, or even to abandon his cherished programs.

This case is a study of the relationship between the management of an assertive Presidency and the realities of American politics.

The Presidency's Climate: 1950

1950 was a year of confusion and adjustment, of clarification and transition in United States foreign policy. In that year the nation had to make a slow and painful adaptation to new responsibilities and a new world position. The United States had only recently rejected isolationism and accepted the United Nations; only recently had this nation become the organizer of new and dynamic alliances.

The necessary adjustments were rendered more difficult by the emergence of the Soviet Union as a menacing imperialist power, by the loss of the Chinese mainland to Communist domination, and the eruption of the Korean conflict on June 25, 1950, when troops of the North Korean "Democratic People's Republic" struck southward across the 38th parallel in an unprovoked surprise attack on the lawfully established Republic of Korea. Before the year was out, Communist China itself intervened in the Korean conflict on a massive scale.

Those charged with the responsibility of conducting United States foreign policy were also facing up to a formidable internal ordeal. In February, Senator Joseph McCarthy of Wisconsin was making a series of speeches implying that the State Department was "thoroughly infested" with Communists. The Senator offered to name 205, 57, or 81 employees —the number varied frequently—"who were known to the Secretary of State as being members of the Communist party and who nevertheless are still working and shaping the policy of the State Department." The McCarthy crusade eventually linked itself to the considerable Republican agitation on Far Eastern policy and thus assured itself the support of such leading Republicans as Senators Kenneth Wherry, Robert A. Taft, and Styles Bridges. By March and April, Wherry was declaring that the Secretary of State "must go" because he was a "bad security risk," and Taft was condemning "the pro-Communist group in the State Department."

But the man who bore the brunt of these pressures, President Harry S. Truman, was not without resources. In 1948, less than two years before these hard events, he had won re-election to the Presidential office in one of the most remarkable contests in the nation's history. His opponent, New York Governor Thomas E. Dewey, was hailed as a sure winner by the professional public opinion polls and seemingly by the man in the street. Indeed, before the Democratic nominating convention in Philadelphia, a concerted movement of party chieftains, ranging from Chester Bowles of Connecticut to Governor J. Strom Thurmond of South Carolina, sought to prevent Truman's renomination, but they failed when they could not agree on a substitute candidate. In the ensuing electoral campaign, Truman won over the voters chiefly by his famous whistle-stop talks whose hallmark was free-swinging oratory accompanied by shouts from the crowd, "Give him hell, Harry," or "You tell it to 'em, Harry." The surprise victory enveloped Truman in a new prestige and seemed to endow him with an undeniable mandate for the foreign and domestic programs on which he had campaigned.

By 1950, Truman had already achieved, or had well under way, major undertakings in the field of foreign affairs. The European Recovery Program, or Marshall Plan, was repairing the damage of World War II with miraculous speed. It was bringing the Western European economy into an era of unprecedented productivity. Greece and Turkey had been saved from possible Soviet domination by the promulgation and administration of the Truman Doctrine in 1947. This was the beginning of the successful policy of containment levied against the threat of the Soviet Union: a pliant, adjustable holding operation along the whole periphery of Soviet domination. Containment was practiced in various ways—in the 1948 Berlin airlift, in economic and defense measures in Greece and Turkey, in the establishment of the North Atlantic Treaty Organization, and later in the American military response to the invasion of South Korea. President Truman demonstrated well his capacity for enterprising innovation in foreign affairs when in his inaugural address of 1949 he proposed the imaginative Point Four program that offered hope and assistance to peoples of "underdeveloped" areas in their ages-long drive to master the essentials of a satisfactory human existence.

Harry Truman Views Foreign Policy / Harry Truman, a creature of benign circumstances, had certain attractive personal qualities that could be exploited to the advantage of himself and his position. He was well known for his abundant courage and his readiness to make decisions. He had the air of a man who will do the best he can, and is sure his best will be pretty good. Further, as befits the democratic cliché, he was a man of the people. Unlike his predecessor, a Hudson Valley patroon, and his successor, who derived from the professional military, Truman depended upon politics for a living and excelled in the standard skills of his trade. He played the game strictly according to the rules, was both at ease and effective in mingling with his fellow politicos, and showed the flair of the seasoned campaigner for remembering people and places. "He remembered everybody's name," said a boat chief of the cruiser *Augusta,* which carried Truman to Potsdam. "We don't see how he did it."

It was while the 1950 international domestic pressures were at their worst that the United States government was faced with establishing substantial working relationships with both Yugoslavia and Spain. Both were dictatorships, one Communist, the other Fascist. Some Americans, both inside and outside the government, conscious of the nation's status as a democracy, viewed with extreme distaste the prospect of cooperating with a dictator. The United States, they pointed out, was already engaged in what was tantamount to war with the Communist alliance. How then could the nation actively assist what had been one of the most hostile and articulate members of that alliance, Yugoslavia?

Others saw the matter in a wholly different light. To them, Yugoslavia and her leader, Tito, symbolized a successful breach in the Communist wall. Tito had broken with Stalin in 1948. In the interval since then, the Soviet Union had been levying the most intense pressures to bring about Tito's overthrow; for the United States not to come to his aid would be foolhardy and unthinkable.

Spain was no less a subject of debate. A Fascist dictatorship imposed on Spain at the cost of one million lives during the bloody Spanish civil war was not admired in this country, nor were the close ties between Franco, Hitler, and Mussolini soon forgotten. Yet those ties had dissolved in 1945 when Italian partisans killed the Duce and when Hitler later shot himself as the Allies closed in on Berlin. As ideology separated Tito from Stalin, death separated Franco from Hitler and Mussolini. The passage of time had done much to soften the revulsion of many Americans toward both dictators.

As far as the President was concerned, however, Franco's Spain was still not a fit object for American aid. Truman was interested, rather, in making the most of the foreign policy opportunities presented by the events in Yugoslavia, and his authority counted for a great deal. "I make American Foreign policy," Truman told an informal gathering at the White House in 1948. He was substantially, although not completely, correct. The President's constitutional position as beneficiary of the executive power clause, as maker of treaties, as commander-in-chief, as nominator of ambassadors and ministers, as author of messages to Congress, and in other particulars, enable him to exercise wide initiative in proposing new foreign policies for the nation. He has an even stronger position in the actual conduct of affairs with foreign nations that Thomas Jefferson described as "executive altogether." The President's primacy in the field of foreign affairs is also heightened by the fact that the executive office has the capacity for secrecy, dispatch, unity, continuity, access to information, and flexibility of means, all of which the legislature does not possess at all, or possesses in far less degree.

Nevertheless—and here is where Truman's statement must be qualified —Congress too can act with great impact in certain sectors of foreign affairs. Although the President proposes, as political scientist Edward S.

Corwin has put it, Congress "disposes." The Senate's advice and consent is required for treaties and major appointments. If the President needs new laws and more money, Congress can limit and reduce funds and be downright ingenious in the way it attaches strings to the money it provides. It can adopt crippling amendments, launch hostile investigations, and pass adverse resolutions. The modern era of gigantic foreign aid programs, like the Lend Lease program of World War II, the postwar European Recovery Program, and Point Four, all depended upon congressional approval revealed in the form of new legislation and ample appropriations.

Like other aid programs, the one for Yugoslavia would have to run the legislative gantlet. Truman would have to propose new legislation and Congress would have to "dispose" of his request. On the basis of the five years of the Truman Presidency that had thus far elapsed, what the President would do, if he chose to act, was to some extent predictable. Aid to Yugoslavia conceivably might be advanced as a project in bipartisan foreign policy.

Bipartisanship had already brought about aid to Greece and Turkey, the European Recovery Program, the North Atlantic Pact, and membership in the United Nations. The scope and coverage of bipartisan foreign policy fluctuated at times so that it did not apply to American policy in Japan, at least up to 1950, to the military government in Germany (although it did in 1948 in the crisis of the Berlin airlift), and, above all, to China. The origination of Point Four was not an act of bipartisanship, but a major political stroke of the President.

Truman the Active, Truman the Passive /   In Truman's dealings with Congress, two quite contrasting approaches of means and manner were apparent, one "strong" and the other "moderate." He was characteristically congenial, cooperative, and even deferential toward Congress. While his predecessor, Franklin Roosevelt promulgated lists of "must" legislation, Truman was given simply to stating his requests for new legislation, making no follow-ups, and exerting no pressure of any kind. The moderate approach was especially dominant in Truman's first several years in office when he used the veto power sparingly, filled the most important posts of his Administration with members and former members of Congress, and made several surprise visits to the place of his former employment, the Senate.

Truman's "strong" approach recurred in the latter part of his first term and in much of his second. It was spurred by his great 1948 election victory. A "strong" Truman used the veto power more freely and with occasional verbal muscle. The Taft-Hartley veto of 1947 is studded with such terms as "startling," "dangerous," "unworkable," "arbitrary," "un-

necessary," "impossible," "clumsy," "drastic." To the 81st Congress—the
Congress that would consider the question of aid to Yugoslavia and inject
the question of aid to Spain—Truman was administering generous doses of
his "strong" approach. Shortly after his electoral triumph in 1948, he
threatened, on the occasion of a Jackson-Jefferson day dinner, to tour the
country to force congressional enactment of Democratic platform pledges
if obstructionism by "the special interests," as he called them, continued.

In the first session of the 81st Congress, Senate Democratic leaders had,
at Truman's request, opened a bipartisan fight on the filibuster, the enduring stumbling block of civil rights legislation. In the second session, Truman
at one juncture threatened to carry his controversial national health program to the "people" in his fight against "the special interests." The vote of
Democratic legislators on the repeal of the Taft-Hartley Act, he declared
in the same session, would be regarded in the White House as a test of
party loyalty.

Debating Foreign Economic Policy /   One other element of the political mood in 1950 needs mentioning. There was a large measure of disagreement between Congress and the executive branch concerning the proper
scope and direction of foreign economic policy. Congress responded to the
military crisis in Korea with lavish military appropriations. But Congress
was far less ready to accept and act upon a premise that the President and
the executive branch were urging, namely, that the economic, military, and
moral factors in the international crisis should be treated as interdependent.

For all President Truman's success in implementing the Marshall Plan
and for all the general enthusiasm of the initial response to his "bold
new program," Point Four, there were plentiful signs of a tendency on
the part of Congress and its leaders to downgrade foreign economic policy.
Senator Robert A. Taft, the Republican leader, for example, took exception to the preamble of the Point Four legislation because he saw in
its language "a permanent policy of giving our money away." Senator Tom
Connally, Democratic chairman of the Foreign Relations Committee, questioned the proposed participation of the United States in the United Nations
technical assistance programs. "I don't see why in the world we need to
turn this over and let us put up the money and let the United Nations run it
. . . and mess it all up," he once commented. Congressman Christian A.
Herter, a future Secretary of State, successfully led a move in the House
to cut $20 million from the Point Four authorization.

Congressional chariness such as this was soon to come up against an unexpected circumstance: an opportunity to pry loose a satellite state from
the domination of Soviet Russia. That opportunity grew directly from a
state of domestic crisis in Communist Yugoslavia.

Yugoslavia: Truman Sees a Chance

Tito, the dictator at bay, was born Joseph Broz on May 25, 1892, in the Croatian village of Kumròvec, then part of the Austro-Hungarian Empire. In World War I, he fought in the Austrian army until his capture by the Russians. Soon after the Bolshevik Revolution broke out, he joined the Red International Guard. Upon returning to Yugoslavia in 1920, he worked in a mechanic's shop in Zagreb and joined the Yugoslav Communist party. In 1934, he adopted the name of Tito, a common one in his part of the country, and he returned to Moscow to work in the Balkan Secretariat of the Comintern, specializing in Yugoslav affairs. In 1937, he became Secretary General of the Communist party in Yugoslavia and made a notable reorganization of the party leadership.

When the Axis invaded Yugoslavia in World War II, Tito organized a guerilla force. His success against greatly superior Axis strength was well nigh miraculous. He outmaneuvered his chief competitor and fellow countryman, Mihajlovíc, for the West's support in 1943, and in 1945, he took over the Yugoslav government. He served simultaneously as Prime Minister, Minister of Defense, and Secretary General of the Communist party. King Peter II abdicated in 1945 and, in 1946, Mihajlovíc was tried and executed on contrived charges of collaborating with the Nazis. Among those subsequently convicted of similar crimes was the Roman Catholic Archbishop Alojzie Stepinac.

Until 1948, Tito collaborated with the Soviet Union, visiting there annually and introducing in his own country such major Soviet expedients as the nationalization of industry, collectivized farms, and the secret police. He cooperated closely with the Soviets in foreign affairs, encouraged the Pan-Slavic movement, and contributed tirelessly to anti-American propaganda.

In March 1948, the sturdy U.S.S.R.-Yugoslav cooperation was displaced by open conflict. The Central Committee of the Communist Party of the U.S.S.R., without first informing Tito, circulated to the members of the Cominform a letter containing a number of accusations against the leaders of the Yugoslav Communist party. Typical of the "errors" cited were slander against the Soviet Union, shadowing of Soviet citizens in Yugoslavia by the secret police, and absence of democracy in the Yugoslav Communist party. In a note to Tito, the Soviet Communist party reminded the Yugoslav leader of Trotsky and his fate. Tito's real crime was insubordination: He refused to permit the interests and policies of his country to serve the national purposes of the U.S.S.R. Yugoslavia, in a word, was misplaying its role as satellite.

Formidable pressures were unloosed against Yugoslavia by the U.S.S.R.

either directly or through the Cominform. "Healthy elements" in the Yugoslav Communist party were urged to overthrow the errant leadership. The various satellite countries began to reduce drastically their trade with Yugoslavia. Prior to the break, the Yugoslav economy was supported chiefly by trade with the states of Eastern Europe. By 1950, dealings with that area constituted only 12 per cent of Yugoslavia's total trade. Armed provocations became a commonplace on Yugoslavia's borders. The embattled Yugoslavs meanwhile were redoubling their denunciations of the West.

Tito's Yugoslavia was more sincerely and thoroughly Communist than the regimes of the neighboring satellite states. The Yugoslav revolt of 1948 against the U.S.S.R. signified no weakening of the nation's commitment to Communism. The revolt was a rejection of Stalinist Communism and Soviet imperialism expressed through the Cominform, which insisted upon imposing on the satellites what in Tito's judgment was a perversion and betrayal of the true doctrine. This clash of national will with international Communism remained an impenetrable enigma to some in this country, who, as events were to prove, could not grasp the possibility of a fissure in the Communist monolith. To them, one Communist was just like any other Communist. No national interest, in their view, could possibly prevail against the iron will of the Kremlin.

Yugoslavia was a land of poverty. Its economy could not produce sufficient goods for export to pay the bill for its huge industrialization program and at the same time give its citizens a living standard anything like that of Western Europe. Indeed, only the barest quantity of consumer goods was produced. Economically, Yugoslavia depended on the exporting of food and raw materials to purchase chemicals, textiles, machinery metals, and machinery manufactures. Yugoslavia's major economic asset consisted of nonferrous metals—copper, lead, antimony, quicksilver—vital to the military economies of the United States and its European allies.

A most important aspect of Yugoslavia in the eyes of the East and West was her army. Estimated at thirty divisions (between 350,000 to 500,000 troops), the Yugoslav army was the largest in non-Soviet Europe. In 1950, France had only three divisions, Italy but seven. The Yugoslav army was generally considered to be well-trained, especially in mountain warfare. It was equipped chiefly with military stocks of World War II and its fighting ability had been amply proven in its lengthy wartime involvement with the Germans.

In 1950, Yugoslavia's approach to foreign relations was shaped primarily by her break with the Soviet Union. Causes pursued prior to the break were redefined, enmities reduced, and tensions eased. Yugoslav relations with Greece were "normalized" for the first time since the Greek civil war. Tito ceased giving aid to Greek guerillas and contributed constructively to the termination of the civil war. Hundreds of Greek children abducted into Yugoslavia during the late hostilities were being returned to their homeland. Yugoslavia's tensions with Italy slackened, although Trieste persisted as an issue. Trade with the United States and Western Europe increased, especially in nonferrous metals. Hopeful signs were discernible in the Yugoslav domestic scene that a significant effort (supported by high officials and party intellectuals) to establish liberalism as a way of life within the framework of the Communist regime was well under way. Legislation was said to be in preparation that would establish reforms in the communal code, the law on misdemeanors, and the law on court procedure. The courts, under the proposed reforms, would be strengthened at the expense of state administration, and the participation of the defending counsel increased at the expense of the public prosecutor.

Although in the United Nations Yugoslavia continued to plead the cause of Communist China and had carefully avoided taking sides in the Korean conflict, the Soviet attack on Korea in June 1950 came as a rude shock to Yugoslav leaders who now discovered what delusions they had been entertaining about Soviet policy. The Korean venture could be seen as another phase of Soviet imperialism. A similar attack, it was all too apparent, could be launched against Yugoslavia. In the summer of 1950, the Soviet image was undergoing substantial redefinition in Yugoslav party circles. The view that the Soviet Union was no longer a Socialist but a Fascist state was expressed indirectly but unmistakably by Milovan Djilas of the Yugoslav Politburo in a series of articles in *Borba,* the official party newspaper. Yugoslav military leaders were reported to be re-examining the question of whether their country could remain neutral in a general European war in which the aggressor's army conceivably might bypass Yugoslavia in an effort to obtain its neutrality. Up to this juncture in its crisis with the U.S.S.R., Yugoslavia's position had been that it would fight only if attacked.

The United States appeared to labor under no illusions that Tito was now, or in the foreseeable future would be, an ally. The shooting down of American fliers who had mistakenly ventured over Yugoslavian territory in 1948 was still fresh in the minds of the President and the Congress. Tito, in truth, was as staunchly devoted to Communism and as contemptuous of the "bourgeois imperialist West" as was the Soviet Union. In a speech in February 1950, Tito told the United States that Yugoslavia would "go naked if necessary" rather than submit to political pressure to bring about a change in foreign policy. Yugoslavia, he went on, would never sell "its principles at any price."

Something of Truman's perspective on Yugoslavia during its down-the-line Communist phase was shown when he later told this story of a clash he had had with Tito:

A short time after the Germans surrendered in Trieste, Tito announced that he was going to occupy the territory. I called Eisenhower, and Marshall, and the Chief of Naval Operations, and I asked the Commanding General of the Armed Forces in Europe how long it would take to get three divisions to the Brenner Pass. He needed, he told me, a couple of days. I asked the Chief of Naval Operations how long it would take to bring the Mediterranean Fleet into the Adriatic. He said about three days. I said to Tito: "Come over, Tito, I'll meet you at the Brenner Pass in about three days," and he didn't come.

U.S.-Yugoslav Relations: The Thaw /   Notwithstanding Tito's pointed reservations, Yugoslav-United States relations grew steadily and constructively in 1950. United States financial assistance to Yugoslavia, a form of association reaching as far back as the Second World War, was on the rise. Shortly before the Korean conflict, the Export-Import Bank allotted two loans to Tito totaling $40 million. Secretary of State Acheson announced that the United States would extend to Yugoslavia another loan of $15 million to be used for mining, agricultural, and industrial equipment. A Yugoslav application for a $25 million loan from the International Bank for Reconstruction was simultaneously under active consideration.

The seriousness with which the United States viewed its relations with Yugoslavia was underscored by the appointment early in 1950 of George V. Allen as the new ambassador to Belgrade. A distinguished career officer of the foreign service, Ambassador Allen sought to establish the tone and theme of U.S.-Yugoslav relations when he presented his credentials in Belgrade with the statement that "The policy of the United States is based upon the strictest noninterference in the internal affairs of Yugoslavia, just as it is with regard to all other countries." Allen was not the only new American face on the Yugoslav scene. In September a delegation from the U.S. Congress arrived in Belgrade as the guests of Tito and the Yugoslav parliament. The visiting legislators included Senator Claude Pepper (Democrat, Florida), Senator Owen Brewster (Republican, Maine), Congressman Harold D. Cooley (Democrat, North Carolina), and Congressman William R. Poage (Democrat, Texas).

In the latter part of 1950, a new and wholly unanticipated force, in the form of a calamitous summer drought, brought the U.S. and Yugoslavia into closer relationship. Persistently through the spring and summer, the rainfall of Yugoslavia dropped off markedly. The March rainfall was 63 per cent of a 15-year average, April, 84 per cent; May, 46 per cent; June, 21 per cent; July, 55 per cent; August, 12 per cent; and September, 37 per cent. Much of the corn crop failed to mature and the wheat harvests were decidedly off. In terms of the average yield for 1947–1949, the percentages for 1950's production were as follows: corn, 59 per cent; wheat, 88 per cent; rye, 83 per cent; barley, 87 per cent; oats, 79 per cent; rice, 100 per cent; vegetables and melons, 57 per cent; potatoes, 67 per cent; edible fats, 88 per cent; sugar, 108 per cent; beans, 72 per cent; peas, 57 per cent.

It was apparent to American eye witnesses on the Yugoslav scene—to our agricultural attaché in Belgrade, to newsmen, businessmen, and congressional visitors—that because of the severity of the drought, Yugoslavia would have great difficulty in avoiding economic collapse. Such a disaster would be but a prelude to a quick overthrow of Tito and resubjugation of his country to the Soviet Union. A time for decision was at hand.

The Stop-Gap Program /   On October 20, the Yugoslav ambassador in Washington presented in behalf of his government a formal request for aid to the Secretary of State, Dean Acheson. Acheson and the Truman Administration needed no convincing that the need was grave and that speed was of the essence. To do any good, shipments of food would have to begin at the earliest possible hour. In the approaching winter, ocean transport would be exceptionally difficult, as would distribution inside Yugoslavia because of the virtual inaccessibility of some parts of the country in that season.

How was American assistance to be provided? Where would the money and the foodstuffs come from? They could not come via new legislation because Congress was not in session. It was an election year, with the voters trekking to the polls in less than two weeks. Most senators and congressmen were not in Washington; they were in their home states and districts, mending political fences. President Truman, accordingly, could not immediately look to the legislature for authority and funds to cope with the rapidly developing Yugoslav crisis. Legally, to be sure, the Constitution empowered him to call Congress into special session. Politically that step was out of the question. The fate of Yugoslavia weighed less in legislators' eyes than the urgency of the coming elections.

President Truman took the only course available: He improvised a stop-gap program, drawing upon extant legal authority and funds, to bolster the faltering Yugoslavs until a more adequate program could be requested when the new Congress convened. To fashion his stop-gap program, the President stretched his available legal authority to the utmost. Indeed, the stop-gap program, one spokesman for the State Department candidly acknowledged, "utilized existing legislative authority on an emergency basis for purposes not specifically contemplated when the laws in question were being considered by Congress."

In seeking out money and legal authority, the President relied upon each of three principal organizations and programs in the field of government: the Export-Import Bank, the European Recovery Program or Marshall Plan, and the Mutual Defense Assistance Program.

Created in 1934, the Export-Import Bank had as its purpose, according to Congress, "to aid in financing and to facilitate exports and imports and the exchange of commodities between the United States and any of its territories or insular possessions and any foreign country or the agencies or nationals thereof." The Bank's loans were made for specific purposes and with a reasonable assurance of repayment. As a rule, the Bank extended credit only to finance purchases of materials or equipment produced or manufactured in the United States and the technical services of United States firms and individuals as distinguished from outlays for materials and labor in the borrowing country or purchases in third countries.

Yugoslavia was no stranger to the Export-Import Bank. There was outstanding a credit of $15 million extended by the Bank to Yugoslavia to develop its export capacity. In keeping with the Bank's legal authority and operations, the credit was originally earmarked for raw materials and equipment to maintain and expand Yugoslavia's vital export industry. For purposes of the stop-gap program, however, $6 million of the $15 million credit was diverted to finance food shipments to commence at once.

Some weeks later, after Congress had reconvened, Senator Owen Brewster, Republican of Maine, questioned the legality of the diversion of funds during Senate floor discussion. A former governor and congressman, a formidable investigator of defense contracts in World War II, Brewster was known for his ready facility in debate.

> MR. BREWSTER: There seems to be rather a strain in the authority in making this form of action in connection with the Export-Import Bank. Did the Committee [Senate Foreign Relations Committee] go into that question?
>
> MR. CONNALLY (Democrat, Texas. Chairman, Senate Foreign Relations Committee): A strain in the authority?
>
> MR. BREWSTER: Yes; that it was somewhat beyond the contemplated scope of the Export-Import Bank's authority. Has there been any precedent for giving aid of this character by the Export-Import Bank?
>
> MR. CONNALLY: It is a loan, is it not?
>
> MR. BREWSTER: I do not understand it is.

A second phase in the stop-gap program called for several moves by the Economic Cooperation Administration (E.C.A.), the administrative agency of the United States government chiefly responsible for the European Recovery Program, more popularly known as the Marshall Plan. Since Yugoslavia was not a member-country of the Marshall Plan, the E.C.A. could not, under its available statutory authority, confer benefits directly upon it. E.C.A., nonetheless, handled the situation by imaginative indirection. Two Marshall Plan countries, Italy and Germany, with E.C.A.'s full encouragement, speedily supplied Yugoslavia with $11.5 million worth of flour. E.C.A., in return, granted Italy and Germany additional Marshall Plan funds to make up for their contribution to Yugoslavia. With their new funds, Italy and Germany were able to purchase approximately 140,000 tons of United States wheat valued at $12 million. Weeks later, in Senate debate, Senator William Knowland (Republican, California) characterized the legality of the whole procedure as exceedingly dubious and Senator Brewster suggested that "When the next E.C.A. appropriation comes before us . . . it would be appropriate to consider at that time making clear that further ventures of this character are not to be encouraged."

The third main prop of the stop-gap program was the Mutual Defense Assistance Program. M.D.A.P., as it was known in Washington officialdom, was the channel through which United States military and economic defense assistance passed to its NATO allies. Yugoslavia, needless to say, was not part of NATO. This, however, did not deter the Truman Administration from arranging through M.D.A.P. to supply foodstuffs to Yugoslavia to meet the immediate and sizable needs of its armed forces. The effect of this move was to lift an enormous burden from the Yugoslav government in its struggle to feed its citizenry in the oncoming winter. The assistance was to be provided subject to consultations with the NATO countries and the negotiation of a suitable agreement with the Yugoslav government.

The latter was undertaken on November 20. Ambassador Allen addressed a note to L. Mates, Yugoslav Deputy Minister for Foreign Affairs, offering to supply the assistance their countries had been discussing informally. The aid was subject to four conditions:

(1) That Yugoslavia use the assistance "exclusively for the purpose for which it is furnished, namely, in furtherance of the purposes of the Charter of the United Nations, to prevent the weakening of the defenses of the Federal People's Republic of Yugoslavia."

(2) Yugoslavia agrees "not to transfer to any other nation the assistance furnished pursuant to this agreement without the prior consent" of the United States.

(3) Yugoslavia was to extend to the United States "reciprocal assistance by continuing to facilitate the production and transfer to the United States, in quantities and upon such terms and conditions as may be agreed upon, of raw and semi-processed materials required by the United States as a result of deficiencies or potential deficiencies in its own resources. . . ." The terms to be arranged were to give due regard to Yugoslavia's own requirements for domestic use and commercial export.

(4) Yugoslavia was to make available funds for use by the United States for administrative expenses incurred within Yugoslavia in connection with the United States aid.

In a note of November 21, Mates declared that his government was "in full agreement" with the terms of Ambassador Allen's letter. In addition to the Mates-Allen exchange of contractual letters, another essential procedural step was an identical letter released by the White House on November 24 and addressed by President Truman to the chairman of the Senate Foreign Relations and Armed Services Committees and the comparable committees in the House.

> The drought, the consequent crop failure, and the imminence of famine in Yugoslavia is a development which seriously affects the security of the North Atlantic area. These events dangerously weaken the ability of Yugoslavia to defend itself against aggression, for, among other consequences, it imperils the combat effectiveness of the Yugoslav armed forces.
>
> Yugoslavia, moreover, is a nation whose strategic location makes it of direct importance to the defense of the North Atlantic area. This importance derives from Yugoslavia's geographic relationship to Austria on the north, where the occupation forces of certain North Atlantic Treaty countries, including the United States, are on duty, Greece on the south, and Italy on the west.
>
> As a result of these factors, an immediate increase in Yugoslavia's ability to defend itself over that which would exist if no assistance were supplied will contribute to the preservation of the peace and security of the North Atlantic area. The governments of the other nations which are members of the North Atlantic Treaty have been consulted on this point. It is a settled premise of our foreign policy that the peace and security of the North Atlantic area is vital to the security of the United States.
>
> Accordingly, I have determined that it is essential in order effectively to carry out the purposes of the Mutual Defense Assistance Act of 1949, as amended, to use not to exceed $16 million of the funds appropriated for the purposes of Title I of the Act to provide food for Yugoslavia in an amount equivalent to the immediate food requirements of its armed forces. This use of these funds is part of the interim aid program to meet the immediate emergency pending further action by the Congress.
>
> This letter constitutes the notification required by Section 408(c) of the Mutual Defense Assistance Act, as amended.

The section of the Mutual Defense Assistance Act referred to by the President provides:

> Whenever he determines that such action is essential for the effective carrying out of the purposes of this Act, the President may from time to time utilize not to exceed in the aggregate of 5 per centum of the amounts made available for the purposes of any title of this Act for the purposes of any other title. Whenever the President makes any such determination, he shall forthwith notify the Committee on Foreign Relations of the Senate, the Committees on Armed Services of the Senate and of the House of Representatives, and the Committee on Foreign Affairs of the House of Representatives.

Owen Brewster Is Not Moved /   Senator Brewster was unimpressed by the Administration's legal and policy justification for extending M.D.A.P.'s benefits to Yugoslavia. No doubt his lack of enthusiasm stemmed directly from his belief that one Communist is identical to any other Communist. Although this line of belief was by no means representative of Congress in general, it did have a significant following among both senators and congressmen. At any rate, Senator Brewster typified the opposition to the Administration's plan as he sparred with Senator Fulbright, an Administration spokesman.

> MR. BREWSTER: In cases of mutual-defense aid to other countries funds have been diverted, but it is true, is it not, that Yugoslavia is not a member of any of the groups contemplated?
> MR. FULBRIGHT: That is true. But there was a reservation in the act for a certain percentage of the aid to be used in emergency conditions, which was not allocated for Yugoslavia. It was my understanding that when we passed the act we certainly anticipated it could be used, for example, in Austria, which was not a party to the treaty.
> MR. BREWSTER: Has Yugoslavia undertaken any of the obligations associated with any of the countries that are parties to either the mutual-defense agreement or the North Atlantic Pact?
> MR. FULBRIGHT: No.
> MR. BREWSTER: If we are relying upon this military aid, why do we not have some kind of obligation on their part that they will come to our aid if we need aid? I think it is about time we should find whether we can secure any help from these people.
> MR. FULBRIGHT: Personally, I would say it was premature to make that a matter of any public recognition.

In its final form the stop-gap program, as pulled together from its several sources—E.C.A., M.D.A.P., and the Export-Import Bank—called for outlays in nine major food categories and for the necessary ocean transportation.

The total outlay of $31.4 million was reported by the New York *Times* to be only about half of the over-all needs outlined by the Yugoslav government. Improvisation and executive resources had been exhausted. For the sizable and urgent unfilled need, the Truman Administration had no choice but to seek new legislation and fresh appropriations from Congress.

The Executive Branch Prepares Its Program

To move ahead in this next phase, the Administration had to assemble a specific and comprehensive estimate of Yugoslavia's needs. The types of assistance that the United States could render under an enlarged program had to be established and deliveries had to be scheduled. The economic agencies of the executive branch most concerned—the Agriculture Department, the Economic Cooperation Administration, and the Export-Import Bank—had to be brought into a consensus as to the roles and policies of each. The implications of the Yugoslav question had to be related to several leading aspects of United States foreign policy.

Leadership in these several areas was provided only incidentally by President Truman and chiefly by his principal agency in the field of foreign affairs, the State Department. The events now to be recounted will doubtless suggest that the formation of a considerable quantity of policy does, and probably must, commence in the executive branch without the President's active intervention. The executive departments and agencies (as will be seen) bear the brunt of a good deal of the initiative, so much so that policy appears almost to develop automatically.

The focal point of action for an expanded program of aid to Yugoslavia through the enactment of new legislation was the Assistant Secretary of State for European Affairs, George Perkins. Appointed to the post by President Truman, Perkins had previously served as executive vice-president of the drug firm Merck and Company, as an officer in the chemical warfare service of the War Department in World War II, and as a high-ranking official in the E.C.A. As Assistant Secretary of State for European Affairs, Perkins was concerned with the development of United States foreign policy toward the Soviet Union, toward other countries behind the Iron Curtain, and toward the European countries in front of it.

On the question of large-scale United States assistance to Yugoslavia, Perkins, aided by the experts of the various country desks, had to determine the extent of the Yugoslav shortages and explore both the seriousness of the Soviet threat to Yugoslavia and the implications of United States assistance in terms of their potential impact on the NATO countries and Greece and Turkey. These countries were consulted by the State Department and all agreed as to the vital importance of the defense and survival of an independent Yugoslavia and hence the desirability of massive United States assistance. Analyses had to be prepared in the Department of Yugoslavia's relations with Greece, Turkey, Austria, and Italy, and of Yugoslavia's conduct in the United Nations.

To obtain a systematic statement of Yugoslavia's needs, in terms of both stop-gap assistance and an expanded program of aid based on new legislation, the State Department relied heavily upon both Ambassador Allen and our agricultural attaché at Belgrade. A career foreign service man, Allen had recently served as Ambassador to Iran and Assistant Secretary of State for Public Affairs, which involved steering the controversial Voice of America program through an intensely violent period of congressional attack. A former high school teacher and newspaper reporter, Allen entered the foreign service in 1930, after a year in the Census Bureau, and quickly acquired his lasting reputation as an articulate, hard-headed negotiator and administrator. The agricultural attaché, John J. Haggerty, a career man of the Agriculture Department, traveled extensively in Yugoslavia to observe drought conditions and the state of agricultural production at first hand. At the suggestion of the United States Embassy, the Yugoslavs, according to Haggerty,

> got up a special emergency food-planning group. As a matter of fact, I told the Minister of Agriculture who we would like to have in that group, and it was set up accordingly. The chairman of the special group is the vice-president of the federal planning commission. We have the Deputy Minister of Agriculture, the Deputy Minister of Foreign Trade, and the Deputy Minister of Internal Trade, and among those individuals they can pull all strings in the Yugoslav Ministry of Railways, Ports, Harbors, and Works.

When the estimates of Yugoslavia's specific and total needs were finally organized, the departments and agencies of the United States executive branch that conceivably might be concerned reviewed the situation in terms of what might be done and how to do it. The Commodity Credit Corporation, the Department of Agriculture, the Economic Cooperation Administration, the Export-Import Bank, and the Defense Department through the Joint Chiefs of Staff all engaged in these consultations. The commodities to be made available, their quantities, prices, and shipping schedules all had to be worked out. The specific roles of such operating agencies as the Commodity Credit Corporation, the Export-Import Bank, and the E.C.A. had to be decided upon. In the negotiations involved, the State Department provided over-all political and policy guidance and general leadership.

It was in the State Department also that legislation was drafted embodying the expanded emergency relief program. On November 10, Jack K. McFall, Assistant Secretary of State for Congressional Relations, transmitted to Frederick J. Lawton, Director of the Bureau of the Budget, a draft bill with the usual request in such circumstances: "It will be appreciated if you will consider this bill and the supporting material, and will advise this Department whether they are in accordance with the program of the President." Accompanying the draft bill was a lengthy memorandum entitled "Yugoslav Aid Program," which reviewed Yugoslavia's plight, the nature of American assistance thus far rendered, and the plan for future action. The memorandum also pointed out that alternative sources of assistance such as the International Bank and the Monetary Fund had been looked to, but neither of these had been considered appropriate. Granting funds for consumable items such as foodstuffs was not the established function of the International Bank. In his letter to the Budget Director,

McFall also noted that "There is under preparation a proposed Presidential message to be used in transmitting the bill and accompanying material to Congress."

The Budget Bureau Analyzes the Aid Plan /   The Budget Bureau, which is responsible for asserting and protecting the interests of the President, and for seeing to it that the views and positions of the executive departments and agencies concerned with a given proposal for new legislation are adequately coordinated, now pursued a characteristic course of conduct. With the State Department's materials at hand, the Budget Bureau took up a series of questions, some of them in close detail, with the departments and agencies whose interests or cooperation were clearly involved in the emergency relief program. These were the Department of Agriculture, the Export-Import Bank, and the Economic Cooperation Administration. With the Department of Agriculture, for example, the Budget Bureau explored whether wheat under the jurisdiction of the Commodity Credit Corporation could be used for relief as well as could wheat under section 32 of the Agriculture Act of 1949; whether section 416 of that act could be interpreted, or needed to be amended, to permit the perishable foods there referred to, to be distributed by the United States and Yugoslav governments in lieu of having that function restricted to private organizations; and whether the Agriculture Department could waive or reduce its customary 1 per cent charge for procuring foods, in view of the temporary nature of the program.

At the Budget Bureau stage seven questions were also explored that most likely would arise when Congress later considered the emergency legislation. (1) How could we be sure that assistance to Yugoslavia would be used for the objectives we favored and not to subsidize experiments in collectivism? (2) To what extent might the present Yugoslav shortages be due to lowered peasant productivity caused by enforced collectivization? (3) Might not Yugoslavia's lack of foreign exchange and gold reserves be attributable to her program of nationalization and building up of heavy industry? (4) How does the average caloric intake of the Yugoslavs compare, say, with that of the West Germans? (5) Why is it necessary to seek this appropriation during the present "rump" session of Congress rather than await the next regular session? (6) Is Tito of a mind to join the Organization for European Economic Cooperation? (7) If so, how quickly could the step be taken and what would the reactions of the member countries be?

With the unhurried deliberation of an organization with a favor to bestow, the machinery of government ground on. Meanwhile, the winds blowing off the Adriatic were turning chill, and in the highlands of Croatia,

Bosnia, and Montenegro, came the first harbingers of the Yugoslavian winter.

On November 25, Roger W. Jones, Assistant Budget Director for Legislative Reference, wrote to the Secretary of State to acknowledge the draft bill. He pointed out that "Certain changes . . . , which appear desirable and are understood to be acceptable to your Department, are reflected in the revised draft which is attached. You are advised that enactment of legislation in the form of the attached draft would be in accord with the program of the President." The revisions made in the draft bill included a reduction of an original request for $50 million of assistance to $38 million, the elimination of a section calling on the Reconstruction Finance Corporation to advance the funds required to carry out the act, and the elimination of another section providing that funds made available under the act could be used to reimburse the Export-Import Bank for expenditures it made to send emergency food shipments to Yugoslavia.

The President Makes a Quiet Request / On November 29, 1950, President Truman dispatched a special message addressed to Congress requesting the enactment of emergency legislation to enable the Administration to take care of the remaining food needs of Yugoslavia. The President was employing what at most was a "moderate" approach. The message was quietly and logically factual. There was no strident verbiage, no suggestion that the legislation requested was in anything approximating the "must" category. The President, after reviewing the Yugoslav-U.S.S.R. break and its implications, the summer drought in Yugoslavia, and the response of the stop-gap program, got to the heart of the matter:

> Now that the Congress has reconvened, I believe it appropriate to request a special authorization to meet the balance of the essential food needs of the Yugoslav people until the next harvest. Action should be taken promptly. Shipments of the remaining supplies needed must be started before the end of December, if the bulk of the food is to be available for distribution in the critical winter period. The additional aid needed is estimated at $38 million. This amount, plus the amount provided under existing authority, will only be sufficient to bring the Yugoslav diet up to a bare subsistence level.

The President stressed that United States aid to Yugoslavia would not be without conditions and safeguards. "We have received satisfactory assurances from the Yugoslav Government," he declared, "first, that all assistance furnished by the United States will be given full and continuous publicity through the press and radio in Yugoslavia; second, that the aid will be distributed equitably and fairly among the Yugoslav people; and third, that this distribution will be under the observation of persons designated by the United States."

The President closed on an exhortative note:

> It is my earnest hope that the Congress will, at this session, provide the 38 million dollars necessary for shipments of food to Yugoslavia. In this way we can help preserve the independence of a nation which is defying the savage threats of the Soviet imperialists, and keeping Soviet power out of one of Europe's most strategic areas. This is clearly in our national interest.

In reality, the message on Yugoslavia was a minor incident in the President's and his Administration's official day. The massive armies of Communist China had just invaded Korea, prompting General Douglas MacArthur, commander of the United Nations forces, to declare that a "new war" had commenced. Secretary of State Acheson termed the breaking events "a situation of unparalleled danger." The day the message on Yugoslavia was received in Congress was one of the most urgent activity in the White House. Spurred by the new crisis in Korea, President Truman progressed through a series of meetings on the subject with the National Security Council, the Joint Chiefs of Staff, and the cabinet. Secretary Acheson passed much of his day in closed consultations with the Senate Foreign Relations Committee. The White House was in touch with London and Paris to arrange a conference "at the highest levels" between the allied powers on the subjects of the Far East and Germany.

Simultaneously with his proposal for Yugoslavia, the President was submitting a batch of requests for legislative action, at least several of which were prompted by the turn of events in Korea. He was asking Congress for more than $80 million in supplemental cash and the release of $126 million of obligational authority to speed up the execution of existing defense and security programs. He requested additional funds to enable the Coast Guard to control the anchorage and movement of foreign flag vessels in United States waters and the Justice Department to enforce the new Internal Security Act. More money was requested for the National Bureau of Standards for its guided missiles program, for the continuation of rent control operations by the Office of the Housing Expediter, for the Office of Education and its school construction program, and for the Commerce Department for its highway construction projects in Central America. On November 30, the day after submitting his special message on Yugoslavia, the President, spurred by the onrushing armies of Communist China in Korea, requested a fresh appropriation of $18 billion for military purposes. In his demands upon Congress for the several measures made necessary by the Korean crisis, the President, in manner and tone, was more insistent and more forceful than in his recommendations on Yugoslavia. He clearly and characteristically was setting priorities in his legislative program in reflection of his own assessment of the competing events on the world stage. Yet he was also seeking to preserve a balance among the parts of his program by giving the Yugoslav request enough play to prevent its being unduly overshadowed by the dramatic events in Korea.

In addition to the President's message, the Administration had in readiness for the Yugoslav project detailed plans to govern the distribution of the $38 million requested among the various food categories on which there were shortages in Yugoslavia.

As projected by the Truman Administration, the emergency relief program was to come to an end with the crop harvest in the spring and summer of 1951. The President and his aides did not contemplate the creation of any special and complicated administrative mechanism for the operation of the program. Rather, it was planned to have the emergency relief program handled in much the same way as the stop-gap program. The principal operating responsibility in the United States would repose in the State Department. The procurement and the shipment of food would be carried on by the established procurement agencies, chiefly the Commodity Credit Corporation and the Department of Agriculture.

At the Belgrade end of the venture, responsibility would be vested in the United States ambassador to Yugoslavia. Aided by a small staff recruited for the purpose, he would oversee the conditions and safeguards referred to in the President's message.

Action in the Senate and the President's Worries / The Administration's bill for Yugoslav emergency relief was referred to the Senate Committee on Foreign Relations whose ensuing hearings were conducted entirely in executive session. The public and the press were therefore excluded and a transcript of the hearings was never published. In its report on the bill to the Senate, the committee disclosed that its hearings commenced on December 4 when it heard three Administration witnesses: George Perkins, Assistant Secretary of State for European Affairs; Stanley Andrews, Director of the Office of Foreign Agricultural Relations of the Department of Agriculture; and John J. Haggerty, agricultural attaché at the United States Embassy in Belgrade who had recently returned to Washington. The three witnesses were said in the committee report to have "discussed drought conditions and the political conditions of the proposed assistance." On the following day, December 5, General Omar N. Bradley, Chairman of the Joint Chiefs of Staff, testified in support of the bill.

While his executive colleagues were carrying the Yugoslav cause on Capitol Hill, President Truman, at the White House, was almost wholly engrossed in the mounting crisis in Korea. The dispatches from the fighting fronts made grimly clear that the onsurging Chinese might sweep General MacArthur's United Nations armies into the sea. The General himself was exciting no little consternation in the White House by declaring publicly that the orders he was under, barring attacks on the Manchurian bases of the Chinese invaders, were gravely hampering his command. Truman was spending most of his day in consultations with Secretary of State Acheson, Secretary of Defense Marshall, General Bradley, and W. Averell Harriman, the Foreign Aid Coordinator. British Prime Minister Attlee was arriving for a week of conferences at the White House.

On December 6, the Foreign Relations Committee voted to report the emergency relief bill (S. 4234) favorably to the Senate. Next day, Senator Connally, the committee chairman, presented the committee's report (No. 2588) on the bill on the floor of the Senate. While the Yugoslav bill was thus progressing, the President was confronted with another crisis, this one of a legislative character: Twenty-four Republican senators requested that he submit whatever agreements he might reach in his conversations with Prime Minister Attlee to the Senate for its advice and consent.

On December 8, Senator Scott Lucas of Illinois, the Democratic floor leader, asked and received unanimous consent for the consideration of the bill. Senator Connally proceeded to state the case for the bill. A man who fitted the stereotype of the old-fashioned senator, Connally was addicted to dark clothes, broad black hats, and black string ties. A faithful supporter of the Roosevelt-Truman foreign policies, a Shriner, and a thirty-third degree Mason, he was known for his flavorful wit and unsparing mimicry. In his presentation of the bill, Connally was assisted by occasional remarks from Senator Kenneth McKellar, Democrat of Tennessee and Appropriations Committee Chairman. "If any Senator two years ago," McKellar began, "had suggested that I would today be standing on the floor of the United States Senate advocating $30 million for aid to Communist Yugoslavia, I should have called him to order." In his argument in behalf of the bill, Connally stressed that Yugoslavia was deserving of help as the only state once under Soviet domination that has successfully defied its master, that United States help was vital if Yugoslavia was to preserve its independence, and that Yugoslavia possessed the largest standing army in Europe outside the U.S.S.R. This army had no little value as a deterrent to potential Russian aggression.

After Connally had completed his presentation, Senator John Stennis (Democrat, Mississippi) posed several pointed questions. Had the funds of the $31 million stop-gap program all been spent? (Connally did not know; it was of course at least in the process of being spent.) Would the additional $38 million be sufficient to meet the emergency? ("We think it will be sufficient until the next harvest.") What is the attitude of Tito and the people of Yugoslavia toward this aid? ("They want it because they are hungry. . . . There has been an increasing expression of their interest in the west rather than in the east.") Were there any expressions before the committee from the [Yugoslav] people? ("We had nothing direct.")

Also speaking for the bill was the Democratic floor leader, Senator Lucas, who saw a fundamental distinction between Stalinist and Titoist Communism. "Soviet imperialist Communism," he noted, "seeks to rob all states of their independence. Titoism seeks the independence of Communist states from Soviet dictatorship." Senator Flanders (Republican, Vermont) contended that Yugoslavia would became "a serious menace" if it passed under Soviet control. "Its long coastline gives ideal location for nests of submarines."

The Rough Treatment of S. 4234 / By no means did the emergency relief bill encounter altogether smooth passage. It was pointedly attacked in debate.

"A Communist is a Communist. Communist ideology is diametrically opposed to everything that every red-blooded American stands for today." (McCLELLAN, Democrat, Arkansas)

"It was Tito who shot down American flyers only a few years ago." (McMAHON, Democrat, Connecticut)

"He [Tito], in the Communist tradition, has persecuted religious persons, has been anti-Christ and anti-God, has suppressed freedom of assembly, and freedom of worship." (McMAHON)

But the most serious challenge to the bill was represented by several amendments, offered on the floor, which touched off a debate on world issues. Senator William F. Knowland, Republican of California, a dignified, tenacious man, long an articulate critic of the Truman Administration's policies toward Nationalist China, and in turn needled with the title, "The Senator from Formosa," proposed the following amendment to the bill: "This act shall not become effective until at least $38 million of the $75 million appropriated for the purpose of carrying out section 303 of the Mutual Defense Assistance Act of 1949, as amended, has been expended or obligated for expenditure for assistance to the Republic of China."

In offering his amendment, Knowland stressed that he favored aid to Yugoslavia, just as in the past he had supported the North Atlantic Pact, aid to Greece and Turkey, and the European Recovery Program. But, he contended, "while we have been closing the door in Europe we were leaving it wide open in Asia." He discerned a basic inconsistency in the Truman Administration's policies toward Yugoslavia and Nationalist China. "On Formosa today," he observed, "there exists a legal government of the Republic of China. They have more than 600,000 non-Communist troops. It doesn't make sense to help Yugoslavia and not give even infinitesimal help to Chiang." Knowland went on to observe that in the past two years, two different amounts of $75 million had been "authorized and appropriated," but that only an "infinitesimal amount, if any, has been spent." To this, Senator Fulbright, who often spoke for the Administration on foreign policy, countered that it was "incorrect to say that money was appropriated for the Republic of China. Money was appropriated to be spent in that general area."

Although his amendment was eventually ruled out as not germane, Knowland carried on by moving that the entire emergency relief bill be sent back to the Foreign Relations Committee with instructions that a grant of assistance to Chiang's National Chinese government be added as a precondition to any grant to Yugoslavia. The senator's motion was defeated by the narrow margin of three votes, 42 to 38; 16 senators did not vote. Senator Knowland was supported by every member of the top Republican hierarchy and two Republican members of the Foreign Relations Committee, H. Alexander Smith of New Jersey and Bourke Hickenlooper of Iowa. Among the Democrats backing the motion were Chavez of New Mexico, McCarran of Nevada, McClellan of Arkansas, and O'Connor of Maryland. The Truman Administration would never have prevailed had not five Republicans abandoned their party brethren to vote against the Knowland amendment. The Republicans who saved the Administration's day were Aiken and Flanders of Vermont, Margaret Chase Smith of Maine, Charles W. Tobey of New Hampshire, and Alexander Wiley of Wisconsin.

A second major challenge to the Administration bill—and one that would prove successful—took the form of an amendment offered by Pat McCarran, Democrat of Nevada. "The President is hereby authorized to spend," the amendment read, "not in excess of $50 million of the funds heretofore appropriated for expenses necessary to carry out the provisions of the Economic Cooperation Act of 1948, as amended (Public Law 759, 81st Congress), for the purpose of providing emergency relief assistance to Yugoslavia under the authority of this act." Although ostensibly providing more money for Yugoslavia than the Administration had asked for, the McCarran amendment differed from the original version of the bill in one most vital aspect that the Administration was certain to regard as highly disadvantageous. The Administration's measure for Yugoslav emergency relief called for fresh appropriations. The McCarran amendment entailed no new appropriations, but in effect would take money hitherto appropriated for the Marshall Plan and transfer it to Yugoslavia. The assistance already projected for the Western European countries participating in the Marshall Plan would be reduced in order to obtain funds for Yugoslavia.

In justifying his move, McCarran declared that his amendment was prompted by a desire to "conserve appropriations" and by the fact that the gold reserves of E.C.A. countries "had been increasing sharply in the July-September quarter of this year." Avowing that he did not want in any way to impair the Marshall Plan, McCarran said he was acting with the knowledge that "E.C.A. had a heavy carry-over last year, and this year the E.C.A. will have a larger carry-over because the economies of the participating European countries have improved during that period of time." Congress, he believed, should stop making appropriations if sizable carry-overs are likely from appropriations already made. If, because of some unanticipated circumstances, E.C.A. appropriations should run low and more funds should be needed before June 30, McCarran concluded, "I am sure Congress will be in a position to provide them."

Among the additional amendments that were offered from the floor was one requiring that "at least 50 per cent of the gross tonnage of any equipment, materials, or commodities made available under the act and transported on ocean vessels, shall be transported on United States flag commercial vessels, if available," and another requiring that "nothing in this act shall be interpreted as endorsing measures undertaken by the present government of Yugoslavia which suppress or destroy religious, political, or economic liberty, and the Yugoslav Government shall be so notified when aid is furnished under this act. . . ."

On December 11, the emergency relief bill finally passed, 60 senators voting "yea," 21 "nay," and 15 not voting. The bill's support was bipartisan in character and drawn from the major sections of the country as evidenced by the favorable votes of Ellender of Louisiana, Knowland of California, McCarthy of Wisconsin, and Tydings of Maryland. A liberal Republican like Bridges of New Hampshire supported the bill, as did Democrats Johnson of Texas, Kefauver of Tennessee, Tydings of Maryland, and George of Georgia. Representative of the opposition were Hickenlooper of Iowa, Bricker of Ohio, McClellan of Arkansas, and McCarran of Nevada.

The Presidential Strategy and Pat McCarran / Notwithstanding the floor crises and limiting amendments, the President was apparently satisfied with the progress of the Yugoslav project. He did not actively intervene in its behalf at this stage. There were good reasons why he should not do so. To be well-assured of its passage, he required support from congressional Republicans. His relations with that party at this juncture were decidedly uneasy. There were, of course, the many Republican legislators who had joined in requesting the President to submit his agreements with Prime Minister Attlee for senatorial review. Perhaps even worse were the well-founded reports that an even larger number of Republicans would demand the resignation of Secretary of State Acheson, who was now a favorite target for Senator McCarthy and the critics of the Administration's China policy. Such an environment was hardly propitious for a Presidential "hard sell" on Yugoslavia.

Truman was also thoroughly engrossed in other crises and undertakings demanding his attention and energy. His full week of conferences with Prime Minister Attlee did much to advance the coordination of Anglo-American policies in Korea but failed to solve such knotty issues between their countries as the recognition of Red China, giving it a seat in the United Nations, and policy toward Formosa. With the Communist Chinese continuing their successful drive, Truman was conferring constantly on the Korean situation with his chief diplomatic and military subordinates. He was also pondering the declaration of a state of national emergency to invoke important statutory powers, and exploring the possible appointment of Dwight D. Eisenhower, president of Columbia University, as supreme commander of the North Atlantic defense forces, in preparation for new eruptions of trouble in the European area.

Spain: McCarran Speaks for Franco

In assessing the President's conduct in the face of the limiting Senate amendments to the Yugoslav emergency relief bill, it is necessary to discuss here another episode, one for which President Truman openly but futilely expressed his distaste, which occurred shortly before the advent of the Yugoslav bill. On August 1, 1950, Senator Pat McCarran, Democrat of Nevada, frequent foe of the Truman Administration, and a master craftsman of the legislative "rider," introduced an amendment to the General Appropriations bill for 1951. In its most essential part, the McCarran amendment provided "That of this appropriation (that is, the total sum of the General Appropriations bill) $100 million shall be used only for assistance to Spain. . . ."

McCarran, in effect, was proposing to aid Franco, dictator of Spain, as Truman later was to propose aiding Tito, dictator of Yugoslavia. Both situations were governed by the deteriorating events in Korea, which to many legislators made the bringing of the Western alliance to full strength the number-one imperative. Our principal Western allies, while actively supporting the policy of aid to Yugoslavia, were hostile to aid to Spain. They vividly remembered Franco's traffic with Hitler in World War II. Our allies' position doubtless steeled President Truman in his opposition to aid Spain.

Senator McCarran, a personal friend of Franco (who, like Tito, had over the years built up an ample record of unfriendliness to the United States), accompanied his amendment with an extended exposition of his special concern for Spain. "If there is one nation of the world," the Senator declared, "which has consistently through all the ages and through all the years fought, opposed, and indeed defeated Communism, it is Spain."

Only yesterday, he pointed out, "the leading citizen of Spain" counseled his people that it is better "to die physically than to die spiritually" in the struggle against Communism.

So loathsome was the menace of international Communism (particularly in view of its recent thrust into South Korea), that the bitter Spanish civil war memories faded away in the United States; so, too, did the sense of disgust with Franco's religious repression, his police state apparatus, and his unrepentant Fascism. The important thing seemed to be that he, also, was opposed to Communism, and against that redoubtable opponent, one could never have enough allies.

The Justification of Spanish Aid / Why a loan for Spain? It was necessary, said McCarran, "to strengthen her own internal economy, to prepare for the emergency of war; to prepare her organized army, now in existence and only recently alerted to the conditions prevailing in Korea, because of which Spain might become involved at any moment." The fact that Spain was a dictatorship did not impress McCarran. "It is time," he said, "that the little things which have from time to time swayed or colored our judgment be laid aside. Our boys are dying in Korea."

In the ensuing discussion McCarran, on the basis of data supplied by the Spanish Embassy in Washington, described the several purposes for which the $100 million would be allotted: the purchase of tractors and fertilizers, construction of airports, machinery, and equipment to promote mineral production, equipment for electric power plants, and the development of the railway system. When McCarran had finished his presentation, one senator after another rose to speak in his support. Only Senators Wayne Morse (Republican, Oregon) and Herbert Lehman (Democrat, New York) vigorously protested the loan. The Truman Administration leaders in the Senate were noticeably silent. Their chief contribution was an amendment, which was adopted, calling for the $100 million loan to Spain to be provided outside of all other allocations for foreign aid. In other words, *additional* money would be appropriated for Spain. In that way, other nations receiving American aid under the Marshall Plan and other programs would not suffer a cut in the dollar amounts allotted them, as they would if the McCarran amendment were adopted.

The Truman Administration's reaction to the proceedings on Capitol Hill was an unhappy one, forcefully expressed. The Senate passed the McCarran amendment, and the next day Secretary of State Acheson candidly informed a news conference, according to the New York *Times*, that "the prospect of putting Spain into the Marshall Plan was unwelcome." Acheson also took pains to make clear that money was already available for "a justifiable loan" to Spain. While discussing Spain, Mr. Acheson noted the utter lack of success of some months of effort by the Administration to induce the Franco regime to adopt more democratic processes of government.

Mr. Acheson's remarks were followed by a blast from President Truman likewise denouncing the bringing of Spain into the Marshall Plan. The President termed the action "entirely out of place." Spain, Mr. Truman pointed out, could apply to the Export-Import Bank for a loan and would get it, he added, if sufficient collateral were assured.

Needless to say, the principal beneficiary of a loan to Spain, General Francisco Franco, was no great favorite of Truman's. "I never had any use for Franco," he once privately remarked. "That's all that needs to be said. I never gave him any house. He wouldn't let a Baptist be buried in daylight. That's the truth. He had to be buried at night in plowed ground." Viewing relations with Franco Spain from this emotional perspective, Truman remained unconvinced that aid to Spain was truly in the American interest.

The Truman-Acheson statements occasioned no surges of joy among the Democratic leadership of the Senate, including the party's floor leader, Scott W. Lucas of Illinois who felt constrained to defend himself and his fellow leaders by announcing to the world that Administration Democrats had acted as "realistic" men in the fracas of the preceding day. A canvass of the Democratic Policy Committee, he said, had clearly shown that under no circumstances could McCarran have been defeated.

Meanwhile the altered McCarran amendment progressed with almost equal serenity through the House of Representatives. A spate of economizing in the conference committee, which took up the General Appropriations bill in behalf of the two houses, reduced the outlay for Spain to $62.5 million, the total that was finally enacted.

In the face of the known and seemingly adamant opposition of the President and the Secretary of State, there was some speculation that Truman would veto the huge omnibus bill, although a glance at history showed that presidential vetoes of appropriation bills were most unusual and nearly always were overridden. Some observers believed that the President was legally free to treat the loan merely as an authorization, and therefore something that was not mandatory. In the latter interpretation, he would be free to hold back on the actual extension of credit to Spain. The step, these veteran observers admitted, had the serious drawback of exposing the President to the risk of a serious political tussle with Congress.

It is just this kind of situation that was to prompt Truman to write in his *Memoirs,* "Every President knows and must know that the congressional control of the purse has to be reckoned with." Yet he was also to write, "I never hesitated to veto any bill presented to me when I was convinced that it failed to serve the best interests of the majority of the people in all parts of the country. I found it necessary to veto more major bills than any other

President, with the possible exception of Grover Cleveland." The kind of dilemma the Spanish rider put Truman in—to veto or not to veto—doubtless contributed to the following bit of philosophizing he once indulged in. "Now the running of government," he mused, "is, of course, a highly practical matter. You do not operate somewhere in a theoretical heaven, but with a tough set of tough situations that have to be met—and met without hesitation. It takes practical men to run a government."

Still another course open to President Truman, in coping with the McCarran rider, was suggested by an Administration aide in an "off-the-record" discussion with the New York *Times*. The aide confided that he would not be at all surprised if the President proceeded to impound the loan to Spain. The United Press was even more positive concerning the likelihood of this step in quoting Senator Walter F. George (Democrat, Georgia), who was close to the Administration, to the effect that President Truman might very well impound the appropriation for Spain. The tactic of impounding was not unknown to Truman. Previously in his Administration, he had ordered the impounding of $873 million of an appropriation designed to increase the Air Force from 48 to 70 groups. With equal success, he had once held up the expenditure of a part of a huge rivers and harbors appropriation. Under the procedures of impounding, the President, through appropriate directives to the Treasury and the Budget Bureau, prevents the release of funds appropriated by Congress to the departments and agencies charged with their expenditure.

When the spiraling rumors of the likely impounding eventually reached the attention of Pat McCarran, the senator declared emphatically that all the fuss about the subject was ridiculous, that there was nothing for the President to impound. While McCarran freely conceded that the President might impound any appropriation passed by Congress, he pointed out that the provision affecting Spain in the General Appropriations bill was not, in any manner, shape or form, an appropriation. "Our amendment," declared the senator, "directs the E.C.A. to issue notes which will be purchased by the Treasury Department. . . . It seems to me that there is nothing for the President to impound." The senator's comment ended the public discussion about impounding.

Still another course open to the President, and one that White House aides in cautious off-the-record remarks gave credence to, was the time-honored course of inaction. The McCarran rider directed E.C.A. to make the loan to Spain through the Export-Import Bank. Both agencies were within the President's control, and doubtless, according to the aides, he would find a way to forestall their action. Certain legislators, who preferred to remain nameless, saw the President as possessing the authority to delay indefinitely, and possibly block completely, the Spanish loan.

The burning speculation about Truman's likely course was finally snuffed out on September 6 when he signed the document. Simultaneously, he issued a statement, drafted in the State Department and revised in the Budget Bureau and Justice Department, setting forth his position on the Spanish rider.

> I also feel obliged to comment upon the provision of this bill which authorizes loans for the purpose of assistance to Spain. I do not regard this provision as a directive, which would be unconstitutional, but instead as an authorization, in addition to the authority already in existence under which loans to Spain may be made.
> Spain is not and has not been foreclosed from borrowing money from this Government. Money will be loaned to Spain whenever mutually advantageous arrangements can be made with respect to security, terms of repayment, purposes for which the money is to be spent, and other appropriate factors, and whenever such loans will serve the interests of the United States in the conduct of foreign relations.

The Truman Administration remained silent on the subject of Spain until November 15, when, through a press release issued by the E.C.A., the following arrangements for loans to Spain were announced.

"United States loan aid for Spain," the statement read, "will get underway immediately, with the Export-Import Bank of Washington acting as the operating agency." The E.C.A. announcement declared that the loan program had been worked out "at the direction of President Truman in accordance with the Congressional authorization in the General Appropriations Act of 1951." Strictly speaking, the Export-Import Bank's loan policy is controlled by the National Advisory Council on International Monetary and Financial Problems; "It is known, however," the New York *Times* reported confidently, "that the question has never come before that top coordinating agency."

The E.C.A. disclosed that a procedure for granting loans to Spain had been worked out at the President's direction by the Export-Import Bank, the State Department, and E.C.A. Individual loans would be made for specific projects which bore promise of making a substantial contribution to the Spanish economy. The loans would be used to purchase commodities, equipment, and services for each project requiring dollar financing.

Applications for loans woud be made to the Export-Import Bank, which would do the negotiating and processing for approval by the E.C.A. administrator. The terms and conditions of specific loans would be determined by the administrator in consultation with the National Advisory Council.

The E.C.A. took pains to emphasize that it would not establish a mission in Spain as it had in the Marshall Plan countries. The Export-Import Bank would be responsible for checking on projects in Spain to see that the

dollar-financed commodities and services were being used for their specified purposes. In appropriate instances, the agreements for specific loans
would carry provisions to facilitate United States acquisition of strategic
materials, especially tungsten, in which it is actually or potentially deficient.
The customary over-all lateral agreement, which incorporated the basic
understandings between the United States and the individual countries
it assisted, was not prepared in the case of Spain. The E.C.A. announcement disclosed that only "project loans" would be made, and these to
private companies in Spain. The role of the Spanish government would
be limited to that of guaranteeing all loans. Spain, it was clear, would not
be brought into the Organization for European Economic Cooperation.

The great unanswered question, or indeed mystery, lurking in these
last events was how the Spanish government had now come to be regarded
as "a good credit risk," while, but a few months before, the Export-Import
Bank had reached a wholly opposite conclusion. At a press conference
on November 16, the day after the E.C.A.'s momentous announcement,
President Truman maintained that his position on the question of loans
for Spain had not changed at all. "Unfortunately," said the New York
Times, ruminating editorially on these late events, "the matter has been
handled clumsily and we have again played into Franco's hands. His press
will undoubtedly claim another victory without any concessions."

Before many a week had passed, United States military representatives
arrived in Spain to commence far-reaching negotiations leading to a major
American military construction program there and large-scale assistance
to the Spanish armed forces. In February 1951, President Truman acknowledged in a statement to the press that on the basis of the Defense
Department's new estimate of Spain's strategic value, United States policy
toward that country was undergoing change.

In the House of Representatives: Formidable Opposition / As for
the Yugoslav emergency relief bill, it was, while advancing in the Senate,
under simultaneous consideration in the House of Representatives where
it was known as H.R. 9853. Hearings on the bill were conducted by the
House Committee on Foreign Affairs, with the identical witnesses who
appeared before the Senate Foreign Relations Committee present plus
Ralph S. Trigg, president of the Commodity Credit Corporation whose
expressed views were closely coordinated with those of his executive colleagues.

The Foreign Affairs Committee reported the bill favorably to the House,
without making any consequential amendments of its text, and on December 12 the Rules Committee secured the adoption of House Resolution
878 that set the terms of debate: "not to exceed 3 hours, to be equally
divided and controlled by the chairman and ranking minority member of

the Committee on Foreign Affairs, the bill shall be read for amendment under the 5-minute rule."

In the ensuing debate in the Committee of the Whole, which took place on December 12 and 13, those arguing in behalf of the bill were led by congressmen from both parties. Their cooperation symbolized the bipartisan character of the bill's support. The substance of their presentation was similar to that of the proponents of the bill in the Senate.

The opposition's presentation, however, was more pointed and vigorous than in the Senate. Representative Leo Allen (Republican, Illinois), a ranking member of the Rules Committee, declared that the bill would give $38 million "to the most ruthless Communist dictator in the history of the world to spend where, how, and when he sees fit, without giving one promise to the Government of the United States." Congressman Lawrence Smith (Republican, Wisconsin): "To do business with Tito is to do business with the Devil," and Congressman Alvin O'Konski (Republican, Wisconsin), in the same vein: "In taking up truck with Tito, we are taking up truck with the most brutal, the most daring, the most cold, and the most dictatorial murderer next to Joe Stalin himself."

"Mr. Chairman," said Congressman Eugene Cox (Democrat, Georgia), "this mushy, moonshine, artificial stuff as represented by this committee sickens me." And again, is there "anything of sanity and strength . . . left to us besides Westbrook Pegler, Fulton Lewis, George Sokolsky, and the Chicago *Tribune?*"

Events far across the world cast their shadow upon the debate:

> Congressman GEORGE A. DONDERO (Republican, Michigan): "Is Yugoslavia a member of the United Nations?"
> Congressman JOHN M. VORYS (Republican, Ohio): "Yes."
> Congressman DONDERO: "Is there one Yugoslav alongside our men in Korea today?"
> Congressman VORYS: "No."

The freedom issue persisted as it had in the Senate. "How shall we calibrate the resentment of the religious people of Yugoslavia," observed Congressman Feighan, "at a regime which has confiscated every Catholic school, every Catholic hospital and orphanage and old-folks home, that has dissolved the religious orders freely serving the poor and the sick, that has murdered 378 priests whose names are known, and holds 400 or more in prison today."

Like the Senate, the House considered a dozen or more amendments offered by those supporting as well as those opposing the emergency relief bill. Among the principal amendments was one by Congressman Burleson identical with Senator McCarran's. Congressman Walter Judd (Republican, Minnesota) wanted the United States to condition its assistance upon a pledge from Tito that the collectivizing of Yugoslavia's farms and the exporting of its food would be stopped. Congressman Hesselton (Republican, Massachusetts) successfully moved that "All of the funds made available under authority of this act shall be utilized to the fullest practicable extent in the purchase of the commodities from the surplus commodities in the possession of the Commodity Credit Corporation."

The bill was finally passed with 225 yeas, 142 nays, and 62 not voting. Support for the bill was bipartisan in character and drew widely from the geographic sections of the country. Allen of Louisiana and Allen of California voted for the bill, as did Celler of New York, Wigglesworth of Massachusetts, and Mansfield of Montana. The ideological range extended from the New Deal-Fair Deal Democrat Monroney of Oklahoma to the Conservative Republican Martin of Massachusetts. The bill's opposition had a similar diversity, extending from Davis of Georgia to Davis of Wisconsin and White of California to Furcolo of Massachusetts. The ideological spectrum was covered from the ultra left wing Marcantonio to the conservative Halleck.

The bill now passed into the hands of the conference committee, consisting of five members of each house appointed to reconcile the differences between the two houses. The conferees apparently reached agreement with little difficulty. Illustrative of the decisions made was a change in the House version of the bill requiring Yugoslavia to agree to take "all necessary actions" to reduce its relief needs, encourage increased production and domestic distribution of foodstuffs, and lessen the danger of similar future emergencies. The words "all necessary actions" in the House amendment were designed to make the self-help feature of the program as explicit and forceful as possible. The conference adopted the less sweeping verbiage "appropriate economic measures" as "language conforming more nearly to this purpose." Doubtless, the sensitivities of the Yugoslavs were uppermost in the conferees' thoughts.

The House and Senate adopted the conference committee report without change.

Truman Declares an Emergency / As the Yugoslav project was weathering its crucial days in Congress, President Truman was absorbed in readying the country for extended war in Korea and possible trouble elsewhere. He declared a state of national emergency and in a radio and television address called upon the people for work and sacrifice to build an arsenal of freedom. He appointed Charles E. Wilson, former president of General Electric, as Director of Defense Mobilization and requested from Congress authority to create major defense agencies. Secretary of State Acheson was proceeding to Europe to hasten the integration of the

North Atlantic defense system under its newly appointed supreme commander, General Eisenhower. Much of the President's own time was committed to meetings with the National Security Council, the chairman of the Joint Chiefs of Staff, the cabinet, and the legislative leaders of both parties. Small wonder that the President was able to train his eye only occasionally on the progress of the Yugoslav legislation.

Truman apparently was also persisting in the judgment that the Yugoslav project required no special White House pressure. No fireside chats were envisioned or undertaken; legislative leaders were not convened in a White House meeting as a step toward eliminating the more objectionable amendments from the legislation; there were evidently no telephone calls from the President and his aides to legislators to buck up their resistance to the opposition's moves. As in the Senate stage, the President in the House and conference committee stages seemed satisfied with the evolution of the emergency relief program.

The Bill Becomes Public Law 897 / On December 20, Speaker Rayburn and the President *pro tempore* of the Senate, Kenneth McKellar, affixed their signatures to the enrolled bill, S. 4234. On the same day, the Secretary of the Senate reported that the enrolled bill had been presented to the President of the United States. The Yugoslav bill was by no means the only Presidential enterprise in the field of foreign affairs to reach a successful climax. At this juncture, President Truman announced publicly his refusal to dismiss his Secretary of State, as many Republicans in the House and Senate were demanding. Truman's negotiations to bring General Eisenhower into the vital European sector were at last resolved when the North Atlantic Council appointed the General as supreme commander of the NATO defense forces in Western Europe.

The Yugoslav bill was sent simultaneously to the President and to the Bureau of the Budget, which, following its usual procedures, solicited the views of the executive departments and agencies most concerned. Assistant Secretary of State McFall advised the Budget Director by memorandum on December 20 that "The Department strongly recommends the prompt approval of this enactment." In a memorandum of December 21 to the Assistant Budget Director for Legislative Reference, James Cooley, General Counsel to the E.C.A., wrote to explain just what his organization understood the aid arrangements to be. The E.C.A., he explained, was proceeding on the assumption that Congress had intended the $50 million figure to include approximately $12 million of the E.C.A. funds that had already been allotted to Germany and Italy, and that these funds would be used to provide Yugoslavia with the emergency relief that the President desired. Counsel Cooley went on to point out that the E.C.A. was working on the further assumption that no part of its funds would be used to meet administrative expenses. It was under these circumstances, he added, that the E.C.A. favored the Yugoslavia Aid Bill being enacted into law.

Having made its position on Yugoslavian aid clear, E.C.A. busied itself with other matters. It remained then for the Bureau of the Budget to grant its approval and for the State Department to make its views known.

On December 28, the Assistant Budget Director for Legislative Reference wrote to William J. Hopkins, Chief Clerk at the White House, to tell him that the Department of State had recommended approval of the bill and that the Economic Cooperation Administration had interposed no objection to its approval. The Bureau of the Budget also recommended that the bill be approved.

Some days later, on January 2, 1951, a message from the President, in writing, communicated to the Senate by one of his secretaries, announced that the President had approved and signed S. 4234. The Yugoslav emergency relief bill was designated in this final stage as Public Law 897. It was now the law of the land, authorizing the President to spend up to $50 million of the funds previously appropriated under the Economic Cooperation Act for the purpose of providing emergency relief assistance to Yugoslavia. No assistance could be conveyed until that country agreed to make local currency available to the United States to pay the latter's local currency administrative and operating expenses in Yugoslavia under the act; "to give full and continuous publicity" to United States assistance; "to permit persons designated by the Government of the United States to observe and supervise without restriction the distribution by Yugoslavia of . . . assistance"; to permit the distribution of assistance to the people in Yugoslavia "without discrimination as to race or political or religious belief"; to provide relief for needy persons and children and for medical purposes; and "to take all appropriate economic measures to reduce its relief needs, to encourage increased production and distribution of foodstuffs within Yugoslavia, and to lessen the danger of similar future emergencies."

The relief act called for the use of surplus commodities of the Commodity Credit Corporation "to the fullest practicable extent." At least half of the gross tonnage of assistance was to be transported in United States flag commercial vessels at their usual market rates. The President or Congress by concurrent resolution could at any time terminate the operation of the act.

Putting the Act to Work / The Emergency Relief Act was now ready for the next stage, its implementation. Although Congress and the President had joined in formulating the policy on which the Act was based, its implementation depended wholly upon the President and his subordinates in the departments and agencies of the executive branch. What follows is more or less typical of the implementing stages of legislation, and especially of foreign aid legislation.

The administration of the Yugoslav Emergency Relief Act was arranged for in two basic documents, the first an agreement signed at Belgrade on January 6, 1951 by U.S. Ambassador George V. Allen and Yugoslav Foreign Minister Edvard Kardelj.

The heart of the Allen-Kardelj agreement, Article II, set forth a series of conditions on which U.S. assistance would be granted. (1) The Yugoslav government would give "full and continuous publicity through the press, radio, and all available media in Yugoslavia to the assistance furnished by the United States Government . . . and will allow the United States Government the use of such media as may be required."

(2) The Yugoslav government "will permit and facilitate in every way the freedom of representatives of the Government of the United States of America . . . without restriction, to observe, supervise and report on the receipt and distribution in Yugoslavia of commodities and other assistance." The Yugoslav government will grant to representatives of the U.S. press "full freedom to observe and report."

(3) The Yugoslav government agreed to make available to the U.S. government funds "to meet its expenses in Yugoslavia in connection with the administration and operation" of the assistance program.

(4) All assistance made available under this agreement "will be distributed equitably among the people of Yugoslavia without discrimination as to race or political or religious belief."

(5) Proceeds realized by the Yugoslav government from commodities sold under this agreement will be used "to provide relief to needy persons and to children for charitable and medical purposes or for such other purposes as may be mutually agreed to."

(6) The Yugoslav government "will take all appropriate economic measures to reduce its relief needs, to encourage increased production and distribution of foodstuffs within Yugoslavia, and to lessen the danger of future conditions of food shortage."

The second basic document establishing the administration of the Emergency Relief Act was Executive Order 10208, issued by President Truman on January 25, 1951. The order, a brief one as executive orders go, contained these central provisions:

(1) "The Secretary of State is authorized and directed to perform the functions and exercise the powers and authority vested in the President" by the Yugoslav Emergency Relief Act of 1950.

(2) "Of the funds heretofore appropriated to carry out the Economic Cooperation Act of 1948 (62 Stat. 137), as amended, $37,800,000 are withdrawn from the Economic Cooperation Administration and are transferred to the Department of Agriculture to be administered under the said

Yugoslavia Emergency Relief Assistance Act of 1950 as directed by the Secretary of State."

The relief program was not a grant of dollars, but of funds usable only for the purchase of commodities. In all, the stop-gap program and the emergency relief assistance program, in terms of the commodities to be purchased, involved 6,039,000 metric tons of foodstuffs. The great bulk of the purchase was from stocks held by the U.S. Government. At least 72 per cent of the commodities to be acquired under the program were to come from surplus stocks of the Commodity Credit Corporation of the Department of Agriculture. The remaining 28 per cent were to be purchased in the open market. Yugoslavia distributed the commodities through regular commercial channels at reasonable prices and, on occasion, free to those of its citizens unable to pay for them.

Aftermath: Yugoslavia, Spain, and the Dollar / The Yugoslav Emergency Relief Assistance Act was the forerunner of the more extensive Yugoslav-United States cooperation and collaboration that steadily unfolded in 1951. Events provided the spur. Throughout the earlier half of 1951, rumors flamed persistently of an impending Soviet attack on Yugoslavia. In April, President Truman set aside up to $29 million in military aid funds to provide raw materials and similar supplies "in amounts and kinds equivalent to certain consumption needs for supporting [Yugoslavia's] armed forces." In June, Britain, France, and the United States agreed to put up some $150 million with 62 per cent of the total supplied by the United States, to meet Yugoslav foreign trade deficit in the next year. Yugoslavia also became a regular recipient of "military end-items" under the Mutual Security Act. Each step of this deepening rapport evoked gnashing denunciations from the Soviet Union.

For its part, Yugoslavia permitted some relaxation of its internal regime. The most spectacular evidence of what proved at most a mild adjustment was the conditional release of Archbishop Aloysius Stepinac from prison. In the United Nations Yugoslavia viewed somewhat more critically the relationship of Communist China to the Korean conflict. A marked cordiality began to grow between Yugoslavia, Greece, and Turkey. A series of official missions by the political and military leaders of those countries laid the basis of a five-year treaty of friendship and collaboration, ultimately signed at Ankara on February 28, 1952.

In the decade and more since the Emergency Relief Act, Yugoslavia has wavered, sometimes violently, on the tightrope it has continued to walk between East and West. In 1953, Yugoslavia undertook several measures of certain appeal to congressional opponents of the Emergency Act. A new constitution was adopted by the Yugoslav national assembly and for the first time since 1946 government measures were severely criticized in parliamentary debate. A drastic cutback in collectivized farms occurred, with 2,000 of 7,000 rural collectives undergoing dissolution.

When Stalin died, a Yugoslav spokesman took care to stress that his death and the anticipated changes in Soviet policy would not alter Yugoslavia's policy toward the West. Khrushchev's eventual triumph in the internal power struggle in Moscow was welcomed in Yugoslavia and in 1957 the new Russian leader met with Tito in Rumania. Secretary of State John Foster Dulles also included a visit with Tito on his itinerary.

Meanwhile, in the late 1950's, Tito, as if to show his continued independence, trod hard on several occasions on the toes of both East and West. The trials of Milovan Djilas and Vladimir Dedijer for "hostile propaganda" against the state in 1955 offended the Western world as did the arrest of a number of Social Democrats in 1958. In that same year, the Communist world press launched fierce attacks upon Tito, precipitating a crisis almost comparable to the one of a decade earlier. The Chinese Communists were the most violent and the Soviet Union commenced an economic boycott by withdrawing credits it was to extend to Yugoslavia and by refusing to complete deliveries of wheat in accord with a previous agreement. The United States again rushed in with assistance. With the dawn of the 1960's, Tito was still insisting that Yugoslavia must remain outside the two great blocs of power and the Chinese Communists were denouncing the Yugoslav leader as "the tool of American imperialism."

Spain, meanwhile, was reaping even larger benefits from American policy. In the spring of 1951, she received over $17 million in grants to be used for various economic developmental purposes. In July of that year, after a trip by Admiral Forrest Sherman to Spain, President Truman announced that United States policy toward that country would hereafter be shifted on advice of the Defense Department and based upon strategic evaluations. The shift resulted in an agreement signed on September 26, 1953 providing for the construction and joint use of naval bases at Cadiz and Cartagena and air bases near Madrid, Sargossa, and Seville; U.S. assistance in organizing and equipping the Spanish armed forces; and economic aid to Spain, which by 1960 was well advanced toward the billion dollar mark in United States outlays. Spain was admitted to full membership in the Food and Agricultural Organization, the United Nations Economic and Social Council, and eventually into the United Nations itself. In 1959, President Eisenhower made a state visit to Madrid, meeting Franco as a fellow opponent of Communism.

Thus, within less than a decade, Presidential leadership and congressional response, combined with military necessity and Cold War pressures resulted in a significant shift in American foreign policy toward two nations at opposite ends of the nominal political spectrum, yet two nations curiously similar in their totalitarian leadership.

The President's Role: A Summing Up

The two episodes discussed here reveal important facets of the American Presidency. In the Yugoslav incident, the President, reacting to an urgent crisis, made a moderate departure in the American foreign aid policy as it had been defined between 1948 and 1950. He carried Congress along with him with a minimum of kicking and screaming from his implacable critics. To achieve this result, the President did not have to expend vast amounts of his personal prestige, or rally the nation; instead, he was able to preside as a foreman over a smoothly functioning executive assembly line, adding a bit of oil here and pushing a switch there. In short, this is a classic illustration of Presidential initiative and relative congressional cooperation.

In the Spanish episode, we see Congress attempting to seize the initiative in a delicate matter of foreign affairs in yet another moderate departure from the foreign-aid consensus presented by congressional power over the purse. The President did not want to act. His Secretary of State was comparably cool to the proposal. However, the executive family was not without rifts. Dominant opinion in the Pentagon and in the civilian leadership of the Defense Department had concluded that bases in Spain and an alliance with Franco would greatly enrich the American defense effort. When this Pentagon attitude was coupled with the solid congressional support for Franco, President Truman was forced to bend with the wind or risk defeats in more vital areas of his foreign and domestic policy. A knock-down fight against such odds would have been a serious hazard for Harry S. Truman in November 1950. As a result of Truman's perception of this situation, his role was muted. Apart from a few minor expressions of discontent, he bowed to the inevitable, encouraged, perhaps, by his awareness that aid to Spain was still within his executive control and that the last word had not been written with the passage of the McCarran rider.

There are larger themes suggested by these events that deserve further exploration. To begin with, one can consider how much the Spanish and Yugoslav affairs were essentially determined by the interaction of Harry Truman's administrative style with the objective realities of the situation. To ask this question is to suggest that Presidents differ in their administrative styles and that the differences matter. How much the presence of a Franklin D. Roosevelt, a Dwight D. Eisenhower, or a John F. Kennedy in the White House in 1950 would have changed the basic administrative response is a provocative, if highly hypothetical, query. Franklin Roosevelt, a man often portrayed as consummate master of the Presidential office, might have adopted quite different tactics. Whatever line he might have taken—from radiation of the famous FDR personality on the cold countenance of Senator McCarran, to a judicious application of the buggy whip of patronage to the opposition's shoulders—it does not strain history to see Roosevelt as a more activist respondent in the Spanish affair.

Eisenhower, in contrast, for all the personal prestige that he brought to the Presidency, could not view the White House in such enthusiastically personal terms. He did not like to go the mat with Congress. Because of his deep belief in the primacy of Congress as the nation's legislative organ, he tended to intervene only when Presidential prerogatives were inescapably challenged. One can visualize him making rather unfriendly remarks about Senator McCarran to Sherman Adams or to George Humphrey, but refusing "to get involved in personalities." In sum, nothing in Eisenhower's conception of the Presidency would lead one to assume that he would have intervened more forcefully than Harry Truman.

John F. Kennedy, a lean and jealous guardian of Presidential power, bears a strong resemblance to Harry Truman. That is, his powerful rhetoric in defense of White House authority and leadership in the dusk of crisis is coupled with a distinct tendency to duck. His experience as a congressman and as a senator leads him to make shrewd and telling estimates of the balance of congressional forces. Where he can persuade and operate, he moves forward. Where he encounters the congressional wall, he is as likely to redefine his goal as to press the issue.

More than personal styles need to be considered, however. The two cases discussed here raise a number of questions as to the adequacy of our institutional machinery to respond in Cold War conflict. For example, the absence of an item veto for appropriation bills made Truman's problem much sharper than it need have been. He was forced to accept or reject the appropriation bill in its entirety. Authority to perform surgery on the McCarran rider was denied him. The choice of, in effect, shutting down the executive branch for want of funds, was not particularly real. Virtually all Presidents have urged that the power to exercise an item veto be provided by Constitutional amendment. Whatever Dwight Eisenhower's perspectives might have been when he first came to office and spoke of getting on splendidly with Congress, even he came to feel that an item veto was essential. Some students of constitutional law have suggested that if a clause were inserted into each appropriation bill, empowering the President to strike out items, the hurdle of a Constitutional amendment could be scaled. Whether Congress would so willingly expand Presidential power and shrink one of its major legislative weapons is more than a little doubtful.

Another institutional facet is the relation of President Truman to the party system in these episodes. The President and his party leaders in Congress hardly constituted a "team" during the Spanish debate, as the contretemps between Lucas and Truman graphically illustrates. In fact, Truman may be seen as the victim of hearty bipartisanship in Congress over aid to

Franco, an indication that this much-praised state of two-party agreement may sometimes operate against a President as well as for him. In the Yugoslav undertaking, the conditions that Congress implanted in the Emergency Relief Act handicapped the freedom of the President to conduct subtle negotiations with a sensitive and suspicious Communist leader. The strings that Congress tied on the package almost bound the President's hands.

A final aspect of the Presidential position worth noting is the tradition of Presidential dependence on annual congressional authorization for foreign aid. In 1961, President Kennedy urged Congress to break with this tradition and allow long-term loans to be made by the Treasury on a five-year basis so that aid programs would not have to run the yearly gantlet on Capitol Hill. As of this writing, the prospects for his proposal are fair. Certainly such a general restructuring of the aid process would provide the President with precisely the elements of flexibility and cash needed in the Yugoslav instance.

It would not be difficult to dwell longer on the conduct of the American Presidency in respect to the Spanish and Yugoslav incidents. Yet there is a danger in placing too heavy a speculative load on a narrow foundation. With a hundred such cases to examine in depth, we would still have only part of the view from the executive desk at 1600 Pennsylvania Avenue. As Harry Truman was so fond of remarking, "No one can make decisions" for the President. "No one can know all the processes and stages of his thinking in making important decisions. Even those closest to him, even members of his immediate family, never know all the reasons why he does certain things, and why he comes to certain conclusions."

The President suffers isolation in the midst of vast power. He must manipulate eighteenth-century tools to meet twentieth-century problems. That is what this case is about.

Sources

PRIMARY

> *Congressional Directory.*
> *Congressional Record.*
> Council on Foreign Relations, *The United States in World Affairs.*
> *Federal Register.*
> *Hearings on Yugoslav Emergency Relief Assistance Act of 1950* (H.R. 9853), House Committee on Foreign Affairs, November 29 and 30, 1950.
> The New York *Times.*
> *State Department Bulletin.*
> Excerpts from Mr. Truman's *Memoirs* (Volume I, Copyright © 1955 and Volume II, Copyright © 1956) used with the permission of Time Inc. Excerpts from *Truman Speaks* used with the permission of Columbia University Press and the author.

SECONDARY

AREY, HAWTHORNE. *History of the Operations and Policies of the Export-Import Bank of Washington.* Washington, 1953.

ARMSTRONG, HAMILTON FISH. *Tito and Goliath.* New York, 1951.

BROWN, W. A., and R. OPIE. *American Foreign Assistance.* Washington, 1953.

DRASKOVICH, SLOBODAN. *Tito, Moscow's Trojan Horse.* Chicago, 1957.

GURIAN, WALDEMAR, ed. *Soviet Imperialism: Its Origins and Tactics.* Notre Dame, 1953.

KORBEL, JOSEF. *Tito's Communism.* Denver, 1951.

MCVICKAR, CHARLES. *Titoism: Pattern for International Communism.* New York, 1957.

PRIDONOFF, ERIC. *Tito's Yugoslavia.* Washington, 1955.

ULAM, ADAM. *Titoism and the Cominform.* Cambridge, 1952.

Bookies and "Bugs" in California:

Judicial Control of Police Practices

"Science has perfected
amplifying and recording
devices to become
frightening instruments of
surveillance and invasion
of privacy, whether by the
policeman, the
blackmailer, or the
busybody. That officers of
the law would break and
enter a home, secrete such
a device, even in a bed-
room, and listen to the
conversation of the
occupants for over a
month would be almost
incredible if it were not
admitted."
—SUPREME COURT
JUSTICE
ROBERT JACKSON

"Even Daddy Warbucks in
the nationally syndicated
comic strip, 'Little Orphan
Annie,' learned to his
anger that agents of 'the
Syndicate' were tapping
his calls."

Alan F. Westin

COLUMBIA UNIVERSITY

CRIMINAL trials hold an unending fascination for most Americans, and for many of the same reasons that people flocked to see trial by combat in Norman England or witches hanged at Salem. At its rational best, the courtroom is a superb snapshot of the human condition and its byways: the prosecutor's quest for punishment in the name of "the People," the defense counsel's wall of sheltering objections around his client, the stream of witnesses dropping bits and pieces of "the Truth," the defendant's outraged innocence or brotherly plea of justification; the mixture of community passions and pity called a jury; and the ambiguous presence of the judge as participant-referee. Criminal trials are also the setting for passionate debates over bedrock principles of American democracy— from police practices and the definition of crimes against state and nation to the conditions of fair trial and appeal. These debates will often widen into celebrated arguments over constitutional history, the standards of judicial review, and the line between judicial and political functions. From their start in a local police court or federal courthouse, such trials can run a judicial gantlet which, if survived, leads to the cavernous majesty of the Courtroom of the United States Supreme Court.

This case presents just such an episode.

Enter the Friendly Restaurateur

Long Beach—California's fifth largest city—lies seventeen miles due south of downtown Los Angeles. Its eight and one-half miles of broad white beachfront along the Pacific Ocean make it a resort playground for the Angelinos and Southern Californians generally. The rich oil field under its harbor, a naval base, and several shipbuilding yards are part of a 150 million dollar port complex; these assets, along with medium-sized industrial plants (aircraft assembly, chemicals, seafood canning, and rubber products) free the city's 350,000 residents from total dependence on feeding and amusing the sun-worshippers and yachting parties.

One of the restaurants in Long Beach that Duncan Hines did not recommend in the 1950's was the Red Onion Café at 123 American Avenue, nestled among several thriving bars. On April 1, 1952, its owner, Patrick Irvine, a genial, heavy-set, fifty-year-old Irish-American, was not behind the cash register trading April Fool's Day banter with his customers. Instead, looking a trifle paler than usual, he was seated beside an officer in the Superior Court of the State of California in and for the County of Los Angeles, Department of Long Beach, charged with violating Section 337a of the California Penal Code. Sanitary conditions at the Red Onion Café were not at issue, for restaurateur Patrick Irvine was in court that morning in his sometime capacity as one of Long Beach's leading bookmakers.

California, home of such celebrated race tracks as Santa Anita, Hollywood Park, and Tanforan, permits betting on horse races only at the pari-mutuel windows at the tracks themselves (from which the State skims off, in taxes, a rich percentage of the betting pools). Section 337a of the State Penal Code makes it a crime for anyone other than the track ticket-sellers to:

(1) engage in pool-selling or bookmaking;
(2) keep . . . any room, shed, tenement, tent, booth, building, float, vessel, place, stand or inclosure . . . with a book or books, paper or papers, apparatus, device or paraphernalia, for the purpose of recording or registering any bet . . . or wager upon the result . . . of any trial . . . or contest of skill, speed or power of endurance of man or beast . . . or mechanical apparatus . . . or upon the result . . . of any lot, chance, casualty, unknown or contingent event . . . ; [or]
(3) [hold] any money, thing or consideration of value, or the equivalent or memorandum thereof, staked, pledged, bet or wagered . . . upon the result [of such contests].

Violation of Section 337a is punishable by thirty days to one year in the county jail if the judge sets a "misdemeanor" sentence, or a year in the state penitentiary if the judge deems the offense a felony.

On the evening of January 5, 1952, Patrick Irvine and his wife, Mildred, had been in the living room of their home at 3916 East 2nd Street. At 7 P.M., Detective Inspector Everett Kennedy of the bookmaking detail of the Long Beach police department opened the front door of the Irvine house with a specially made key. Accompanied by a police sergeant, he walked into the living room and announced, "Pat, this is an arrest." Irvine's dog began to bark angrily at the Inspector and had to be tied up in the kitchen. A half-hour later, three newspaper photographers arrived to take pictures of the arrest and to follow Irvine down to the police station to record his "booking." Thus was completed the first formal step in the case of *The People of the State of California v. Patrick Irvine, Morris Jamoke Lippe, and Pete Emil Curti.*

Minor offenses committed in Long Beach are handled by the city prosecutor and heard in the municipal court. More serious crimes, under which bookmaking is placed, are heard in the California Superior Courts.

In most states, criminal prosecutions are initiated by having an indictment voted by a grand jury. In others, such as California, prosecutions may be initiated by the district attorney filing a verified complaint in Municipal Court charging a defendant with committing a crime. A preliminary hearing is then held before a magistrate who decides whether there is "probable cause" to place the accused on trial. If probable cause is found, defendant is held in custody (or released on bail). An "information" is then filed by the district attorney in Superior Court and the trial is thereby launched. Probable cause was found in the case of Irvine and his two employees and the district attorney of Los Angeles County filed an information on February 13, 1952 charging five counts of felony:

Count 1 charged Irvine, Lippe, and Curti with conspiracy to violate Section 337a. It was charged, as one of several "overt acts" proving this conspiracy, that the three men had purchased federal wagering tax stamps.

Count 2 charged defendants with "wilfully, unlawfully, and feloniously engaging in poolselling and bookmaking."

Count 3 charged the keeping of premises at 10851 South Chestnut Street, Los Alamitos, and 3916 E. 2nd Street, Long Beach, with paraphernalia for recording and registering bets on horse races.

Count 4 charged them with receiving money and memoranda thereof for wagering on horse races.

Count 5 charged the recording and registering of bets on horse races.

On March 3, Irvine, Lippe, and Curti each pleaded not guilty as charged on each count of the information and demanded trial by jury.

Pat and the "Mike"—Trial in Superior Court

The trial opened on April 1, 1952, three months after the arrest. It was held in Superior Court for Los Angeles County, Department E of Long Beach, Judge Ralph K. Pierson presiding. Each of California's fifty-eight counties has a Superior Court. In large counties with heavy case loads, this Superior Court is divided into departments, Los Angeles having 120 departments at the present time. The judges are elected on a county-wide nonpartisan ballot for six-year terms.

On April 3, after the jury was selected and the clerk had read the information, the veteran Deputy District Attorney for Los Angeles County, Thomas W. Cochran, rose to deliver his opening statement.

The People would show, Cochran said, that Irvine and his two employees, Lippe and Curti, had conspired to engage in and had engaged in bookmaking activities at Irvine's home and at a second location, 10851 South Chestnut Street in nearby Los Alamitos. The evidence of these activities would be of several types. First, there would be proof that Irvine, Lippe, and Curti had each applied for and secured a $50 wagering stamp from the tax division of the federal Internal Revenue Bureau. (In 1951, stemming from Senator Estes Kefauver's dramatic hearings into organized crime, Congress had passed an act requiring all persons receiving wagers to apply for a license stamp, pay a $50 fee, list their place of business, and pay a 10 per cent special tax on all amounts wagered with them. Failure to obtain the stamp and pay the tax is punishable by a fine of $1,000 to $5,000. Congress was quite aware that state and local police would hurry to see who applied and where they were doing business. Indeed, the legislation specified that payment of the tax and fee would not operate to bar state prosecutions for wagering or give any immunity to those registering, and the applications were made public records open for inspection.)

Second, Deputy District Attorney Cochran continued, the People would introduce recorded conversations and summaries of conversations overheard among Irvine, Lippe, Curti, and Mildred Irvine proving that bookmaking was being carried on at Irvine's home and over his telephone. Cochran described how these conversations were secured and gave samples of what the talks contained.

Third, the People would prove that Curti and a woman named Audie Greer had taken betting records from the South Chestnut Street house and had delivered them by car to Irvine's home. That fact would be shown on the basis of a police trap by which, on January 5, the papers being carried by Curti and Audie Greer were impregnated with a fluorescent powder visible only under a fluoroscope. Traces of the powder were found, Cochran explained, on Irvine's hands and on bookmaking records in his bedroom desk at the time of his arrest on January 5.

Cochran instructed the jurors that his description of these facts and events, being an opening statement for the prosecution, "was not evidence." That would have to "come from the witnesses." It was only a general, chronological narrative of "what I believe and expect that the evidence in this case will prove."

The attorney for Irvine, Lippe, and Curti was Andrew H. McConnell of Long Beach. This was not the first time that "Andy" McConnell had been Irvine's counsel. "As a criminal lawyer," he recalled, "I had represented Irvine and his brother Joe, and many of their employees, for a number of years on charges of violation of the [liquor] prohibition laws, and later of the horse-racing laws of this State." McConnell, who was 72 years old in 1952, had served as a criminal prosecutor in Montana for his first decade of law practice, first as a member of the state attorney general's staff and then as county attorney in Helena, Montana. In 1923, he moved to California and, like many former prosecutors, became a defendant's lawyer in criminal cases. He was to be Irvine's lawyer throughout all stages in the California courts.

Following Cochran's opening statement to the jury for the People, McConnell would ordinarily have made a comparable statement for the defense. He chose to waive that right, however, and Judge Pierson directed the People to put on its witnesses.

Enter Russell Mason, the Happy Wirer /   Cochran called as his initial witness a man who was to be perhaps the second most important figure in the case, Russell Dean Mason. His special connection with the investigation was quickly developed by the questioning:

> MR. COCHRAN: Mr. Mason, what is your business or occupation?
> MR. MASON: Recording engineer.
> MR. COCHRAN: Will you tell the jury just briefly, please, what a recording engineer is?
> MR. MASON: A person that makes it their [sic] business to use recording equipment to record voices, sounds, or any types of noises, picked up from a microphone and run through various amplifiers and so forth, into a recording machine. . . .
> MR. COCHRAN: How long have you been engaged in that work, Mr. Mason?
> MR. MASON: Since 1928.
> MR. COCHRAN: Have you devoted practically your entire time to the work of a recording engineer since that time?
> MR. MASON: Since about the last 10 or 15 years exclusively in that type of work.

Cochran then brought out by his questioning that Mason had done such recordings previously for the district attorney's office of Los Angeles County and had appeared in California and federal courts as "an expert on recording devices." Mason then explained the process by which sounds in a room (including human voices) are picked up by a sensitive microphone and transmitted by wire to a listening post where the sounds can be heard through earphones or recorded automatically on magnetic tape.

Having qualified Mason as an expert and described the eavesdropping process, Cochran was now ready to let Mason tell his story.

MR. COCHRAN: Now then, I want to direct your attention to the premises, Mr. Mason, located at 3916 East 2nd Street in the City of Long Beach. Are you familiar with the location of those premises?

MR. MASON: I am.

MR. COCHRAN: Did you have occasion sometime around December 1 of 1951 to go to those premises with any police officers from the Long Beach Police Department?

MR. MASON: Yes, sir, I did. . . .

MR. COCHRAN: Did you at or about that time do anything in respect to the installation of wire or wiring?

MR. MASON: Yes, sir. I strung a wire up the alley . . . north about three-fourths of a block, on poles, and terminating at a garage.

Mason indicated that he did not complete the wiring job on December 1; he had to wait several days until a time when the Irvine house was empty and he could enter.

MR. COCHRAN: Tell the jury what you did on December 3rd.

MR. MASON: On December 3rd, it was during the evening, I took my truck and drove down to this address, parked in the alley, took off one of my ladders [from] the truck and carried the wire that I had strung up previously up to the roof of . . . 3916 East Second, which is composed of some garages with living quarters up above. And I bored a hole in the roof, stuck my wire through the roof. I came downstairs [into Irvine's house] . . . crawled up into a little hole in the closet and installed a microphone above the light in the fixture box. . . . Then I went back to the place we term as the listening post . . . I connected up the equipment, connected the wire to the preamplifier, connected the preamplifier to the recording equipment, and turned it on "on" position.

Mason continued this part of his account by noting that he made several tests (with officers talking from Irvine's house), that he instructed the police officers at the listening post in the proper operation of the equipment, and then left in his truck with his wife, who had come along to aid him in secreting the microphone.

Tapping, Bugging, and the Law / At this point, some background on Mason's art is essential. Mason was not a "wiretapper," in the proper use of that term, since he had not made a connection to the telephone instrument or lines in order to overhear both sides of the telephone conversations on Irvine's wire. He was an "electronic eavesdropper," someone who uses sound equipment to overhear and record (if he desires) the conversations of people in rooms, autos, apartments, or offices, including their conversations into the telephone instrument. This is often called "bugging" or "a mike job."

The legal basis of wiretapping and electronic eavesdropping in 1952 was complex. Federal law on both subjects was governed by Supreme Court interpretations of the Fourth Amendment to the federal Constitution, which provides: "The right of the people to be secure in their persons, houses, papers, and effects, against unreasonable searches and seizures, shall not be violated, and no warrants shall issue, but upon probable cause, supported by oath or affirmation, and particularly describing the place to be searched, and the persons or things to be seized." In the area of "bugging," the Supreme Court had held in *Goldman v. United States* (1942)[1] that there was no violation of the Fourth Amendment when federal officers placed a sensitive microphone device on the wall of a room adjoining that of a suspect. And in *On Lee v. United States* (1952), a 5–4 vote had upheld police recording of a store-owner's conversations obtained by concealing a radio transmitter on the person of a federal "undercover agent" who entered the store and talked to the owner-defendant. In these cases, the Supreme Court had not squarely faced the problem of unauthorized entry to install listening devices, since entry was not considered by the Court in the *Goldman* case and the agent was invited into the store in the *On Lee* case. State law on "bugging" was widely permissive. Several states, such as California and Massachusetts, authorized police use of dictographs. Other states had held that bugging did not violate the anti-wiretapping statutes because there was no connection to the telephone circuit.

Federal law as to telephone tapping moved along a different channel. In *Olmstead v. United States* (1928), a 5–4 decision of the Supreme Court ruled that wiretapping did not violate the Fourth Amendment. According to Chief Justice William H. Taft for the majority, telephone users projected their voices outside the home; in addition, there was no seizure of anything tangible and no actual physical invasion of a person's premises. Justices Oliver Wendell Holmes, Jr. and Louis D. Brandeis each contributed famous dissents challenging wiretapping as a "dirty business," a fundamental invasion of the citizen's constitutional privacy, and an inherently unreasonable method of police search. From 1928 through the time of Irvine's trial (and today) wiretapping has never been held to be unconstitutional.

In 1938, the Supreme Court took a vague provision of the Federal Communications Act of 1934 (Section 605: "[N]o person not being authorized by the sender shall intercept any communication and divulge or publish the meaning of such intercepted communications to any person . . . .") and read this to forbid federal officers to intercept telephone calls and use the evidence in federal trials. This was the so-called "first *Nardone* case." In the "second *Nardone* case" in 1939, the Justices said evidence obtained by

---

[1] Official citations for all cases mentioned will be found in the Table of Cases at the end of this chapter.

wiretapping leads was also inadmissible, since it was the "fruit of the poisonous tree." In 1942, however, the Court ruled that Section 605 was not violated by federal agents who listened to telephone conversations by means of a microphone on the wall of an adjoining room (*Goldman v. United States*). Finally, as far as the effect of Section 605 on the states, the Court held in *Schwartz v. Texas* (1952) that the states could decide whether evidence obtained by state police through wiretapping in violation of Section 605 should be admitted in their courts.

State law as to wiretapping in 1952 was outwardly restrictive but was almost wholly ineffectual. Only one state (New York) supervised police wiretapping by court order; several states, such as Louisiana, gave police the right to tap wires on their own authority; thirty-eight states had statutes generally forbidding any person to intercept telephone or telegraph messages. However, none of these thirty-eight statutes specifically mentioned police officers as persons forbidden to tap telephones, and no state before 1952 had interpreted its law to forbid police interceptions. In addition, more than half of the states in 1952 allowed evidence obtained illegally—including wiretap evidence—to be used in criminal trials.

California Blazes a Trail / California's law on wiretapping dated back to 1861.[2] In that year it enacted the first anti-tap statute in the nation, a law forbidding interception of telegraph messages. In 1905, a scandal in which a newspaper reporter bribed telephone operators to let him listen to calls going to a rival paper, led California to extend the anti-tap law to telephonic communications. Although this provision, listed as Section 640 of the Penal Code, bars "every person" from tapping, only private wiretappers had been successfully prosecuted down to 1952. Neither police officials nor technicians employed by them were even indicted under Section 640, much less convicted, in those forty-seven years.

As for electronic eavesdropping, California passed a statute on this subject in 1941, again in response to sensational disclosures. During the 1930's, the California press had featured stories of police eavesdropping in regular criminal investigations, such as the bug that Los Angeles Police Captain Earl Kynette had secreted in the bedroom of Raymond Lisenba, the "rattlesnake murderer." However, between 1938 and 1941, incidents involving more than common criminals began to appear. In Pasadena in 1938, a recording device placed by private detectives was discovered in the hotel room of a New York lawyer who represented an

---

2 The California Constitution, article I, section 19, contains a provision on searches and seizures that varies by only one word from the Fourth Amendment to the federal Constitution. The California clause has been interpreted as not forbidding wiretapping or eavesdropping by police.

Eastern bank being sued for over a million dollars by a California gold
mine operator. Also in 1938, Captain Kynette and his men were found to
be eavesdropping on the home of an investigator for the "reform" political
movement in Los Angeles. What moved the legislators to swift action,
however, was the uncovering in 1940 of an elaborate dictograph apparatus
in a suite of the Hotel Senator in Sacramento, occupied by the speaker of
the state assembly, Gordon Garland. It turned out that this installation had
been ordered by the state director of motor vehicles, a political opponent
of Garland's, and had been installed by the governor's military aide "to
get at the bottom of lobbying."

Within a few months, another listening apparatus came to light, this one
installed throughout Los Angeles City Hall by an investigator hired by reform mayor Fletcher Bowron, who wanted to get proof of official corruption. The California legislature responded immediately by passing Section
653(h) of the Penal Code, which provides:

> Any person who, without consent of the owner, lessee, or occupant, in-
> stalls or attempts to install or use a dictograph in any house, room, apart-
> ment, tenement, office, shop, warehouse, store, mill, barn, stable, or
> other building, tent, vessel, railroad car, vehicle, mine or any underground
> portion thereof, is guilty of a misdemeanor.

As a result of powerful pressure from law enforcement officials, acting
through the California Peace Officers Association, the legislature went on
to say in Section 653(h):

> provided, that nothing herein shall prevent the use and installation of dic-
> tographs by a regular salaried peace officer expressly authorized thereto
> by the head of his office or department or by a district attorney, when
> such use and installation are necessary in the performance of their duties
> in detecting crime and in the apprehension of criminals.

At the time of the Irvine investigation, then, California had a broad
statute forbidding "every person" to tap telephone lines, without specific
exception for the police, but the law had never been used to prosecute the
steadily-wiretapping California police departments in the 1930's and
1940's. On the eavesdropping side, California law specifically permitted
use of "dictographs" by police on authorization of superior officers, and
officers were busily "bugging" throughout the state.

More On Mr. Mason: The Law Enforcers' Friend / That was the
law in California and in the nation on December 3, 1952, when Russell
Mason connected his microphone to a ceiling fixture in the hall of Patrick
Irvine's home and ran the wires to a listening post in a nearby garage. As

Cochran continued his examination of Mason, further details of the eavesdropping operation were unfolded:

> MR. COCHRAN: After [the installation] had been done did you receive
> some complaints from the officers in respect to the audio features of this
> reception?
> MR. MASON: Yes, sir, I did.
> MR. COCHRAN: What was that date?
> MR. MASON: That was around the 8th, December 8th.
> MR. COCHRAN: . . . And did you move the microphone on that date?
> MR. MASON: Yes, sir, I moved it from the original place over the light
> fixture in the hall to over the light fixture in the bedroom.

The reason for this re-entry, Mason explained further, was the complaint from officers at the listening post that there was "a hum" on the line
which prevented "a good clear recording." Moving the microphone on
December 8, however, did not solve this problem. The officers continued to
complain of humming sounds. So Mason went back to Irvine's house a
third time.

> MR. COCHRAN: Did you have occasion on a still later occasion to do
> anything further in respect to that equipment?
> MR. MASON: Yes, sir. It was on about December 28th.
> MR. COCHRAN: Did you have further talks with the officers concerning
> the [humming] sounds?
> MR. MASON: Yes, sir.
> MR. COCHRAN: Pursuant to that conversation did you again enter those
> premises and change the location of the microphone?
> MR. MASON: Yes, sir, I did. . . . . I placed it over a hole I made directly
> inside of the bedroom closet door.

During each of these visits to move the microphone, Mason testified, he
had the police officers go into Irvine's living room and bedroom and talk
aloud so that reception could be tested and adjustments made. Mason's
direct examination concluded with his account of removing the microphone
on January 5, 1952, during the arrest. With Irvine, Inspector Kennedy,
several police officers, and three newspaper photographers watching him,
he climbed down from the attic holding the wires and the disconnected
microphone.

Mason was cross-examined extensively by defense attorney McConnell,
who led him through a series of questions about the fidelity of room recordings, the various entries to Irvine's home, and the exact manner in
which the microphone was placed and moved. McConnell brought out the
fact that the microphone would and did pick up conversation into the

telephone, and if the party calling Irvine were talking loudly enough, both sides of the conversation might be overheard.

Mason did not testify again in the Irvine case. However, his pre-1952 activities as a "recording engineer" were to figure prominently in the press during later stages of the Irvine appeal and its aftermath. Mason started as an amateur radio operator in 1916, studied sound recording at a Western Electric Company training course for motion picture work, and began doing microphone eavesdropping as a private investigator in 1928. He moved to Los Angeles in the late 1930's as a full time "recording engineer," and was soon doing 25 per cent of his work for private clients and 75 per cent for police agencies. Operating under the firm name of Western Television and Sound Laboratories, his eavesdropping assignments included work for police departments in San Francisco, Oakland, Long Beach, Los Angeles, San Diego, and other cities. He also worked for the district attorney in Los Angeles and other counties, as well as for such public agencies as the State Medical Board, State Narcotics Bureau, and state attorney general's office. Between 1940 and 1956, Mason estimated that he had installed over 500 "bugs" in California for law enforcement officers —in offices, stores, homes, hotel rooms, and automobiles. Between 1940 and 1950, he was employed as the "official eavesdropper" for the Los Angeles district attorney's office, during which time, he recalled, he had as many as seven microphone installations a week in operation.

In 1947, Mason's activities became a bit too public for his own good. An eavesdropping system he had installed in the State Building in Los Angeles was accidentally discovered. Mason had been hired by a special agent in the attorney general's office who wanted to check into the conversations of some state officials. In the course of installing his microphones, Mason had made some connections to the telephone switchboard and this activity provided the basis for his indictment—not under Section 640, for wiretapping, but rather under a malicious-mischief law, for making unauthorized repairs on telephone equipment. He was given a 90-day suspended jail sentence and placed on probation for one year. His law enforcement clients probably accounted for this light sentence. Rumors that Mason's operation had provided him with "bulging files" on state officials must have worried some of California's public servants because a mysterious fire broke out in the middle of the affair, completely destroying his laboratory and filing cabinets.

Microphones and Stomach Pumps: When Is Process Due? / Meanwhile, the fruits of Russell Mason's efforts at 3916 E. 2nd Street were ready to be presented to Judge Pierson and the jury. The People's second witness was Officer Jack Calori of the Long Beach police department's bookmaking detail. He described his actions in November and December in following defendants Lippe and Curti as they drove to Irvine's house from the South Chestnut Street house and from the Red Onion Café; then, he was asked by Cochran to relate the conversations of Lippe and Irvine which he had heard while at the listening post on December 4. McConnell was on his feet at once.

> At this time, your Honor, in order to save time, I wish to interpose a standing objection to the admission of any evidence purporting to relate any conversation heard or registered by use or means of the microphone or listening device installed in the apartment of Patrick Irvine at 3916 East 2nd Street, Long Beach, California . . . without the knowledge and consent of the defendant Patrick Irvine or his wife, Mildred Irvine, upon the ground and for the reason that the installation of said listening device was a violation of the constitutional rights of the defendant Irvine as set forth in the Fourth Amendment to the Constitution of the United States. . . . This same exact provision is found in the Constitution of California as Section 19. . . . [In support of this contention], I wish to call your Honor's attention to a case [that] possibly you know, the federal case of *People v. Rochin,* and later termed the case of *Rochin v. the State of California.*

The *Rochin* case, which McConnell and Judge Pierson proceeded to discuss, had been decided by the United States Supreme Court on January 2, 1952 and had been well publicized in California newspapers. Its facts were summarized by Justice Felix Frankfurter in his opinion for the Court:

> Having "some information that [the petitioner here] was selling narcotics," three deputy sheriffs of the County of Los Angeles, on the morning of July 1, 1949, made for the two-story dwelling house in which Rochin lived with his mother, common-law wife, brothers and sisters. Finding the out-side door open, they entered and then forced open the door to Rochin's room on the second floor. Inside they found petitioner sitting partly dressed on the side of the bed, upon which his wife was lying. On a "night stand" beside the bed the deputies spied two capsules. When asked, "Whose stuff is this?" Rochin seized the capsules and put them in his mouth. A struggle ensued, in the course of which the three officers "jumped upon him" and attempted to extract the capsules. The force they applied proved unavailing against Rochin's resistance.

Rochin was then handcuffed and taken to a hospital. He was strapped to a table and his mouth was forced open.

> At the direction of one of the officers a doctor forced an emetic solution through a tube into Rochin's stomach against his will. This "stomach

pumping" produced vomiting. In the vomited matter were found two capsules which proved to contain morphine.

Charged with possession of morphine, Rochin was tried, convicted, and sentenced to 60 days in prison. "The chief evidence against him was the two capsules," Justice Frankfurter noted. Rochin appealed his conviction to the California District Court of Appeal. Even though that court held that the police officers "were guilty of unlawfully breaking into and entering defendant's room and were guilty of unlawfully assaulting and battering defendant while in the room" and even though they were also "guilty of unlawfully assaulting, battering, torturing and falsely imprisoning the defendant at the alleged hospital," the district court affirmed the conviction because of the California rule allowing illegally obtained evidence in court. The California Supreme Court denied Rochin's petition for a hearing.

The United States Supreme Court had unanimously reversed Rochin's conviction, with eight Justices participating (Justice Minton did not take part). Justice Frankfurter's opinion, joined by five of his colleagues, held that Rochin had been denied that "due process of law" guaranteed by the Fourteenth Amendment to the federal Constitution against infringement. ("No State shall . . . deprive any person of life, liberty, or property, without due process of law. . . .") The existing Supreme Court test of whether due process had been violated, said Frankfurter, is whether the state had deprived a person of rights "implicit in the concept of ordered liberty" and "so rooted in the traditions and conscience of our people as to be ranked as fundamental," these two being quotations from earlier opinions by Justice Benjamin N. Cardozo. Frankfurter went on:

> Applying these general considerations to the circumstances of the present case, we are compelled to conclude that the proceedings by which this conviction was obtained do more than offend some fastidious squeamishness or private sentimentalism about combatting crime too energetically. This is conduct that shocks the conscience. Illegally breaking into the privacy of the petitioner, the struggle to open his mouth and remove what was there, the forcible extraction of his stomach's contents—this course of proceeding by agents of government . . . [constitutes] methods too close to the rack and the screw to permit of constitutional differentiation.

On the issue of allowing the evidence to be used, Justice Frankfurter had commented tartly: "[T]o sanction the brutal conduct [by allowing the evidence] . . . would be to afford brutality the cloak of law. Nothing would be more calculated to discredit law and therefore to brutalize the temper of a society." Justices Black and Douglas based their votes to reverse the conviction on the ground that Rochin had been deprived of his privilege against self-incrimination in the Fifth Amendment to the federal Constitution which provides that "No person . . . shall be compelled in any criminal case to be a witness against himself. . . ." This Amendment, Black and Douglas said, was a limit upon the states as well, through the Fourteenth Amendment.

When McConnell raised the *Rochin* case in his objection to Officer Calori's testimony about eavesdropped conversations, Judge Pierson called McConnell and Cochran into his chambers. This was done so that the legal discussion would not be heard by the jury and possibly influence their determination. In Judge Pierson's chambers, Cochran argued that "the Rochin case turns entirely on due process," and on the shocking physical character of stomach pumping, while the conduct in Irvine's case involved no such physical mistreatment. He added that the law in California ever since *People v. Mayen* in 1922, which had been followed "no less than 200 times" by California courts, is that evidence inadmissible in federal trials or obtained in violation of the California constitution is admissible in the state courts if otherwise relevant and trustworthy.

Judge Pierson was persuaded by Cochran's argument and overruled McConnell's objection. He also rejected another defense objection that admission of the conversations would be a violation of Section 640 forbidding telephone tapping and disclosure. When the judge, counsel, and stenographer returned to the courtroom, the examination of Calori resumed. He gave a very brief description of conversations overheard on December 4 and 17 and, after desultory cross-examination, left the stand.

"Babe Gave me Three Horses in that Race. . . ." /   The next witness, Officer Charles Gautt, provided extensive testimony about conversations in the Irvine house, beginning with talks on December 17, 1951. Judge Pierson instructed him not to summarize the conversations but to relate them in dialogue from his notes, "One voice said this, another voice said that. . . ." Gautt did so:

> One voice said "Joe wanted 40 and I figured I would hold him 60." The other voice said "Joe only wanted 10 dollars." And the same voice said something about paid 5.60. . . . The first voice said something about laying off money you haven't got and "When you lay it off my book, that's two separate books, just as separate as if you was giving it to Joe Irvine or somebody else as far as my book is concerned."
>
> The second party said, "Then I made a mistake. I had 45-across on the board. We made it 6-across. Bob only wanted 15-across. Bruce had enough on that horse."
>
> The first party said something about "It goes on his sheet or don't give it to him." The second party said, "Babe gave me three horses in that race. She come in with 5-and-5."

Gautt provided five typewritten pages of testimony from the conversation of December 17. Although the reels of tape were later introduced as an exhibit in the trial, along with transcripts paralleling the portions the officers were reciting from their notes, the tapes themselves were never played to the jury.

Officer Gautt also gave testimony describing how the fluorescent powder "plant" was arranged. When enough incriminating conversation had been assembled, the police were ready to make their arrest; they wanted to do so in a way that would seize physical evidence and establish proof of the relationship between bookmaking at South Chestnut Street and Patrick Irvine's bookmaking at his home. On several occasions, Curti and a woman had been observed driving from the South Chestnut Street house to Irvine's, carrying bundles the officers believed to be bookmaking records. At 5:35 P.M. on January 5, Gautt related, Curti and the woman (Audie Greer) left the South Chestnut Street house by car. Gautt followed, dressed in plain clothes and in an unmarked car. At a prearranged point, he moved ahead of the Curti car. Then two motorcycle officers and a patrol car containing Officers Jacobsen and Dulaney stopped both Gautt's and Curti's cars. Everyone was told to get out and stand with his hands up. The officers explained that a liquor store had been held up and all new Fords of dark color were being stopped because that was the type of vehicle used by the bandit. A gun was "found" in Gautt's belt and he was ostentatiously taken to the patrol car. Curti's person and car were searched, and Audie Greer's bundle of papers were examined. This examination was done by Officer Jacobsen, whose hands had been dusted with an invisible white crystalline powder, which was now on the bundle of papers being carried to Irvine's home.

The police gave Curti time to get to Irvine's and soon heard him (over the microphone) telling Irvine about being stopped at a roadblock for some liquor bandit. At 7:00 P.M., immediately after Curti and Audie Greer left the house, the officers entered and arrested Irvine. An immediate examination of Irvine's hands under ultraviolet rays disclosed fluorescent powder on them and on the betting papers in the drawer of the desk in Irvine's bedroom.

The next police witness, Officer Leonard Hermansen, provided page after page of dialogue overheard between December 3 and January 5. Many of these snatches of talk, unlike those recited by Officers Calori and Gautt, were conversations into the telephone:

> I heard the sound of a 'phone being dialed. I heard Mr. Irvine's voice. . . . I heard Mr. Irvine say, "Can I speak to Jamoke?" Then I heard Mr. Irvine say, "In the first place you've got the horse down wrong." Then I heard him say, "In the 8th, 2 to win." Then I heard him say "King's Boy,

2 to win. In the fourth, Handy Display. In the fifth, Limbo Junior, 2 to win. I've got some more for you. In the third, Clam Digger. . . ."

Another sample of these talks into the telephone, heard on December 29 was:

> I heard Mr. Irvine say, "How're you doing, Pete?" I heard him say, "Tropical, 37, 64, 9.11, 96, one and one criss-cross. Whitman, one to place, criss-cross." Then I heard him say, "You made a mistake on Nelson. You paid him 7.20 for the $5 he bet and that 7.20 was payment for only $2."

Mrs. Irvine was a working helpmate to her husband, and her telephone conversations were also recorded and testified to by Officer Hermansen. For example:

> I heard the 'phone ring and I heard Mrs. Irvine's voice. I heard her say, "Wait a minute. I was down getting my laundry." Then I heard her say a lot of "Um-hums." Then I heard her say, "I'll write them down and mark them across the board. F-9, F-34, T-910."

We Had a Little Key . . . And No Warrant /   After Officer Hermansen had spent a day reciting his notes, McConnell cross-examined him. Irvine's counsel particularly wanted to know how the police and Mason had entered Irvine's house to install and then move their listening equipment. Hermansen replied that he had simply "unlocked the door and walked in."

> MR. MCCONNELL: Did you have a key?
> MR. HERMANSEN: I did.
> MR. MCCONNELL: Did Irvine give it to you?
> MR. HERMANSEN: No.
> MR. MCCONNELL: A pass key?
> MR. HERMANSEN: No, it was a regular house key.

McConnell was to return to this point later.

After Officer Donald Dulaney had testified about the roadblock affair and the arrest of Curti, Officer Lewis Jacobsen was called. He was an expert on bookmaking language and operations, having had six years on the bookmaking detail and a special course on "vice control administration" at the University of Southern California, taught by a Los Angeles police department expert. Jacobsen explained fully that the ledgers, markers, betting sheets, and other materials found in Irvine's home and the conversations testified to were standard bookmaking materials and procedures.

During cross-examination, McConnell again raised the issue of the police entries. Jacobsen replied that the officers had a key.

> MR. MCCONNELL: I show you a key here and ask you, Is that the key that you used, if you would know?
> MR. JACOBSEN: Yes, that is the key.
> MR. MCCONNELL: Where did you get it?
> MR. JACOBSEN: I got it from a man that makes keys for a livelihood.

McConnell led Jacobsen to explain that on "the first or second of December," the locksmith was brought to the Irvine house while the Irvines were out. "He had an apparatus . . . that . . . you push into the lock to locate the tumblers and then file the key until it opened the lock."

After Audie Greer (now a state's witness), Officer Frederick Good, and Detective William Stovall had added details on the surveillance and arrest of the Irvine defendants, Inspector Everett Kennedy took the witness stand. He described the events of the arrest of January 5, 1952, including the fact that he "told Irvine that we had planted a microphone in his house and that we had listened to conversations for over a month." McConnell then pressed hard at the basis for the arrest and its circumstances:

> MR. MCCONNELL: Did you enter with the use of this key that I have just shown you or did you just knock at the door and have it opened?
> MR. KENNEDY: Didn't knock at the door. Sgt. Jacobsen put that in the lock and opened the door.

McConnell then asked what Inspector Kennedy said to Irvine about searching the house:

> I told Mr. Irvine that we had made a legal arrest, that we had the right and we intended to search the entire house for evidence in our case, and that we were looking specifically for old records, and if he would tell us where they were it would keep us from searching the house.
> MR. MCCONNELL: That statement of yours, that you had made a legal arrest, and that you had a right to search the place, that wasn't based on any search warrant you had in your possession, was it?
> MR. KENNEDY: I had no search warrant.

The final witness for the People was Officer Ralph Bradford, a handwriting expert, who testified that the betting records, the signatures on the federal wagering forms, and other physical evidence were all in the handwritings of Lippe, Curti, and Irvine.

It was now noon of Friday, April 11, 1952. Mr. Cochran announced, "The People rest."

When Silence is Golden /   On Monday, April 14, when the trial re-convened, McConnell announced:

Ladies and gentlemen of the jury, your Honor, Mr. Cochran. The defend-ants will not take the stand in this case and will rest their defense upon the presumption of innocence, their rights under the Constitution of the United States and this state, and upon the factual weakness of the People's case on all counts, particularly on that in regard to conspiracy.

Normally, at this point in the trial the defense attorney would have "made his case." The defendants would have been called and examined about the charges, their characters and accomplishments unfolded to the jury, and witnesses produced to support the defense version of the central events and motivations.

Why McConnell chose not to put Irvine, Lippe, Curti, and Mrs. Irvine on the stand is not difficult to imagine. Effective denial of the State's facts about the bookmaking activities was impossible. Furthermore, putting Irvine on the stand to bring out his good character would have entitled the prosecution to cross-examine the defendant on his past activities. A brief look at Irvine's biography, as he wrote it in a long letter in 1954 to the court authorities, indicates why McConnell probably wanted to avoid that.

Irvine's letter described his early life in Wyatt, Louisiana, a hip injury that made manual labor difficult for him, and his early wanderings about the country in the 1920's and early 1930's. Then, it went on to narrate:

So I came back to Long Beach, California, early in 1938, and was given an opportunity to make a living in bookmaking in a small way. During 1938 I married the lady who is now my wife, and in 1939 bought a lot and built the home in which I still reside. In 1940 I was arrested and con-victed of bookmaking and served a year in jail, starting July, 1941. During this time my home was supported by my wife, who was employed by the Associated Telephone Co. Upon my release from jail in May, 1942, I was employed by the California Shipbuilding Co. at Long Beach, California, and worked there until the end of 1944, when my physical handicap again forced me to discontinue manual labor. During this period I bought a restaurant in the 100 block, on American Avenue, Long Beach, which I have operated at various locations in that block ever since. In 1948, I again started bookmaking, in a small way, and continued until my arrest for bookmaking in 1952.

The police record on Irvine, which was carefully nestled in Cochran's briefcase in the event that Irvine took the stand, would have added some further painful details for the defense to overcome. Irvine was first arrested in Gainesville, Texas in 1927. His California dossier started with a prohibition act violation in Long Beach in 1930. Between 1931 and 1946, Irvine had been arrested seven times in Long Beach on charges including vagrancy, burglary, running a lottery, and drunkenness. Apart from paying fines and receiving suspended sentences, he had served a year in county jail for bookmaking in 1941.

Irvine's explanation of his conduct would ordinarily have been another major part of the defense case. In his 1954 letter, Irvine provides us with about what he would have said had he testified on this point. While admitting that what he did was a violation of law, he added:

> I consider it a minor offense, considering the fact that the State of California has declared itself in, to the extent of several million dollars a year, on funds realized from betting on horses. I mean the State's cut from legalized racing, and betting under the Pari-mutual [sic] System. . . . I fail to understand how the law can make it a crime to engage in horse race betting to the extent of a few thousand dollars, on one side of the fence, and declare it legal to bet a million a day on the other side. Another thing I feel is wrong, is the giving of a monopoly to the horse-racing fraternity, to the extent that it is illegal to make any kind of a bet on any other kind of sport. There have been more men ruined and homes desolated and broken up by the Pari-mutual system, than there ever has been by hand-book makers. Most bets with bookmakers are very small. If a man bets a dollar with a bookmaker, even one every day, he would lose only seven dollars in a week. I know, in my own case, that I have refused bets from my clients when I knew that they were overextending themselves.

Given the solid factual basis of the state's case, then, and the perils of testimony by the defendants, no witnesses were put on for Irvine and his colleagues.

With the defense having rested, Cochran made the first closing statement. He laid out for the jury each of the elements of proof of bookmaking in violation of Section 337a, and he maintained that the testimony in the trial had "clearly established" that these charges were valid. McConnell's closing statement was part law and part an appeal to the jury's discretion. He challenged the legality of the police intrusions into Irvine's privacy and called on the jury to consider this in their deliberations. He also pointed to the widespread betting done off-track by many thousands of persons and said that these defendants had not done anything terribly wrong, even if it might have been forbidden by statute.

Enter the "Twelve Good Men and True" / After a short rebuttal from Cochran, Judge Pierson read a series of instructions to the jury to guide them in their deliberations. Such instructions are often based upon drafts submitted by the government and the defense, with the judge accepting those he feels correct or formulating his own versions. Over McConnell's objections, Judge Pierson accepted two key instructions from the People and read them to the jurors. The first advised the jurors to ignore "any trespass which you may find to have been committed." The defendants might sue the police for trespassing but that, said the Judge, "has no part in this trial." The other disputed instruction told the jurors to consider all evidence introduced "irrespective of the manner by which such evidence has been obtained . . .", specifically, the evidence obtained by the planted microphone. Such evidence, Judge Pierson said, "is legally admissible in this State the same as any other competent evidence."

At 4:28 P.M. on April 14, the jury retired. At 8:00 P.M., after their dinner, they returned to the courtroom to hear the counts of the information read to them again.

At 11:58 A.M. the next day, April 15, the jury returned and announced its verdict. The three defendants were found "not guilty" on the conspiracy charge of Count 1. Irvine and Curti were found "guilty" of the other four counts and Lippe was found "guilty" of counts 2, 4, and 5. The three men were continued at liberty, on bail, and May 9 was set for a hearing on probation requests, on McConnell's motion for a new trial, and on sentencing (if a new trial were denied).

At the hearing on May 9, McConnell tried to convince Judge Pierson that a new trial was called for, especially because of the *Rochin* case. He acknowledged California's admission rule, "and I am not asking your Honor to be a crusader or to overrule those decisions of the higher court. . . ." But here, he argued, there was an "aggravated breach of the defendant's constitutional rights," and the verdict should be put aside. Judge Pierson was still not persuaded. "No matter how I might feel about that type of evidence," the Judge responded, no physical violence was used and the *Rochin* case was not in point. "If the [California] Supreme Court, as you say . . . [sees] fit to change the law, let them do it in this case. The motion for a new trial will be denied."

On May 14th, Judge Pierson announced his sentence. First, he commented:

> I do not make the laws that govern this country and I realize at times it is pretty difficult to . . . legislate people's morals. Yet . . . these laws are made and it is like playing a football game. We have rules by which we play and we have rules by which we live. Now, if anybody else . . . was going to take it into their own hands and determine what rules they would abide by and what rules they would not abide by, then organized society, as such, is just not going to function.

Judge Pierson added:

> What is Mr. Irvine's attitude? Mr. Irvine says in effect, "I don't give a darn. I am going to live this way, the way I want, and I am going to do this." Now I cannot subscribe to that. . . . I have never felt good after I sent a man to jail. It makes me upset . . . but Irvine cannot get by with deals like this and someone has to impress him and I am going to be the one that has to decide the matter.

Then Judge Pierson announced Irvine's sentence: on Count 2, one year in county jail; on Count 3, six months imprisonment, to be suspended if Irvine paid a fine of $1,500 in three installments within ninety days, plus three years probation; on Counts 4 and 5, six months imprisonment (suspended) on each and a three-year probation. Lippe and Curti were each sentenced to six months in prison (five of which were suspended), a $500 fine, and three-year probations. McConnell asked that Irvine be freed on $3,000 bond, since he had filed an appeal. This was done, and after Judge Pierson delivered a short lecture to Patrick Irvine, the trial in Superior Court was officially at an end.

Along the Appellate Avenues

After trial in the Superior Courts of California, a defendant's next step is the District Court of Appeal. California has five district courts located geographically throughout the state; District 2 is for Los Angeles. In the Los Angeles District Court, there are four divisions, each with three justices. Vacancies on the District Court of Appeals are filled by the governor. At the first state-wide election more than fifty days after appointment, the electorate votes by answering the ballot question, "For Associate Justice, District Court of Appeals, Second Appellate District, Division Three. Shall Jonathan J. Jones be elected to the office for the term expiring January 1968?" Election is for a 12-year term.

Irvine, the only one of the three defendants to take his case to appeal, had his case heard in Division Two, District Court of Appeal for the Second Appellate District, before Presiding Justice Minor Moore and Associate Justices W. Turney Fox and Marshall F. McComb. In his written brief and oral argument, McConnell presented two points: the first went to the violation of due process, the second dealt with the "improper" instructions given by Judge Pierson. Mrs. Elizabeth Miller, Deputy Attorney General of California, submitted a brief for the People and made the oral argument. Mrs. Miller, a seasoned appellate lawyer, was born in Middle River, California and was graduated from Mills College and the University of Southern California Law School. Once the *Irvine* case left the Superior Court level, she and other members of the attorney general's staff would be responsible for defending the conviction (and the means employed to obtain it) against attack from Irvine's counsel.

On October 2, 1952, the District Court unanimously affirmed Irvine's conviction, reciting the prevailing rule on admissibility of illegally obtained evidence and finding no error in the charges to the jury.

McConnell then took Irvine's case to the final judicial tribunal in California, the Supreme Court, located in San Francisco. This body has a chief justice and six associate justices, selected in the same manner as district justices and for 12-year terms. The Supreme Court does not have to hear every case presented to it but has discretion to review those appeals which it considers important to consider. Only about one out of five requests for hearings is granted. On October 30, 1952, by a 5–2 vote and without issuing an opinion, the California Supreme Court refused to hear Irvine's petition. The two dissenters, Justices Carter and Schauer, were long-standing dissenters from the California admissibility doctrine. Irvine now faced the question whether he should try to appeal his case to the United States Supreme Court.

So far, only minor reports of his arrest, trial, conviction, and appeal had been carried in the California press. More newsworthy people and more serious crimes in which "bugging" was being used had been occupying public attention. The complete wiring of gambler Mickey Cohen's new house by the Los Angeles police at the time of its construction and the planting of a microphone in a Kleenex box beside the bed of a woman suspected of involvement in San Francisco and Los Angeles gambling operations were examples of the leading incidents. At the time that Irvine was being tried, a case that received great publicity was the bugging, by Russell Mason, of the bedroom of James Tarantino, a gossip-sheet publisher who was prosecuted and convicted of blackmailing California celebrities. Another central development in this period, stemming from the Mickey Cohen microphoning installation, was a suit filed in 1951 by A. L. Wirin, counsel of the American Civil Liberties Union Chapter of Southern California; this suit sought to enjoin Los Angeles Police Chief William Parker from using public funds to install "illegal" dictographs and microphones. Parker, who became chief in 1950, had issued Order No. 826, in 1950, authorizing bugging as long as prior permission was had by the police officers and confidential reports of the results were filed.

In November 1952, Irvine and McConnell began to consider strategy for appealing to Washington. McConnell, who was not experienced in arguing appeals before the Supreme Court of the United States, contacted a Washington attorney to argue the petition for certiorari, which asks the Justices to review the case. Under the Court's rules before July 1, 1954, a petition for certiorari had to be accompanied by a printed copy of the record;[3] in Irvine's case, this meant the printing of the 995-page transcript of the proceeding in Superior Court. The Washington attorney estimated the cost of such a printing at $3,500. Printing the clerk's transcript and the brief in support of the petition, plus the attorney's fee for filing the petition for certiorari, would cost $5,000 more. If the petition were granted, there would be an additional fee for writing a full brief and making the oral argument. Irvine did not have $8,500-plus.

Enter Morris Lavine, Appealing / Faced with this situation, McConnell called a Los Angeles specialist in appellate work, Morris Lavine, and asked him to handle the case. Lavine, who had entered law practice in Los Angeles in 1918, had a reputation as a skillful defendant's lawyer in criminal and civil liberty cases. When he was not arguing his own cases, he was often ghost-writing appellate briefs for other lawyers. He had also represented such prominent California businessmen as oil millionaire Edwin Pauley, the famous evangelist, Aimee Semple McPherson, and many indigent defendants, for whom he served as court-appointed counsel in both state and federal courts.

Lavine had argued quite a few cases in the United States Supreme Court—*Lisenba v. California,* a Los Angeles wife-murder case; *Penfield Co. v. S.E.C.,* a case on the distinction between criminal and civil contempt; *Adamson v. California,* an important case for constitutional doctrine involving the murder conviction of Admiral Dewey Adamson; *Phyle v. Duffy,* on the right of a prisoner sentenced to death to have a hearing on a prison doctor's determination of his sanity; *Zap v. United States,* on the government's search rights in a defense contract plant; and *Kawakita v. United States,* a death sentence for treason.

With this background, Lavine was able to tell McConnell that printing the record was not an absolute requirement. Under the rules then in force in the Supreme Court, the Justices could grant permission to file for a petition of certiorari and use the typewritten record of the lower court reporter. This was done when the cost of printing the record was beyond a defendant's means and the requirement would prevent presentation of important federal questions; Lavine had obtained such leave in the *Kawakita* case. He offered to handle the appeal for $1,000. If the petition were granted, he would be paid an additional sum for his time and trip to Washington. Actually, Lavine was attracted strongly to Irvine's appeal. "The case fascinated me," he recalled; "imagine placing a microphone in a married man's bedroom, after entering his house like an ordinary

---

[3] Under the rules after July 1, 1954, a printed record is required only after a petition for certiorari is granted.

burglar with special keys . . . to catch a man making book!" Later he
added, "It was the type of appeal I would rather handle than go to a show."

Lavine's motion to proceed on the typewritten record and his petition
for certiorari (with accompanying brief in support of the petition) were
filed in the Supreme Court on January 1953. The mathematical chances of
having one's petition granted are strongly against a petitioner. At the term
of Court during which Lavine filed, 665 petitions for certiorari were filed
but only 104 were granted. "The Supreme Court," Chief Justice Fred
Vinson once noted, "is not, and never has been, primarily concerned with
the correction of errors in lower court decisions."

> In almost all cases within the Court's appellate jurisdiction, the petitioner
> has already received one appellate review of his case. The debates in the
> Constitutional Convention make clear that the purpose of the establishment
> of one supreme national tribunal was, in the words of John Rutledge of
> South Carolina, "to secure the national rights & uniformity of Judgmts."
> The function of the Supreme Court is, therefore, to resolve conflicts of
> opinion on federal questions that have arisen among lower courts, to pass
> upon questions of wide import under the Constitution, laws, and treaties
> of the United States, and to exercise supervisory power over lower federal
> courts. If we took every case in which an interesting legal question is
> raised, or our *prima facie* impression is that the decision below is erroneous,
> we could not fulfill the Constitutional and statutory responsibilities placed
> upon the Court. To remain effective, the Supreme Court must continue to
> decide only those cases which present questions whose resolution will have
> immediate importance beyond the particular facts and parties involved.

Irvine proved to be fortunate in his relations with the Justices. Leave to
proceed on the typewritten record was granted and the Court examined
Irvine's petition for certiorari. Lavine argued that four fundamental questions should be passed on by the Justices. Two related to the federal wagering stamp and its use in Irvine's trial. The other two revolved around the
eavesdropping, arguing that due process demanded rejection of such evidence and that the use here deprived Irvine of his right to a fair trial.

On March 9, 1953, the Supreme Court granted the petition for certiorari.
Lavine began writing his brief, and attorneys for the People began writing
theirs.

Keeping the Wolf From the Door / Perhaps the most serious block to
Irvine's chances for success in the Supreme Court was the leading case of
Wolf v. Colorado (1949). Earlier, in *Weeks v. United States* (1914), the
Supreme Court had held that evidence obtained in violation of the con-
stitutional guarantees of reasonable search and seizure could not be used in
federal courts. In *Wolf v. Colorado,* the Court held that "the security of

one's privacy against arbitrary intrusion by the police" is part of a person's right to due process under the Fourteenth Amendment and states were bound by this restriction. However, the Court also held that it would *not* invoke the *Weeks* rule and require states to bar such illegally obtained evidence; six Justices felt that the choice between exclusion or other civil and criminal remedies against the police should be up to the states to determine. Since thirty-one states admitted illegally obtained evidence in 1949, the majority said that exclusion was obviously not considered by the nation to be essential to ordered liberty in a free society. If the *Wolf* case were held to control, Irvine's conviction was likely to be sustained; if he could fit his case into the *Rochin* compartment, he might escape the *Wolf* rule.

When *Wolf* was decided, the Supreme Court majority supporting the rule consisted of Chief Justice Fred Vinson and Associate Justices Felix Frankfurter, Stanley Reed, Robert Jackson, Harold Burton, and Hugo Black. The three dissenters had been Justices Frank Murphy, Wiley Rutledge, and William O. Douglas. When Irvine's case was argued before the Supreme Court, on November 30, 1953, the Court's personnel had undergone several changes, none of which seemed especially heartening to Irvine's prospects. Two of the dissenters in *Wolf,* Murphy and Rutledge, had died in 1949 and had been replaced by Tom C. Clark and Sherman Minton, men who had established themselves quickly as conservatives in the area of civil liberties and criminal procedure. In place of Chief Justice Vinson sat Earl Warren of California, whose career as crusading district attorney of Alameda County, attorney general, and anti-crime governor gave little indication that he would be generously disposed toward a clearly guilty bookmaker or that he would be strictly inclined toward the California police.

Actually, the area of search and seizure was so confused and fluid that rigid "bloc" analysis of the Justices was unwise. One could never quite tell how the Court would treat such cases. Justice Black, for example, a stout exponent of the "absolute" Bill of Rights and of maximum civil liberties activism from the Court, seemed to view the Fourth Amendment as less absolute than other Amendments.[4] He had joined the majority in *Wolf* and in other search cases affirming convictions against claims of Fourth Amendment deprivations. Justice Frankfurter, on the other hand, generally described as an exponent of judicial self-restraint and permissive toward state action, had written the outraged opinion of the Court in the *Rochin* case and had dissented vigorously in the wiretapping decisions

---

[4] It should be noted that the Fourth Amendment's command is that searches and seizures not be "unreasonable," while the First Amendment states that "Congress shall make *no* law" abridging freedom of speech, press, assembly, and religion. This difference in standard has affected Justice Black's reaction to search-and-seizure cases.

in the *Goldman, On Lee,* and comparable cases. He had also written the opinion in the *Wolf* case, to further compound the complexities.

Actually, the Supreme Court of 1954 would be considering electronic eavesdropping from a remarkably broad base of experience. Jackson and Clark had been attorneys general of the United States and had authorized F.B.I. wiretapping. Both had refused to prosecute state officials for violation of Section 605 of the Federal Communications Act. Black, during his years as a United States senator, had outraged conservatives by subpoenaing the original copies of telegraph messages from Western Union to show how utility companies were lobbying to defeat New Deal legislation. Shortly after graduation from law school, Frankfurter had served in the United States attorney's office for the southern district of New York under Henry Stimson and had formed the opinion there that wiretapping and eavesdropping were simply not essential to effective law enforcement. He had grown more convinced of this view as the years had passed. Warren, as already noted, had been a California prosecutor when wiretapping and eavesdropping were standard procedure for prosecutors. As governor, he had deplored political wiretapping but had not opposed police use of the technique.

The experience of these Justices was not precisely in point for the *Irvine* case, however, and it is generally risky to assume that men carry all of their pre-Court views into their opinions when they become Justices. All that this biographical data suggests is that the Court's members had informed ideas about this field and that discussion at the conference table was likely to be lively.

The briefs in the *Irvine* case arrived at the Supreme Court in the fall of 1953. Irvine's, 54 pages long, was filed on October 31; the 69-page brief for California arrived on November 23. Earlier, on March 9, 1953, the Supreme Court had narrowed some of the issues in the *Irvine* case by deciding, in *United States v. Kahriger,* that the federal wagering tax was constitutional. Six Justices held that it did not intrude on the reserved powers of the states or violate the bookmaker's privilege against self-incrimination. The use of the stamp as evidence in a state prosecution had *not* been passed upon in the *Kahriger* case, and this remained as part of the debate in the briefs for Irvine and California.

Oral argument before the Supreme Court was held on November 30. It is here that the Justices, by questions to counsel about the facts and the implications of the arguments being offered, begin to get the intimate "feel" for the case that is essential to wise judgment.

The Rewards of Library Work /   The clerk of the Supreme Court had notified counsel that the case had been "set down" to be heard on Monday, November 30. Whether it would actually be argued then or later in the week depended on how many opinions the Justices would have to deliver that Monday, a fact the Court keeps secret until the time of delivery. Lavine recalled that he "left Los Angeles by train Friday night and arrived in Chicago Sunday morning."

> I went to the Cook County law library upon arrival and reviewed all the prosecution cases until closing time and then left for my train for Washington. Arriving Monday morning I immediately went to the Supreme Court building from the station, reported in to the clerk, and went to the Supreme Court's law library. I wanted to read the original record in *Wolf v. Colorado*.

The reason for Lavine's last minute research was that the Supreme Court's opinions in the *Wolf* case had disclosed nothing of the facts in that case.[5] All that had been said was that Colorado police had obtained evidence illegally. Actually, the *Wolf* case involved an entry, without a warrant, into a doctor's office. The doctor's notebook had been opened and carried away, and the names found there had served to lead the police to its key witness in the abortion prosecution of the doctor. The notebook itself was introduced in evidence at his trial. Lavine continued:

> I had gone through the record, familiarizing myself with the facts of Wolf, when at about 11:45 I received a phone call in the library from the clerk, telling me to be sure to be in court at its opening—that I was first up for argument, the calendar was clear and I would open [the appeal] as soon as the admissions [of new members of the Bar of the Supreme Court] were through.
> I barely had time to address the court when Justice Frankfurter shot this question at me:
> "How do you distinguish this case on the facts from *Wolf v. Colorado?*"
> I answered: *"Wolf v. Colorado* was an abortion case, where the officers after seizing records in the doctor's office went out to the patients whose names they secured. They didn't find the patients in the office and they didn't place a microphone in the doctor's office to listen to him. In the *Irvine* case, the officers made a key to the house, and like common burglars, went in and placed a microphone to learn if he was taking bets . . . and listened to this married couple for a month to get information about bookmaking."

Lavine recalls that Justice Frankfurter "looked surprised when I was

---

[5] The facts *were* described in the opinion of the Colorado Supreme Court, however, although not in the detail that Lavine found in the original record of the *Wolf* case.

able to give the facts of the *Wolf* case. Ignorance of facts asked by the court often throws lawyers completely off balance."

Frankfurter then asked Lavine: "Do you think it was worse than taking records from a doctor's office to get the names of his patients?" "I do," Lavine replied. "It is as bad as sticking a stomach pump into a man to compel him to throw up the evidence, as in *Rochin*. . . . I can't think of any more shocking invasion of privacy than to stick a microphone into a man's bedroom secretly."

When the State's turn came, the oral argument was presented by Mrs. Miller, deputy attorney general, and Clarence Linn, then assistant attorney general and now a municipal court judge in San Francisco. Several of the Justices bore down heavily on counsel for the State, revealing their shock at the facts. Chief Justice Warren read Section 653h of the California Penal Code to Linn, and asked whether the consent of the chief of police or district attorney had been secured to place the microphone. Linn stated that he believed no such permission had been obtained. The Chief Justice remarked that such unauthorized use seemed to be a crime on the part of the police officers. Linn, who had argued the *Rochin* case In the Supreme Court, tried to veer the argument back to the *Wolf* principle and away from *Rochin*. However, the questioning concentrated heavily on the police conduct, with little discussion on the value of excluding illegally obtained evidence.

When the oral argument was concluded, several lawyers in the Courtroom congratulated Lavine on having won his case, since the questions from Warren, Frankfurter, Jackson, and others seemed to indicate deep dissatisfaction with California's position. "Everyone thought the Chief was with me," Lavine noted, "but knowing his attitude toward bookmaking, I did not feel that way."

After hearing oral argument, the Supreme Court considers the case at the conference held at the end of the week. Full discussion is held among the Justices and a vote is usually taken the same week that the case is argued. Then drafts of the opinion for the Court and any concurring or dissenting opinions are written by the individual Justices and circulated to other members of the Court for comment. The case is then "brought back" to conference and a final vote is taken. (Between the first conference vote and the final one, Justices can and often have changed their position as they reflect on the issues or read the drafts.) The debate in the conference room on the Irvine case was unusually heated and what had seemed a rather tawdry little appeal when it first arrived at the Court now seemed to be developing into a hearty *cause célèbre*. (It is significant to note that no organization filed a "friend of the court" brief in support of Irvine's civil liberties claims, although such intervention is common in such cases as this. Neither the Southern California Civil Liberties Union nor the American Civil Liberties Union entered the case; nor did any of the various bar associations or other groups that had ideological interest in vindicating freedom from police eavesdropping on bedroom conversations.)

Five Justices Make a Court: The Jackson Opinion / The Supreme Court's ruling in the *Irvine* case was handed down on February 8, 1954. The Court had voted 5–4 to affirm the conviction. There were five opinions: one by Jackson for himself, Warren, Reed, and Minton; one by Clark concurring in the majority result; a dissent by Black for himself and Douglas; a dissent by Frankfurter for himself and Burton; and an additional separate dissent by Douglas.

Jackson's opinion for the Court began by disposing of the claims for reversal based on the federal wagering act. Without discussing the question of self-incrimination, Jackson said that the act had been held constitutional in the *Kahriger* case; the information it required was intended to be made public; and the act specifically stated that no one should be exempt from prosecution by state law for engaging in such taxed activity.

"But the questions raised by the officers' conduct while investigating this case are serious," Jackson continued. These were clear violations of the citizen's constitutional right to privacy:

> Each of these repeated entries of petitioner's home without a search warrant or other process was a trespass, and probably a burglary, for which any unofficial person should be, and probably would be, severely punished. Science has perfected amplifying and recording devices to become frightening instruments of surveillance and invasion of privacy, whether by the policeman, the blackmailer, or the busybody. That officers of the law would break and enter a home, secrete such a device, even in a bedroom, and listen to the conversation of the occupants for over a month would be almost incredible if it were not admitted. Few police measures have come to our attention that more flagrantly, deliberately, and persistently violated the fundamental principle declared by the Fourth Amendment.

Jackson reviewed the *Wolf* case's unwillingness to apply the exclusionary evidence rule to the states and said, "That holding would seem to control here." As for *Rochin,* that case had rested upon

> an element totally lacking here—coercion . . . applied by a physical assault upon his person to compel submission to the use of a stomach pump. This was the feature which led to a result in Rochin contrary to that in Wolf. . . . However obnoxious are the facts in the case before us, they do not involve coercion, violence or brutality to the person, but rather a trespass to property, plus eavesdropping.

To reverse Irvine's conviction, even though it was not within the *Rochin* rule but because it was "more shocking, more offensive" than the situation in *Wolf,* said Jackson, would leave the Court's rule of due process in search and seizure cases "so indefinite that no state court could know what it should rule in order to keep its processes on solid constitutional ground."

In support of this position, Jackson explained that until 1949 the Fourth Amendment had never been held to be incorporated into the Fourteenth, and thirty-one states had not installed the exclusionary rule. States "may wish further to reconsider" their evidentiary principle in light of *Wolf.*

> But to upset state convictions even before the states have had adequate opportunity to adopt or reject the rule would be an unwarranted use of federal power. The chief burden of administering criminal justice rests upon state courts. To impose upon them the hazards of federal reversal for noncompliance with standards as to which this Court and its members have been so inconstant and inconsistent would not be justified. We adhere to Wolf as stating the law of search-and-seizure cases and decline to introduce vague and subjective distinctions.

Jackson's opinion concluded with the comment that there is "no lack of remedy if an unconstitutional wrong has been done in this instance without upsetting a justifiable conviction of this commonplace gambler." The Federal Civil Rights Act (originally passed during reconstruction) makes it a crime for any person under color of law willfully to deprive anyone of his rights and privileges secured by the federal Constitution. Carefully indicating that he was speaking only for himself and Chief Justice Warren in this suggestion (and not for Justices Reed and Minton who joined the rest of this opinion), Jackson said: "We believe the Clerk of this Court should be directed to forward a copy of the record in this case, together with a copy of this opinion, for attention of the Attorney General of the United States."

(When Jackson delivered this opinion orally in the Courtroom, he commented extemporaneously that he and the Chief Justice would have to pay the postage for this forwarding since the Court disapproved of the action.)

The Reluctant Consent of Justice Clark / Justice Clark wrote a short concurring opinion joining in the result but not in all the reasoning of the Court's opinion. If he had been on the Court when the *Wolf* case had been decided, he said, he would have voted to apply the exclusionary rule in search-and-seizure cases to the states. Since the Court refused to overturn that precedent, he would vote "reluctantly" to stick to its letter rather than "sterilize" the rule by a "case-to-case approach" that would make for "uncertainty and unpredictability." He added, "Perhaps strict adherence to the tenor of [the Wolf] decision may produce needed converts for its extinction."

Black and Douglas See Self-Incrimination /   Justice Black, joined by Douglas, maintained that the Court should have reversed Irvine's conviction because it was based on evidence from the federal wagering act "extorted from him by the Federal Government in violation of the Fifth Amendment." Black and Douglas, who had dissented in the *Kahriger* case, said that even though that act had been held constitutional, the use of confessions forced by it to convict defendants in state courts should have been held unconstitutional. "I believe this frustrates a basic purpose of the Fifth Amendment—to free Americans from fear that federal power could be used to compel them to confess conduct or beliefs in order to take away their life, liberty or property."

Black added one last paragraph, objecting strongly to the call for action by the attorney general as suggested by Jackson and Warren. That is "inconsistent with my own view of the judicial function in our government. Prosecution, or anything approaching it, should, I think, be left to government officers whose duty it is."

The Anti-Mechanics of Frankfurter and Burton /   Justice Frankfurter, joined by Burton, dissented from what they regarded as the "mechanical" application of the due process clause and of the *Wolf-Rochin* precedents. Judicial construction of due process calls for flexibility, a "gradual process of judicial inclusion and exclusion," as the Court had said in the nineteenth century. Even though physical violence was absent in Irvine's case, "we have here . . . a more powerful and offensive control over the Irvines' life than a single, limited physical trespass." It would be highly unwise to "announce a new absolute, namely, that even the most reprehensible means for securing a conviction will not taint a verdict so long as the body of the accused was not touched by State officials."

Frankfurter replied in detail to Jackson's argument questioning the efficacy of the exclusionary rule. He concluded that to suggest other means to reach the illegal actions of the Long Beach police was shirking the Court's duty. A new trial was demanded.

And Douglas Also Cites the Fourth Amendment /   The final opinion, by Justice Douglas, related fully the "revolting" conduct of the police. Such "unconstitutional evidence" cannot be used in state trials, Douglas said: "It is no answer that the man is doubtless guilty. The Bill of Rights was designed to protect every accused against practices of the police which history showed were oppressive to liberty. The guarantee against unreasonable searches and seizures contained in the Fourth Amendment was one of those safeguards." Deploring the original departure from principle of the *Wolf* case, Douglas challenged the idea of a remedy in prosecution by the attorney general. He described the overburdened status of the civil rights section of the Department of Justice and the "hostility" that Federal Civil Rights Act prosecutions of police officers had received from the Supreme Court in the past. He also added an appendix to his opinion showing how few prosecutions had been brought under that act. "[A]s long as courts receive the evidence," he ended his opinion, "the police will act lawlessly and the rights of the individual will suffer. We should throw our weight on the side of the citizen and against lawless police. We should be alert to see that no *unconstitutional* evidence is used to convict any person in America."

The Aftermath of Irvine's Trials

After a petition for rehearing which Lavine submitted was quickly denied by the Supreme Court, Irvine's appeal was finished. No higher court was available. But while this specific case was done, the impact of the *Irvine* ruling was only beginning.

The *Irvine* case drew little immediate attention from the national press. Contrary to the reception of "big" Supreme Court decisions, most leading newspapers ignored *Irvine* completely. A few had minor news accounts. Only a handful wrote editorials. The St. Louis *Post-Dispatch,* on February 9, 1954, wrote the strongest editorial comment, denouncing it as "a judicial outrage" and a "terribly wrong decision."

> There are a shocking number of things wrong with this 5-to-4 decision, but undoubtedly the most distressing aspect of it is the fact that Chief Justice Warren is on the side which shuts its eyes to justice under the Constitution. Indeed it is by the vote of the new Chief Justice that the scales tip against the civil rights views of Justices Black, Douglas, Frankfurter and Burton and in favor of the strange position of Justices Reed, Jackson, Clark and Minton.

Justice Clark's "astonishing position" in following a rule he considered unwise was also criticized.

> Justice Clark is not obligated to follow any decision he does not believe in. Can it be that he is so little familiar with the history of the bench on which he sits that he does not know that Justices and the Court have reversed themselves many times when convinced of error?

Reviewing the facts and noting that what happened to "this miserable gambler can overtake any other citizen," the *Post-Dispatch* lamented that "once again the Supreme Court has joined in eroding the liberties of the American people. . . . A judgment so rank will not stand for long. The quicker it is expunged the better it will be!"

California Digests the Decision / Reaction in California law enforcement circles was swift. In some ways, it resembled the stunned sensation of a man long used to kicking a mule who suddenly finds that the mule has kicked back, even lightly. The possibility of federal prosecution, while not terribly real, had at least been raised and the California police became a bit edgy.

Reflecting this feeling, the district attorney of Los Angeles County, S. Ernest Roll, sent a letter on February 15, 1954, to the attorney general of California, Edmund Brown, asking for an official opinion as to the meaning of the *Irvine* ruling for California law enforcers. Specifically, Roll wanted to know whether a district attorney should refuse to prosecute new cases and move to dismiss existing cases based primarily on evidence such as in *Irvine* and whether police agencies must "completely refrain" from such conduct hereafter. Roll also asked whether it would make any difference in either answer if the "bug" were installed in an office, hotel room, or place of business rather than a home.

Brown's answer was given on September 4, 1954. Briefly put, his rulings were:

(1) District attorneys can prosecute cases based on evidence as in Irvine's and they will not incur liability by doing so. This conclusion was based on the majority holdings of *Wolf, Irvine,* and the California cases rejecting the exclusionary evidence rule. But, Brown went on to state, the district attorney's oath is to maintain and uphold the United States and California Constitutions. That oath "commits him to a duty to defend and protect the rights of the people guaranteed thereunder . . . [and] conviction of the guilty by deprivation of constitutional rights imperils the freedom of the innocent." The district attorneys must therefore review all such cases and decide whether it would be in the interests of the people of California to prosecute them.

(2) Police officials who use such methods in private homes may be liable for both civil and criminal penalties. This applies as well to bugging in offices, hotel rooms, and places of business. This conclusion was put with a clarity that even a Los Angeles policeman could grasp:

There can be no room for quibbling over the "holding" of the *Irvine* case. The articulate premise of the decision is that the officers involved violated Irvine's constitutional rights. Therefore, law enforcement officers who engage in such conduct violate their oath to support and follow the Constitution of the United States and the Constitution of the State of California.

To determine exactly what police conduct would be illegal, Brown reviewed the federal cases thoroughly. He concluded that the basic offense in the *Irvine* case was the trespass on Irvine's property, the unlawful entry. Listening without trespass had not been condemned. As for California's law allowing police to use dictographs, Brown brushed this statute aside swiftly, ruling that it could give no officer any right to violate the Constitution of the nation or state and police conduct "should be governed accordingly."

Many enforcement officials in California made hostile comments on the decision. Chief William Parker of Los Angeles and the city attorney saw the *Irvine* case as resting upon "a complete absence of facts on the question of the reasonableness of the quest under the circumstances." Clarence Linn commented later, "I believe that a man's home is his castle, but if he turns it into a bookmaking establishment, the reason for the rule ceases to exist."

How police officials would react, in practice, to the ruling of Attorney General Brown remained to be seen.

Justice Reads the Record / Another attorney general had to be reckoned with—United States Attorney General Herbert Brownell. When the record of the *Irvine* case and the Supreme Court's opinion reached the Department of Justice, a full investigation was ordered, to be conducted by the Federal Bureau of Investigation. The F.B.I. soon discovered that Russell Mason and the Long Beach police *had* been authorized to install a microphone in Irvine's house, contrary to what Assistant Attorney General Clarence Linn had thought and had informed Chief Justice Warren during oral argument. Assistant United States Attorney General Warren Olney III (himself a Californian and a Warren protégé) headed the Justice Department's criminal division. He stated officially that the eavesdropping had been done "under orders of the Chief of Police, who in turn was acting with the full knowledge of the District Attorney."

When an F.B.I. agent interviewed Morris Lavine during the investigation, Lavine stated that Irvine would neither make a complaint nor aid in the prosecution of the officers. With his home and his restaurant in Long Beach, and given his criminal record, Irvine "would be harassed by the police for the rest of his life," Lavine said. Both Irvine and Lavine urged the Justice Department to drop the prosecution. While he and his counsel had invoked every possible guarantee of the state and federal constitutions during his trials, Irvine was too skilled a handicapper of realities (as well as of horses) to "take on the Los Angeles police force."

Looking over these facts, the Department of Justice concluded that it was "doubtful" whether a successful prosecution under the Federal Civil

Rights Act could be maintained. It was decided that "it would be both use-
less and inadvisable to present [the] matter to the Federal grand jury."
This decision, Olney has explained, "was largely influenced by the belief
that the Government . . . would not be able to satisfy the rigid standard
of intent [knowingly to deprive a person of his constitutional rights] imposed by the Supreme Court" in cases construing the Civil Rights Act. Particular mention was made of *Screws v. United States,* a Civil Rights Act
case decided in 1945. There, the court had reversed the conviction of a
Georgia sheriff who had beaten a handcuffed Negro prisoner to death; a
"specific intent" to deprive a person of rights expressly given by the Constitution or by court decisions interpreting the Constitution was required,
the majority ruled, and this element had not been found in the trial in
Georgia. Those elements, Olney felt, would impair any possibility of proceeding against the Long Beach police. Consequently, the matter was
closed.

The Nation Surveys Its Party Line /   While the California community
was digesting the *Irvine* case, a flood of wiretapping and eavesdropping incidents throughout the country focused public attention on the issue.

In the states, eavesdropping news seemed everywhere. During February
1955, a central wiretap station in New York City was discovered; this
listening post permitted its enterprising private-detective installers to monitor over 100,000 telephone lines in the plush mid-Manhattan area. Also in
1955, the district attorney of Philadelphia took it upon himself to release
to the press the full transcripts of telephone taps he had ordered made on
the lines of out-of-town Teamsters Union organizers whom the D.A. alleged were intending to raid a local union; no prosecutions were ever
initiated against the wiretapped visitors. In 1954, an investment broker and
a private detective in Chicago were caught tapping the line of a company
the broker was thinking of purchasing. Also in Chicago in 1954, a local
labor racketeer tapped the phones of the persons complaining about him
to a federal grand jury. Taps by Maryland police in bookmaking cases in
1954–55 became so widespread that the Baltimore *Sun* attacked "wide-
open, indiscriminate uses of wire tapping" in the state. In Las Vegas,
Nevada, the public learned that hidden microphones were used by a newspaper editor to get proof of connections between state officials and prominent gamblers; in addition, it was revealed that many of the local brothels
wired their rooms to collect "useful information" about important clients.
In New Jersey, a state investigation in 1956 concluded that prosecutors
and state troopers were tapping telephones despite the 1930 New Jersey
statute forbidding such conduct. Private eyes were also doing a thriving
business in the Garden State. These instances were paralleled by disclosures
in Detroit, Kansas City, Portland (Oregon) and many other communities.

Clearly, wiretapping and bugging were no longer—if they had ever been—
a phenomenon restricted to the "eavesdropping capitals" of Washington,
New York, and Los Angeles.

The years 1954 and 1955 also saw a series of dramatic and influential
congressional hearings into electronic eavesdropping. At one point, a
private wiretapper even demonstrated to the congressmen at a committee
hearing how he could sit in a legislator's outer office reading a magazine
while secretly recording telephone calls made from the inner office. The
display of parabolic microphones, transistor recorders, and "Buck Rogers"
sound equipment, all in working order and not in blueprints, had a profound
effect on the congressional investigators and their reaction was registered in
the alarmed stories featured in the press. Proof of more than the usual concern of editors of liberal weeklies and civil libertarians was the fact that
two major television networks raced one another in 1955 to see which
could broadcast the first exposé of electronic eavesdroppers. Reverend
Billy Graham's organization made a movie entitled *Wiretapper* depicting
the religious conversion of a man named Jim Vaus whose presalvation
occupation had been that of a "professional earphones man" for both the
police and gambler Mickey Cohen. The mass media featured articles on
wiretapping excesses steadily in this period, and even Daddy Warbucks in
the nationally syndicated comic strip, "Little Orphan Annie," learned to
his anger that agents of "the Syndicate" were tapping his calls.

Even more important than this concern by itself was the fact that, for
the first time since the 1920's, the states began to do something legislatively
about wiretapping and the newer electronic eavesdropping developments.
The cold statistics of state action between 1954 and 1958 reveal something
of a civil liberties revolt by the legislatures. Eighteen states held legislative
debates over tighter control laws in that four-year period. Three states—
Maryland, Nevada, and Oregon—joined New York in putting police wiretapping under tight court order controls, while writing clear and modernized
prohibitions against private-eye wiretapping. Two states, Pennsylvania and
Illinois, banned all wiretapping completely, whether done by police agencies or by private persons, and excluded all wiretap evidence from their
state courts. Five states went beyond telephone tapping and enacted controls on all types of electronic monitoring—by radio, microphone, or electric beam. Three states had judicial rulings that declared wiretapping to be
illegal under existing state laws and excluded wiretap evidence from state
trials. One state, Texas, passed a law making Section 605 of the Federal
Communications Act binding within the state for purposes of determining
the admissibility of evidence obtained by wiretapping, in short, excluding
all such evidence. Some municipalities passed ordinances to control wiretapping excesses. Baltimore, for example, enacted an ordinance in 1954

requiring the city police to obtain a court order before tapping telephones within the city limits.

Furthermore, these laws were not left to languish on the statute books. A deputy inspector and two plain-clothes men of the Brooklyn, New York police force were dismissed for illegally wiretapping, and the two plain-clothes men pleaded guilty to criminal charges. Private tappers in New York, Chicago, and Portland (Oregon) were indicted and convicted. Included in this group was John Broady, probably the top New York wiretapper, who was sentenced to prison for two-to-four years and disbarred as an attorney. Even the federal government became active in enforcement of Section 605 against *private* violators. Between 1954 and 1961 there were twelve prosecutions brought involving twenty wiretappers. Ten of the cases resulted in convictions, and the wide distribution of cases—in Texas, Maryland, Louisiana, California, New York, North Carolina, Oregon, and Arkansas—made the new enforcement policy nation-wide. In New York, the Secretary of State moved to withdraw licenses from private detectives who wiretapped or eavesdropped illegally, and this action cut private wiretapping facilities in New York even further.

California Changes its Mind /   In this new climate of public opinion on privacy, eavesdropping, and law enforcement, the State of California was not left untouched.

In 1955, the California Supreme Court found itself faced with the appeal of Charles H. Cahan and fifteen others, charged with conspiracy to engage in bookmaking in violation of Section 337a. An officer of the intelligence unit of the Los Angeles police, with Chief Parker's permission, had entered Cahan's house "through the side window of the first floor" and had supervised the installation of a mike under a chest of drawers. Lines were strung to a nearby garage where a listening post and recording station was established. It was almost a perfect duplication of the *Irvine* situation.

This time, the California Supreme Court did not brush the appeal aside. Instead, a 4–3 majority overruled *People v. Mayen* and its successors and placed California in the list of states that excluded illegally obtained evidence.

The presence of the United States Supreme Court's opinions in the *Irvine* case hung like fallout over the majority opinion. California Justice Roger Traynor noted the caustic censure by the Supreme Court of such methods of getting evidence, while noting that here the Los Angeles police blithely admit to kicking doors in and forcing windows to gain entry.

Thus, without fear of criminal punishment or other discipline, law enforcement officers, sworn to support the Constitution of the United States and the Constitution of California, frankly admit their deliberate, flagrant acts in violation of both Constitutions and the laws enacted thereunder. It is clearly apparent from their testimony that they casually regard such acts as nothing more than the performance of their ordinary duties for which the City employs and pays them.

After discussing the *Wolf* and *Irvine* cases, Justice Traynor said,

> Pursuant to the suggestion of the United States Supreme Court [in *Irvine*], we have reconsidered the rule we have heretofore followed [as to exclusion]. . . . [W]e have concluded . . . that evidence obtained in violation of the constitutional guarantees [should be] inadmissible. . . . We have been compelled to reach that conclusion because other remedies have completely failed to secure compliance with the constitutional provisions on the part of police officials with the attendant results that the courts under the old rule have been constantly required to participate in, and in effect condone, the lawless activities of law enforcement officers.

Reaction to the *Cahan* decision was sharp among many law enforcement officers. Chief Parker condemned it bitterly. Assistant Attorney General Linn said it was "the Magna Carta of the criminal. In this electronic age, it is equivalent to a law disarming police officers, saying they cannot carry guns." District Attorney Roll of Los Angeles, however, praised the ruling, an action somewhat curious and not a little unexpected in light of his long record of authorizing microphone and wiretap installations by Russell Mason. Praise for the ruling came from most California newspapers, the local bar associations, and civil liberty groups. Two years later, Attorney General Edmund Brown reviewed experience under the *Cahan* rule and declared that its "over-all effects" had been "excellent."

This was not to be the only major development in California stemming out of the post-*Irvine* mood. In 1957, the California Senate Judiciary Committee held far-ranging hearings into wiretapping and bugging in the state. The extensiveness of police and private-eye taps was laid on the record, primarily through the reluctant testimony of law enforcement officers and technicians they employed. (Russell Mason, for example, detailed his bugging services for dozens of state and local law enforcement agencies throughout the state. He also provided an account of how he bugged auto salesrooms, department stores, and hotel lobbies for their owners, as well as placed a mike in a casket during a private investigation involving a leading California mortuary.)

On August 7, 1957, the California Supreme Court held that the suit brought by Civil Liberties Union attorney, A. L. Wirin, for an injunction to stop Chief Parker from using public funds to install dictographs, could be maintained. The Court said that Parker's pleadings in the courts below in the injunction suit had indicated that he intended to continue authorizing such conduct, and he had not changed his position after the *Irvine* decision in 1954. Unless there is a clear finding when the case goes back to trial that Chief Parker is not authorizing and does not intend to authorize dictograph surveillance, Wirin should have his injunction granted.

(Some California police officials take the view that it was the Los Angeles police department that brought all the "Cahan trouble" on state law enforcers. Every case in the California appellate courts between 1940 and the *Irvine* decision that had involved wiretapping and bugging had come from Los Angeles. Other police departments in California had used eavesdropping information for leads to regular evidence and had not presented testimony on eavesdropped conversations to the courts.)

Following the *Wirin v. Parker* decision, Chief Parker stipulated that he would authorize no more dictographs. However, from 1957 to the present, he has criticized the *Cahan* and *Parker* rulings, claiming that the rise in the crime rate in Los Angeles and California is directly traceable to these handcuffs placed on law enforcement. Supporters of the *Cahan* ruling have challenged his figures and the battle about causation is still being waged.

All attempts by Chief Parker and the California Peace Officers Association to have the state legislature change the *Cahan* rule or authorize wiretapping and eavesdropping by court order have thus far failed. In the new atmospheres in California, several private detectives have been tried and convicted of unlawful tapping. In February 1961, Russell Mason, who had said that his work had shifted to 75 per cent private and only 25 per cent for police after the *Cahan* decision, was arrested and held for trial in Los Angeles on charges of illegal telephone tapping for a private client in a divorce case.

The Supreme Court Also Reconsiders /   The most recent reverberation from the *Irvine* case came in June 1961 from the United States Supreme Court. In *Mapp v. Ohio,* a 5–4 majority overruled the *Wolf* precedent and announced a new constitutional rule of due process: "all evidence obtained by searches and seizures in violation of the Constitution is . . . inadmissible in a state court." The "swing" Justice in the *Mapp* case and the man who wrote for the Court was Tom C. Clark.

Dolly Mapp had been arrested in 1957 by Cleveland police officers and had been convicted under an Ohio statute that punished the knowing possession of obscene books or pictures. The police had gone to Miss Mapp's home (the second floor of a two-family house) on information from an informant that someone in connection with a bombing was there and also that large amounts of "policy paraphernalia" were in her residence. When the police arrived, they knocked and asked for admittance. Miss Mapp asked whether they had a search warrant and when they said they did not, she refused them entry. The officers called their headquarters and waited outside the house. Three hours later, additional officers arrived, pried off the outside screen door, attempted to "kick in the door," and finally broke a pane of glass to open the door from the inside. As Justice Clark described the next sequence of events:

It appears that Miss Mapp was halfway down the stairs from the upper floor to the front door when the officers, in this highhanded manner, broke into the hall. She demanded to see the search warrant. A paper, claimed to be a warrant, was held up by one of the officers. She grabbed the "warrant" and placed it in her bosom. A struggle ensued in which the officers recovered the piece of paper and as a result of which they handcuffed appellant because she had been "belligerent." . . . Running roughshod over appellant, a policeman "grabbed" her, "twisted [her] hand," and she "yelled [and] pleaded with him" because "it was hurting."

Miss Mapp was then forced by the policemen to go upstairs to her bedroom where her room and furniture were searched. Then the entire second floor was searched, and, finally, the first floor and basement of the house. Partly in Miss Mapp's quarters and partly in the basement, the officers found several pictures and pamphlets which served as the key pieces of evidence in Miss Mapp's trial. (Miss Mapp and another witness testified these had been left by a boarder who had just gone to New York.) The police did not prove at the trial that any search warrant had even been issued by a judge and the Supreme Court thought it highly doubtful that one had been obtained. Miss Mapp received a one- to seven-year prison sentence.

Justice Clark Reviews the Record / Justice Clark's discussion focused primarily on developments between the *Wolf* case in 1949 and the situation in 1961. He noted the California Supreme Court's switch to the exclusionary evidence rule and their conclusion that other remedies had simply failed to protect privacy and secure police compliance. Now, the Supreme Court must "close the only courtroom door remaining open to evidence secured by official lawlessness in flagrant abuse" of the constitutional right to privacy. Clark noted that the Court did not hesitate to enforce the rights of free speech, free press, and a fair trial upon the states; the same standard, he said, should be applied to the right to privacy enunciated in *Wolf*. To protect the right to fair trial, the Supreme Court excluded all coerced confessions from use in state courts, despite the accuracy of such confessions. Finally, Clark stated that ever since the case of *Boyd v. United States,* in 1886, the Supreme court had noted a close connection between the Fourth Amendment's right to privacy and the

Fifth Amendment's guarantee against self-incrimination; this relationship strengthens the argument for a rule of exclusion in both situations.

Clark's peroration reflected the passion that the illegal search cases evoked from the Justices:

> The ignoble short cut to conviction left open to the States tends to destroy the entire system of constitutional restraints on which the liberties of the people rest. Because [the right of privacy] is enforceable in the same manner and to like effect as other basic rights secured by the Due Process Clause, we can no longer permit it to be revocable at the whim of any police officer who, in the name of law enforcement itself, chooses to suspend its enjoyment.

Black and Douglas Add Some Fuel /   Justice Black wrote a concurring opinion. Reflecting on the *Wolf, Rochin,* and *Irvine* cases, he reminded his readers that he and Douglas had never accepted the "shock-the-conscience test" used by the majority in those rulings. Speaking of *Irvine,* he commented that "the five opinions written by the Court in that case demonstrate the utter confusion and unceraity that had been brought about by the *Wolf* and *Rochin* decisions. . . ." This confusion promised to end only now, when the Court was installing a "precise, intelligible and more predictable constitutional doctrine. . . ." Assuming that this new doctrine rested on the complementary relation of the Fourth and Fifth Amendments, Black said he would change his previous position (that the Fourth Amendment did not require exclusion of evidence) and would support exclusion for all illegal search-and-seizure cases.

Justice Douglas' concurring opinion added a further reason for abandoning the *Wolf* rule. That doctrine had encouraged federal and state police to engage in "working arrangements," obtaining evidence illegally and using it in the state courts. Now, this practice would stop.

Four Read the Record Differently /   Four Justices dissented—John Marshall Harlan, Felix Frankfurter, Charles E. Whittaker, and Potter Stewart. Harlan, who had replaced Robert Jackson after the latter's death in 1954, wrote an opinion for himself, Frankfurter, and Whittaker that the late Justice Jackson would have warmly applauded. The Court, said Harlan, "has forgotten the sense of judicial self-restraint" and the respect for precedents that should always be its guides. Dolly Mapp's counsel had not cited or relied upon the issue of the *Wolf* case; there had not been a full discussion in the briefs or in oral argument on that issue. Yet the majority "reached out" to overturn the *Wolf* rule. Such conduct conflicts with the Court's principle that constitutional issues should not be reached unless unavoidably presented in a case. The *Mapp* appeal *had* presented a serious and important issue—the punishment of the "mere" knowing of possession of obscene materials. This, Harlan said, is what the Court should have ruled upon, and nothing else. The first thing wrong with the majority's opinion, therefore, is that it should not have been written in this case. (Counsel for Miss Mapp, when asked during oral argument whether he was asking the Court to overrule *Wolf,* replied that he was not—that he had never heard of that case. Only one brief paragraph in the "friend of the Court" brief for the Ohio Civil Liberties Union and the American Civil Liberties Union has asked for reconsideration of *Wolf.* In oral argument, the Ohio Civil Liberties Union counsel did develop this point in response to direct and obvious interest from several of the Justices. Justice Clark noted in his majority opinion that proper objection to the search had been made in the Ohio courts and in the appeal papers to the Supreme Court of the United States. Justice Douglas said the "casual arrogance" of the police in this case made it a proper case for reconsidering the *Wolf* assumptions about police conduct.)

Turning to the merits of the *Wolf* rule, Harlan remarked: "The preservation of a proper balance between state and federal responsibility in the administration of criminal justice demands patience on the part of those who might like to see things move faster among the States in this respect." Each state has special problems of law enforcement, state-by-state experimentation is progressing well, and it was a mistake for the Supreme Court to "fetter" the states as it had done here. Discussing the analogy to coerced confessions, Harlan said this doctrine rested not on disciplining the police but on the violation of the defendants' rights when states wrung admissions from them while they were held in custody; the violation took place in court when the confession was admitted.

In counterpoint to Clark's peroration, Harlan wrote:

> I regret that I find so unwise in principle and so inexpedient in policy a decision motivated by the high purpose of increasing respect for constitutional rights. But in the last analysis I think this Court can increase respect for the Constitution only if it rigidly respects the limitations which the Constitution places upon it, and respects as well the principles inherent in its own processes. In the present case I think we exceed both and that our voice becomes only a voice of power, not reason.

Justice Stewart's separate dissenting opinion agreed with Harlan that the *Wolf* case should not have been reconsidered. Stewart did not state his views on the merits of requiring exclusion. He did state, however, that the Ohio obscene materials statute was a violation of freedom of thought and expression, and he would have reversed Dolly Mapp's conviction on that ground.

And the Friendly Restaurateur? /   What about Patrick Irvine? All too often, treatments of constitutional law cases trace the doctrinal developments and leave readers completely in the dark as to the fate of the litigants. This practice is particularly misleading because attention to the fate of criminal defendants shows that more than a few times, the public interest stimulated by an unsuccessful appeal produces pressures that lead government to suspend a deportation, reinstate an employee, or fail to press a contempt prosecution.

After the Supreme Court affirmed his conviction, Irvine asked Judge Pierson for a rehearing on probation. He filed a statement saying that the condemnation of the police tactics in his case should lead the court to deal lightly with him, and he promised to "plow a straight furrow" in the future. The probation officer was unimpressed and recommended that his original sentence be confirmed. Judge Pierson felt differently, however, and he considerably reduced the sentence. In place of one year in county jail, Irvine was ordered to serve sixteen days in jail, two days a week for eight weeks. He was allowed to pay his fine over thirty-six months rather than ninety days. For three years, he gave full-time attention to the Red Onion Café, plowing the "straight furrow." On May 3, 1957, his three-year period of probation was ended. Having fulfilled all the parts of his sentence and probation, Irvine applied to the court again. California law permits a defendant who shows proof of rehabilitation to have his conviction wiped off the books officially. This is done as an encouragement to offenders to become law-abiding citizens. (The federal government does not have this procedure, although many jurists and students of criminology have strongly urged Congress to adopt it.) Irvine's probation record was examined in Superior Court and found to be satisfactory; his verdict of guilty was set aside, a plea of "not guilty" was officially entered, and the information was ordered to be "dismissed." On August 7, 1958, Patrick Irvine died. Whether or not his memory is warm in the hearts of Long Beach horse-lovers and gourmands, his case has become a permanent addition to the nation's constitutional literature.

Patrick Irvine and the American Judicial Process

The *Irvine* case and its aftermath provide the raw material for a variety of observations and speculations about the operations of the judiciary in our political system.

The Costs of Constitutional Justice /   First, *Irvine* illustrates the American judicial process in its textbook splendor. The Supreme Court of the nation, the appellate courts of California, the United States Attorney

General—all became deeply involved over the manner in which a petty bookmaker was caught and tried. Moreover, justice had come cheaply. It cost Pat Irvine about $2,500 to carry his case from Superior Court in Long Beach to the Courtroom in Washington, D.C., which is a lot of legal attention for the money. Such economy was possible because the record did not have to be printed, because Irvine's counsel fees were decidedly modest, and because he had no witnesses to pay or expensive exhibits to prepare at his trial. Other defendants in criminal cases, such as Frank Costello, have spent $50,000 to travel the same route as Irvine. Indicted political groups, such as the Communist party's national leadership, spent more than $100,000 in their trials. On the other hand, a defendant with no resources at all may be involved in a case of serious importance to American constitutional law. If so, he can ask to have counsel appointed for him, from trial court to United States Supreme Court. These court-appointed counsel are often leaders of the Bar or ambitious young lawyers. The case reports are filled with superb legal defenses that did not cost indigent defendants one cent. This has led one astute commentator to conclude that the rich and the poor are equally well defended in our appellate courts; it is the middle-class defendant with his average-priced and often average-quality lawyer who often fails to get imaginative and energetic representation.

When large corporations are defendants in antitrust cases brought by the government, costs are usually gigantic. Wall Street legal estimates are that Du Pont has spent $20 million in the past decade contesting Justice Department efforts to force Du Pont to dispose of its stock interest in General Motors. Even cases that do not reach the appellate courts can be enormously expensive. In February 1960, the federal district court in Tulsa, Oklahoma dismissed a federal antitrust suit against twenty-nine oil companies. The courtroom was crowded—with seventy-five defense lawyers. Senior counsel drew $1,000 a day and junior associates $500–$750. To keep themselves busy, some of the junior counsel calculated that the trial alone had cost the oil companies $50 a minute. Total costs were estimated at between two and three million dollars. The district judge lectured the government stiffly for bringing an unwarranted case. The oil companies, although pleased with their "vindication," could not deposit that lecture in their checking accounts.

When individuals or groups are not prosecuted but choose to bring test cases to vindicate what they consider "their rights," justice can be costly. When Joseph Burstyn challenged the denial of a license by New York to a movie he was distributing, the case that we know as *Burstyn v. Wilson* (1952) cost him about $55,000. The National Association for the Advancement of Colored People estimates that it cost "well over $200,000" to get to the Supreme Court in the famous school segregation case, *Brown v. Board of*

Education (1954). Today, the average cost of Supreme Court cases testing Southern compliance with the *Brown* ruling runs "between $50,000 and $100,000." These expenses are substantial because of the lengthy trial court record in desegregation cases. If regular lawyers' fees were included, the figures per case would be higher, but counsel from the NAACP's national office are paid annual salaries and local cooperating lawyers are paid only $25–$50 per diem while the trials are in progress. When large corporations challenge government regulation, the costs are invariably large. In the case involving President Truman's seizure of the steel mills in 1952, *Youngstown Sheet & Tube Co. v. Sawyer,* over $1,500,000 was spent by the steel companies in direct legal costs and counsel fees. Both Joseph Burstyn and the steel companies, of course, were able to deduct these expenses from their income taxes as business costs required to defend their property rights. Patrick Irvine could not deduct his $2,500, just as the average citizen cannot deduct the cost of fines for speeding or littering the streets. Religious and civil liberties groups, being tax exempt, do not consider deductibility when they litigate.

Some organizations active in bringing constitutional test cases have perfected techniques of cheap appeal. If the trial records can be kept very slim—which means that constitutional argument instead of extensive factual testimony is presented in the lower court—then the route to the Supreme Court is not prohibitively expensive. The American Civil Liberties Union's general counsel budgets "$1,500–$2,500" for the average case that the ACLU sets up from trial court to Supreme Court. Some cases cost them more. *Wilkenson v. United States* (1961), involving the refusal of a witness before the House Committee on Un-American Activities to answer questions about Communist affiliations, cost the ACLU $3,900.

The government has costs too, sometimes matching and sometimes exceeding those of its adversaries in constitutional cases. The giant antitrust suits against Du Pont, the United Shoe Machinery Corporation, or the electric companies convicted of price-rigging in 1961 entail vast outlays by the government in investigative costs, the time of government economists, accountants, and lawyers. Adding to the expense is the preparation of exhibits, and the regular legal printing costs (whether done by private printers, as for U.S. attorney's offices, or by the Government Printing Office for government presentations before the Supreme Court). Of course, the government also collects as a result of some of its litigation—fines, penalties, taxes contested or unpaid, and moneys improperly charged the government by persons contracting with it. In Patrick Irvine's case, the state of California had the cost of the time of its deputy district attorney, assistant attorney general, and deputy attorney general in trying the case, preparing briefs, and arguing appeals. Since neither California nor the federal government keeps separate case records of their costs in each item of litigation, figures are not available as they are for private parties.

Liberty, Due Process, and Judicial Discretion /   Second, *Irvine* presented the Supreme Court with a problem of "federalism"—the application of federal constitutional standards to the police practices and courtroom procedures of the states. *Irvine* typifies the "Fourteenth Amendment due process" cases, such as those involving the right to have counsel, protection against the third degree and coerced confessions, and freedom from double jeopardy. Procedural due process is an area that the public regards as in the special care of the judges, especially in cases of minor criminal offenders like Pat Irvine and Dolly Mapp. When the courts issue rulings affecting labor-management relations, or adjusting the boundaries between church and state, or altering the power balance between President and Congress, there is usually much more public debate over the judiciary's qualifications for deciding these questions of "economics" or "politics."

Even in the procedural area, there is some ambivalence in public attitudes toward judicial assertiveness. When the judges invoke procedural rules to void the convictions of persons the community is anxious to punish —Communists or rapists or airplane dynamiters—public belief in fair procedure can be subordinated to the desire to "get" society's enemies. Supporters of civil liberties then hasten to defend full constitutional procedures for everyone accused of crime, and a meaningful debate will be under way over key procedural rules, as with the boundaries of the privilege against self-incrimination or reasonable search.

There is, however, another kind of situation in which the judges use their broad discretion over fair procedure to strike disguised blows for liberty. At times, majorities on our courts will view a political conviction or a censorship move as unwise and dangerous, but not so clearly violative of a constitutional limitation that the court's majority can properly declare the measure invalid. (Some liberal activist judges may urge doing so, but will be out-voted.) Within such cases, there will often be errors in the trial or in the administrative process—involving instructions of judges, comments by prosecutors, statements of witnesses, and adherence to the agency's own rules in administrative cases. The judges have broad discretion either to call these errors "harmless" or to brand them as so serious that a new trial is required. Because decisions of this kind will turn on the facts and circumstances in each specific case, the judges do not worry unduly about making "bad law" for the future by this tactic. Such reversals thus produce a two- to four-year delay and give the community a chance to regain its perspective and equilibrium, while avoiding a direct showdown between the judiciary and the political authorities, and leaving unimpaired the general constitutional authority of government officials to protect the public in "true" danger situations. Judges do not advertise their use of this technique, though it is at least as old as the medieval era when British courts used technical procedural rules to free defendants from the impossible harshness of the English criminal code. The United States Supreme Court put its finger on the scales of liberty in this manner in several "internal security" cases between 1954 and 1957 involving deportations, loyalty programs, and state investigations. When American courts are accused of using procedural technicalities, the judges are sure to reply with an icy stare of denial. This is part of the public ritual, designed to quiet the fears of the unsophisticated. Students of our judicial process should still appreciate this method as one of the major, though not overworked, weapons in the judicial arsenal.

The Varieties of Constitutional Experience / Third, as mentioned earlier in discussing the costs of constitutional cases, the *Irvine* case was a criminal action brought by the State, in which Irvine defended himself and, while doing so, made certain constitutional claims. This is only one type of constitutional format. In other major types, the federal or state governments may bring civil suits, as for tax arrears, or to condemn land, or to dissolve a trust. Interest groups such as the National Association of Manufacturers or Jehovah's Witnesses may sponsor cases or support individual plaintiffs who challenge legislation or administrative regulations. Private persons, in their roles as taxpayers or parents of school children or doctors facing penalties for disseminating birth control information may sue to have the government restrained from carrying out a law. Individuals and groups may sue one another and, in the course of the cases, raise basic constitutional issues. In these types of cases, many of the judicial ground-rules will be quite different from those in the *Irvine* case. Burdens of proof and presumptions of innocence will shift, different canons of statutory construction may be applied by the courts, and the general willingness of the judges to overturn government action may rise and fall in significant degrees. In short, although *Irvine* reveals the basic mold of the judicial process, other types of cases will present contrasting patterns in their rise, progress, and resolution in the courts.

Courts and the Political Process / Fourth, *Irvine* illustrates that American public law is not made in solitary majesty from the white marble temple of the Justices but is usually fashioned in a continuous interacting process with the political agencies of government. The Supreme Court—in the cases that come to it—legitimates some acts and invalidates others. Those measures invalidated are then reconsidered by the policy-makers. If the Court's basis for invalidation was a constitutional ground, the policy-makers may do one of several things. They may dutifully obey the Court, abandoning their previous lines of policy. They may defiantly repeat the challenged action and make the courts rule again, and again, and again; many southern officials in segregation cases are content to adopt one subterfuge after another rather than comply with decisions they regard as politically and constitutionally "insufferable." Policy-makers may seek and sometimes secure a constitutional amendment to authorize their program. (The Sixteenth Amendment, for instance, gives the United States power to tax incomes directly.) More commonly, policy-makers simply remodel their statutes or practices in order to accomplish some or all of the desired results while side-stepping the judicial objections. Usually, tests will be made in the courts to see whether the new measures are constitutional, or just what the limits of the Court's rule were, and the process begins again.

Where the Court's rulings in federal cases are not based on constitutional grounds but rest on statutory construction, the policy-makers are in a far stronger position. When Congress disagrees with the Supreme Court's reading of a statute, the congressmen can simply rewrite or repeal the statute. This was done some fifty times by Congress in economic matters between 1944 and 1961, overturning about seventy-five Supreme Court rulings. The Court has always accepted these revisions as within congressional power—what Congress says, Congress can un-say. Some Justices (especially those who dissented from the earlier judicial interpretation) regard the revisions as a proper and democratic interaction between those who make and those who expound legislation. Other Justices, a bit offended by congressional revision debates that condemn "judicial legislation," have felt that if Congress had spoken more clearly when it originally drafted the legislation, the Court would not have had to fill in the gaps in a way that the congressmen later disapproved.

In the *Irvine* chain of cases, the Supreme Court, between 1954 and 1961, performed in a perfect illustration of this judicial-political interaction. The majority made general guiding comments about the reasonableness of state police practices and the values of exclusion. The Court's "guides" were received, sifted, and evaluated by state law enforcement officers, lawyers, executive officials, and the state courts and legislatures with varying results. However, with the Court's declaration in the *Mapp* case, we see the Justices taking the issue "out of politics." A judicial floor was imposed and state experimentation with exclusion is no longer possible. If neither Supreme Court reversal nor constitutional amendment overturns the *Mapp* rule, policy-makers could try to use Congress' power over the appellate jurisdiction of the Supreme Court to bar the Justices from hearing state search-and-seizure cases. This was the technique attempted by critics of the Supreme Court in 1958, when the Jenner bill sought (unsuccessfully) to withdraw appellate jurisdiction from the Justices in cases involving state antisubversive laws, state teacher loyalty programs, state requirements for admission to the bar, and several federal areas as well. Whether the Justices, if such measures were passed, would follow a single reconstruction-era precedent and acquiesce in such congressional action is doubtful. The effect of cutting off Supreme Court review here would be to leave in force the definitions of due process reached by each of fifty state supreme courts, and that would place a severe strain on the self-restraint of the Supreme Court.

Judicial "Activism" and Judicial "Self-Restraint" / Fifth, the *Irvine* case set off a lively debate among the Justices over the proper role for the national judiciary in due process cases. The fight—to hear each group describe the other's position—was between "mechanistic" rules and "subjectivity." Political scientists often call the debate one between "judicial activism" and "judical self-restraint." Some commentaries suggest that the division is an all-inclusive split within the Supreme Court. Several facts might be noted about this characterization.

If we classify the politically sensitive litigation coming before the contemporary court, we find cases presenting issues of equality, property, liberty, and fair procedure. In the equality cases, such as those dealing with Negro civil rights, the Justices have usually been united in a policy of active intervention against state segregation laws. In property cases, such as challenges to the constitutionality of federal regulation of industry or state and federal welfare programs, the Court has been almost as united behind self-restraint, or nonintervention. A deep split is found then in only two of these areas: in fair procedure, as we saw in *Irvine-Mapp,* and in liberty cases, particularly as to government's power to set loyalty standards, censor literature and movies, or give aid to religious enterprises.

Another fact to note about the activism-restraint terminology is that, to be used properly, it should be taken as shorthand for a number of variables in judicial attitudes, not just the degree of intervention by courts: Judges divide into those who view rights enumerated in the Constitution as "absolutes" and those who see these rights as competing with others and, therefore, "relative" in each specific setting. The "absolutist" may be a liberal in his political philosophy, such as the first John Marshall Harlan or Hugo Black, or he may be a staunch conservative, such as Justices Stephen J. Field and George Sutherland. The same is true of the "relativist," with Justice Felix Frankfurter as a liberal exponent of this position and Chief Justice Charles Evans Hughes as a conservative. And there is also a division between those who see all rights in the Constitution as equivalent in value and those who see some (such as the First or Fifth Amendments) as "preferred" to others, commanding greater respect from political authorities, and thus requiring greater protection from the courts.

Still another thing to note about the activism-restraint terminology is that, even as to the degree of court interference with the elective agencies, these two positions may not exhaust the meaningful positions actually held within the Court. A third major view, one which would be best illustrated by Justice Robert Jackson, could be called "selective intervention," or the "equilibrium" theory of judicial review. Here, the Justice does not adopt the full rigors either of activism or restraint but suggests that the central cases should be viewed pragmatically. The Court should adjust the conflicting claims of liberty and authority, state and nation, private and public sector, etc. to retain those "great balances" that the founding fathers struck on such questions and that our political system has continued. This leaves the question of intervention to be decided on the basis of the key imponderables—whether the court's ruling will command obedience in the community; whether the political process has become clogged or is in a moment of localized hysteria that can be overcome; and various other considerations of a similar nature. This third position obviously gives the greatest discretion of all three to its exponents, and in the sense that the Justice's decisions are always unpredictable in the great cases, it makes him a fluid and shifting figure within the Court, as Robert Jackson was.

National Standards and Local Option in Constitutional Law /   Sixth, what about the merits of requiring or making optional the exclusionary evidence rule? Does *Irvine* and its aftermath shed any light on that?

On the one hand, the experience of California in reconsidering its admissibility rule and adopting exclusion can be seen as a vindication of discretionary flexibility in the Jackson mode. Let the states alone to consider the problem and you encourage concern for constitutional rights at the grass roots. The debate in the California courts and legislatures served to focus public attention on the police conduct and the civil liberties violations. By 1961, seven formerly permissive states had shifted to the exclusionary rule. "Discretionary flexibility"—the sharp lecture but not the federal sanction—can be seen as successful here in helping the state governments to move toward reform, and by themselves, with the maximum effect this has on local police behavior, local public opinion, and the like.

On the other hand, is that enough? Between 1954 and 1961, violations of search-and-seizure rules were repeatedly carried on by the police in states admitting illegally obtained evidence. Whether their practices were worse, or only better reported, than those in states with exclusion is the key factual question. Clearly, no one on the Supreme Court when the *Mapp* case was decided had any conclusive figures on that issue. Conclusive figures probably do not exist and it is difficult to see how they could be gathered short of an enormous, multimillion dollar research project in fifty states that somehow would be able to get "inside" the local police departments for accurate observation. When the facts are not available in constitutional cases, the area of ideological debate widens to fill the vacuum. At least in the twenty-six exclusionary-rule states, many exclusionary supporters would argue, defendants are not being convicted through such "unconstitutional evidence." And, they would continue, the move of additional states to exclusionary rules is proof that the public really cares about its constitutional right to privacy. Thus the Court should institute total exclusion in recognition that this is required by community feelings about ordered liberty in a free society. In an ironic sense, therefore, the very "success" of the *Irvine* doctrine can be turned into an argument for the *Mapp* majority.

Planning the Future in Search-and-Seizure Cases / Seventh, a host of intricate yet vital questions confronts the judges, criminal lawyers, and legal commentators who must estimate the potential sweep—and the practical limits—of the *Mapp* rule. To sample these problems:

(a) What about prisoners now in jail who were convicted years ago on the basis of evidence obtained by illegal searches on the part of state police? Are these prisoners entitled to file writs of habeas corpus, cite *Mapp v. Ohio,* and win either release from jail or a new trial? In a comparable due process area—denial of the right to a free transcript where this is a condition of appeal—the Supreme Court ruled that a prisoner denied such a transcript in 1935 was entitled to a new trial in 1958.

(b) What about the admissibility in state courts of wiretap evidence obtained by state police, in violation of the Federal Communications Act? The *Schwartz* case in 1952 said admission or exclusion of such evidence was up to the states. That ruling, however, was made when the *Wolf* doctrine was in its prime. Now, will the Court invoke the *Mapp* principle when the next conviction based on state wiretaps comes before the Justices?

(c) With *Wolf* overruled, how will the Court deal with the critical problems of "reasonableness" as to police searches and seizures? For example, "Andy" McConnell, trying criminal cases in California after the *Cahan* decision in 1955, believes that the "probable cause" doctrine is "nullifying" all the good promised by the exclusionary evidence rule. The "probable cause" doctrine works as follows: "A police officer," says McConnell, tells the Court that 'Some person whom I have never met, but whose voice I recognized because on former occasions he gave me correct information, called me on the telephone and told me there were bookmaking operations at No. 654 Jones Street.' The officer rushes there, without a warrant, and searches the premises." The California District Court of Appeal has upheld such justification, and McConnell notes that he has lost several cases on the basis of this convenient and manipulatable "exception" for the police. In the *Mapp* case, possibly because of the aggravated physical character of the search, the Supreme Court of the United States did not let such a "tip" justify the search. But if no physical mistreatment is present, and no electronic surveillance, what will the Supreme Court do with "probable cause"? Also, what constitutes "consent" to a search? How much looking around during a lawful arrest becomes a search requiring a warrant?

Many more such queries could be raised. The important point to appreciate, for our purposes, is the range and complexity of such questions.

The "Court" is Nine Men /   Finally, the *Irvine* case and its aftermath illustrate the irreducible element of personality in the judicial process. The Supreme Court is not a collectivity nor is there some deep allegiance to its institutional prestige that persuades the justices to put aside their convictions on public law issues. The Supreme Court, precisely described, is nine middle-aged to elderly lawyers; what five or more of them say is the highest constitutional law of the land, and a new justice or a change of heart by a justice can change that law overnight.

The *Irvine* case demonstrates these points nicely. This was one of Chief Justice Earl Warren's first cases. He came to it with his judicial philosophy largely unformed. Between 1954 and 1961, Warren was to move from the position represented by his vote in *Irvine* (with Jackson, Reed, Minton, and Clark) to a firm alliance with the liberal activists, Black, Douglas, and William J. Brennan, Jr. If there is any vote that Warren cast in his first year that he has come to regret, it probably was his vote in *Irvine*. Jackson's suggestion that the Supreme Court could discharge its own duties with a referral to the Department of Justice would not satisfy the "mature" Chief Justice Earl Warren. Had Irvine's appeal reached the Court in 1955, or 1958, or 1961, the odds are heavy that Warren would have voted to reverse the conviction, and this would have swung the decision in Irvine's favor.

Then there is Mr. Justice Clark. In 1954, his vote could have led the Court to discard the 1949 *Wolf* rule and introduce the *Mapp* doctrine of 1961. Why did Clark choose to hold back? His vote determined other 5–4 rulings of the Court between 1949 and 1954, including some which overturned existing precedents. His written opinion, with its public confession of discomfort with the *Wolf* rule, does not provide any satisfactory answers. Perhaps twenty years from now, some letter or memorandum, or some recollection of a former law clerk, will indicate whether an incident around the conference table, an article or report on police problems and practices, or some assumption about the consequences of exclusionary rules that he later abandoned led Clark to this curious fidelity to a wobbly precedent that four colleagues were prepared to bury. Furthermore, Clark's stand in the *Irvine-Mapp* cases is even more unusual in light of his general tendency to uphold police powers and to view the need for order with utmost sympathy. As a man whose major pre-Court career had been as a prosecutor in the Department of Justice, and as a man chided by his critics as the "cop on the Court," Clark's votes with the liberal activists against police misconduct and in "threat" to crime control indicates the highly personal and variable aspects of judicial voting behavior. Few Justices can be dipped in analytical formaldehyde and classified neatly by specie, for they are constantly hopping off "their" page in the album.

Looking back at the *Irvine* case and its doctrinal aftermath, an observer from another political system might read the *Mapp* case and remark, "Well, that debate is over." It would be the mark of emerging sophistication in the student of American government (and a last tribute to Patrick Irvine's beloved profession) to respond at that point, "Would you care to bet on that?"

Table of Cases, in Order of Citation in the Text

Sources

THE primary sources for *Irvine v. California* and its treatment here have been
the transcript of proceedings in the Los Angeles Superior Court (deposited in
the Library of the United States Supreme Court) and the petitions and briefs
filed in the Supreme Court, copies of which are in the Court's library and are
given to leading law schools. The copy I used is at the Columbia University
Law Library. Court records from California were also consulted, such as the
probation reports for Patrick Irvine and the records relating to his resentencing.
Newspaper clipping files on wiretapping and eavesdropping in California were
examined for the period 1938–1961 covering the Los Angeles *Times,* San
Francisco *Chronicle,* Los Angeles *Mirror-News,* and Sacramento *Bee.* Persons
directly involved in the Irvine trial and appeals, notably Morris Lavine, A. H.
McConnell, and Clarence Linn, aided with recollections, materials, and memorandums. The law clerks to the Justices of the Supreme Court during the 1953
term were contacted and several aided me in dealing with oral argument and
the mood within the Court. My own files on wiretapping and eavesdropping
in the United States from the 1850's to the present were drawn upon for developments in other states and for editorial and public opinion.

The most useful printed and secondary sources have been: *Report of the
California Senate Judiciary Committee on the Interception of Messages by the
Use of Electronic and Other Devices* (1957); the hearings and materials of
the United States Senate Subcommittee on Constitutional Rights, on eavesdropping and wiretapping, published between 1958 and 1961; "State Police, Un-
constitutionally Obtained Evidence and Section 242 of the Civil Rights Statute,"
7 *Stanford L. Rev.* 76 (1954); and Dash, Schwartz, and Knowlton, *The Eavesdroppers* (New Brunswick, N.J.: Rutgers University Press, 1959). For the
author's views on wiretapping, eavesdropping, and the judicial process see
Westin, "The Wire Tapping Problem: An Analysis and a Legislative Proposal,"
52 *Col. L. Rev.* 165 (1952); "Wire-Tap: The House Approves," *New Republic,*
June 20, 1955, p. 13; "Wiretapping: The Quiet Revolution," *Commentary,*
April 1960, p. 333; Testimony of Alan F. Westin, Before the Senate Subcommittee on Constitutional Rights, Washington, D.C., May 18, 1961.

Sources

THE primary sources for Irvine v. California and its treatment here have been the transcript of proceedings in the Los Angeles Superior Court (deposited in the Library of the United States Supreme Court) and the petitions and briefs filed in the Supreme Court, copies of which are in the Court's library and are given to leading law schools. The copy I used is at the Columbia University Law Library. Court records from California were also consulted, such as the probation reports for Patrick Irvine and the records relating to his resentencing. Newspaper clipping files on wiretapping and eavesdropping in California were examined for the period 1938–1961 covering the Los Angeles Times, San Francisco Chronicle, Los Angeles Mirror-News, and Sacramento Bee. Persons directly involved in the Irvine trial and appeals, notably Morris Lavine, A. H. McConnell, and Clarence Linn, aided with recollections, materials, and memoranda. The law clerks to the Justices of the Supreme Court during the 1953 term were contacted and several aided me in dealing with oral argument and the mood within the Court. My own files on wiretapping and eavesdropping in the United States from the 1950's to the present were drawn upon for developments in other states and for editorial and public opinion.

The most useful printed and secondary sources have been: Report of the California Senate Judiciary Committee on the Interception of Messages by the Use of Electronic and Other Devices (1957); the hearings and materials of the United States Senate Subcommittee on Constitutional Rights, on eavesdropping and wiretapping, published between 1958 and 1961; "State Police, Un-constitutionally Obtained Evidence and Section 847 of the Civil Rights Statute," 7 Stanford L. Rev. 76 (1954); and Dash, Schwartz, and Knowlton, The Eavesdroppers (New Brunswick, N.J.: Rutgers University Press, 1959). For the author's views on wiretapping, eavesdropping, and the judicial process, see Westin, "The Wire-Tapping Problem: An Analysis and a Legislative Proposal," 52 Col. L. Rev. 165 (1952); "Wire-Tap: The House Approves," New Republic, June 20, 1955, p. 13; "Wiretapping: The Quiet Revolution," Commentary, April 1960, p. 333; Testimony of Alan F. Westin, before the Senate Sub-committee on Constitutional Rights, Washington, D.C., May 18, 1961.

How to Get into TV:

The Federal Communications Commission and Miami's Channel 10

Victor G. Rosenblum

NORTHWESTERN UNIVERSITY

"I feel sorry for you, Mr. Mack. In my opinion you are to be pitied, because I think you have been used as a tool in this unfortunate mess. It seems to me that the best possible service that you could render now as a member of the Federal Communications Commission would be to submit your resignation."

—COMMITTEE CHAIRMAN OREN HARRIS

REGULATORY agencies must grapple with many practical problems. The Miami Channel 10 case provides an illustration of some of these problems. In the pages that follow we will see how one federal agency, the Federal Communications Commission, has reacted to a series of influences—rational and irrational—involved in the allocation of a single television station in a single city. In considering the record of events, we will examine the process by which the FCC allocated Channel 10 originally, the revelations of the congressional investigation into the FCC's policies and practices, the judicial and administrative consequences of the investigation, and the subsequent steps taken by the FCC in reallocating the Channel.

It took eight years to dispose of the Channel 10 case. Volumes of testimony have been laboriously compiled, and hundreds of thousands of dollars of public funds have been expended—all with the hope of illuminating the "true" story of the allocation of Channel 10. Not all the facts have been documented, however, and the student of administrative politics may find himself sometimes in the uncomfortable position of drawing inferences from a story to which only partial visibility has been given.

Nevertheless the case raises and illustrates many important questions about the regulatory process in practice: How do regulatory agencies reach decisions? What are the standards that guide decision-making? Is the process controlled by independent experts or do pressure politics play an active, if not sordid, role in formulating agency decisions? What are the methods and techniques of influencing judgments? Have flexibility and speed been hallmarks of the regulatory commissions or have policy conflicts, confusion, and delay emerged as obstacles to effective action? Do the regulatory agencies comprise a "headless" fourth branch of the government, or are they hydra-headed entities subject to control by the legislature, the executive, and the groups they are designed to regulate?

The FCC, Channel 10, and the Licensing Process

The activities of the federal regulatory Commissions cover a wide and heterogeneous range of duties—including rate-making, licensing, policing, and even subsidizing. The nine leading Commissions can be classified into four general types according to their areas of jurisdiction. Two regulate practices that cut across industry generally: the Federal Trade Commission (unfair trade practices and deceptive advertising), and the National Labor Relations Board (unfair labor practices and collective bargaining). Three commissions regulate carriers: the Interstate Commerce Commission (rail, motor, and water carriers), the United States Maritime Commission (ocean carriers), and the Civil Aeronautics Board (air carriers). Two agencies regulate finance and credit: the Securities and Exchange Commission (stocks and bonds, the issuance of securities generally, and holding companies) and the Federal Reserve Board (money and credit and the reserves and policies of member banks). The remaining two commissions have control over the gas, electric, and communications industries. The Federal Power Commission deals with electrical and gas utilities, while the Federal Communications Commission is concerned with regulation of the telephone, telegraph, and broadcasting industries.

The discussion of the Channel 10 case that follows centers on the allocation of a channel for a television station—a function assigned by Congress to the Federal Communications Commission. Established in 1934, pursuant to the Federal Communications Act, the FCC is composed of seven members appointed by the President, with the advice and consent of the Senate, for seven-year, staggered terms. The chairman is designated by the President and the Commission is required to have bipartisan representation with no more than four members belonging to the same political party. Major problems currently facing the FCC concern allocation and renewal of radio and television channels, competition and concentration of control, and regulation and advancement of the art of airwave communications. The magnitude and financial significance of these problems have made the FCC a prime target over the years for investigations of the pressures of power politics.

The problem of allocating a scarce number of broadcasting channels among a large number of applicants is continually before the FCC, and continually poses a severe test to the decision-making abilities of the commissioners. In 1960, there were only 580 authorized television channels in the entire United States. The consequence of such a situation is that the Commission's power to allocate a channel becomes the power to convey rich rewards and handsome privileges. Each license awarded gives to one applicant the opportunity to make large profits, and, in effect, denies to all others the chance of entering the field. In one case, a licensee, whose original investment was $186,000, sold his channel for $2,400,000 only five years after the FCC had conferred its award on him. And four years later, this same channel was resold, this time for $6,300,000. In such a situation it is not surprising that the competition among applicants is often fierce and that it is guided in practice by principles of jungle warfare.

The Supreme Court's Image of the Licensing Standard /   Early in 1940, before the allocation of TV channels became a major problem, the U.S. Supreme Court gave explicit support to the broad discretionary powers of the Federal Communications Commission in the area of licensing. Called upon to construe the intent of Congress in the Communications Act of 1934, which established the FCC, a unanimous Court found congressional intent to be that "in granting or withholding permits for the construction of stations, and in granting, denying, modifying or revoking licenses for the operation of stations, *'public interest, convenience or necessity'* was the touchstone for the exercise of the Commission's authority."

Justice Felix Frankfurter, who wrote the opinion, maintained that the criterion of "public interest, convenience or necessity" was "as concrete as the complicated factors for judgment in such a field of delegated authority permit." In short, Congress could not reasonably have been expected to impose more specific standards to guide the agency's decision-making. The Court recognized at the same time that "public interest, convenience or necessity" would serve as a "supple instrument for the exercise of discretion by the expert body which Congress has charged to carry out its legislative policy." As a consequence, questions of how to ascertain the public interest when the Commission's licensing authority is invoked "were explicitly and by implication left to the Commission's own devising, so long, of course, as it observes the basic requirements designed for the protection of private as well as public interest."

Underlying the Communications Act, Justice Frankfurter stressed, was the recognition by Congress of the dynamic factors characteristic of the evolution of broadcasting and of the "corresponding requirement that the administrative process possess sufficient flexibility to adjust itself to these factors." The Court, like Congress, made no effort to define "public interest, convenience or necessity." Concrete definition was a matter for the agency. Could such a standard be flexible as well as concrete? Let us see how it was applied by Hearing Examiner Herbert Sharfman, who was assigned by the Commission to preside over the initial stages of the Channel 10 case.

"The Public Interest" Through the Eyes of the Hearing Examiner / The two major steps in an administrative proceeding are the public hearing

before an agency Examiner and the final decision rendered by the agency members. The Examiner—generally a lawyer and a career civil servant—is the only one who hears all the evidence and is familiar with the entire record. He has no staff to dig out information for him, and he relies solely upon the evidence produced by the applicants. His role, therefore, is essentially a passive one. The initial decision of the Examiner, written at the conclusion of the hearing, serves merely as a recommendation to the agency; it is not, in any sense, final. The agency members may choose to be guided by what the Examiner has recommended, or they may ignore him completely. They may or may not agree with his conception or application of "public interest, convenience or necessity." The commissioners are not legally bound by any finding of fact by the Examiner. Presumably, this "maybe" policy is necessary in order to allow maximum play for flexibility and expertise; but it may, as we shall see, also allow play for less wholesome factors.

For thirty-two days, between June 22 and December 17, 1954, hearings on the allocation of Channel 10 were held in Washington before Examiner Herbert Sharfman. The Channel was to broadcast to the semitropical Dade County area of Florida, an area with a population in excess of 900,000—a figure that does not reflect the enormous annual influx of tourists. The total TV area also included much of Broward County, thus today providing a two-county audience in excess of 1,500,000, and growing at a rate of almost 100 per cent per decade. The stakes were high.

Miami and Miami Beach have, in effect, been allocated three channels for commercial television. Two additional channels on ultra high frequency (UHF) since have been granted. (Most television sets are not equipped for UHF, however, and commercial broadcasting on such channels has not proven economically feasible.) In addition, the Miami area is served by an educational channel.

The four applicants for the construction of Channel 10, the third of the prime television stations in the area, were all presented as substantial citizens. They were, indeed, typical applicants.

The call letters of WKAT stood for the first applicant, A. Frank Katzentine, president, director, and sole stockholder in the radio station. A resident of the Miami area since 1925, Katzentine had served as a Miami Beach Municipal Judge from 1928 to 1930, and as Mayor from 1932 to 1934. He was one of the founders of the Variety Children's Hospital of Miami Beach. He was a prime mover in the establishment of an Inter-American Cultural and Trade Center in Miami. He was head of the Crime Commission of Greater Miami. He was also principal owner of two canned music organizations and a recording company, as well as owner and president of radio stations WKAT and WKAT-FM in Miami. Associated with Katzentine in his proposal were: John I. Prosser, general manager of

WKAT radio who was described by Examiner Sharfman as "an outstanding religious leader, serving as first reader of the First Church of Christ, Scientist, Coral Gables, and on the radio and television advisory committee of the Greater Miami Council of Churches"; Mrs. Katzentine, who wrote, produced, and broadcast daily radio programs of interest to women for a number of years over WKAT and "has been active as chairman of local fundraising drives for the American Red Cross, Miami Heart Institute and American Cancer Society"; Arthur P. Smith, Jr., chief engineer, who was identified as an expert in photography and gem cutting "and is one of the country's leading amateur astronomers"; and A. Wampler, stepfather of Mrs. Katzentine and business manager of WKAT radio since 1937, who was to serve as agricultural program coordinator on the television station. The WKAT petitioners acknowledged that Wampler's only identification with farming had been before 1924, when he owned and operated a farm in Missouri.

The second applicant, L. B. Wilson, was president of L. B. Wilson, Inc., which owned WCKY, Cincinnati, Ohio. Wilson had owned a home in Miami Beach for twelve years prior to becoming a legal resident of the area in 1953. He died on October 28, 1954, in Cincinnati. Of the persons designated as beneficiaries under Mr. Wilson's will, only Clarence H. Topmiller, executive vice-president of L. B. Wilson, Inc., was expected to play an active part in the day-to-day operations of the TV station. Topmiller had been with WCKY and the Wilson organization since 1931 when he joined the station as a transmitter engineer, except for two years during World War II. He became president on Wilson's death. It was noted that he was an elder in the Madison Avenue Presbyterian Church of Covington, Kentucky, that he was active in Cincinnati civic affairs, and that in connection with community contacts, he was in the Miami area for five weeks during September and November 1953 and April and May 1954.

The third hopeful petitioner, Frank Bryson, President of North Dade Video, Inc., had lived in the Miami area since 1931 where he was head of a steel fabricating and sales company. He was active in Red Cross and Community Chest drives, but had no broadcast experience. He and the executive vice-president, Angus W. Graham, who was a general contractor and had served as chairman of the Dade County Board of Public Instruction from 1951 to 1954, expected to rely heavily on Walter Compton, general manager of a Washington, D.C. television station, for the development and management of the proposed station. Compton had originated the first regularly scheduled daily news program in television, had scheduled the first program to originate from the White House, the first telecast of surgery from an operating room, and the first regularly scheduled religious program on a Washington television station during his years with WTTG. Compton was to serve as vice-president and general manager if North Dade Video were awarded the channel. Another North Dade organizer was William E. Eichenbaum, a former Chicagoan who became a Miami resident in 1948. Eichenbaum, a real estate promoter and developer, testified that if North Dade were awarded the channel, he would be interested in profiting from a later sale of his interest under the "capital gains" provision of the tax law, and thereby would enjoy a substantial profit.

Public Service Television, Inc., the fourth applicant, was a subsidiary of National Airlines. G. T. Baker, president, chairman of the board, and principal stockholder of National Airlines was also president and a director of Public Service. He had resided in Florida since the early 1930's and in Miami since 1946. He was a director of the First National Bank of Miami, a national director of the National Conference of Christians and Jews, a member of the Florida State Chamber of Commerce, and a member of the transportation and communication committee of the United States Chamber of Commerce. He had no broadcast experience, but expected to devote 75 per cent of his time to the day-to-day operations of the proposed station. National Airlines' Board of Directors had authorized him to devote all of his time to the station if that were, in his judgment, necessary. Associates of Baker included George W. Gibbs, Jr., director of National Airlines and a resident of Jacksonville, Florida (who had been half-owner of an Orlando, Florida radio station), and Jerome A. Waterman, a department store executive and motion picture theatre-owner from Tampa, Florida. Waterman had served earlier as Commanding Officer of the First Air Force of Embarkation at Miami, was active in veterans' affairs, and was cited in the hearing record as "the first Tampa resident to bring an art exhibit to Tampa from New York's Metropolitan Museum of Art." Another Public Service officer who was also a director and member of the executive committee of National Airlines, Robert P. Foreman, was singled out for his civic activities as a Boy Scout committeeman and as an official in Amateur Athletic Union swimming meets in Florida.

(This concentration on the private lives and community activities of applicants is frequent in the regulatory process. A similar focus is often found when parties apply for franchises, licenses, or charters before other agencies such as the ICC, SEC, FPC, and Federal Home Loan Bank Board.)

Sharfman, the Hearing Examiner, was a career employee at the Federal Communications Commission. He had served as an attorney in the agency's Rate Section of the Common Carrier Branch from 1946 to 1950, in the agency's Office of Opinions and Review from 1950 to 1952, and as a Hearing Examiner since 1952. The purpose of the hearings as specified in the Commission's Order of Designation of January 5, 1954 was "to determine on a comparative basis" which of the contending groups would best serve the public interest, convenience, or necessity. To select the best applicant, the FCC would have to establish a significant difference among the applications as to (1) the background and experience of each of the applicants having a bearing on its ability to own and operate the proposed television station; (2) the proposals of each of the applicants with respect to the management and operation of the proposed station; and (3) the programing service proposed in each of the applications.

Under the procedures of the Commission in effect at the time of the hearing, each of the applicants was called upon to submit "Points of Reliance" —the factors considered by them to be of basic importance in guiding the Commission in directing the hearing and framing of the decision. The purpose of this procedure was to narrow the issues on which evidence could be admitted, and thus to reduce the size of the record. Although at first glance it appears that this procedure permits the applicants to determine the standards for agency decision-making, it should be noted that the "Points of Reliance" were drawn for the most part from the principles enunciated in previous FCC decisions and were not unique to the Channel 10 proceeding.

Attorneys for all four applicants agreed on May 24, 1954 on the following "Points of Reliance":

(1) The applicant and its officers, directors and stockholders, individually and collectively, offer greater experience, diversification and capacity for rendering a program service of merit to the Miami area.

(2) The applicant and its proposed managing heads possess experience and training superior to that of the management heads proposed by others, insuring superior management, capable of being translated into maximum service to the area.

(3) Its proposal offers more meaningful integration of ownership and management when consideration is given to the requirements of television broadcast station operation.

(4) Its program proposals are better balanced and have been more realistically conceived, and its plans and preparation for management, equipment, studios, personnel and budget allocation afford greater assurance that its objectives will be carried out.

(5) Whole aspects of the proposal reflect greater maturity of thinking and judgment, with practical application to the rendition of a reliable, sound operation in the public interest.

(6) Its proposal offers greater diversification and less concentration of ownership or control of the media of mass communication.

If the "Points of Reliance" clarified the criteria, it was not because they were precisely phrased. In fact, this system has since been abandoned.

The Parties' Claims to Preference /   As none of the applicants was hesitant in extolling his own superiority, the factor that could serve as the basis for choosing among them had to be found elsewhere. WKAT maintained that its complete local ownership, integration of ownership and management, and record of participation in civic affairs, as well as its self-proclaimed "outstanding record of past performance as a broadcasting licensee in serving the community interests of the Miami area," accounted for its superiority over its opponents and qualified it to be recipient of the channel. In the hearing transcript that ran over 5,000 pages, there were numerous statements in support of WKAT's record of public service. In religious programing, for example, it had cooperated actively with the Miami Council of Churches. *This We Believe,* an interfaith program, and *Religion in the News* were regularly scheduled features on the station. In educational programing, the station worked closely with the University of Miami and Dade County schools. There was also testimony to show WKAT's cooperation with Chambers of Commerce, including a regular weekly half-hour program, *Breakfast Roundtable,* sponsored by the Miami Chamber of Commerce, and its cooperation with labor organizations, including the first regularly scheduled program in the Miami area offered free to organized labor. WKAT cooperated also with the Weather Bureau in establishing a network of amateur stations for rapid communication of hurricane warnings.

The L. B. Wilson Co. claimed that its proposal was superior to the others because Wilson was the only applicant to attempt to ascertain the community's needs. The applicant had enlisted the services of four widely recognized civic leaders of Miami as a Program Advisory Committee to assist in the preparation of its program proposals. Wilson also claimed to offer greater assurance than the others of its ability to put its program proposals into practice. It asserted that its proposals were "honest, straightforward, and sincere," implying, of course, that the others were not.

North Dade claimed preference on the ground that it had no interests other than the proposed television station, that Walter Compton, its vice-president and general manager was "the only person in this proceeding who has any industry-recognized background in television," and that it was superior in diversification of background of its principals.

Public Service, Inc. based its claim on its self-proclaimed "superiority in meaningful participation in civic affairs resulting in tangible and physical benefit to the Miami community; its aggressive and demonstrated successful management team that retains and jealously guards the responsibility and control which we expect of a responsible licensee; . . . the record of the stewardship of the National Airlines public trust to serve the public interest; and its superiority in the planning of its locally originated programs in the categories of news, religion, and educational type programs as well as planned remote telecasts."

The attorneys for the applicants often pictured their competitors as in-

competent and nefarious. National Airlines was charged by its opponents
with having violated Civil Aeronautics Board regulations in at least three
instances; L. B. Wilson was charged with having sold time on WCKY, its
Cincinnati station, on the basis of the number of listener responses, and to
have booked one commercial after another during the best evening hours,
leaving virtually no prime time for quality programing. Principal owners of
North Dade, who were also officials of the Dade County Board of Public
Instruction, were accused of having their Board positions to favor their
own business associates. And WKAT was accused of having violated FCC
regulations for minimal FM broadcasts, of hiring "free-lance" disc jockeys
who were paid on the basis of the commercial time they sold for their own
programs and who regularly and without correction by management
delivered overly long commercials in poor taste, of broadcasting horseracing information and results that might encourage illegal gambling, and of
offering "retreaded radio" instead of creative programing.

Examiner Sharfman weighed all the charges carefully. Before announcing his conclusions, he suggested that

> The tone of this initial decision is somewhat less strident than it would
> have been had the Hearing Examiner accepted without reservation the ac-
> cusations of misconduct and tongue-clucking observations about their com-
> petitors which the parties have launched. From the advocate's viewpoint,
> it is easy and perhaps good tactics in the abstract to emphasize and even
> magnify an adversary's purported derelictions. It is a function of decision
> to achieve a proportioned result.

In reaching his "proportioned result," Sharfman appeared to give considerable weight to the charges against National Airlines and not to discard
as inconsequential those against WKAT. The Examiner found that in the
three instances cited by the opponents of Public Service, Inc., National
Airlines had taken action without first obtaining the required approval of
the CAB. In the "Key West Episode," National had cut down its round-
trip schedule to Key West from four flights to one flight a day without prior
approval of the CAB and without the ten-day advance notice to the Post-
master General required by the Civil Aeronautics Act. In the "National-
Caribbean Atlantic Control Case," National had entered into an agreement
with the West Indies air carrier whereby National would acquire voting
control of Caribbean through an exchange of stock, without prior consent
of the CAB as required by Section 408 of the Civil Aeronautics Act. The
third episode was the "Aerovias Affair" in which the compliance attorney
of the CAB alleged that National had acquired without Board authorization
an undisclosed interest in Aerovias Internacional, a Cuban corporation.
The parties subsequently agreed to dismiss the complaint when National
stated that all dealings with Aerovias had been discontinued.

While admitting that subsequent CAB route awards to National "at least indicates that National Airlines is not under a cloud in its regulatory relationships," the Hearing Examiner felt that "the several affairs described indicate a certain individualistic attitude on the part of Mr. Baker (the president of National and of Public Service Television), which is perhaps to be expected in one who has been the dominant figure in building up a large business, and a distaste for regulatory restraint when its requirements clash with immediate objectives." Thus National Airlines' involvement in "administrative displeasure" was found by Examiner Sharfman to be "of consequence."

The Examiner spent considerable time probing WKAT's broadcasting of horseracing information. At one stage, the FCC had renewed WKAT's license on a temporary basis. It was finally renewed unqualifiedly only after Katzentine wrote to the Commission in November 1951 assuring it that broadcasting of racing results was being delayed and that all racing programs had been cleared with the State Racing Commission. An advertisement from the Miami *Herald* of January 21, 1948 accounted for intense criticism of Katzentine by his opponents. The ad, phrased in the argot of the horse tout, read in part:

> 20 to 1 Longshot. And few handicappers will give you this 1, 2, 3 chance. But Wednesday is the day. Also for "Dark Sleepers" that should amaze you how easy they should romp home under the wire. I know something Wednesday. I urge and implore you, don't go track Wednesday before you get my Dark Sleeper. If you miss me today Blame Yourself. I will also include free probable $150 for $2 daily double.

At this point the following material was set off in a box:

> Free Code Horse Goes Today—Also Reports on Coming Longshots—Tune in W-K-A-T at 10:15 a.m.

Katzentine was taken to task by his opponents for not forcefully repudiating such advertisements. Asked in cross-examination what he would have done if the ads had been called to his attention, he indicated that he wasn't sure just what he would do.

> Q. You had no objection, then, to your name being used as part of an advertisement of a racing tout?
> A. Obviously we sold him time on the station. I don't think I could object to him calling attention to his broadcasts.

The Hearing Examiner did not share counsel's "professed disapproval" of Katzentine's response. Sharfman admitted that Katzentine was in a difficult position on the stand, that he could not feasibly castigate the sponsors, and that he gave the only honest answer he could give.

On the subject of length of commercial announcements, the executive vice-president of WKAT acknowledged that "in practically all the so-called 'free-lance' programs" (programs in which the announcers and disc jockeys are paid on the basis of the number of spot announcements sold by them for their own programs), "we have been guilty of allowing spots well over a minute in length." Katzentine testified that he never discharged or threatened to discharge anyone for excessively long commercials. He declared that he "could fire everybody in there, but I wouldn't have any disc jockeys if I did." Neither excessive advertising nor WKAT's failure to adhere to FCC requirements for a six-hour minimum broadcast day for FM stations seemed as significant to the Examiner as the examples of National Airlines' involvement with "administrative displeasure." Sharfman was also more displeased by L. B. Wilson's excessive commercialism on WCKY in Cincinnati than by Katzentine's use of free-lancers on WKAT. No negative inferences were drawn in the Examiner's conclusions from the functions of the WKAT free-lancers and the length of their spot announcements, though he referred disapprovingly to the "monotonous diet" of WCKY's nighttime schedule of country music and commercial announcements. While recognizing Wilson's "strict business probity," he pointed out in reference to WCKY that "one of the functions of a licensee is to try to raise the tastes of its listeners, and it does not necessarily discharge its responsibilities by catering exclusively to what it feels is the most representative mass interest."

Sharfman noted that a Grand Jury had looked into the affairs of the North Dade officials who were connected with the Dade County Board of Public Instruction. The Grand Jury neither returned indictments nor brought charges of wrongdoing; it merely cautioned against conflicts of interest. Despite WKAT's charge that North Dade officials acted "in direct defiance of the Grand Jury's recitation of public policy requirements," the Examiner felt that he could not "at this distance and with the meager facts in the record" pass upon matters involving "general ethics as well as local patterns and law."

Sharfman recommended that WKAT be awarded Channel 10. He did not seek to develop his decision through systematic consideration of each of the six Points of Reliance. He pointed out, rather, that "a judgment as to which applicant will best serve the public interest, convenience and necessity is not to be based solely on a mathematical formula which dictates an award to the possessor of the greatest number of plus factors. . . ." Of basic importance in a comparative proceeding, he felt, were the criteria of local ownership, integration of ownership and management, and participation in community affairs.

The Examiner, using, perhaps subconsciously, the terminology of the race track, proceeded to award WKAT a "clear lead" in the composite consideration of local ownership, integration of ownership and management, and civic participation. "When this is coupled with the assurance of operation in the public interest inferable from its long past broadcast record as a whole, it is apparent that the greater likelihood it offers of fulfilling its promises are a formidable challenge to any competitor who would try to overtake it."

Public Service and North Dade, like WKAT, were owned by local residents, but the Examiner was impressed with the fact that WKAT was "100% locally owned," whereas the other applicants were "not all as intimately indentified with the area as Mr. Katzentine."

The Examiner's evaluation of civic participation by the respective applicants led irrevocably toward the award of the channel to WKAT. Sharfman noted that "it cannot be gainsaid" that Katzentine's record has been "outstanding."

Sharfman's position on civic participation, as it was phrased in his report, appeared to be that self-interest of the participant detracts from the recognition awarded him, and that self-interest is inherently greater when the participant in civic activities is a corporation rather than a private individual. Katzentine, in the Examiner's judgment, participated in civic activities as an individual whereas Baker participated as a corporate representative.

Sharfman then proceeded to analyze WKAT's "substantial record of broadcast service to the community." He found that WKAT "was sensitive to a representative variety of the community's activities and conscientiously attempted to play a significant role in its life." Insofar as broadcasting of racing information was concerned, he took "official notice" that WKAT was only one of a number of stations that broadcast horseracing programs that "may conceivably have been of some aid to illegal gambling." Viewing WKAT's performance "in the round" and "as a whole," the station's record was held "a meritorious one."

"The Public Interest" Through the Eyes of the FCC Commissioners / After the Examiner's decision was issued on March 30, 1955, each of the three unsuccessful applicants filed his exceptions to that decision and appealed to the Commission to reverse the Examiner. Pursuant to the agency's rules, the final decision awarding the channel rested with the seven commissioners. A favorable vote by at least four commissioners could assure victory for an applicant under all circumstances, four constituting a quorum. An applicant might still be victorious with only three commissioners' votes as long as at least four but no more than five votes were cast. The practice of the commissioners was to cast their votes in the same order as the Justices of the Supreme Court, with the most recently appointed

commissioner voting first, the others (with the exception of the Chairman) voting in order of ascending seniority, and the Chairman voting last.

Who were these seven men who wielded the agency's final power to award the channel? On the basis of party affiliation, four were Republicans, (Rosel Hyde, John Doerfer, Robert E. Lee, and the Chairman, George McConnaughey); two were Democrats (Robert Bartley and Richard Mack); and one was independent (E. M. Webster). Hyde and Webster were career employees of the agency; the other five gained their appointments through political patronage.

The Chairman, George McConnaughey, had been made Chairman of the Ohio Public Utilities Commission some years before by Governor John Bricker. At the time of the appointment of McConnaughey to the FCC in 1954, former Governor, and now Senator, Bricker was Chairman of the Senate Interstate and Foreign Commerce Committee, which has jurisdiction over FCC policies and appointments. Doerfer, a member of the Wisconsin Public Service Commission from 1949 until his appointment to the FCC in 1953, had the sponsorship of Governor Walter J. Kohler and of Senators Alexander Wiley and Joseph McCarthy from that state. Robert E. Lee, who had no experience whatever in the regulatory field when he was appointed to the FCC in 1953, was a close political associate of Senator McCarthy of Wisconsin when the late Senator was at the height of his power. A former FBI agent and staff official of the House Committee on Appropriations, Lee was an active participant, allegedly at Senator McCarthy's behest, in the bitter and successful 1950 senatorial campaign against Millard Tydings of Maryland.

As for the Democrats, Bartley had worked for several government agencies, for a regional broadcasting network, and for the National Association of Broadcasters prior to his elevation to the FCC by President Truman in 1952. He acquired political renown primarily by virtue of being the nephew of Speaker Sam Rayburn of the House of Representatives. Mack, a former official of the Florida Public Service Commission and a so-called "Eisenhower Democrat," had been suggested frequently for appointment to the federal regulatory agencies by Senators George Smathers and Spessard Holland of Florida. President Eisenhower had to appoint a Democrat to the FCC in 1955 when he declined to renew the appointment of another Democrat, since four Republicans, the statutory maximum, were already on the Commission. He chose to follow the recommendations of the Florida senators and of Chairman McConnaughey. He named Mack.

Republicans McConnaughey, Doerfer, and Lee as well as Democrat Mack, then, were appointed by President Eisenhower. Republican Hyde of Idaho, a lawyer with the FCC since its creation in 1934, had been elevated by President Truman from general counsel of the agency to commissioner in 1946. He was renominated by President Truman in 1952 and served as

Chairman for eighteen months prior to President Eisenhower's appointment of McConnaughey as Chairman in 1954. The Commission's independent, Webster, a lifelong resident of the District of Columbia, had first joined the FCC in 1934 as a member of its engineering staff. He achieved recognition as an expert in communications engineering as a result of his work with the Commission and as Chief Communications Officer of the Coast Guard. President Truman appointed him to the Commission in 1947 to fill out an unexpired two-year term, and then reappointed him for a full seven-year term in 1949. Commissioner Webster retired in 1956 and was replaced by Democrat T. A. M. Craven whose background and experience as an engineer were quite similar to Webster's. He had been chief engineer of the FCC from 1935 to 1937 and served a seven-year term as a commissioner, noncontroversially, from 1937 to 1944. He declined reappointment by President Roosevelt in favor of private radio engineering practice and was a consulting radio engineer in Washington, D.C. at the time President Eisenhower appointed him in May 1956.

McConnaughey was not reappointed at the expiration of his term. He was replaced by a respected government career official, Frederick W. Ford. A former chief of the hearing division of the FCC's broadcasting bureau from 1947 to 1953, Ford served as an assistant attorney general in the Department of Justice immediately prior to his appointment to the FCC in August 1957.

Routine hearings had been held by the Senate Interstate and Foreign Commerce Committee on the appointment of each of the Commissioners, as required by law. With the exception of the hearings on Lee and McConnaughey, approval by the Committee and the Senate had been perfunctory. There was some opposition to Lee at his hearing because of his intimate political ties with Senator McCarthy and his role as organizer of the radio program Facts Forum, which promoted the ultraconservative views of a wealthy Texas oilman, H. L. Hunt.

In McConnaughey's case, outright opposition to his appointment was voiced by Senator Estes Kefauver. The Senator's opposition was to have repercussions when the Channel 10 case unfolded. McConnaughey had been counsel for the Ohio Bell Telephone Company and other communications companies after leaving the Ohio Public Utilities Commission. Therefore Kefauver maintained that it was improper to appoint to the Commission "an attorney for someone who is going to have substantial matters before the FCC." McConnaughey retorted, with support from Senator Bricker, that "a general practicing lawyer who has happened to represent a utility company or two along with general clients is certainly capable of rendering public service."

It should be pointed out that candidates for high judicial office as well as those for high administrative positions frequently are appointed in recognition of past service to politically valuable causes. The difference between such judges and administrators, however, is the requirement of both law and tradition that once a man sits on the judicial bench he is insulated and isolated from "off-the-record" representations that might influence his decisions; but neither law nor tradition isolates the regulatory agency commissioner from political pressures. On one hand, appointment to high judicial office may repay, but not often create, a political debt. On the other hand, both repayment and political debt-creation may be present in the appointment of a commissioner. Under such circumstances there is a real question whether all commissioners can or do reach their decisions objectively and on the merits of the case, or whether their decisions are in practice more representative of the "who-owes-what-to-whom" principle.

Counsel for the four Miami applicants participated in oral arguments before the Commission—a procedure like that before an appellate court—on July 18, 1955. Written briefs in behalf of each of the applicants, the record of the original hearing, and the opinion of the Examiner were already on file with the Commission. Unlike an appellate court, which would have announced its decision within no more than several months of the oral argument, the decision of the Commissioners was not announced until February 1957, some eighteen months later. What did the opinion of the Commissioners in the Channel 10 case indicate about the basis of the decision they rendered?

Of the more than 50,000 words that comprised the Commission's decision, the bulk repeated the findings of the Hearing Examiner. The major areas of difference between the Commission and the Examiner were the evaluations of civic participation by WKAT and Public Service, comparison of WKAT's record of compliance with regulatory agency requirements with that of the parent company of Public Service, and the weight accorded WKAT's use of free-lance talent and its past broadcasting of horseracing news.

As for civic participation, the Commission noted that, of the WKAT principals, only the Katzentines were active in community activities, whereas at least five officials of Public Service, Inc. had outstanding records of civic participation. Sharfman's discounting of civic participation in the interests of a corporation was explicitly rejected. The Commission said:

> The Examiner's conclusion is noted to the effect that the extensive civic record attributable to Public Service must be deprecated to some extent due to business motivations. This would not conform to Commission practice. The motive for public service is not the test; rather it is the record compiled. Moreover, such a test if applied to one applicant, would of necessity —were it practicable in a given case—be for application to the others, a matter not considered by the Examiner.

The Commission concluded that WKAT and Public Service were "in balance" in civic participation, and both were well ahead of North Dade and Wilson. While seemingly unaffected by the reports of National Airlines' conflicts with the CAB, the Commission criticized WKAT vigorously for cutting down its FM broadcasts from the minumum of five hours daily called for by the FCC to three hours. While not of a disqualifying nature the violation is "a matter which must be weighed comparatively as being adverse to WKAT."

The Commission expressed serious reservations over WKAT's past use of free-lance talent and its declared intent to use such talent in its TV operation if it were awarded the channel:

> Involved is a matter of maintaining complete licensee responsibility and supervision over an important segment of station programming and service to the public. When responsibility is not seriously assumed, and furthermore is permitted in part to be assumed by non-staff individuals, interested in increasing their earnings by promotion of excessive advertising which reduces the program service to the public, a serious demerit must be visited upon the licensee involved.

The Commission also disagreed forcefully with the Examiner over his evaluation of WKAT's horseracing broadcasts. It was not that WKAT carried horseracing information per se that upset the Commission; rather it was that

> certain of these programs were sponsored, announced and advertised by individuals engaged in selling to the public so-called "tip sheets." . . . The Commission recognizes that the sale of "tips" on racing has been legalized in the State of Florida, but believes that the use of licensed broadcast facilities for the advancement of such service does not indicate as high a degree of licensee responsibility as is desired.

The Commission construed these weaknesses in WKAT's past to detract from the station's rating on the criterion of integration of ownership and management. Whereas Examiner Sharfman had given WKAT clear preference in this category, the Commission awarded a "distinct preference" to Public Service.

For similar stated reasons, the Commission ranked WKAT last on the suitability of its program proposals. It concluded that "criticism must be found and demerit attached" to the proposed adoption of free-lance practices for the television operation.

The Commission also alleged its concern about advancing diversification of control in the media of mass communications. It gave North Dade and

Public Service "definite preference" over WKAT and a "slightly lesser preference" over L. B. Wilson, since North Dade and Public Service were in no way associated with other media of mass communications.

The Commission then summed up its findings:

> Public Service has made a creditable showing in all factors, and is superior in one. No detracting considerations diminish its presentation. It yields to WKAT a moderate preference in residence and a more distinct one in experience, but these are overbalanced in the context of this proceeding by the preferences it carries over WKAT in integration of ownership with management, diversification of the media of mass communications, programming, and diversification of business interests of principals. It yields to North Dade a moderate preference in experience and a slight preference in residence, but, more important to the outcome herein, it has received preference over North Dade in integration of ownership with management, and in civic participation, and no demerit attaches to its showing.

It concluded that an award to Public Service "would best serve the public interest, convenience and necessity." The opinion represented the views of four of the Commissioners; Mack, Lee, Doerfer, and Chairman McConnaughey. Craven declined to vote, and Bartley and Hyde dissented.

The Dissents of Commissioners Hyde and Bartley / Commissioner Hyde felt that an applicant's "primary interest" as well as his background and experience should be the basis on which the channel recipient is chosen. "I think that operation of a television station on Channel 10 in Miami is important enough to warrant the full attention of an applicant who would make it a primary interest and therefore, would favor granting the application of L. B. Wilson, Inc." The death of L. B. Wilson himself did not disqualify the organization in Commissioner Hyde's judgment as the organization would continue to function and be controlled and guided by his business associates of long standing.

Commissioner Bartley voted to uphold the decision of Examiner Sharfman. He agreed with Sharfman's findings and conclusions and announced at a later point that he was particularly doubtful, in view of claims of financial woes National Airlines had made before the CAB, that its wholly-owned subsidiary would have the financial ability to live up to its proposals.

Following the award by the Civil Aeronautics Board of a New York-to-Miami route to Northeast Airlines and the complaint by National Airlines that such action would destroy them financially, the other contestants for Channel 10 petitioned the FCC to reopen the record in the case and to schedule further hearings on the capacity of Public Service to carry out the construction, programing, and management commitments it had undertaken. With Commissioners Bartley and Hyde again dissenting, and Ford (who had been in office less than two weeks) and Craven abstaining, the Commission on September 11, 1957 rejected the petition by a 3-2 vote. Doerfer, Lee, and Mack found "nothing therein to warrant a rehearing with respect to the financial qualifications of Public Service. No showing is made of present financial inadequacy or any reasonably inferable condition approaching it."

As to Baker's claim before the CAB that the route award to Northeast Airlines would have dire effects on the financial future of National, the Commission termed the claim "an argument of advocacy rather than an admission against interest." The CAB failed to find any evidence of destructive financial effect, and the FCC should not "superimpose our judgment over that of the CAB in a matter peculiarly within the Board's expert field of knowledge and regulatory jurisdiction."

In his dissenting statement, Commissioner Bartley stressed his feeling that petitioners had made a sufficient showing of new developments to warrant reopening the record and conducting additional hearings. The majority's award was based in large part on the integration of ownership and management by Public Service. Since the CAB's actions could adversely affect the proposed integration of Baker and since the question of National's financial abilities was a serious one, the dissenters felt further hearings should be held to determine whether the original proposal by Public Service could still be carried out.

The Commissioners' Votes

We have discussed thus far the two occasions on which the Commissioners voted in the Channel 10 case, February 11, 1957 and September 11, 1957. There was an earlier, though not binding vote as well, on December 21, 1955, when instructions were given to the agency's opinion-writing staff to prepare an opinion "looking toward" award of the channel to Public Service. The vote at that time was 3–2–1 with Republicans Doerfer, Lee, and McConnaughey voting for Public Service; Democrat Bartley and Independent Webster for WKAT, Republican Hyde for L. B. Wilson, and Democrat Mack abstaining. The vote of December 21, while sufficient under the agency's internal rules to set the opinion-writing section to work, would have been insufficient to make the award to Public Service. The law requires approval by a majority of the quorum present in order to have binding action by the agency. With three of the six votes cast for Public Service, a fourth vote, Mack's would have been necessary for Public Service before the award could be made.

FCC Votes on the Channel 10 Award: 1955 and 1957

December 1955

WKAT	PUBLIC SERVICE	L. B. WILSON	NORTH DADE	ABSTAIN
Bartley (D.)	Chairman McConnaughey (R.)	Hyde (R.)	—	Mack (D.)
Webster (Ind.)				
	Doerfer (R.)			
	Lee (R.)			

February 1957

WKAT	PUBLIC SERVICE	L. B. WILSON	NORTH DADE	ABSTAIN
Bartley (D.)	Chairman McConnaughey (R.)	Hyde (R.)	—	Craven (D.)
	Doerfer (R.)			
	Lee (R.)			
	Mack (D.)			

Craven had replaced Webster between the time of the vote on instructions and the vote making the award. No one knew for sure that Craven would not participate. Thus Mack's vote remained crucial in the eyes of the applicants. If Mack voted for Public Service, the National Airlines' subsidiary would have received the channel regardless of how Craven voted. Any other vote by Mack would have prevented the award of the channel to Public Service.

In the September decision, with McConnaughey no longer on the Commission, Bartley and Hyde united in their dissent, and the positions of Craven and Ford unknown, any defection by any of the men favoring Public Service would have jeopardized the Public Service victory. A switch of Mack's vote at this point, for example, would have required reopening the case for further proceedings by the agency. Even an abstention would have led to reopening the case if either Ford or Craven joined Bartley and Hyde. It is important to keep these points in mind when evaluting at a later stage the pressures exerted on Commissioner Mack.

The Scene Shifts to Court and Congress

So far, the Channel 10 decision appeared to have been a rational one by dedicated public servants in a complicated area of the regulatory process. There were differences of value and of perspective, reflecting alternative notions of the public interest in awarding television channels. However, it was not long before events were to reveal that other forces and motives were at work in the decisions of the Commission.

The FCC, through its decision and order of February 7, 1957 allocated to Public Service Television, Inc. a channel potentially worth millions of dollars. No one could expect that the other contestants, especially WKAT, which had been the Hearing Examiner's choice, would merely watch such a succulent economic plum elude their grasp. Judicial review of administrative action may be sought by an injured party after he has exhausted his administrative remedy. Having failed to convince enough commissioners to reconsider or reverse the decision, WKAT brought suit against the FCC in the Court of Appeals for the District of Columbia in the hope, however remote, that the judiciary might reverse the agency's decision.

While the case was pending before the Court, some seemingly unrelated activity was going on in Congress. A new subcommittee of the Committee on Interstate and Foreign Commerce of the House of Representatives had been established on April 11, 1957 and had given a $250,000 budgetary appropriation. The Special Subcommittee on Legislative Oversight, as it was named, had the baptismal blessing of Speaker of the House Sam Rayburn, the Texas Democrat who had been responsible for drafting much of the legislation creating the major regulatory agencies. It is time, the Speaker had declared on one of the rare instances in which he left the rostrum and took the floor, to "see whether the laws have been faithfully executed [by the agencies] and whether or not administratively some of these laws or the intent of some of these laws are being disregarded. I have heard such complaint many times." Democrat Oren Harris of Arkansas, the Chairman of the Committee on Interstate and Foreign Commerce, announced that Congressman Morgan M. Moulder of Missouri, also a Democrat, would serve as chairman of the Subcommittee.

On April 18, Representative Moulder outlined the scope of the Subcommittee's activities. Its declared purposes were to examine the execution of the laws by the agencies administering laws within the legislative jurisdiction of the Committee, and "to see whether or not the law as Congress intended in its enactment has been and is being carried out or whether it has been and is being repealed or revamped by those who administer it."

Several months later the Subcommittee selected as its general counsel Bernard Schwartz, a 34-year-old professor of constitutional and administrative law at New York University Law School. The New York *Times* described Professor Schwartz as "a man with bounce and brilliance," with "fantastic drive," and as "an only son who swallowed books as others might ice cream."

Schwartz proceeded to build upon an earlier investigation of the FCC by the House Antitrust Subcommittee that had criticized the agency vigorously for its many private conferences and discussions between Commission members and industry representatives on pending cases. In January, Schwartz prepared a stinging report on the FCC that was then "leaked" to the newspapers. Referring to the Federal Communication Commission as "the Supreme Court of the communications industry," the report proposed that the first subject for the new Subcommittee to probe should be the alleged deviation by members of the FCC from the judicial standards of conduct that Congress intended them to follow. Schwartz claimed to have evidence that:

> A commissioner was fully reimbursed by the industry for the expenses incurred by him and his wife in attending an industry convention at which he delivered an address. This commissioner also claimed from and was paid by the Government his full expenses (travel and per diem) to attend the same convention.

> Members of the Commission have had their room, board, and other expenses (e.g., café, valet, golf fees, etc.) paid by the industry while attending industry conventions. At the same time, these commissioners have claimed and received per diem from the Government for living expenses incurred by them in attending the same conventions.

> Members of the Commission engage in constant fraternization with individuals and corporations who appear as litigants before the Commission.

> Members of the Commission have received for personal use color television sets and other communications equipment, as well as free service contracts.

In making these charges, Schwartz did not take his own staff associates into his confidence. For example, quotations from these charges against the FCC appeared in Drew Pearson's column of January 22 before Stephen J. Angland, who was supposed to be in charge of the FCC phase of the Subcommittee's investigation, had seen the text of it.

After the "leak" in Pearson's column appeared, Schwartz, unknown to the Subcommittee members, gave the complete text of his memorandum to William Blair of the New York *Times* and the *Times* published the text along with a front-page story of the charges against the FCC, on January 23.

The spectacle of a "runaway" counsel bringing charges against both the regulatory agencies and his own Subcommittee at the same time was made to order for a sensation-mongering press. Whether the events had any bearing on the original objectives of the Subcommittee seemed immaterial. This was news, colorful and dramatic; the public was interested in reading about it. Subcommittee Chairman Morgan Moulder, a quiet, self-effacing former judge, seemed to echo, rather than lead, his chief counsel. Oren Harris, the garrulous and back-slapping, but thoroughly sophisticated, chairman of the parent Interstate and Foreign Commerce Committee now had to face a barrage of potentially hostile newspaper publicity if he sought to make the Subcommittee's inquiry follow paths other than those advocated by Schwartz. The Subcommittee met behind closed doors for four and a half hours the day the *Times* printed the Schwartz memorandum. At its conclusion, Harris announced that the Subcommittee would conduct a "comprehensive investigation" into charges that FCC members had allowed the industry to give them color TV sets and to pay their bills when they and their wives attended radio and television conventions.

While the dispute over the nature and scope of the Subcommittee's inquiry in light of the "Schwartz memorandum" was raging, some items in an earlier column by Drew Pearson were momentarily ignored. Discussing the award of Channel 10 in Miami to National Airlines, Pearson had focused on "the strange role played by FCC Commissioner Richard Mack." Mack was described as "an alleged Democrat who voted for Mr. Eisenhower" and was appointed by Eisenhower to the FCC when the Commission was faced with the unfavorable recommendation of Examiner Sharfman, "which the White House wanted to reverse." Pearson, in his usual "insider" style, said in his January 17 column, "There are reports that before he was appointed Mack promised Thurman Whiteside, a Miami attorney close to National Airlines, that he would vote for National Airlines." Jack Anderson of Pearson's staff had called Mack and learned from him that Mack, a Miamian, had borrowed money from Whiteside and still owed him "a couple of hundred dollars."

Meanwhile, new evidence of the pervasive problem of conflicts of interest emerged with the newspaper story charging Chairman Harris with 25 per cent ownership in television station KRBB of El Dorado, Arkansas. Shortly after the newspaper stories appeared, Harris announced that he sold his 50 shares of stock in the station for the same $500 cash down payment and $4,500 promissory note he had used to buy the stock the year before. "I'm out of the TV business," Harris declared, "I got tired of being harassed and it didn't mean a thing to me anyway."

Bitterness, recrimination, exposés, and harassment seemed to be the standard ingredients of the Subcommittee's inquiry. When, if ever, would they consider the basic problems of the agencies? Jack Gould, the radio-TV critic of the New York *Times* raised this question in a searching article on February 2. What never has been adequately appreciated, he stressed, is the magnitude and complexity of the decisions that a commissioner is expected to make. "He's always going to be in somebody's frying pan." Gould then proceeded to point out some of the hard realities of administrative politics.

It is certainly not classified information that major concerns in broadcasting engage in lobbying. But there is also what might be loosely defined as "the Congressional lobby." Members of Congress, through their personal secretaries, will undertake to arrange appointments at the F.C.C. for one of their constituents who has a matter to discuss with the commission. This type of accommodation may be innocuous enough but it has gone on for years and hardly enhances an F.C.C. commissioner's sense of independence. Realistically, it's a form of "pressure." If it isn't, then why doesn't everyone deal with the F.C.C. directly?

Gould went on to exhort the Subcommittee to proceed with the major problems of regulation. But his words fell on deaf ears as the Subcommittee continued to focus on the narrower but more sensational issues. John C. Doerfer, Chairman of the FCC, was due to testify on the following day to answer the charges in the Schwartz memorandum and to defend the agency's record. Doerfer directly challenged Schwartz's accuracy and integrity. He said in his prepared statement that Schwartz's confidential memorandum is the work of a man "who either does not understand or does not wish to understand the responsibilities of the FCC."

> This memorandum makes it appear that the members of the Federal Communications Commission are judges and only judges. It implies that most of their time is spent in deciding cases between litigants. Your counsel should have learned that this is not the fact. In probably 90 per cent of our work we do not act as judges but as legislators and executives.
> The Federal Communications Commission has the responsibility for making rules to govern the regulated industries. These rules, subject to broad standards set by Congress, have the force of law. In making these rules we are acting as legislators, not as judges. . . .
> It is naive to think that it is possible to legislate without conversations and conferences with people who know problems of the particular industry.
> Your counsel also forgot to tell you that for many years it has been the practice for almost all of the regulatory [agencies] to meet freely with the people [they regulate] and to discuss the problems of the industry with them.

Doerfer denied that the payment of commissioners' expenses by industry at conventions is a sin. The conventions consist of people who are competitors among themselves. It is hardly likely that any one of them would allow another to be favored. As for the color TV sets, they are not "play toys" for commissioners but one of the "tools of their trade." Television sets from industry have been used by commissioners to obtain information and observe industry practices almost from the beginning of television broadcasting. New sets are furnished whenever there is a substantial technical improvement. Chairman Doerfer also defended the legal right of commissioners to receive honoraria for talks at conventions. He cited Section 4 (B) of the Communications Act, passed by Congress in 1952, which authorizes commissioners to receive "a reasonable honorarium or compensation" for delivery of publications or papers. He charged Schwartz with acting with "questionable propriety" in failing to discuss Section 4 (B) in his memorandum and in leaking the memorandum to the press without any reference whatever to the rights of the members of the FCC.

In the course of the questioning following Doerfer's prepared statement, there was considerable spirited sparring between Schwartz and Doerfer; but during the three days of vigorous and vituperative exchanges, there was scarcely a mention of the agency's basic or long-range problems.

Could the Subcommittee change the direction of its inquiry? Not in the eyes of many observers. As Columnist Doris Fleeson put it in her column of February 4, the Subcommittee had begun "as inexorably as fate an examination of what Speaker Rayburn contemptuously called 'fly-specked' scandal." Miss Fleeson predicted that the hearings would continue along present lines until their "doubtless bitter conclusion. The FCC will be a violently shaken agency. The Subcommittee and its staff may continue in a turmoil. . . ."

On February 8, a story in the Tulsa (Oklahoma) *Tribune* filed from its Washington office said Schwartz had received $400 in expense money from the Subcommittee for four weekends in New York and that part of the money was earmarked for hotel expenses despite the fact that Schwartz still maintained his own apartment in New York. Schwartz termed the story "sheer nonsense" and charged that "powerful interests will stop at nothing to block the probe of the FCC." Chairman Moulder asserted that the fuss was over a "technicality," and that Schwartz had actually lost money leaving New York to take the Subcommittee post.

The Subcommittee held two lengthy and stormy closed-door sessions on Monday, February 10, the first session without Schwartz and the second with him. At the close of the first it was reported that the Subcommittee had voted 6 to 5 to keep him as counsel at least temporarily. Just how temporarily was made clear when it was announced at the conclusion of the second session that Schwartz had been fired by a 7 to 4 vote. Shortly after his firing, Schwartz accused the members who ousted him of being in "an unholy alliance between big business and the White House" and of having fired him knowing that he had evidence of payment of money to a Federal Communications Commissioner in a television case. In the furor, Morgan Moulder resigned as Chairman and Oren Harris announced that he would personally assume the Chairmanship of the strife-torn Subcommittee.

There were acid comments in the press over these developments. James Reston suggested in the New York *Times* that "any attempt to analyze who's ahead in the current battle over the Federal Communications Commission recalls Mark Twain's question 'Who won the San Francisco earthquake?' "

Schwartz States His Case /   When the Subcommittee reconvened for a public session on February 13, Chairman Oren Harris announced at the outset that he wanted "to say publicly that I feel personally that I have now the greatest challenge of my life. I will stand or fall on the success of this investigation." Schwartz, now appearing as a subpoenaed witness, was asked to develop his charge that an FCC Commissioner had accepted money in a comparative television license case: the saga of the Channel 10 case began to unfold before the Subcommittee.

The Commission's vote, Schwartz explained, was 4 to 1 in favor of Public Service Television:

> We have ascertained that in preliminary instructions to the staff to write the opinion, only the three Republicans were for Public Service Television. These preliminary instructions required final ratification by the Commission, and a fourth vote was necessary for there to be a full majority of the Commission in favor of the ultimately winning applicant.

The fourth vote was, of course, that of Commissioner Mack.

The names of men who had never been mentioned in Examiner Sharfman's initial decision or in the FCC's final decision were introduced at this point by Schwartz:

> Commissioner Mack was appointed to the FCC during the summer of 1955. Before that time, Commissioner Mack had been a member of the Florida Railroad and Public Utilities Commission.
>
> In the first place, he was close to Mr. Thurman A. Whiteside, in fact close is not a strong enough descriptive word. He has stated to our investigators that they were extremely intimate since boyhood and he used the simile, "We were like brothers."
>
> Mr. Whiteside is an attorney who has a reputation in Florida as the investigators have developed this, to use the colloquial term, "a fixer." He was involved with Judge Holt, who was the subject of impeachment proceedings in Florida, and Mr. Whiteside himself has been, and I believe still is, subject to disbarment proceedings.
>
> The second person the Commissioner was close to was Mr. Perrine E. Palmer. Mr. Palmer was a leading Miami political figure, and after the war, Mr. Mack, Commissioner Mack, had worked for Mr. Palmer's construction company.
>
> The third important person to whom Mr. Mack was close was Mr. Jerry W. Carter, a member of the Florida Railroad and Public Utilities Commission.

In developing Mack's relationship with Thurman Whiteside, Schwartz said that Mack had admitted to Subcommittee investigators that he had received several thousand dollars from Whiteside. Herbert Wachtell, one

of the investigators to whom the admissions were allegedly made, then
rocked the hearing with his statement that he had had two interviews with
Commissioner Mack and

> that on the second of these two interviews, which was in many ways the
> key one, the entire conversation, unknown to Commissioner Mack, was
> wire recorded.

In response to Representative Bennett's question whether the wire recording contained significant information, Investigator Wachtell replied:

> Oh, yes; this is a recording of the entire interview in which Commissioner
> Mack acknowledged receiving the money, acknowledged that substantial
> portions of these loans had been forgiven, acknowledged he had no specific
> recollection of ever making any single repayment, acknowledged that he
> knew Mr. Whiteside was representing National Airlines, acknowledged
> that he had told people that he had pledged his vote to Mr. Whiteside and
> National Airlines and acknowledged that he then voted for Public Service.

Although the recording had been made at Schwartz's suggestion, no
member of the Subcommittee had any knowledge of its existence. Mack's
frankness in response was probably explained by his assumption that these
were talks between insiders in the political system and would not be used
against him.

When the hearing adjourned at 2:15 that afternoon, it was clear that,
as extraordinary and unorthodox as his methods were, Schwartz had made
a case against Commissioner Mack.

The "Man in the News" sketch of Richard Alfred Mack in the New
York *Times* of February 14 listed "affable" as the adjective most often
used by his friends to describe him. Florida's newspapers unanimously
praised his appointment to the FCC in 1955. While Chairman of the
Florida State Railroad and Public Utilities Commission, Mack was largely
responsible for requiring utilities under the Commission's jurisdiction to
submit their financial records for detailed examination, despite their
vehement opposition, when they applied for rate increases. After graduation
from the University of Florida in 1932 he worked as an insurance sales-
man, credit manager for the General Motors Acceptance Corporation in
Miami, and as office manager for a farm supply firm in Miami. He rose to
lieutenant colonel in the infantry in World War II. "Washington knows
him as a sociable and suave man who has a good sense of humor and
enjoys displaying it."

"Affable" Commissioner Mack labeled Schwartz's charges as "without
foundation." He said he would not resign as a member of the FCC and, in

a letter to Chairman Harris, he requested "an early opportunity to appear before your committee and answer the unsubstantiated charges, accusations, innuendoes, and distortions so recklessly made by Bernard Schwartz." Mack also said that he had told J. Edgar Hoover that he wants to cooperate in every way possible with the FBI investigation of Schwartz's charge.

At the session on February 17, the Subcommittee continued the questioning of Schwartz who, at the outset, placed in the record an affidavit by A. Frank Katzentine, the owner of WKAT and loser to Public Service Television of Channel 10.

Katzentine had made the affidavit a year earlier, on February 15, 1957, a week after the Commission announced the award of the channel to Public Service. In it, Katzentine discussed some of the rumors, "leaks," and pressures that developed between the time of the Examiner's decision and the Commission's award of the channel.

He charged specifically that Mrs. Dwight D. Eisenhower's brother-in-law, Colonel George Gordon Moore, and Thurman Whiteside, Mack's longtime friend and associate, had used their influence to bring about the award to National Airlines' subsidiary. The affidavit also suggested that Katzentine was no shrinking violet when it came to pulling political high-tension wires.

> Sometime in the late summer or early fall of 1955 I received a phone call from a trusted friend, at my home, and he told me he had bad news for me. He said I was going to lose the channel 10 hearing even though we had a favorable decision from the examiner. I asked him how he knew, and he said he had been out with two of [National Airlines Chairman] Ted Baker's best friends the night before and that Col. Gordon Moore was engineering this application for National Airlines and that they were sure to win. This was after we had received the decision from the examiner. I immediately communicated this information to Paul Porter, our attorney in Washington. I later learned that Colonel and Mrs. Moore had been the house guests of Mr. Baker for quite a visit, and their pictures appeared in the paper here with Mr. and Mrs. Baker. I also later learned that Colonel Moore was engaged in a business in the Dominican Republic with one of the directors of National Airlines. Paul Porter has that information.
>
> I asked this friend to do what he could to circumvent such an act, and he called some powerful Republicans in Washington who likewise said there was no chance for WKAT, that I was a Democrat, and they were going to give it to Mr. Baker, president of National Airlines.

The name of Senator George Smathers of Florida, who in addition to being a member of the powerful Senate Committee on Interstate and Foreign Commerce was also executor of the L. B. Wilson estate, then entered the proceedings for the first time. Katzentine said:

Sometime later I was called at my home by one of the Florida Senators, George Smathers, who said he didn't think it was fair for National Airlines to have a television station, and that he felt WKAT deserved it for the public service WKAT had done, but that I had better find out where Richie Mack stood; did I know any friends of Mack. I told him, "No." I didn't know who he was associated with. George suggested I call Perrine Palmer, Thurman Whiteside, and his former roommate in college, William Gaither. I did call Mr. Gaither and Mr. Palmer. I knew Mr. Palmer well, but I did not know Mr. Gaither well. Perrine Palmer volunteered to go see Thurman Whiteside, known as Whitey Whiteside, and he came back to my office and said he had talked with Whiteside and Whiteside had told him that he had pledged Richie Mack to vote for National Airlines. Palmer volunteered to contact Richie Mack and try to get him to do what was right and give an honest vote on the merits, but I determined to go see Whiteside, whom I knew slightly. I did go to see him and told him what Mr. Palmer had told me. He said "Yes," he had talked to Richie Mack; that he was asked to do so by Mr. Robert Anderson, now Judge Anderson, one of the attorneys for National Airlines; that he would give the shirt off his back to Mr. Anderson; that he, Whiteside, was employed to do this task for National. I said, "Is this legal work, for if it is it is the strangest employment I ever heard of." I also asked him if he was to receive a fee and this he did not answer but continued to say he would do anything in the world for Bob Anderson. I told him that at my age, and what I thought was my reputation in the community, I hated to humble myself by coming to him, but our whole lives had been spent in preparing for television and it meant a great deal to my wife and me and the long-time associates of ours at WKAT. I told him I was not going to be craven about it but that I felt he ought to release Mr. Mack from any pledges. This he refused to do.

Katzentine then invoked the aid of the Chairman of the Florida Railroad and Public Utilities Commission to get Mack "released from his pledge."

Later Mr. Jerry Carter, chairman of the Florida Railroad and Public Utilities Commission, Mr. Palmer, and I went to Washington and Mr. Palmer and Mr. Carter tried to get Mr. Mack to seek release from his pledge, and he told them, so they reported to me, that he "was over a barrel" but that he would come to Miami and talk to Whitey Whiteside and try to get released. Mack did come to Miami but told Palmer that Whitey refused to release him or at least that is what Mr. Palmer told me Mack said.

Another reference in the affidavit to the informal network of communication surrounding the regulatory agency's work was Katzentine's statement that an FCC employee came to Harry Plotkin, a member of Arnold, Fortas and Porter, WKAT's lawyers, and told him the FCC's opinion-writing staff had been ordered to write up a report for National Airlines. Upon hearing this, said Katzentine, "I contacted [Florida Senators] Spessard Holland and George Smathers and Senator Magnuson [Chairman of the Senate Interstate and Foreign Commerce Committee]." The affidavit did not state whether Katzentine asked for or received assistance from them.

The last politically prominent person to be brought in by Katzentine was Senator Estes Kefauver of Tennessee. Katzentine had contributed to Kefauver's campaign for the presidential nomination and claimed the Senator as one of his friends.

> About the 1st of January 1957 Richie Mack came to Miami, and he had a long talk with Perrine Palmer, and Perrine Palmer told me that Richie Mack had said that I was out and that the reason was that I was a friend of Estes Kefauver and his supporter. I promptly wrote a letter to Estes Kefauver requesting him to call Palmer, for I did not wish to tell my friend such news, but that Palmer would tell him. I am told by Mr. Palmer that he reiterated the statement made by Commissioner Mack to Estes Kefauver.

Following his introduction of the Katzentine affidavit, Schwartz's exchanges with members of the Subcommittee took on an amicable note. He reviewed what he could recall in the files in order to assist the Subcommittee in investigating the charges against Mack and the allegations of Katzentine. Oren Harris expressed his appreciation for this.

Sharfman Explains His Decision /   The first witness after the Subcommittee ended what a Washington practitioner termed "its era of Schwartzmanship" was the Hearing Examiner in the Channel 10 case, Herbert Sharfman.

Sharfman reiterated his judgment that, on the whole, WKAT was the best-qualified applicant for the channel.

Asked by Representative O'Hara how he went about writing his decision, the Examiner offered this interesting description of his decision-writing process:

> I suppose it would be intellectual dishonesty to say there is not a certain amount of prejudgment in these matters, and perhaps rationalization, after a person, perhaps by intuition or osmosis, or whatever it is, feels a certain one of the applicants is the best qualified of the applicants, and then perhaps he does attempt to rationalize or to justify his own decision.
>
> But in this case, and I have tried this in my other cases, I write the facts first and then go over the findings of fact, and then determine whether— to see where the findings of fact lead me.
>
> In this case, I felt that the overriding factor was the fact that the local ownership, the civic participation, and what I thought was the general good broadcast record of Mr. Katzentine—that broadcast record was, of course,

the subject of criticism in the case, and I considered those criticisms. But I felt that overall, in the round, I felt that his broadcast record was a good one.

Representative Williams asked whether anyone had tried to influence or exert pressure on the Examiner. Sharfman stated that no one had done so.

Representative Moulder sought to determine whether any of the Commissioners had discussed the case with the Examiner:

> MR. MOULDER: While you were hearing the evidence or at any time prior to your final decision did you meet Mr. Mack?
> MR. SHARFMAN: No. I have never met Mr. Mack.
> MR. MOULDER: My additional question goes to this point: While you were hearing the evidence or after the case had been assigned to you, did any other member of the Commission discuss with you the merits of the case?
> MR. SHARFMAN: No, sir, never.
> MR. MOULDER: In any manner whatsoever?
> MR. SHARFMAN: No, sir; no Commissioner has ever discussed the merits of any case with me.

Chairman Harris sought to determine whether the Examiner was so convinced of the correctness of his decision that reasonable men could not have reached a different conclusion.

> THE CHAIRMAN: Did you state to anyone that you thought that this was a rather shameful decision?
> MR. SHARFMAN: Shameful decision? I do not think I have ever used that term. I said, as I said I was surprised at the decision, because of all the decisions I have rendered, this was the one case that I felt that I would be upheld, and I was surprised that I was not.
> But I do not feel, as I have indicated before, that reasonable minds could not have come to a different conclusion.

The Entry of Thurman Whiteside /   Circuit Judge Robert H. Anderson of Dade County, Florida, former attorney for National Airlines and the man to whom, according to Frank Katzentine's affidavit, Thurman Whiteside would give "the shirt off his back," took the stand at the beginning of the afternoon session. The objective of the investigators was to learn the relationship between National Airlines' lawyers and Thurman Whiteside. After identifying himself as a Miami resident for twenty years, circuit judge since January 12, 1956, and former senior partner in Anderson, Scott, McCarthy and Preston, one of Miami's oldest and most respected law firms, Judge Anderson stated that he knew surprisingly little about the association of Whiteside with National's lawyers to assist them with the Channel 10 matter.

JUDGE ANDERSON: My partner, Paul Scott, handled National Airlines' affairs, and of course I knew the case was in the office.

Scott came to me sometime in the fall of 1955 and suggested we associate local counsel in the case. And I suggested Mr. Whiteside. He asked me if I would talk to Mr. Whiteside and I told him I would and I did.

THE CHAIRMAN: Would you relate the nature of your discussion with Mr. Whiteside?

JUDGE ANDERSON: Yes. I told Mr. Whiteside about the case, told him that we wanted him to become associated in it, and I asked him what his fee would be. He told me that he would not charge any fee. I explained to him that that would be a very unsatisfactory way to handle the matter, and I remember quite clearly that his reply was, well, he did not know what good he could do.

MR. HALE: His reply was what?

JUDGE ANDERSON: He did not know what good he could do. And my recollection about it is, that I agreed to go into the case, but the matter of compensation was left open. I reported back to Scott what had transpired between Whiteside and me, and Scott took over from there.

Representative Hale tried to find out why Whiteside was retained by Anderson's law firm.

MR. HALE: An ordinary lawyer in towns outside of Washington does not have much experience of that kind of practice, is that not true?

JUDGE ANDERSON: That is right.

MR. HALE: Had Mr. Whiteside had experience in that kind of practice?

JUDGE ANDERSON: Not that I know of.

Representative Flynt finally drew an admission that a factor other than Whiteside's excellence as a lawyer may have led Anderson to seek his assistance.

MR. FLYNT: Did you ever ask Mr. Whiteside to confer with any member of the Commission?

JUDGE ANDERSON: No.

MR. FLYNT: Did you ever suggest to him, through any other person, that he contact any member of the Commission?

JUDGE ANDERSON: No.

MR. FLYNT: Specifically, did you ever ask him to contact Commissioner Richard A. Mack?

JUDGE ANDERSON: I don't think that I did. I may have.

MR. FLYNT: About when would that have been, if you did?

JUDGE ANDERSON: Well, it would have been about the time that I talked to him. It would have been in the fall of 1955.

MR. FLYNT: Would it have been in that initial conference that you had with him?

JUDGE ANDERSON: I think so.

MR. FLYNT: Or a subsequent conference?

JUDGE ANDERSON: I do not recall ever having had but the one conference with him: I may have had more. But the initial one, as you term it, was the only one that I definitely recall.

MR. FLYNT: Do you now think that you did discuss the possibility of his talking to Mr. Mack?

JUDGE ANDERSON: I think so.

MR. FLYNT: You think that that was brought up at that time?

JUDGE ANDERSON: I think so.

MR. FLYNT: Was that the main purpose that you wanted Mr. Whiteside associated in the case?

JUDGE ANDERSON: Well, let's put it this way: It was a fact that was not completely overlooked. I knew that Mr. Whiteside and Mr. Mack were good friends. I knew that quite well. And it probably influenced my selection of him.

Representative Moss led Judge Anderson to make his admission more explicit.

MR. MOSS: Well, now, when you discussed with Mr. Whiteside the question of retaining him, did you at that time also discuss with him the possibility of his contacting and discussing the case with Commissioner Mack?

JUDGE ANDERSON: We talked about that.

MR. MOSS: You did then discuss it with him at that time?

JUDGE ANDERSON: Yes.

The specific assignment Anderson had in mind for Whiteside was finally drawn out by Representative Peter Mack (no relation to Commissioner Richard Mack). Anderson had learned that in December 1955 instructions had been issued to the agency's opinion-writing section to prepare an opinion looking toward the award of the channel to Public Service. At that time, Doerfer, Lee, and McConnaughey had voted for the National Airlines' subsidiary; Bartley and Webster for WKAT, and Hyde for L. B. Wilson. Mack had not been present and had cast no vote.

JUDGE ANDERSON: My recollection is that Mr. Mack had not voted in the case and had not indicated how he would vote, and I was interested in finding out first whether he was going to participate in it.

MR. MACK: And you hesitated to ask Mr. Mack, even though he was a friend of yours?

JUDGE ANDERSON: That is right.

At the conclusion of Judge Anderson's testimony this much was clear: Anderson's partner, Paul R. Scott, had talked to him about the need for additional counsel after the hearings before Examiner Sharfman had been completed, the record closed, and the Examiner's decision for Katzentine announced. It was after that time but before the FCC's final decision that the effort was made to retain Whiteside.

Judge Anderson's former partner, Scott, who was general counsel and a director of National Airlines as well as one of the organizers of Public Service Television, was more expansive than the Judge on the theme of the role contemplated for Whiteside:

> MR. SCOTT: Well, I would put it this way: I know very little about the practice before the federal regulatory agencies, because I never had done that type of work. But when I found that our opposition was actively talking and having people of influence talk to the Commissioners, it seemed to me if we could get someone who was a friend of one of the Commissioners, it might be desirable.

Scott said that he knew Senator Holland had talked to Commissioner Mack in behalf of Katzentine "because Senator Holland told me that he did" before he knew that Scott had any interest in the matter. Representative Hale wanted to know Scott's estimate of Whiteside's success.

> MR. HALE: Looking back on the matter, you think Mr. Whiteside was useful to you in the case; do you not?
> MR. SCOTT: I am not sure that I do.
> MR. HALE: What is the basis of your doubt, Mr. Scott?
> MR. SCOTT: Well, I do not know whether or not Mr. Mack—Mr. Whiteside was a deciding factor in Mr. Mack's vote or what he did.
> Now I know that he must have done something, because of his telling me later that he had to withdraw his promise to be of help. So that evidently indicated that he had tried to do something.
> Now I just do not know.
> MR. HALE: Didn't Mr. Whiteside ever later receive a fee from National Airlines?
> MR. SCOTT: Never at any time.

Whiteside withdrew from the matter allegedly because of pressure from Katzentine, who in his own capacity as a lawyer had undertaken an action against Whiteside on behalf of another client.

> MR. BENNETT: Did Whiteside indicate to you that Katzentine had something on him that he did not want to reveal; is that the kind of pressure?
> MR. SCOTT: His exact words were that Katzentine was using blackmail on him.

Representative Bennett and Scott had another interesting exchange on the process of decision-making by an administrative agency.

MR. BENNETT: If you had not been informed that people like Senator Holland were speaking in behalf of your adversary would you have sought the services of Mr. Whiteside in the capacity that you were seeking it?

MR. SCOTT: No, sir.

MR. BENNETT: Did you feel that aside from the fact that somebody might have the private ear of Commissioner Mack, that your firm had put in a good case and would stand on the merits of the facts that were presented to the examiner and to the Commission?

MR. SCOTT: Well, I feel this way, Congressman: I listened to quite a bit of that proceeding over there before the examiner, and it is very difficult for me to see how anyone can, after going through all those reams of testimony, decide that one is any better than the other. As I say, it looks to me as though any one of them could do the job.

MR. BENNETT: How do you assume the Commissioner reaches his decision on it? If I understood you correctly, what you are saying is that the evidence in a case of this kind is such that a Commissioner might decide for any of the parties.

MR. SCOTT: Yes, and it seemed to me if the Senators of the State came and said to me "I know all of these fellows and they are all right but I think this one is a little better than the rest of them," that would have a lot of influence with me.

MR. BENNETT: You think that would be enough to tip the scales?

MR. SCOTT: I think it would be; yes.

MR. BENNETT: That is why you wanted somebody to help tip the scales in your direction?

MR. SCOTT: At least not let them tip too far the other way.

The objectives and tactics of National Airlines in exploiting Whiteside's relationship with Mack were now quite clear. But what of Katzentine's objectives and tactics? Were they more honorable or more respectful of administrative integrity than National's? These questions were dominant as Katzentine took the stand the following morning, February 19.

The Busy Life of Colonel Katzentine / The voluble, effusive former Air Force colonel told the Subcommittee at the outset that he had sent copies of his now famous affidavit to his counsel, Paul Porter, and to Senator Estes Kefauver. Describing Senator Kefauver as "about the closest friend I have in Washington," he proceeded to deny that he sent a copy of the affidavit to the Senator "to use it possibly in connection with an investigation." He sent the copy, rather, in order to have the salient information "preserved."

Representative Bennett confronted Katzentine with an exchange of cor-

respondence between the WKAT owner and Senator Kefauver pertaining
to the channel award that predated the appointment of Richard Mack to
the Commission. The letter of June 6, 1955, read in part:

> Now "Keefe," down to my case.
>
> We have won a magnificent decision, which I wish you would read—it
> can be obtained from Paul Porter's—but I am troubled that politics may
> intervene between the examiner's report and the final decision. I do not
> believe there is a dishonest man on the FCC, and I do not believe that
> politics per se would persuade any of these gentlemen, but I do feel that
> your offer to help could be useful now.
>
> If you could let it be known that you are my friend and I am not a
> rascal and scoundrel, as I have been charged by an attorney, Leo Resnick,
> attorney for the L. B. Wilson estate, . . .

After discussing briefly the major points in Examiner Sharfman's decision, the letter returned to the matter of the senator's help.

> I would greatly appreciate your talking to Paul Porter in confidence and
> telling him how you can help me. It may be that nothing should be done
> but I just would like to eliminate the possibility of any political she-
> nanigans.
>
> I have today received a letter from Spessard Holland which in confi-
> dence I quote: "I have had the opportunity of talking with Chairman
> McConnaughey about the long delay on the part of the FCC in making the
> decision in the Miami TV problem. I particularly emphasized how this has
> deprived the greater Miami area of additional VHF service. I also have
> again told him of the fine record made by you with WKAT and I urged
> that prompt action be taken in this case." I do not see how Spessard could
> do more for me than that and I do appreciate it.
>
> Incidentally, George Smathers is the executor of the L. B. Wilson estate,
> but he told me in his office in Washington last week that he felt I deserved
> the grant here, regardless of his position with regard to the estate.
>
> I am sorry to burden you, and if it is going to hurt you in any way for-
> get it.
>
> With kindest personal regards and love to Nancy,
>
> As ever,
>
> A. FRANK KATZENTINE

Senator Kefauver's answer of June 13 said that the Senator had been
waiting for "a go ahead sign from you." It went on:

> In incidental conversation I have talked with Bob Bartley, Frieda Hen-
> nock, and Commissioner Lee by letting them bring up the subject in some
> way. I think this is the best way to be helpful.
>
> But if there is anything in the way of a more direct approach to anyone

that I can make or be useful to you let me know about it, because it would break my heart if you did not get final approval of the Commission.

Sincerely,

ESTES KEFAUVER

The letters made it clear that Katzentine had begun to seek ex parte political pressures even before Richard Mack replaced Frieda Hennock on the FCC. They made an earlier statement by Katzentine that "I never tried to influence anybody to vote for WKAT" seem at best an exaggeration.

Additional evidence introduced into the record by Representative Flynt showed that the Katzentine organization's attempts at influence went beyond Senators Kefauver, Holland, and Smathers into the highest executive echelon of the Republican party. Downey Rice, a Washington lawyer, and former chief investigator for the Kefauver committee, had written on October 13, 1955 to Dan Sullivan, a witness for Katzentine in the Channel 10 hearings. He wrote to tell him of his thorough discussion of "the Channel 10 problem" with Paul Porter, who was Katzentine's counsel and a former FCC Chairman. It was generally agreed, Rice wrote, that "the place to go was as high up in the circle of close Eisenhower associates as possible. It had occurred to Paul Porter to get Nixon through having [Eastern Air Lines President] Eddie Rickenbacker contact Bill Rogers in the Justice Department." Rickenbacker, as head of Eastern Airlines, was a fierce competitor of National and, needless to say, an opponent of the award to Public Service; and Rogers, who was later to become attorney general, was a close friend of the Vice President. Rice preferred to try to reach Nixon through the Vice President's administrative assistant, Bob King. Rice, Sullivan, and King were all former FBI agents.

> I set it up and saw King for over an hour in Nixon's office yesterday. At the outset we knew that the problem had to be presented carefully. It had to be strong enough to make Nixon do something and yet we did not want to bring a reaction anywhere which would mitigate against Frank if Baker was knocked out.
>
> King was most cordial and attentive. He took notes and seemed to grasp the problem and to see it our way. I think the fact that he was told that Smathers had the story had the effect of forcing some action. Obviously they cannot afford to risk exposure by Democrats of an "influence deal."

Rice said King understood that Katzentine was "not only a Democrat but even worse, a Kefauver Democrat." Rice "guessed" that:

> Nixon will simply telephone to his friend Bob Lee and tell him that there were some loaded rumors afloat and that Lee would do well to carefully consider any action being taken by the Commission with an eye to the probability that if said action was questionable, prompt unfavorable pub-

licity could be expected. No attempt was made to arrange with King to let us know what action was taken. It did not appear that this was in good taste, but I feel certain we are going to get immediate results.

Referring to another "lead" which might bring Republican Senator Alexander Wiley into the picture on WKAT's side, Rice commented, "Action by Nixon compared with action by Wiley would be like comparing an atomic cannon with a popgun."

Two letters from the past were also introduced indicating that the utilization of political endorsements in Katzentine's behalf was virtually a hallowed custom. One was a letter of July 15, 1951, from Jerry W. Carter, the National Democratic Committeeman of Florida, to the Federal Communications Commission. The other, dated July 19, 1951, was written to the FCC by the then-Chairman of the Railroad and Public Utilities Commission of Florida, Richard A. Mack. The assumption was obvious in Carter's letter that since the majority of FCC members at that time were Democrats, they should favor loyal, life-long Democrats like Katzentine in their decisions. The letter was simple and concise:

GENTLEMEN: It is my pleasure and privilege to recommend to you Mr. A. F. Katzentine, the owner and operator of radio station WKAT of Miami, Fla. Mr. Katzentine has been a loyal Democrat all his life and to my personal knowledge has supported the Democratic party, Democratic committee, and all of its candidates for the past 15 years, and is entitled to all of the consideration that a good citizen and a good Democrat is entitled to.

I personally take great pleasure in recommending and requesting that you give him and his company every consideration possible.

Richard A. Mack, the commissioner who was to become the center of the current controversy, wrote at that time:

This commission has been informed that Mr. A. F. Katzentine, owner and operator of radio station WKAT at Miami, Fla., has applied to your Commission for a certificate to operate a television station.

Mr. Katzentine is a pioneer resident of Miami and has been an outstanding business and civic leader for years.

The manner in which he operates station WKAT is a credit to his community and to the State of Florida.

No contract submitted by Mr. Katzentine has been denied by this Commission. This letter is written with the thought that it might be of some assistance to you at such time as Mr. Katzentine's application is considered.

From the material introduced into the record, it appeared that no influential friend or associate of Katzentine's was exempt from being asked to prepare affidavits or write letters.

In the course of Katzentine's subsequent testimony, it was brought out that he had made two trips to Washington to speak with Commissioner Mack and conferred on several occasions with Thurman Whiteside in efforts to have Whiteside release Mack from the alleged pledge he had obtained from Mack to vote for Public Service.

Insofar as his association with Thurman Whiteside was concerned, Katzentine admitted disliking Whiteside intensely but denied categorically that he had ever blackmailed him.

A Friendly Visit to Richie Mack /   Katzentine had asserted in his affidavit and again in a letter of June 4, 1957 to Senator Kefauver requesting an investigation of the Channel 10 case that he had three witnesses who would testify that "Richie Mack was pledged" to National Airlines before the Commission's vote was taken. One of the alleged witnesses was Perrine Palmer, former Miami mayor, public relations consultant, and real estate developer. Palmer was credited with having obtained for Richard Mack his initial appointment to the State Railroad and Public Utilities Commission. The others were Ben Fuqua, a vice-president of the Florida Power Co. and Jerry Carter, Democratic National Committeeman of Florida.

In his appearance before the Subcommittee, Palmer reported that he told the WKAT owner that he personally believed "an airline should not go into the television business and that I would be glad to call Mr. Mack and tell him how I felt about it." Just as Whiteside had done when Judge Anderson asked him to work in behalf of National Airlines, Palmer agreed to the work but declined any fee.

Palmer phoned Mack early in 1956, and Mack told him that the FCC had the matter under consideration "and that a decision would not be rendered for quite some time." Palmer then spoke to Thurman Whiteside and asked him if he would speak to Mack in behalf of Katzentine. "He told me that he had either already spoken to Mr. Mack or promised to speak to him, I forget which, in behalf of National Airlines." Palmer was in frequent touch with Mack. "It seemed like every week that went by Mr. Katzentine called me and asked me, he said, 'Gootsie, what have you done for me today?' And then I would call Mr. Mack."

Despite the frequency of Palmer's calls and visits to Mack, he learned nothing more from Mack about the disposition of Channel 10 than that "There were tremendous pressures being brought on some members of the Commission and that he personally was over a barrel" because he had friend on all sides of the fence.

Shortly before the FCC announced its decision, Katzentine asked Palmer to phone Mack again to see if he could find out when the decision would be made: Palmer answered, "At that time, I believe Mr. Mack told me that the decision would be made shortly, but that it did not look too good for

Mr. Katzentine, and I asked him why. And he said: 'Well, there is too much Kefauver in this situation.' "

Senator Kefauver's efforts to assist Katzentine were brought in again in Fuqua's testimony. In the winter or spring of 1956, he related, McGregor Smith, Chairman of the Board of the Florida Power and Light Co. called Fuqua into his office and told him that on the previous night he (Smith) had had a call "from his old friend and college mate, Senator Estes Kefauver of Tennessee" requesting assistance in connection with Katzentine's application for a TV license. Smith told the Senator he didn't know Richard Mack "too well' but that Fuqua did. "It was agreed between Mr. Smith and Senator Kefauver that I would come to Washington and report to Senator Kefauver and discuss the matter with him. Mr. Smith told me that he wanted to repay a favor that Senator Kefauver had done for him." Senator Kefauver suggested that Fuqua "convey to Mr. Mack the desire that Mr. Katzentine's application for a TV license should have every consideration on its merits." Fuqua communicated all of this to Commissioner Mack. "He was noncommital. He did not appear to want to discuss the situation. I did not press it any further."

Jerry W. Carter, the former Democratic National Committeeman from Florida and present member of the State Railroad and Public Utilities Commission told the Subcommittee that he had testified for Katzentine at the hearing before Examiner Sharfman as a representative of the Florida Railroad and Public Utilities Commission. After Mack's appointment to the FCC, Carter, having heard "so many rumors about different things that had been said that had led me to believe that the decision on this franchise might not follow the law and the evidence," went to Washington to see Mack on his own initiative to suggest that Mack disqualify himself since "there was liable to be some scandal about this." Mack sparred with him, Carter reported:

> We sparred backward and forward, but you cannot go to a man and just open up and tell him you are afraid he is going to do the wrong thing. You have just got to—you say he is a friend and sort of advise him and tell him what is the safest thing he ought to do. You know, you do not find so much in the Bible about avoiding evil as you do about avoiding the appearance of evil.

When it appeared to him that Mack was not about to disqualify himself, Carter told him "that I thought he would be smart just to follow the Examiner's report."

Returning to the allegation in Katzentine's affidavit that "Mr. Palmer and Mr. Carter tried to get Mr. Mack to seek release from his pledge," the Subcommittee members succeeded only in eliciting the information that Carter had played a key role in obtaining Mack's appointment to the FCC and that he had had numerous conversations about Channel 10 with Mack and Whiteside, in all of which he sought to do what he could in Katzentine's behalf. He had "apprehensions" that Whiteside had pledged Mack to vote for National Airlines but "I cannot say" that Whiteside had Mack so bound to him that if "Mr. Whiteside put the finger on Mr. Mack, Mr. Mack had to do what he said."

Thurman Whiteside and the Uses of Friendship /   The exact nature of the Mack-Whiteside relationship was still unclear when Thurman Whiteside took the stand on February 24. It was established that Mack had borrowed money from Whiteside and that he had, in fact, voted for National Airlines. But it was equally well established that Mack had debts of a political nature to other Florida leaders who were working in Katzentine's behalf. Was Mack's decision on Channel 10 the product of his own, independent judgment, or was he ultimately swayed by pressure?

Whiteside, described in an Associated Press dispatch of February 15 as "a balding, 47-year-old barrister whose heavy rimmed spectacles gave him an owlish appearance," had branded as "a big lie," in statements to the newspapers, any implication that he had exerted pressure on Mack to gain Channel 10 for National Airlines. At the outset of his appearance before the Subcommittee, he branded Schwartz "an unmitigated liar" for saying that he (Whiteside) was an attorney employed by either National Airlines or its subsidiary, Public Service Television. Schwartz's allegations, Whiteside said, were "second-hand hearsay premised upon the false Katzentine hearsay-and-gossip affidavit." As to the specific charge of the "pledge," Whiteside testified that Mack "has never been pledged to me for any person or corporation at any time or for any purpose."

In reference to the efforts of Judge Anderson and his former partner, Scott, to retain him as counsel for Public Service, Whiteside said that he declined Scott's offer of a $10,000 fee. He insisted that he "would not accept employment as an attorney or retainer as an attorney and receive or accept any fee, but left it on a personal basis between us." He did, however, volunteer to talk to Commissioner Mack. He then phoned Mack in Washington:

> and advised him of my opinion of the high character, integrity, and reputation in the community of the individuals involved in the National Airlines application, and of my friendship for Robert H. Anderson; and all things being equal, I would appreciate his giving National his consideration.
> He replied in substance that "Frank Katzentine is a friend of mine, as are others involved in the Channel 10 application, but Mr. Katzentine helped me become a Sigma Nu in the University of Florida."
> That was the sum, substance, and effect of our conversation.

Whiteside denied emphatically that he ever, at any time, in any place, directly or through his law partners or associates, received any fees from or on behalf of National Airlines or Public Service Television. The members of the Subcommittee then proceeded to focus on two matters: the details of Whiteside's financial and other transactions with Mack and the nature and source of Katzentine's alleged pressures on Whiteside. The two matters must have been related, the investigators felt. Persistently and grimly they covered the points with Whiteside over and over again in three grueling days of questioning.

Whiteside first enlarged upon his charge of "blackmail" against Katzentine. Whiteside testified that he had a dispute with a former client, Grant Foster, over Whiteside's fees as trustee. Foster retained Katzentine as counsel and Katzentine allegedly threatened Whiteside with suit for misuse of trust funds. Katzentine also told a relative of Mrs. Whiteside's that actions Whiteside had taken as trustee for Foster were likely to be harmful to Mrs. Whiteside's family business. After that, Whiteside phoned Katzentine and asked him to come to his office.

"I told him I was a fighter and, for my part, if I were the only one involved, I would not give in to the kind of actions he would have taken, which were tantamount to blackmail." Upon his wife's request, however, Whiteside agreed to settle the matter. He asked Katzentine to find out what his client was willing to concede on the fee account and promised that he would advise Anderson of his withdrawal of his recommendation of National Airlines. Katzentine appeared pleased with the arrangement, and the fee matter was settled to Whiteside's satisfaction.

> At that time, Perrine Palmer, Jr., was called by Mr. Katzentine to his office, apparently for the purpose to witness my withdrawal by telephone conversation with Commissioner Mack.
>
> Several days following the keeping of this part of the bargain, the closing papers and documents in the Foster matter were executed and delivered by all parties.

After discussion of the "blackmail" episode, the congressmen began to probe the details and ethics of Whiteside's loans to Commissioner Mack. Representative Peter Mack asked whether Whiteside thought it entirely ethical for him to loan money to a member of the FCC "notwithstanding the fact that you are authorized to practice before that Commission?"

> MR. WHITESIDE: Ethical? I don't know that ethics enters into the thing because we have a relationship that goes for 40 years. I think he is still a member of the human race and I have a right to treat him as such.

Turning to Whiteside's various business interests, Representative Peter Mack learned that one of his business ventures consisted of a one-third interest in an insurance agency which had sold insurance to Public Service Television after the FCC's award of the channel to Public Service.

MR. MACK: Does Mr. Mack have an interest in the firm?
MR. WHITESIDE: Yes, sir; he has a one-sixth interest and has had since January of 1953.

Mack's one-sixth interest was a gift from Whiteside and had yielded the Commissioner about $13,000 since 1953, partly in "commissions," on policies written as a result of "leads" supplied by Mack before his appointment to the FCC. The Public Service account was obtained not by Mack or Whiteside but by Charles Shelden, another one-third owner of the agency, who was the "closest of social and personal friends" of Baker, the head of National Airlines. Painstakingly, the Subcommittee members reviewed the payments made to Mack in each year and were momentarily baffled by the fact that no payments were made in 1957. Mack received nothing directly in 1957, Whiteside stated. "His ownership participating interest in this company for 1957 was paid to a corporation named Andar, Inc."

Andar, Inc., the congressmen then learned, was a corporation originally founded as a holding company for a Coral Gables Checker Cab Company in which Whiteside had a financial interest. When the cab company was sold, Whiteside transferred the outstanding stock in Andar to Richard Mack. The company had no assets at the time of the transfer, but after the payment of the $2,250 participating interest in the insurance agency to Andar, Mack received $2,000 in checks from Andar. Furthermore, as Representative Moss brought out, Mack, being the sole stockholder in Andar as a result of Whiteside's gift, would also be the recipient of all future profits. Whiteside agreed that, "Less income taxes, all profits would accrue to him." Commenting on his gifts of interests in business firms to Mack, Whiteside felt that there was a vast difference "between a gift and placing a lifelong friend in a position where he can earn money on an income basis."

Toward the end of Whiteside's three-day stand before the Subcommittee, the conversation again turned to the subject of ethics in regulatory agency proceedings. Representative Williams suggested that since Whiteside was not an attorney of record in the Channel 10 case but conferred nonetheless with Mack about it, then "fixer," the term Schwartz had applied, was indeed the most appropriate term to describe him. Whiteside indicated politely that if Williams were correct, the same could be said of Senators Smathers, Holland, and Kefauver, so far as Channel 10 was concerned.

Whiteside acknowledged that it would not be proper for anyone to attempt to use personal influence in seeking a favorable decision from a friend who was a member of the judiciary, but he felt that commissioners of regulatory agencies are in a different category from judges.

In closing the hearing at 6:45 p.m. at the end of the third and final day of Whiteside's testimony, Chairman Harris grimly quoted to Whiteside section 1505 of the U.S. Criminal Code, which prohibits, among other things, efforts to "influence, obstruct or impede the due and proper administration of the law" in any proceeding pending before any department or agency of the United States.

As Commissioner Richard A. Mack prepared to take the stand the following day, he might well have had in mind the Washington *Post* editorial condemning the "courthouse clique." Little by little, the *Post* declared, "the House Committee on Legislative Oversight had wrested from Thurman Whiteside admission after admission which, pieced together, form a picture of county courthouse finagling at its unloveliest."

The Ordeal of Richard Mack

Commissioner Mack's appearance before the Subcommittee began with an apology that "I may seem a little nervous this morning, which you can well understand." After assuring Chairman Harris that he was ready and anxious to discuss every phase of his conduct, Mack asserted categorically that he had at no time directly or indirectly, pledged his vote to Thurman Whiteside, or to any of the applicants in the proceeding.

He declared that Thurman Whiteside, Frank Katzentine, Ben Fuqua, Jerry Carter, and Perrine Palmer, "all personal friends of mine," talked to him about the Channel 10 matter between the time he was appointed to the FCC and the Commission's final decision. But these conversations, he said, dealt only with requests that he give "consideration" to the character and other qualifications of the respective applicants.

Mack said he did not participate in the Commission's proceedings in July 1955, when oral argument was heard on appeals from the Hearing Examiner's initial decision, and that he was not present and did not vote on December 21, 1955, when the instructions were issued to the opinion-writing section to prepare a decision looking toward award of the channel to Public Service. Mack became "more interested in the proceeding" only after a question was raised by Senators Bible, Payne, and Monroney, in a letter to the Commission, over whether a scheduled airline was qualified under the law to operate a television station. The Commission obtained a ruling from its general counsel that there was no legal objection to such ownership and operation. Mack told the Subcommittee:

> About 3 weeks before the Commission's final decision in the channel 10 case, I received a copy of the decision which had been drafted for the Commission by the Office of Opinions and Review. I studied this docu-

ment and decided, based upon it and the record in this case, that I would cast my vote to adopt the decision.

Mack also told the Subcommittee that he did not discuss his vote with other members of the Commission before casting it; nor did he have any discussions with them about how they would vote. On the basis of the tally, with Republican Commissioners McConnaughey, Doerfer, and Lee voting for Public Service, Democrat Bartley for WKAT, and Republican Hyde for L. B. Wilson, "Public Service would have won had I not voted."

Confronted with the letter of endorsement he had written to the Commission in 1951 in Katzentine's behalf, Mack termed it a "routine" letter that almost anyone could obtain from a public official. As to his ties with the Stembler-Shelden insurance agency, the commissioner asserted emphatically that he did not know until he was informed of Whiteside's testimony before the Subcommittee that the insurance agency in which he held stock handled the insurance for Public Service Television. He promptly "renounced and terminated" his interest in the insurance agency in a special delivery letter mailed to Whiteside in care of Chairman Harris.

Representative Moss reminded Mack of his letter of December 30, 1957, responding to Schwartz's questionnaire, in which Mack had said:

> Neither I nor any member of my immediate family has received any honorarium, loan, fee, or other payment, directly or indirectly, from the time of my appointment to the Federal Communications Commission, July 1, 1955, to the present, by or on behalf of any person, firm, corporation, association, organization, or group having any interest, direct or indirect, in any manner subject at any time to the jurisdiction of this Commission.

Mack denied that his loans from Whiteside were inconsistent with his statements in the letter since "to the best of my knowledge at the time I wrote that letter, Mr. Whiteside was not legally employed nor was he a principal in any of the matters he had mentioned to me. . . . Even today he is not a principal nor has he represented any of the people that you have mentioned, any more than I have any knowledge that Senator Kefauver was involved."

With monotonous persistence, the members of the Subcommittee asked the commissioner to review over and over again his financial relationship with Whiteside, the information conveyed to him by his various friends, and the basis on which he had cast his vote for Public Service Television. So repetitive were the questions and answers at this stage that one might have thought the session was prerecorded and replayed every thirty minutes.

Chairman Oren Harris vigorously pressed Mack on the subject of the commissioner's sense of ethics. "Did it ever occur to you," he asked, that a man who had extensive interests, recognized as a man of wealth as has been testified heretofore, and having matters before a regulatory commission of which you were a member and interested in things on which you must pass your judgment, did it ever occur to you that there was anything wrong or improper for you to be accepting loans on such friendly association during that time?

RICHARD MACK: No, sir, it did not.

As Mack concluded his testimony, Oren Harris commented gravely on the commissioner's admissions. Mack had confirmed that he had invested no money of his own in either of the companies from which he had received a substantial sum. The arrangement for him to receive these sums was made by his trusted friend, Thurman Whiteside, during the time that Whiteside had expressed his interest in behalf of National Airlines' application for a channel worth millions of dollars. Whether true or not, rumors were circulating that Mack had pledged his vote, and Mack knew about the rumors. Harris and Mack, both normally affable gentlemen, were grim and grave. The Chairman felt that the testimony revealed a deliberate conspiracy to achieve undue influence through the instrumentality of the FCC. He concluded:

I do not like to say this, but we have heard you, we have heard you through. I feel sorry for you, Mr. Mack. In my opinion you are to be pitied, because I think you have been used as a tool in this unfortunate mess.

It seems to me that the best possible service that you could render now as a member of the Federal Communications Commission would be to submit your resignation.

Furthermore it seems to me that the President of the United States who is responsible under the law for your appointment, should unhesitatingly under the circumstances revealed during these hearings, make a direct request to you for your resignation and thus employ the necessary action that would reestablish the confidence so vital in this great agency of the Government.

RICHARD MACK: Mr. Chairman . . .

THE CHAIRMAN: You may have an opportunity.

RICHARD MACK: I would just like to make one remark.

THE CHAIRMAN: Yes.

RICHARD MACK: I will certainly most seriously consider your remarks.

On March 3, following the President's request in a note delivered by Presidential Assistant Sherman Adams, Richard Mack resigned from the FCC, still protesting his innocence.

On March 12, Mack returned briefly as a Subcommittee witness to explain additional details about his bank deposits. The session was an anticlimax but revealed a mellower and more introspective Richard Mack than did his earlier appearance. Representative Peter Mack referred once again to the political pressures to which Richard Mack had been subjected. Then for the first time, the former commissioner admitted the ordeal through which he had gone.

> RICHARD MACK: They bothered me. . . . Some of these people involved, getting back to Channel 10 again, some of the people involved in that matter, I had known for years and years. And, as I have testified, they contacted me concerning this matter, now when I used the term "bothered" it is pretty hard to slam the doors on friends and I am sure that you have people up in the legislature. . . .
>
> THE CHAIRMAN: Yes, sir.
>
> RICHARD MACK: That are close personal friends of yours, and they would come in and talk to you. That is the situation I was in. . . . Perhaps the fact that I was an elected official of Florida, on a statewide basis, and maybe my attitude as a Commissioner during the first years I was on the Commission was a little bit like that of a Congressman, you are going to have to listen to them whether you want to or not.

As the Subcommittee completed its investigation of the Channel 10 case and moved on to other cases that were to unearth at later points the gifts of Boston industrialist Bernard Goldfine to Presidential Assistant Sherman Adams and the "fixing" of the television quiz programs, a crucial question remained: What would happen to Channel 10 in Miami?

The Decision of the Court of Appeals and the Rehearing Before the FCC

The appeal that had been taken from the Commission's final decision to the U.S. Court of Appeals was still pending before the judges. Shortly after Mack's resignation, the Commission's attorneys petitioned the Court to remand the case to the FCC for further proceedings. Basing their request on the public charges against Mack before the Harris Subcommittee, the agency lawyers contended that Mack should have disqualified himself and that his failure to do so may have invalidated the agency's decision. In a unanimous decision, Judges Prettyman, Danaher, and Washington granted the agency's request, and called on the FCC to answer three questions:

> —what circumstances formed the basis for the public charges that one of the members of the Commission should have disqualified himself in these proceedings;
>
> —whether any person or persons influenced or attempted to influence any member of the Commission in respect to the present proceedings in any

manner whatsoever except by the recognized and public processes of adjudication, and, if so, the full facts and circumstances;
—whether any party to the proceeding before the Commission directly or indirectly secured, aided, confirmed, ratified, or knew of any misconduct found by the Commission to have occurred.

Horace Stern, a recently retired Chief Justice of the Pennsylvania Supreme Court was retained by the Commission as a special Examiner to conduct the hearings on these questions. The parade of now-familiar names and faces involved in the Channel 10 case shifted back from the House of Representatives to the Federal Communications Commission where it had begun in 1954. Hearings were held from September 8 through October 1, and Judge Stern's decision was announced December 1.

To no one's surprise, the Examiner found that there were "persistent attempts" improperly to influence Commissioner Mack in favor of WKAT on the one hand and National Airlines on the other. The pressures brought to bear on Mack were all the more intense and reprehensible as a result of the "general knowledge" of the Commission's 3–2–1 vote of December 21, 1955, instructing the agency's opinion-writing staff to prepare an opinion awarding the Channel to National Airlines. This led "naturally" to the inference that Mack's vote would be the one finally decisive, "thereby marking him out all the more for intensive solicitation."

Judge Stern reviewed the efforts of Frank Katzentine, Perrine Palmer, Jerry Carter, and Ben Fuqua as well as those of Senators Smathers, Holland, and Kefauver, to influence the commissioner's decision in favor of WKAT. He found that:

All of those thus named—persons to whom Mack was obligated by reason of friendship or political support or both—actually sought his vote for WKAT however vigorously both he and they denied that they asked him for it in so many words. One would have to be quite naïve to accept as a fact that they urged him only to decide the case on the merits,—a request that would properly have merited resentment as implying a lack of confidence in his judicial integrity. Mack certainly knew what was being asked of him.

As to the approaches made to Mack in behalf of Public Service Television, "there was only one such intermediary, but, in the person of Thurman Whiteside, a very powerful one for the purpose." Whiteside's loans to Mack, made without interest and payable on demand, "invested Whiteside with the power to embarrass Mack at any time by a call for payment." Under such circumstances, Whiteside's "recommendation" of National Airlines was tantamount to a request for Mack's vote. In short, all the representations made privately to Commissioner Mack were "grossly improper."

Mack should have disqualified himself, the Special Examiner ruled, despite the commissioner's claim that he was able to reach his decision purely on the merits. It would be quite contrary to our knowledge of human nature, Judge Stern noted, to believe that Mack or anyone similarly situated could perform his duty with any degree of objectivity and necessary impartiality when he was "acting in response to such close ties of friendship and financial favors." The Examiner quoted loftily from Sir Edward Coke's address to his neighbors a few weeks after his appointment as a judge in 1606, in which Lord Coke said that "he that is a judge ceaseth to be a friend." Judge Stern quoted also from the Book of Deuteronomy in the Bible ("a gift doth blind the eyes of the wise and pervert the words of the righteous"), from Seneca ("while you look at what is given, look also at the giver"), and the Canons of Ethics of the American Bar Association ("a judge should not accept presents or favors from litigants or from lawyers practicing before him or from others whose interests are likely to be submitted to him for judgment").

The question whether the parties were acting only "defensively" on hearing rumors that others had contacted Mack secretly was deemed unimportant because the remedy was to call the efforts at improper influence to the attention of the Commission, not to indulge in the same reprehensible conduct.

The Examiner also found that North Dade Video had engaged in questionable conduct in the course of the original proceeding. When North Dade's general manager, Walter Compton, heard rumors that Examiner Sharfman's initial decision would be reversed, he employed former congressman and former FCC member Robert F. Jones for a fee of $2,000 to "counteract the rumor-mongering" and "try to neutralize the pressures." Jones sought to obtain legislation by Congress to prevent airlines from owning television stations. Although there was nothing wrong with this effort at political action, since no FCC personnel were involved, Jones later "did something which must be regarded as imprudent under the circumstances although apparently not ill-intentioned." A memorandum Jones had prepared in October 1956, pointing out North Dade's allegedly superior qualifications for the channel was sent by Jones to Commissioner Craven who had not participated in the agency's decision. Although the memo was not sent to Craven until after the FCC's final decision making the award to Public Service, it was sent before petitions for rehearing were filed. Craven did not vote on those petitions. Judge Stern felt that Jones' "imprudence" would have to be weighed against North Dade in any subsequent allocation of the channel.

The grant of the channel to Public Service should be set aside in light of these findings, Judge Stern concluded, but he did not recommend that any of the applicants be disqualified from ultimate award of the channel. In essence, his recommendation called for a new set of hearings, in which all

four original applicants could participate, but in which the past misconduct of the applicants would be weighed comparatively by the FCC before
the channel was finally allocated. Since the "public interest, convenience
or necessity" must be the controlling consideration for the Commission in
awarding the channel, the wrongdoer should not be repelled by the agency
to the extent of making him "an absolute pariah" in all subsequent proceedings.

The Department of Justice, having been designated by the Court to observe and participate as *amicus curiae,* or "friend of the court," dissented
vigorously from the Examiner's recommendation that no participant be disqualified. Taking issue especially with Judge Stern's interpretation of what
is required and authorized by the standard of "public interest, convenience
or necessity," the attorney general maintained that Public Service, WKAT,
and North Dade should have been permanently and irrevocably disqualified as applicants for Channel 10 since "any applicant before an administrative body that seeks improperly to influence such agency's decision in a
quasi-judicial proceeding should be disqualified."

Contrary to Judge Stern's view, the attorney general argued that the
public interest should not be equated with so narrow a gauge as "best television service." The public interest is best served, rather, by maintaining
and enhancing the "integrity of those quasi-judicial processes from which
Channel 10 and all other licenses spring." The public interest demands that
there be an effective deterrent to attempts at influence that go beyond the
recognized and public processes of adjudication. Disqualification of the
offending parties is the only sanction sufficiently strong to make clear to all
that any applicant resorting to influence beyond the record loses all rights
he seeks. "In sum," the attorney general concluded, "we seek no backward bite for any newly minted standard of conduct. Rather we urge that
the Commission simply announce once again that it will adhere to those
standards which courts as well as itself have long held to govern the activities of the parties."

The Justice Department did not favor an automatic grant of the channel
by default to L. B. Wilson, the only original applicant not found to have
intended or engaged in undue influence. Additional parties should now be
permitted to file applications for the channel along with L. B. Wilson, and
new proceedings should be scheduled, the Department urged.

The attorney general's brief was filed with the FCC on January 14,
1959. Exactly eighteen months later, on July 14, 1960, the Commission announced its decision.

The Commission's Final "Final Decision" / The FCC adopted the
attorney general's view of the public interest insofar as the subject of disqualification was concerned. The Agency ruled that Public Service, WKAT,

and North Dade were barred by virtue of misconduct from consideration for the channel award. The Commission rejected the proposal that new comparative hearings be held, however. It granted the channel to L. B. Wilson, Inc., without affording new applicants who had not been parties to the original proceeding the opportunity to contest the grant in a comparative proceeding. The vote was 4 to 1, with Commissioners Ford, Hyde, King (a Republican from Michigan who had replaced Doerfer in June 1960) and Cross (a Democrat from Alabama who had replaced Mack) in the majority, and Bartley and Craven not participating. Commissioner Lee voted to adopt *in toto* Judge Stern's initial decision.

In sharp contrast to the rambling opinion that accompanied the award of the channel to Public Service Television in 1957, the Commission's opinion this time was terse and succinct. The misconduct of Public Service, WKAT, and North Dade "reflects so adversely upon their character as to demonstrate that they lack the qualifications to operate the station. . . ." The Commission condemned the willingness of the three applicants "to pervert the process of administrative adjudication" and concluded that public interest, convenience, and necessity could not be served were any of the three ultimately to receive the channel. Recognizing that the award to L. B. Wilson under the "peculiar circumstances of this matter [has] resulted in a type of award by default," the Commission limited the initial license it would grant to L. B. Wilson to a period of four months instead of the usual three years.

FCC Votes on the Channel 10 Award: July 1960

WKAT	PUBLIC SERVICE	L. B. WILSON	NORTH DADE	OTHER	ABSTAIN
—	—	Chairman Ford (R.)	—	Lee (R.) (voted to schedule new hearings)	Bartley (D.) Craven (D.)
		Hyde (R.)			
		King (R.)			
		Cross (D.)			

The revocation of the original award to Public Service was to take effect September 15, 1960, but appeals to the judiciary from the Commission's decision by Public Service led the agency to issue an order on September 20 postponing the effective date for setting aside the permit to Public Service until after disposition by the courts of the appeals from the FCC's July 14 decision. On November 20, 1961, after Public Service's appeals failed, L. B. Wilson began operation of the channel.

After eight years of agency proceedings, congressional investigation, and judicial review, Channel 10 in Miami was awarded by default to the only applicant of the original four who was not disqualified by the Commission.

A final tragic footnote to the careers of attorney Whiteside and former Commissioner Mack warrants mention. As of this writing, Mr. Mack lives in seclusion in Florida, his health shattered. Mr. Whiteside is dead; in the spring of 1961, he took his life with a .22 caliber pistol.

The Channel 10 Case in Perspective

How typical of regulatory procedure was the Channel 10 case? It was not, perhaps, typical of all agency procedures, but it nevertheless represented many of the flaws and difficulties faced by all administrative agencies in their regulatory activities. In this single case the FCC reversed its Hearing Examiner's findings, continued its erratic interpretation of "public interest, convenience or necessity," permitted its members to come under the influence of special interests, and allowed "off-the-record" approaches by various legislators.

None of the above circumstances is unique in the FCC's experience. The record shows that the FCC, between 1948 and 1958, reversed Examiners' decisions on television petitions 20 out of 57 times. (The fact that Examiners' decisions are often reversed presents less of a problem than the inconsistent, contradictory reasons for those reversals.) As for the Commission's changeable interpretation of its criteria for awarding licenses, there is a similar haphazardness. James P. Radigan, Jr., of the Legislative Reference Service of the Library of Congress, has found that there are thirteen basic criteria that the FCC weighs in making its awards, yet Radigan also finds that there is almost no discernible consistency in applying those weights. Thus while local ownership may assume overriding importance in one decision, a past broadcasting performance might assume such importance in another decision. As Radigan's study concluded: "Not a single person at the Commission who is concerned with broadcast work will even pretend to demonstrate that the Commission's decisions in its broadcast cases have followed a consistent policy."

These inconsistencies and contradictions create three problems at the same time: they delay important decisions, they frustrate much of the work of the Hearing Examiner, and they enhance the appeal of a "back-door" approach. The greater the range of discretionary power held by the commissioners, the easier for them to yield to sub-, quasi-, and extra-legal pressures.

That the Channel 10 case was a typical illustration of the magnitude of "off-the-record" pressures on agency officials has been borne out by subsequent investigation. The Subcommittee on Legislative Oversight disclosed efforts at ex parte influence of commissioners in at least twelve other television cases. The patterns of behavior of channel applicants, party officials, legislators, and commissioners were similar to those in the Channel 10 case. Only the stations' call letters and the peoples' names were different.

Other agencies have suffered equally from problems of ex parte influence and inconsistent interpretation of standards. This was evidenced by the role of Sherman Adams, former Assistant to President Eisenhower, in intervening "off-the-record" with the Federal Trade Commission in behalf of textile manufacturer Bernard Goldfine; the role of former New Deal official Thomas G. Corcoran in making "off-the-record" visits and telephone calls to Federal Power Commission officials on behalf of Midwestern Gas Transmission Co. while Midwestern's case was pending before the Commission; and the blistering 75-page document submitted as a letter of resignation from the CAB by board member Louis Hector, in the course of which he castigated the agency as "unable to form clear policy," "unable to make sound and comprehensive plans," and "long on judicial form and short on judicial substance." A Washington practitioner, William C. Burt, has described the pressures on agency commissioners as "almost inconceivable." After their appointment they live in a world somewhat akin to Marilyn Monroe's, he maintained, since "everybody who sees them from then on has something in mind." The problem has not escaped the concern of the business community. An article in *Fortune* in June 1961, for example, labeled as the "worst drubbing of all for the public interest" the situation that arises when tractable commissioners, beguiled by blandishments including expense-account entertainment and the promise of jobs after they leave government, slip into the "tender traps of Washington influence peddlers."

What should be done about regulatory problems such as those highlighted in this case? Some commentators find in sordid details like these convincing proof that the regulatory process has failed and that the agencies should be abolished. They maintain that the competition of the market place, dangerous though it may be, is nonetheless preferable to the persistent confusion, uncertainty, and illicit influence that seem to brand the agencies today. Other observers suggest segregating the agencies' legislative functions from their judicial functions. What they urge is leaving the power to make rules unchanged but stripping the agencies of their power to pick a winner from a field of contestants. What they propose is to set up special administrative courts. These courts would then be empowered to handle such "adversary" questions.

When an agency is making rules, the commissioner acts as a legislator. When he weighs the merits of a case, however, he acts as a judge. In order to act as a legislator, he must have access to and familiarity with the broad range of industry problems to which his rule-making is directed. To do that job, the commissioner has to be a mingler. He must go to meetings, attend conventions, and freely associate with leaders of industry. On the other hand, when he acts as a judge, the commissioner must reach his decision isolated from industry influences. Therefore when the commissioner acts as both legislator and judge he at one time creates inherent internal contradictions that inevitably result in weakening one or the other of his functions.

The most prevalent view is that reform, not abolition, is the road to follow. One of the most widely discussed proposals for reform in the past decade was the high priority "Landis Report," written by James M. Landis, former dean of the Harvard Law School, at the request of then-President-elect Kennedy. Landis's suggested remedies focused on reforming the agencies through centralized planning rather than segregating their legislative from their judicial functions.

In brief, the Landis program called for more centralized control by the various agency chairmen, and at the same time it called for more centralized coordination of the activities of all the agencies through the Executive Office of the President. Landis pointed out that in the absence of such planning and coordination, two agencies charged with similar duties—like the ICC and the CAB—might and in fact often do pursue contradictory policies.

Following some of Landis's key recommendations, though ignoring those that would have centralized authority in the Executive Office, President Kennedy sent a Special Message to Congress in April 1961. He advised Congress that he would propose reorganization that would authorize greater delegations of power within the agencies and centralize authority for managerial functions in their respective chairmen. By Executive Order, the President established the Administrative Conference of the United States to study the efficiency, adequacy, and fairness of agency procedures.

When Kennedy's reorganization plans went to Congress, they met a mixed fate. For example, the FCC and the SEC plans went down to rapid defeat. The FTC and the CAB plans squeaked through the Congress by narrow margins some weeks later. A major reason for hostility to these plans can be summed up simply: Legislators view the regulatory agencies as "arms of Congress," hence the task of agency reform is a task to be undertaken by Congress. As an example, basic provisions of the defeated reorganization plan for the FCC were embodied in legislation subsequently passed by Congress in the summer of 1961.

While the prospects for agency reform remain unclear, the realities of day-to-day politics make such reform all the more urgent. The overriding reality is that special interests tend to seek special treatment.

In light of this reality of the American political system, the frank and revealing insight given in 1960 by Senator Everett Dirksen of Illinois into responsibility to constituents in agency matters is worthy of special note.

> Here is Town "A" and there are three applicants for a TV channel. I know every one of them. They are my friends. They vote for me. Some of them may be a little closer than others.
>
> An attorney comes to see me. He is representing Group "X." They are one of the applicants. He says, "Look, we want that television station. Call them up down there. You've got friends down there, haven't you? Call them up and see whether you can't do us some good."
>
> Why, for 26 years my office has been full of attorneys, who come with missions just like that. Now, you see, I can plead the Fifth Amendment, say "I am sorry. I just can't answer your question, I can't make any comment."
>
> He will probably say—"Well, what kind of a friend are you, anyway? Don't you look after your constituents?" So what am I going to say to him? Or am I going to lift the receiver and see what information I get?
>
> These are hard situations and these go on every day. I got a half dozen calls over there in my office I've got to make after a while to some agencies.

This view is not remarkable except for its candor. Men in public life—in both executive and legislative branches—suffer such pressures every day. What is perhaps more important, these same men respond to these pressures.

To label regulatory commissions "independent" under these conditions requires political blinders, for the agencies are in fact the most broadly "dependent" of our government structures.

It should not be our task to make regulatory commissions wholly independent of the President, Congress, and the political system. The pressures of politics, when properly channeled, are creative and vital components of democratic government. Absolute independence of agencies that exercise a combination of legislative, executive, and judicial powers, as the regulatory commissions do, would also impair the "checks and balances" that are basic to our constitutional system. Our task, rather, is to determine how—given the dependence of the Commissions on both President and Congress and their involvement in the political system—we can maximize the fulfillment of their functions with speed, consistency, fairness, and appropriate use of expert knowledge, and minimize the role of illicit influence epitomized by the Channel 10 case. The removal of Richard Mack from the FCC must symbolize something more than a tribal rite. It was more than the sacrifice of an erring human to appease the wrath of some pagan image. It was, in sum, not merely another act that reinforces rather than changes the existing system, but, hopefully, an important sign on the road to reform.

Sources

EMERY, WALTER B. *Broadcasting and Government: Responsibilities and Regulation.* East Lansing: Michigan State Univ. Press, 1961.

FCC v. Pottsville Broadcasting 309 U.S. 134 (1940).

FEDERAL COMMUNICATIONS COMMISSION. In reference to applications of WKAT, Inc.; L. B. Wilson, Inc.; North Dade Video, Inc.; Public Service Television, Inc.; for Television Construction Permit (Docket No. 9321, File No. BPCT-399; Docket No. 10825, File No. BPCT-1645; Docket No. 10826, File No. BPCT-1685; Docket No. 10827, File No. BPCT-1792).

HECTOR, LOUIS. "Problems of the CAB and the Independent Regulatory Commissions." 69 *Yale Law Journal* 931, 1960.

KENDALL, DAVID. "Some Observations about the Administrative Process." 11 *Administrative Law Review* 62, 1958.

KINTNER, EARL W. "Federal Administrative Law in the Decade of the Sixties." 47 *Journal of the American Bar Association* 269, 273, 1961.

LANDIS, JAMES M. "The Administrative Process: The Third Decade." 47 *Journal of the American Bar Association* 135, 1961.

President's Conference on Administrative Procedure. *Report to the President.* Washington, D.C.: Government Printing Office, 1955.

ROSENBLUM, VICTOR G. "Realities of Regulation." 20 *Public Administration Review* 219, 1960.

Special Message of the President to Congress on the Regulatory Agencies. New York *Times,* April 14, 1961.

UNITED STATES SENATE. *Administrative Procedure in Government Agencies* (Report of the Attorney General's Committee on Administrative Procedure). Washington, D.C.: Government Printing Office, 1941.

———, Subcommittee on Administrative Practice and Procedures of the Committee on the Judiciary. *The Landis Report.* Washington, D.C.: Government Printing Office, 1960.

United States House of Representatives, Committee on Government Operations. *Survey and Study of Administrative Organization, Procedure, and Practice.* Washington, D.C.: Government Printing Office, 1958.

———, Special Subcommittee on Legislative Oversight of the Committee on Interstate and Foreign Commerce. *Investigation of Regulatory Commissions and Agencies.* Washington, D.C.: Government Printing Office, 1959.

———, Special Subcommittee on Legislative Oversight of the Committee on Interstate and Foreign Commerce. *Report on Independent Regulatory Commissions.* Washington, D.C.: Government Printing Office, 1960.

WESTIN, ALAN F. "An Inquiry into Our Watchdog Agencies." *New York Times Magazine,* October 23, 1960.

WIBC v. FCC 259 F.2nd 941 (1958).

WKAT v. FCC 258 F.2nd 418 (1958).

5 POLITICAL PARTIES

The Unsolid South:

A Challenge to the Democratic National Party

Allan P. Sindler

DUKE UNIVERSITY

"Have we reached a point, my friends of the Democratic Party, when we no longer believe that the Democratic Party stands for States' Rights? . . . If [the South] . . . [is] defeated, then I say to you that you are witnessing here today the dissolution of the Democratic Party in the South."
——CECIL SIMS
OF TENNESSEE

"To those who say we are rushing this issue of civil rights, I say to them, we are 172 years late. . . . The time has arrived in America for the Democratic Party to get out of the shadows of States' Rights and to walk forthrightly into the bright sunshine of human rights."
——HUBERT HUMPHREY
OF MINNESOTA

SOUTHERN states provided—from the end of the Civil Wa:

until recent decades—the outstanding example of durable sectionalism in American politics. Two factors distinguish the South from the rest of the nation: (1) secession from the Union to form the Confederacy, and (2) persistent Democratic loyalty in presidential elections to the extent of not having gone Republican more than two times in the period from 1876— the end of Reconstruction—through 1944. Of all the American states, the same eleven meet both conditions: Virginia, North Carolina, South Carolina, Georgia, Florida, Tennessee, Alabama, Mississippi, Arkansas, Louisiana, and Texas. The term, "the North," as here used, refers to all states except the eleven Southern states, i.e., the non-South is the North.

Although Americans are today commemorating the centennial of the Civil War, South-North tensions still persist on many fronts. In politics, there are dramatic conflicts between the two, particularly within the Democratic national party. After the Democrats became the majority party in the nation in the 1930's, Southerners began to re-examine seriously their traditional commitment to Democratic presidential candidates. With the new directions that party policy took during the New Deal and the Fair Deal and the political groups and economic interests that became integral parts of the Democratic national coalition, the historic Democratic partisanship of Southerners was increasingly strained. Ultimately that strain led to party revolt by the South.

This case study details the various roads of party rebellion traveled by Southern Democratic leaders in their efforts to increase their region's influence in presidential politics and within the national party. It focuses on (1) the new problems of party loyalty and the related conflicts between state party and national party stirred by the Southern revolt; and (2) the political changes within the South resulting from its defection from the Democratic party in presidential elections.

Scene: The 1952 Democratic Convention

The Difficulties Facing the Democrats /   In the week before their 31st national convention (July 21–26, 1952), as the Democrats began moving into the Conrad Hilton Hotel and the International Amphitheatre in Chicago —the same arena recently vacated by the Republicans—it was apparent to all that the party was in real trouble. The fact that the Democrats after 1932 had enjoyed unbroken control of the White House and nearly unbroken control of Congress (except for 1947–48) was small comfort to the party's leaders. Nor were they comforted by being the majority party in the nation as far as the preference of the man in the street went.

The difficulties stemmed in part, as frequently must happen in any truly competitive party system, from the new strength of the opposition party. At a rousing Republican convention, one that made fascinating television viewing for millions of Americans, General Dwight D. Eisenhower defeated Ohio Senator Robert A. Taft for the presidential nomination. Involved in that outcome was a commitment by the Republicans to a greater degree of liberalism and, even more, to the hard-headed conviction that the General, whatever his political philosophy, could win the election, while Senator Taft—"Mr. Republican"—could not. Among other assets, Eisenhower could be expected to hold a strong position on foreign policy, particularly when it came to the popular dissatisfaction over the Korean war. Republicans also expected to capitalize on Eisenhower's nonpolitical image in castigating the Democrats for numerous instances of corruption in high places of government. In similar fashion, the selection of Senator Richard M. Nixon of California as Eisenhower's running mate would serve, in view of the close identification of Nixon with the exposure of Alger Hiss, to underline Republican accusations that the Democrats had been "soft on Communism."

The condition of their own party no less than the appeal of the opposition ticket contributed to the difficulties of the Democrats. The grand coalition of diverse and often contradictory groups, areas, and interests that Franklin Delano Roosevelt had constructed and led was threatened by disintegration. True, Harry S. Truman had earned his surprise victory in 1948 by hitting hard with the liberal and bread-and-butter themes of the New Deal, but he came nowhere near being the effective and popular leader of nation, party, and Congress that FDR had been. At its 1952 convention, therefore, the Democratic party was faced with making fundamental decisions on leadership succession, group support, and policy direction.

Democratic anxieties were further aggravated by ambiguities and tensions concerning the two key goals of any American major party as it assembles for its quadrennial convention: the designation of a politically effective presidential candidate and the reinvigoration of party unity so that the party can mobilize its full resources in the election. Yet even as the Democrats refurbished the convention hall near the stockyards—replacing the picture of Lincoln with those of Jefferson, Jackson, Wilson, FDR, and Truman—the remoteness of those goals was the ever-present topic of worry and discussion. For the first time in twenty years, the Democratic convention was "open" as to the selection of a presidential nominee. In addition, the threat of a split between Northern and Southern wings of the party hovered over the convention.

President Truman, acting in the belief that the uncertainty surrounding his renomination intentions enhanced his political influence, delayed announcing that he would not run again until late March. On the eve of the convention, in order to reaffirm that position, Truman had National Chairman Frank E. McKinney leak to the press the former's observations that the Presidency was a "man-killing job," and that his response to the question of his availability for another term was: "You wouldn't want to see me carried out of the White House in a pine box." Informed speculation had it that Truman might be prevailed on to accept the nomination in the event the party became hopelessly deadlocked; otherwise, it was understood that the President was out of the running.

Although he was most eager to exert active influence if not direct control over the convention's choice of a presidential candidate, Truman had not been able to find and endorse his successor before the convention began. The difficulties facing Truman were those facing other party chieftains as well: to locate a leader in the authentic tradition of the New Deal and the Fair Deal who could both unify the party and appeal broadly to the voting citizenry.

The omnipresent threat of a sectional split provided the other main source of tension at the Democratic convention. The conflict between the South and the rest of the party was deep-running; its high emotionalism revolved around the issue of extending federal protection of the civil rights of Negroes. The irreconcilability of Northern and Southern views on the matter was illustrated at the 1948 Democratic convention when, for example, Tennessean Cecil Sims and Minnesotan Hubert H. Humphrey spoke right past each other during the sectional fight on strengthening the civil rights plank of the party platform:

> SIMS: "Have we reached a point, my friends of the Democratic Party, when we no longer believe that the Democratic Party stands for States' Rights? . . . If we from the South, having extended the hand of friendship to this Convention, if we are defeated, then I say to you that you are witnessing here today the dissolution of the Democratic Party in the South."

HUMPHREY: "My friends, to those who say we are rushing this issue of civil rights, I say to them, we are 172 years late. To those who say that this civil rights program is an infringement on States' Rights, I say this, that the time has arrived in America for the Democratic Party to get out of the shadows of States' Rights and to walk forthrightly into the bright sunshine of human rights."

At that same 1948 convention, state senator Edgar A. Brown, a power in South Carolina politics, warned, "the people of the [Southern] states have been buffeted around long enough and they are not going to stand for it any longer." And some Southern states made good on their threat to desert the Democratic party in the presidential election of 1948.

The events from 1948 through mid-1952 provided no settlement of the sectional feud. Notwithstanding the endorsement by the 1948 convention of a vigorous civil rights plank, the South used its strength in the Senate to block enactment of any and all of Truman's civil rights program. It was against this backdrop that the regional wings of the national party braced for their encounter during the 1952 convention. Senator Herbert H. Lehman (New York), representative of militant liberals on the matter, told reporters that one of his principal objectives in coming to Chicago was "to fight for a strong and forward-looking platform which will be outspoken and unequivocal on the great issues of our times, including but not confined to civil rights." Might not the South then bolt the party? The CIO's Walter Reuther had an answer to that one. "We do not believe the South will bolt," he wrote in a letter to the platform committee, "but if it so chooses, let this happen. Let the realignment of the parties proceed." The hearings held before the platform subcommittees during preconvention week ran the gamut from plans to ensure world peace, to farm and labor policy, to twice-a-day home mail delivery. The focus of public attention, however, never left the civil rights issue, neither as to the content of that plank nor as to the related plank on strengthening the closure rules of the Senate so as to reduce the ability of Southerners to filibuster bills to death.

The Interplay of Candidate Strategies and Sectional Tensions / It was inevitable that the three sources of Democratic difficulties—the appeal of the Republican ticket, the uncertainty as to presidential nominee, and the possibility of intense sectional discord—would become intertwined in the thinking of many delegates at the convention. Solutions proposed for these difficulties derived basically from one or the other of two opposing strategies.

The *unifier* strategy developed the argument that the Democrats required a unified party in order to defeat Eisenhower: the electoral votes of a handful of big Northern states in combination with those of the Solid South would ensure Democratic victory. What was required was the nomination of a man who could satisfy Northern liberals and Southern conservatives, both at the convention and in the ensuing election. The fact that the Republicans had adopted a weak civil rights plank with which Negro groups were displeased provided, according to the unifiers, elbow room for the Democrats to compose their differences on civil rights.

The alternative *sectionalist* strategy presented the argument that no Democratic candidate could match the personality appeal of Eisenhower, and therefore the emphasis must be on the Democratic party program. The key to party victory, in this view, was to stress the liberal image of the Democratic party with special reference to domestic policies long associated with the New and Fair Deals so that, negatively, Eisenhower could be attacked as a "front man" for Republican "reactionaries" and, positively, the Democrats could once again reactivate those group alignments that had come through to give Truman victory in 1948. This strategy was deliberately indifferent to the possibilities of Southern antagonism and defection; the emphasis was entirely on appealing to the voters of the urbanized and industrialized non-South. The fact that the Republicans had adopted a weak civil rights plank was interpreted, by the sectionalists, as an opportunity for the Democrats to provide the strongest contrast in making an effective appeal to the Negro and other minority ethnic-religious groups.

The strategy of the unifiers was held by Truman, the convention management (National Chairman Frank McKinney, Permanent Convention Chairman Sam Rayburn, etc.), and probably by a majority of the delegates, but its influence was markedly handicapped by the absence of a major presidential aspirant around whom those holding these views could coalesce. Only two of the prominent presidential possibilities met the needs of the unifiers; one withdrew from the contest on the first day of the convention and the other never directly entered the contest.

Vice President Alben W. Barkley, a veteran political leader from the border state of Kentucky, was much beloved personally in the party and enjoyed the respect and friendship of the South notwithstanding his consistent Fair Deal record, which included support for the Truman civil rights program. But when organized labor indicated its opposition to Barkley's candidacy on the grounds that his age (74) precluded political victory, Barkley—after referring bitterly to "certain self-anointed political labor leaders"—publicly withdrew his candidacy on Monday night, the first day of the convention.

The other possibility, Illinois Governor Adlai E. Stevenson, was not a candidate at all. And his noncandidacy was genuine and not to be confused with the sham coyness imposed on aspirants to high office by the prevailing ethic that the office should seek the man and not the reverse. Ever since January 1952, when Truman had first tried without success to interest

Stevenson in the presidential nomination, he had consistently taken the position that he was firmly committed to running for re-election for the Illinois governorship. While Stevenson indicated that he might accede to a genuine draft, he stressed that he would not participate "overtly or covertly, in any movement to draft me" and he would have to be shown the existence of such a genuine draft. After addressing the convention in his capacity as host governor, Stevenson secreted himself for the first three days of the convention at the home of a friend on fashionable N. Astor Street. (The street was promptly invaded by newsmen with portable telephone booths and television trucks.) The governor's cause at the convention was promoted by a volunteer Draft Stevenson Committee, led by a history professor from the University of Chicago and headquartered at the Conrad Hilton Hotel. The Committee operated without permission from or any contact or consultation with Stevenson himself. The ultimate nomination of Stevenson thus was one of the few instances of a true draft of a major-party presidential candidate. But the convention delegates, not possessed of a crystal ball, knew during the first half of the convention only that the apparent unavailability of Stevenson greatly undermined the chances of success of the unifier strategy.

The presidential bid of Senator Richard B. Russell (Georgia) was presumably intended to represent a variation of the unifier strategy, but it never was able to escape the confines of a sectional Southern context. Truman put it succinctly in his *Memoirs:* "Dick Russell . . . had ability, integrity, and honesty. . . . But being from Georgia . . . he did not have a serious chance of being nominated. I believe that if Russell had been from Indiana or Missouri or Kentucky he may very well have been the President of the United States." The inability of a Southern leader to appeal to the non-South was made apparent when, during the preconvention week, Senator Russell appeared to change his mind on the Taft-Hartley labor act and stated that it was "weighted against labor [and] must be supplanted by new legislation. . . ." Organized labor denounced the move as a hoax, since Russell had not only voted for the Act initially but once again, to override the President's veto of it. Right-wing Southerners called Russell on the carpet and had him subsequently explain that he was not in favor of repeal of the Act. Commented the conservative Richmond *Times-Dispatch,* referring to Russell's prorepeal stand, "If the Southern Senators and Governors can forgive this kind of behavior, they can forgive anything."

The sectionalist strategy of ultraliberals was represented by the candidacies of Averell Harriman (New York) and Senator Estes Kefauver (Tennessee). Harriman had been wartime ambassador to Russia and was close to Truman, having been his Secretary of Commerce from 1946–48 and then serving as his Mutual Security Administrator after 1951. The wealthy Harriman, who was neither a particularly effective political speaker nor a dynamic personality, pursued his ambitions with two tactics: (1) pushing a right-down-the-line Fair Deal program for the party; and (2) depending on the hope that his friend, the President, might decide to support him. (Truman had warned those delegates who were hard at work on the platform that "there must be no betrayal of the New Deal and the Fair Deal.")

Senator Kefauver, because of the well-televised revelations of his crime committee on the links between organized crime and urban politicos, had become a household word with the public, but a dirty word with many big-city Democratic leaders. Yet on the other hand, his liberal voting record cut him off from a serious chance for Southern support at the convention. Under those conditions, Kefauver found himself pursuing the same sort of sectional strategy as Harriman.

Thus, as the Democratic convention began, the New York *Times* report was accurate in stating that "no candidate comes to the convention with votes enough to make a good show and no two candidates have sufficient strength between them to form a winning combination." Recognizing that situation, the Harriman and Kefauver forces, in temporary alliance, attempted to stampede a convention majority into endorsing their "the-devil-with-the-South" position—a move designed to repudiate the unifier strategy and to enhance the prospects for their own convention victory. The proximate cause of the sectional controversy that followed thus related to the maneuverings of candidates in an "open" convention. But the underlying causes of that sectional controversy related to the reasons for increasing Southern disaffection with the Democratic party and to the manner in which the South expressed that disaffection in the 1948 presidential election. A review of those factors provides the backdrop necessary to a full understanding of the South-North struggle within the Democratic party at the 1952 national convention.

Background: Smith, Roosevelt, and Truman

For a collection of states to comprise a unified section in national politics presupposes high agreement within each of the states and common agreement among the states on which problems are most important and which attitudes towards those problems are correct. It would be difficult, after all, to envision a group of states without such a sense of unity maintaining a persistent sectional position in national politics. On what, then, does the political solidarity of the South rest?

Although such regional features as a one-crop (cotton) agrarianism, low per capita income, and intense nativism have contributed to the development of the unity of the South, the fundamental determinant of

Southernism has been the presence of the Negro in large numbers relative to the whites, and resulting white supremacy doctrines and patterns of behavior. A South divorced from the problem of race would not have been a Solid South; a South preoccupied with race problems became a Solid South. Broadly speaking, the development of the Solid South involved the actions of the former states of the Confederacy, passively consented to by the North, in fashioning institutions, laws, and practices designed to maintain the free Negro in a position subordinate to that of whites. Whites living in areas with high proportions of Negro population (black-belt whites) were the most aggressive in pursuit of this racial goal, but virtually all whites accepted the necessity and legitimacy of the objectives of race supremacy.

Negro influence in Southern state and local politics was effectively barred by the monopoly position of the Democratic party in combination with the exclusion of the Negro from participation in the nominating process within the Democratic party. The nominating process was the only meaningful point of political choice and control. The hopes of whites that significant political divisions among themselves could be sustained within one-partyism have been only incompletely realized. In the main the South has not been able to secure benefits from its patterns of competition within the dominant Democratic party comparable to those many non-Southern states have had from their patterns of two-party competition between Democrats and Republicans.

The South's commitment to the national Democratic party coincided, during the first three decades of this century, with a period in which the country was "normally" Republican in national elections. As *the* large sectional stronghold of the minority national party (before 1932), the South's influence within the Democratic party naturally was high. The Democratic party thus supported the South's view of the race problem as one to be handled by state authorities. At the same time, the party adequately represented the South's economic interests. Important and continuous influence within Congress was assured the South by virtue of the number of Southern legislators, their high positions on the ladder of seniority, and their cohesion on matters vital to the region—characteristics that remain conspicuous even on the current political scene. In the selection of presidential and vice-presidential candidates also, Southern strength within the party was made relatively secure by the convention rule that required a two-thirds majority for nomination.

Southern loyalty to the Democratic party developed vested interests and emotional attachments within the region over the years, enhancing the capacity of the one-party system to perpetuate itself. Nonetheless, it must be remembered that the South's commitment to one-partyism was a means to an end, not an end in itself. Therefore, the continued satisfaction of the

South with its national one-partyism depended on the sorts of policies endorsed by the Democrats, particularly by the presidential, as distinguished from the congressional, wing of the party. And the presidential candidate's political hue depended, in turn, on the sorts of groups to which the Democrats wished to make an effective appeal in order to become the majority national party. To oversimplify, the question for the future was: would the new non-Southern elements that had been attracted to the Democrats be compatible with Southern influence or would they overwhelm Southern influence within the party on those core matters that agitated the South and gave it sectional unity?

The presidential candidacy in 1928 of New York Governor Alfred E. Smith—a Catholic of recent Irish immigrant stock, a "wet" on the liquor issue, a big-city product, and an ally of Tammany Hall—reflected the conscious attempt of the Democratic party to cut into the Republican loyalties of urban-industrial-immigrant voters in the North. By the same token, Smith's candidacy placed the party loyalty of many Southerners under severe strain. The election resulted in a considerably larger Republican vote in all Southern states, with Republican candidate Herbert Hoover actually carrying five states in the South with from 52 to 57 per cent of the popular vote: Florida, Texas, North Carolina, Virginia, and Tennessee. The Deep South states and black-belt whites—those with the greatest stake in the maintenance of racial supremacy—were most resistant to party defection. While the cracking of the Solid South testified to the capacity of the rim-South states to desert the Democratic party when under sufficient provocation, the special vulnerability of Smith's candidacy in the region made the 1928 election unusual, hence not necessarily a firm indication of continued party bolting by the South.

Contemporary Southern rebellion within and outside the Democratic party stems more directly from events since 1932, when the Democratic party became the dominant national party and espoused the New Deal and the Fair Deal programs. Southern conservatives grew increasingly resentful of the liberal labor, welfare, and economic legislation and of the expansion of national governmental authority and action initiated and supported by Roosevelt and Truman. Even more offensive to Southern sensibilities was the nature of the new group of "partners" with which the South was linked in the Democratic party: organized labor, big-city machines and bosses, ethnic and racial minorities, including the Negro. Perceptive Southern conservatives accurately judged that a Democratic party so constituted not only failed to represent adequately the regional interests of the South in national politics (as they saw those interests), but also threatened to hasten the development and expression of economic conflict within Democratic politics in each Southern state.

The greatest impetus to party revolt was provided by the same aroused racial anxieties that had committed the region to partisan solidarity in the first place. The presidential camp of the Democratic party, allied with political leaders in the key urban and industrial states of the North, increasingly took up the cause of the advancement of the Negro. The political power of the Negro was also rising. Negro leaders spoke less of "racial accommodation" and more of "racial protest." With racist doctrines discredited by Hitler's program of mass extermination of European Jewry, the Southern view on race relations was put more than ever on the defensive and, in the nation as a whole, in the minority. As a final blow, the federal judiciary also became more receptive to Negro efforts to achieve legal equality. In the area of political rights, for example, the U.S. Supreme Court flatly held that the white primary was unconstitutional in 1944.

Incidents symptomatic of rising Southern discontent were not lacking during Roosevelt's term of office. In the 1936 national convention, parts of the South provided most of the minority opposition to the elimination of the two-thirds nomination rule that had been in effect since 1832. The great court reform (or "court-packing") controversy of 1937 split the Democratic party along its conservative–liberal axis. The South emerged as the Court's foremost sectional defender. (Yet another indication of the changed environment for the South is that in recent years the trend of Court rulings has made the South the chief sectional critic of the Supreme Court.) 1938 marked Roosevelt's largely unsuccessful attempts to "purge" several conservative Southern Democratic legislators by intervention in their bids for the primary nomination. In the 1940 convention, Roosevelt had some difficulty in securing approval of Henry A. Wallace as his running mate; more than three-quarters of the South's vote was cast for a Southern opposition candidate. At the 1944 convention, dissident Southerners cast a futile 87½ protest votes for Senator Harry F. Byrd (Virginia) against the renomination of Roosevelt for a fourth term. Then, in alliance with other conservatives, the AFL, and some big-city bosses, Southern delegates succeeded in rejecting Wallace (who no longer had Roosevelt's firm support) and in nominating Senator Harry S. Truman (Missouri) for the vice-presidential post, an important outcome in view of the death, five months after his re-election, of President Roosevelt.

The quarrel of Southern conservatives with Roosevelt was also expressed, though feebly, in presidential elections. Third-party slates of electors were entered in deliberate opposition to FDR in Texas in 1936, in South Carolina in 1940, and in both those states as well as in Mississippi in 1944. The highest proportion of any state's popular vote won by these five insurgent slates was 11.8 per cent, obtained in Texas in 1944. Whatever the eagerness of Southern conservatives to revolt, they lacked a basis for regional mass appeal and, even assuming they had that basis, Roosevelt would have won all four of his elections had every Southern electoral vote gone to the Republicans.

These hard facts no longer existed after President Truman assumed office in April 1945. Truman's lower political standing and influence invited aggressive attack by interests opposed to the policies of his Fair Deal. That such an attack would be forthcoming from the South was virtually guaranteed when, in October 1947, the President's Committee on Civil Rights issued its report and then, in early February 1948, when Truman went on to urge congressional action on some (*not* all) of the Committee's recommendations. The Truman civil rights program urged congressional adoption of the following:

(1) Organizational changes to acknowledge the importance of the government's job of protecting civil rights and to administer civil rights legislation more effectively: a Joint Congressional Committee on Civil Rights, a Division of Civil Rights in the Department of Justice, and the re-establishment of a Fair Employment Practices Commission, which had been operative from mid-1941 to mid-1946.

(2) Additional statutory protection: strengthening of laws protecting citizens in the enjoyment of rights secured by the federal Constitution, anti-lynching law, protection of the right to vote (including prohibition of poll taxes as a condition of voting in federal elections), and prohibition of enforcement of segregation in interstate carriers by the carriers themselves (state laws requiring such segregation had been held void).

At long last, here was the spark that Southern dissidents could use to touch off a large-scale revolt against the national Democratic party.

1948: The Dixiecrats Revolt

The States' Rights (or Dixiecrat) rebellion in 1948, was in preparation well in advance of the Democratic national convention. The rebellion was undertaken on the reasonable assumptions that Truman, as the incumbent President, could not be stopped from securing the presidential nomination and that, in any event, the national platform would include a civil rights plank repugnant to the South. Dixiecrat leaders, therefore, thought in terms of revenge in the election-to-come in exchange for defeat in the convention-at-hand. The immediate goal of the Dixiecrats was to deny to Truman any significant number of Southern electoral votes. The aim, of course, was to bring about his outright defeat, or possibly to deadlock the electoral college and throw the choice of president into the House, or—at least—to make an already defeated Truman lose by that much more. Whatever the result, the national Democratic party would be made to realize its dependency on Southern support. Hence the party would be obliged in the future

to cater more to Southern interests. Since the Dixiecrats were satisfied with
the Democratic party at the state level, these plans for party defection were
confined entirely to presidential politics. There was no clear idea of what
the Dixiecrat movement would do after 1948—much depended, of course,
on how the movement did in 1948.

The impetus behind the Dixiecrat revolt derived from a potent mixture
of racial fears (played up prominently for vote-getting appeal) and of
economic conservatism (consciously assigned a less prominent role). The
judgment of the Little Rock, Arkansas *Gazette* of February 21, 1948 was
accurate: "The race issue is by no means the sole cause of the great division in Democratic ranks. It is no accident that those who are loudest now
in denouncing Mr. Truman are the same Southern Democrats who have
also taken issue with him and with his predecessor on many other matters
—labor legislation, price controls, public power, federal spending, etc." To
that list should be added explicitly the Dixiecrat position in opposition to
federal control of tidelands oil, a position not calculated to alienate the
affections or lessen the financial contributions of the petroleum industry.

That the initiative and drive for the party revolt came from the Deep
South states and black-belt leaders dramatically symbolized the changed
relationship between the South and the national Democratic party. In laying
heavy stress on Truman's civil rights program—"the most vital single issue
facing the country at this time," as former Governor Frank Dixon of Alabama put it—Dixiecrat leaders grossly misrepresented it as seeking "social
equality by Federal fiat," as one "that would eliminate segregation of every
kind from all American life." President Truman's later evaluation in his
Memoirs was in accord with the facts:

> My appeal for equal economic and political rights for every American
> citizen had nothing at all to do with the personal or social relationships of
> individuals or the right of every person to choose his own associates. The
> basic constitutional privilege which I advocated was deliberately miscon-
> strued to include or imply racial miscegenation and intermarriage. My only
> goal was equal opportunity and security under the law for all classes of
> Americans.

The positive themes of the Dixiecrats, consciously broader than the South's
special concern with civil rights, embraced a wide-ranging defense of individual liberties, local self-government, states' rights, and constitutional
processes on economic and other matters.

The central strategy of the States' Righters was to gain control of the
machinery of the state Democratic party in as many Southern states as
possible. Capture of the state party organization would bring with it the
ability to instruct the state delegation as to its participation in the national
convention and, most crucially, to decide what presidential electors were

POLITICAL PARTIES   **242**

to go under what party label. In this sense, the 1948 presidential contest in
the South was fought out within the governing bodies of the state Democratic parties, the focal point being the determination of which electors
were to appear on the ballot, and under what party designation.

The Democratic National Convention, 1948 / Surveying the South-
wide scene just prior to the opening of the Democratic national convention,
it was evident that all the states of the region were hostile to Truman's
candidacy and to his civil rights proposals. Moreover, all but two states had
altered their party rules to redefine loyal Democrats (candidates and voters) in terms of those who supported the Democratic nominees for all
state, county, and local offices. The purpose of the deliberate exclusion
from the party rules of support for the Democratic presidential nominee
was to permit Democrats to vote Dixiecratic without thereby jeopardizing
their standing as good Democrats. The two exceptions were states operating
by the direct primary, Alabama and Florida. In mid-September, in response
to Dixiecrat pressures, the Florida legislature released Democratic party
members from any obligation to vote for the Democratic national ticket.
In Alabama, Democrats remained (technically) obligated to vote for all
party primary winners, including presidential electors.

The willingness to bolt the national Democratic party, however, was by
no means as uniform as the antipathy to Truman and to civil rights. Adherents of the no-bolting view seemed firmly in control of the state party
in Texas, Arkansas, Louisiana, Tennessee, North Carolina, and Florida.
In Georgia, the Talmadge and anti-Talmadge factions, preferring not to
inject the issue of a party bolt into their ongoing gubernatorial contest,
committed themselves (at least temporarily) to working within the national
party. In Virginia, the Byrd organization's inclinations to party rebellion
were sharply modified by the resistance of the state legislature. The upshot
was a decision to encourage the state party convention to reconvene and
consider appropriate action with regard to presidential electors in the event
that Truman was nominated.

The remaining Southern states—Mississippi, South Carolina, and Alabama—went much farther down the road of revolt. At its meeting on
June 22, the Mississippi state Democratic convention passed a set of resolutions that were incorporated as part of the credentials of the delegation
sent to the national convention. These resolutions provided, among other
things, that the Mississippi delegates would withdraw from the national
convention if Truman were nominated, if Truman's civil rights program
were not "publicly condemned," and if the platform did not embody a
positive states' rights plank. These restricted credentials of the Mississippi
delegation further stated that the delegates of Mississippi were "without
power or authority to bind or pledge support of the Democratic Party of

Mississippi, or the Democrats of Mississippi, to support and vote for the nominees of the National Democratic Convention" if any of the conditions cited above were not met. The South Carolina Democratic party, at its May 19 session, instructed its electors to vote against any candidate favorable to civil rights. The Alabama situation crystallized through the outcome of primaries held in May and June to choose Democratic presidential electors and delegates to the national convention, at which the black-belt faction advocated party rebellion and the economic liberal faction (including Senator Lister Hill and Governor James E. Folsom) urged a no-bolting view. Fourteen of the 26 delegates elected were pledged to walk out if the convention adopted a civil rights plank. The other 12 were committed to remain in the convention. All of the winning presidential electors were pledged to vote against any nominee unsatisfactory on the civil rights question.

The Deep South seemingly had picked a most advantageous time to press its regional cause of party revolt. Gloom and disunity hung over the 30th Democratic National Convention meeting at Philadelphia in mid-July. Truman was on the outs with much of his party and in low standing with the public. He was given little chance to win the election by friend, foe, or neutral. Henry Wallace announced that, regardless of what happened at the Democratic convention, he would lead a third-party movement against the Democrats from the Left. The situation appeared sufficiently desperate to impel some Northern liberals and urban bosses to try to ditch Truman at the last minute and to persuade General Eisenhower to run for the Democratic nomination. (Included among these Democratic leaders anxious to drop Truman was Colonel Jacob Arvey of Chicago; gubernatorial nominee Adlai E. Stevenson remained firmly for Truman.) Eisenhower's unequivocal refusal left these would-be insurgents in a rather uncomfortable position. It was in the light of all these splintering tendencies encouraged by the expectation of election defeat and by dissatisfaction with Truman's policies that Permanent Chairman Sam Rayburn's admonition to the delegates should be understood: "The Democratic Party has been the majority party . . . for 16 years, and for God's sake at this Convention let us act like it."

Four major instances of sectional conflict developed at the national convention:

(1) A minority report of the credentials committee, signed by ten members, including Adlai E. Stevenson, urged that the Mississippi delegation not be seated because of the nature of its restricted credentials. The convention, by voice vote, rejected the minority report and adopted the majority report. However, various Northern delegations then requested that the record show their affirmative vote for the minority report; by such means a total of 503 votes not to seat Mississippi was compiled, some 115

votes shy of a convention majority. Since more Northern votes were readily available on behalf of the minority report, it was apparent that the North was, in effect, warning the South to moderate its rebellious tendencies at the convention or suffer retaliatory action. The warning was not heeded by the South, and the seating of the Mississippi delegation inadvertently established a precedent that dissident Southerners would be happy to exploit anew in 1952.

(2) A Southern drive to have the two-thirds nomination rule restored was decisively defeated by voice vote.

(3) Three Southern-sponsored amendments to the platform, each seeking to add an affirmation of the states' rights position, were defeated, two of them by voice vote and the other by vote of 925–309. On the other hand, an amendment to strengthen the civil rights plank by specifying the elements of the Truman program was passed, 651½–582½. The floor fight for the amendment was led by Congressman Andrew J. Biemiller (Wisconsin) and Hubert H. Humphrey (mayor of Minneapolis and senatorial nominee), and its passage was based on the support of the large and medium-sized Northern states as against the opposition of the South, the border states, and many of the small states without regard to region. (President Truman, for tactical and perhaps other reasons, did not support the Biemiller-Humphrey report until after the convention had adopted it.) Convention adoption of the platform precipitated a walk-out by half the Alabama delegation and the entire Mississippi delegation. It led to heated warnings by other Southern spokesmen to the delegates that "You shall not crucify the South on this cross of civil rights."

(4) Truman easily secured the presidential nomination on the first ballot (947½ votes), all of the remaining ten Southern delegations except North Carolina voting solidly for Senator Russell (Georgia) and providing him with virtually all of his 263 votes. The South persisted in its mood of resistance even when Senator Barkley (Kentucky) was placed in nomination, with Truman's blessing, for the vice-presidential spot. Alabama, Arkansas, and Florida supported Senator Russell, and when the Georgia delegation withdrew Russell's name, the other Southern states preferred to pass rather than to second Barkley's nomination. By a nonunanimous voice vote, Barkley was nominated.

The Presidential Election / Their resolve fortified, dissident Southern Democrats adhered to their earlier-formulated plan of holding a Birmingham "conference" on July 17. (Since it was obvious that the Democratic leaders of some Southern states had never warmed to the idea of party rebellion, the Dixiecrats had adopted the device of calling "grass-roots" conferences, open to any and all citizens who believed in states' rights and who opposed the civil rights program.) The States' Rights party was created, a "declaration of principles" was adopted, and a national ticket was nominated: Governor J. Strom Thurmond (South Carolina) for president and Governor Fielding L. Wright (Mississippi) for vice-president. Having formalized their movement, the States' Righters then intensified their efforts to gain control of the state party organizations in order to control the placement of presidential electors on the state ballot.

In four Southern states, Mississippi, South Carolina, Louisiana, and Alabama, the Dixiecrats succeeded in having the Thurmond-Wright electors placed on the ballot under the emblem (the rooster) of the state Democratic party. In all but Alabama the Truman-Barkley ticket was also on the ballot. In Alabama, all of the presidential electors elected in the spring primaries had been pledged not to vote for a nominee unsound on the civil rights question. Because, under state law, there was no method by which the names of the national party nominees could be put on the ballot (and Governor Folsom tried vainly in state and federal courts to compel the Alabama Democratic electors to vote for the national party ticket), Alabama had the distinction of being the only state in the nation in which the Truman-Barkley names did not appear on the ballot.

In Florida, action by the legislature so arranged the ballot form that neither Thurmond nor Truman was given the important advantage of possession of the state party label. In the remaining six Southern states, the state party emblem was assigned to the Truman-Barkley slate, and the Dixiecrats had to content themselves with placing an independent or third-party slate on the ballot. The Dixiecrats, however, did not lack for influential leaders in these states. In Georgia, for example, many of Talmadge's lieutenants worked for Thurmond. And in Virginia the Democratic state executive committee took the unorthodox tack of declaring its neutrality in the presidential race while urging good Democrats to support the party nominees for all other offices!

In the November election, the States' Rights ticket received 2.4 per cent (1,169,312) of the total popular vote, nearly all of it concentrated in the South. Of the Southwide popular vote, Thurmond got 22.6 per cent, Dewey 26.6 per cent, and Truman exactly 50 per cent. The Dixiecrats won the 38 electoral votes of four states, Mississippi, South Carolina, Louisiana, and Alabama. Their total popular vote in these four states was over half their Southwide vote. In the remaining seven states, Thurmond's proportion of the popular vote ranged from 8.8 to 20.3 per cent, and in each of them (with the exception of Georgia), his vote was less than that cast for the Republican Dewey-Warren ticket.

In the four states carried by the Dixiecrats—unlike the situation in Tennessee, North Carolina, and Virginia—Democratic leaders wishing to defect did not have to worry about the possibility of a Democratic split permitting a Republican state victory. In addition, the four were Deep South states, with high proportions of Negro population and of whites acutely sensitive to the race question. The suspicion that the bedrock political appeal of the Dixiecrats lay in exploitation of racial fears of whites has been confirmed. Professor Alexander Heard has noted, "In state after state the Dixiecrats won their greatest support among the whites who live closest to large numbers of Negroes. . . . Many of them [whites] have little in common with the leaders of the Dixiecrats except a susceptibility to Negrophobia." Finally, the four states were the only ones in which the state Democratic label had been assigned to Thurmond. Although the capture of the state Democratic emblem by the Dixiecrats was in good part the product of the factors just discussed, it exerted an independent influence of considerable benefit to the party bolters. By operating under the Democratic label, Dixiecrats gained the support of those who habitually voted the Democratic ticket and strengthened both the legitimacy and attractiveness of their bolt from the national party.

The Dixiecrats Fail—Or Do They? /   There is much to support the view that the Dixiecrat movement was a failure: it neither achieved its immediate aim of defeating Truman, nor demonstrated impressive South-wide backing, nor had any clear future as a party except as a subregional third-party competitor in presidential politics. Its continued exploitation of the race issue might help it retain a following, particularly in black-belt areas, but there was little that the Democratic national party (or the Republicans for that matter) would want or could afford to do to placate the Dixiecrats on that issue.

At the same time, the States' Rights movement could not be dismissed simply as an exercise in the "piracy" of state party labels and in the agitation of the race problem. It was a demonstration, and not just another verbal threat, that the changes in the historic relationship between the South and the Democratic national party could produce a Southern bolt. The big question for the future was whether much of the South was capable of defecting again from the Democratic presidential ticket if there were no Dixiecrat alternative to facilitate defection. Would enough Southern Democratic leaders support the Republican national ticket to constitute another party revolt in 1952?

Since an affirmative answer was evident as early as the preconvention period in 1952, it was a good bet that intense sectional conflict on the issue of party loyalty would materialize at the 1952 Democratic national convention, involving the thorny problems of intraparty relationships raised by the past actions of the Dixiecrats and the anticipated actions of the "Republicrats," both sets of bolters, of course, being from the South.

1952: The Democratic National Convention

Southern Party Defection: The Problem and the Strategy /   The party
loyalty problem at the 1952 convention, however exploited for selfish gain
by the various factions, was a real and not a manufactured problem. The
controlling party factions in Mississippi, South Carolina, Georgia, Louisiana, Texas, and Virginia had adopted a common "wait and see" attitude
as to their stand on the nominees of the national party ticket. Each of these
six states made plans for a postconvention meeting at which time the position of the state party organization and the ballot location of presidential
electors would be fixed. At the same time, they sent to the national convention a delegation expecting to participate as fully as any other in the deliberations and actions of the national party.

The strategy and rationale underlying these Southern actions repay close
study, because they lay bare the heart of the party loyalty controversy as it
has developed within the national Democratic party in recent years. The
basic pattern of Southern defection was set by the Dixiecrats. Then it was
taken up and reaffirmed by the Eisenhower-leaning Southern Democratic
leaders of 1952. In discussing this pattern of defection, the illustrations will
be drawn from 1948 events—since that was the background experience
available to the 1952 delegates—but the discussion applies with equal force
to the events of 1952 as well.

Effective Southern resistance to the nominees and policies of the national
party would be severely handicapped if every Southern Democratic party,
by virtue of its participation in the national convention, was *obliged* to
place the national ticket on the state ballot under the label of the state
Democratic party and, further, to work for (or at least not oppose) the
election of the Democratic presidential candidate. If the obligations of a
state Democratic party were so construed, then the onus of party desertion
would be placed on the Dixiecrats and thousands of Southern votes semi-
automatically cast for the rooster emblem under the Democratic party
would be denied to the cause of rebellion. The obvious solution—escaping
the obligation by not participating in the national convention—would also
stigmatize the Dixiecrats as deserters, reduce or eliminate Southern influence within the convention, and would be certain to produce a national-
party-supported "loyalist" faction within the state. Here, then, was a problem of the utmost gravity to Southern dissidents: the feasibility of party
revolt depended on its solution.

The solution advanced by the Dixiecrats was superbly conceived to
implement their goal, but at the same time it produced a crisis within the
national party as to the meaning of a national party. This centered on the
relationships between the state party (the delegation to national conven-

tions and the presidential electors) and the national party (the national convention and its nominees). In presenting a theoretical justification of their proposed actions, the Dixiecrats, in effect, fully applied their states' rights doctrine to the area of party relationships, assuming the role of regional patriots morally bound to defy the national party.

The Dixiecrats advanced a view of party relationships that assigned to the national party the status of a confederate body in which the constituent units—the state parties—retained nearly autonomous power. Under state laws, over which the national party had no control, the governing state party organs and/or the state legislature had the authority to determine which presidential candidates went on the ballot, and under what label. Lacking authority over these matters, the state delegation could not permit itself to be bound on them by the national convention. By the same reasoning, the state Democratic party emblem or label belonged to the autonomous state party, and the national party could not compel (as a matter of law) the state party to give its label to the national ticket.

On the basis of this rationale, the Dixiecrats asserted the legitimacy of (1) the participation of Southern Democratic parties in the national convention, even though no commitment to abide by the convention's decisions could be entertained, and (2) the postconvention determination of each Southern state Democratic party to confer its support and its label on someone other than the nominee elected by the national convention.

It was understood, of course, that the national convention might object to seating Dixiecratic delegations. If such rejection (or ejection) occurred, it would serve to arouse the South's anger and to buttress the emotional theme that the Democratic national party had deserted the South, and not the reverse. It was also understood that the national party would resent, and might try to punish, Southern Democratic leaders who denied the state party label and their official or personal support to the Democratic national ticket. If the States' Righters achieved their goal, however, the national party would neither be able nor willing to impose punishment. In any event, the Dixiecrats, by controlling the state party, would be operating from a position of strength, one that would be based on the support of their home constituency and would facilitate further resistance to the national party.

The form taken by the 1948 Dixiecrat revolt suggested to the 1952 convention delegates these specific problems:

(1) Would the Democratic national party ticket be on the state ballot (e.g., the 1948 Alabama problem)?

(2) Would the Democratic national party ticket be on the state ballot under the emblem or label of the state Democratic party (e.g., the Mississippi-Louisiana-South Carolina problem in 1948)?

(3) Would the machinery of the state Democratic party be operated for

the benefit of the Democratic national party ticket or, if not, then at least not for the active support of an opposition ticket (e.g., the four states that went for Thurmond and the neutrality of the Virginia Democratic organization, all in 1948)?

In thinking through those aspects of the party loyalty problem, the 1952 delegates did have some guideposts available. In the first place, under existing laws and procedures the state legislatures and the state parties control the placement of presidential electors on the state ballot—not the state delegations, the national government, or the national party. Second, the state party is linked to the national party by the delegation the state party sends to the national convention—though what obligations the state party thereby assumes or the delegation thereby assumes on behalf of the state party were precisely some of the important points in dispute in 1952. Third, a national convention, like any representative body, is the final judge of the qualifications of its members. A convention majority can impose any number of requirements as part of the qualifications of all its members—but a national party is not likely to win an election by booting out delegations sent by a goodly number of its state parties. And no national convention is likely to overlook the practical political consequences of any proposed settlement of such a problem as party loyalty, as sharply distinguished from the abstract merits of one or another suggested solution.

At the 1952 convention, the Harriman and Kefauver followers—pursuing their sectionalist liberal strategy as opposed to the unifier strategy—assaulted the South through the medium of an alleged party "loyalty pledge" to be imposed on all delegates. The setting was most unconducive to a thoughtful and firm settlement of some of the intraparty problems raised by the bolting tendencies of the South. Northern liberals not wedded to Harriman or Kefauver were not united on presidential candidates or on factional leadership. Also, they were uncertain as to how far they were prepared to push the South. Southerners were united in repelling the attack, but were otherwise divided as to whether, and under what circumstances, some states should bolt or should reject the conditions for participation imposed by the convention. The compromise-oriented delegates who leaned to the unifier strategy, not merely deprived of the counsel of their candidate but not even knowing who (if anyone) that candidate was to be, reacted uncertainly to the unclear cues presented during the loyalty pledge hassle.

Rival Delegations from Texas and Mississippi / During the week before the convention, press attention focused on the hearings before the platform committee, at which the supporters of Harriman and Kefauver and other liberals were pressing for a vigorously worded civil rights plank. At the same time, sectionalist liberals also were seeking to exploit the issue of potential party disloyalty by some Southerners. As events turned out, to the surprise of both the Harriman-Kefauver camp and others, it was the latter issue and not the civil rights plank that plunged the convention into bitter sectional controversy.

The opportunity to question Southern intentions concerning the 1952 election arose because contesting delegations from Texas and Mississippi appeared at the convention. In both states, the properly elected delegation was made up of leaders and members of the dominant state faction whose future party loyalty was suspect: the Texas group headed by Governor Allan Shivers and that from Mississippi led by Governor Hugh White, Attorney General J. P. Coleman, and state party chairman Tom Tubb. The rival delegates had little legal standing in terms of the procedures by which they had been selected, but they were party-loyal delegates who had organized a seating contest partly because of their fears concerning the post-convention actions of the regular delegation and partly to exploit the situation to gain advantage in their factional struggle for control of the state party. (Customarily, the faction granted the state's seats at the national convention controls the naming of the state's two members of the National Committee and is recognized by the national party as the legitimate spokesman for the state party.)

The states of the South had provided the conventions of both major parties with a good deal of experience in settling seating contests involving competing delegations. On the Republican side, before 1916, the disproportionate convention representation of moribund Southern Republican parties had encouraged a competition of venal local organizations whose delegation vote frequently was for sale to the highest bidder and/or to the presidential candidate most likely to win the convention nomination. Since 1916, when the relative convention vote strength of such Southern Republican state organizations was sharply reduced, seating contests in those states based on local factional feuds have remained common. As recently as the 1952 Republican convention, the outcome of the Republican presidential contest turned largely on the Taft-Eisenhower struggle on resolving the claims of rival delegations from several Southern states. On the Democratic side, nearly all the seating contests since 1928 related to Southern states. A typical dispute would pit a "loyalist" against a "potentially disloyal" faction in the exact manner of the 1952 events.

In spite of the frequency with which the problem had appeared, the Democratic convention (like the Republican one) had not evolved any firm rules for settling disputes arising out of rival delegations. Typically, the problem was resolved on the basis of political expediency: whether presidential contenders were involved in the dispute, or whether the broad convention desire was to effect a solution that would not handicap the prospects of national party victory in a particular state.

In the 1944 Democratic convention, the "regular" Texas delegation, allied with business conservatism and headed by Governor Dan Moody, had come with restricted credentials stipulating that unless the convention's actions satisfied certain conditions (reflecting economic conservatism) Texas presidential electors would not be bound to support the Democratic national ticket. An insurgent Texas delegation also came to the convention, and pledged itself to abide by the convention's decision on nominees. Rather than decide the problem on its intricate merits, the credentials committee and the convention adopted a purely expedient solution: both delegations were seated, and the state's vote was divided equally between them. Some of the Texas Regulars voted for Senator Byrd in opposition to FDR, and nearly all voted for Truman as the vice-presidential nominee. The insurgent delegation, operating under the unit rule, voted for FDR and for Wallace. Later, the Regulars entered a slate of electors pledged to oppose Roosevelt, which attracted 11.8 per cent of the Texas popular vote.

The 1948 Mississippi seating contest was unusual in that it occurred in the absence of a rival delegation, which meant that a refusal to accept the Mississippi delegation would have denied Mississippi representation at the national convention. Although Adlai E. Stevenson and the nine other signers of the minority report of the credentials committee felt that the highly restricted credentials of the Mississippi group justified convention refusal to seat them, a majority of the delegates supported the view set forth by Senator Carl A. Hatch (New Mexico), the sole speaker for the majority report:

> Your Committee on Credentials, not having any rule or guide by the Convention or by the [National] Committee, decided that in the interest of permitting Democrats to sit in our convention and have a voice, the delegation from Mississippi should be seated. The contention is that they will walk out of the Convention; that is a question to be decided later. Every Democrat should be heard.

The Texas and Mississippi seating contests of 1952, since they involved competing delegations, thus were more akin to the 1944 than to the 1948 precedent. The 1944 solution was inappropriate, however, to the 1952 problem, if only because former Representative Maury Maverick, head of the Texas insurgents, insisted on an all-or-nothing decision: "We don't want any 50-50 split. Kick us out like dogs, or seat us as the only legal delegation from Texas."

On Friday, July 18, 1952 an eight-member credentials subcommittee of the National Committee, headed by Calvin W. Rawlings (Utah), held televised hearings on the contested delegations, focusing on the issue of intended party loyalty. Both Shivers of Texas and Coleman of Mississippi indicated their agreement with the doctrine of "majority rule" at the convention, but neither would definitely commit himself in advance to support of the convention's choice of nominees. The subcommittee unanimously recommended placing the Shivers and Coleman delegations on the temporary roll, but also to provide "adequate chairs at the convention" for the insurgent delegations. (The ambiguity of the latter provision was deliberate; as events turned out, the phrase was intended more to provide a sop to the rival delegations than to provide a base for later convention rejection of the regular delegations.) More importantly, the subcommittee's recommendation urged that the National Committee and the convention accept the following resolution, the authorship of which was generally credited to Jonathan Daniels of North Carolina, a member of the subcommittee: "That it is the consensus of this Convention that the honorable course of every delegate who participates in its proceedings is to support the majority decisions of the Convention here and hereafter."

When the full National Committee met on July 19 to receive and act on this report of its credentials subcommittee, Daniels, editor of the Raleigh, North Carolina *News and Observer* and a loyalist Southerner (who disliked disloyal Democrats even more than he did Republicans—"I think a Dixiecrat is worse than a rattlesnake," he had remarked) candidly defended the resolution and the over-all recommendation:

> I believe . . . that [this report] will make it possible to advance the end of the whole Dixiecrat movement. We don't want any martyrs in Mississippi. We won't let any people go back beating their breasts to Texas saying that they were rejected by the Democratic Party, but we lay it on the line that any Democrat who wants to go home, goes home honestly as an honorable man. . . . I think we have gone far enough in this report, and I think Democrats who want to build the Democratic Party and pull us together, should . . . adopt the report, . . . as a compromise, perhaps, but a creative compromise for a fighting, united Democratic Party in all of the United States.

Three committee members from states supporting Kefauver or Harriman (Oregon, New York, Minnesota) led an unsuccessful drive to undercut the standing of the Shivers and Coleman delegations. Their purpose was partly to pick up the additional delegate support available in the insurgent delegations, but mostly to develop a broad liberal issue to aid them at the convention. Committeeman Monroe Sweetland of Oregon proposed, in the form of a motion, that "we invite them [the leaders of the two delegations that the subcommittee had recommended should be placed on the temporary roll] to appear for a hearing not to exceed five minutes, before this National Committee and tell us at firsthand whether they intend to support the decisions of this Convention." Although the motion passed, the non-availability of the Texas and Mississippi spokesmen put an end to the usefulness of that maneuver. Jacob Arvey, Chicago boss and no friend to the

Kefauver or Harriman candidacy, then proposed that the subcommittee's report be adopted with the added condition that the convention's credentials committee, which had the authority to review the entire problem, be urged to have the chairmen of the four rival delegations restate their position with respect to support of the convention's nominees. The sectionalist liberals, expressing their dissatisfaction with the uncertain nature of the regular delegations' position on party loyalty, moved an amendment to Arvey's motion to the effect that the National Committee place no delegation from either state on the temporary roll. Such action would deny participation to the two states until the third day of the convention when the delegates would act, as the ultimate authority, on the recommendations of the convention's own credentials committee. The amendment was rejected by a 65–22 vote and the Arvey motion was then passed.

The "Loyalty Pledge" Idea Emerges /   After the National Committee had adjourned, Congressman Franklin D. Roosevelt, Jr. (New York) voiced the displeasure of Northern sectionalists at its decision and warned that his group would devise firmer solutions. Roosevelt urged the "fair play" position that neither contested delegation be allowed to vote until after the convention had taken action to resolve the seating contests. (This same problem had attracted wide publicity by disrupting the Republican national convention; it had been handled skillfully by Eisenhower backers to discredit the Taft forces. The Republican solution was to adopt "fair play" procedures whereby delegates whose own credentials were in question were not permitted to vote in the convention on seating other delegates whose credentials also were in question.) On the matter of party loyalty, FDR, Jr. introduced a "loyalty pledge" that would assure "that the nominees of the convention will be placed on the ballots of each state as the Democratic candidates and, second, [that] would bind the Democratic state organizations, represented by the state delegations, to work for and support the nominees of this Democratic convention." Partisans of Kefauver and Harriman, together with some uncommitted liberals, spent Sunday and part of Monday (the opening day of the convention) drafting a suitable text of an amendment to the temporary rules of the convention to accomplish the points set forth by Roosevelt.

At the opening session of the convention, the delegates heard welcoming addresses by various Illinois and Chicago leaders, including one by Stevenson in his capacity as host governor. In view of the rather firm tradition that major presidential aspirants should not take a prominent part in convention proceedings, Governor Stevenson's willingness to make an address lent further support to his oft-stated position that he was not a candidate. His speech itself, however, acquainted many of the delegates for the first time with the incisiveness of his mind and the felicity of his phraseology, and served to heighten the chances of his own nomination.

Senator Paul H. Douglas (Illinois), a former professor of economics, followed Stevenson's brief address with a lengthy speech, complete with footnotes, devoted to a detailed defense of the Administration's handling of the Korean war. After two more addresses of welcome, the session adjourned, to reconvene that evening.

The adjournment period was used by National Chairman McKinney to arrange a conference broadly representative of geographic sections and of presidential candidates in an attempt to reach some common ground on the related but separable problems of the contested delegations and the loyalty issue. The meeting reached wide agreement only on the fair-play solution to the first problem; the liberals' proposals on party loyalty won less extensive support.

In late afternoon, however, delegates were informed—via circulars issued and distributed by the Americans for Democratic Action (ADA), a militantly liberal private organization—of the exact wording of the liberals' proposed resolution, and that even "most Southerners" had agreed to it. The first half of the proposed amendment formalized the fair-play procedure; the remainder, here quoted, dealt with the loyalty problem:

> This Convention believes in the great American principle of majority rule. *Every delegate assumes a moral obligation to support the nominees of this convention and bring about their election.* No delegate shall be seated unless he shall give assurance to the Credentials Committee [of the convention] that he will exert every honorable means available to him in any official capacity he may have, to provide that the nominees of the convention for President and Vice President, through their names or those of electors pledged to them, appear on the election ballot under the heading, name or designation of the Democratic Party. Such assurance shall be given by the chairman of each delegation, and shall not be binding upon those delegates who shall so signify to the Credentials Committee prior to its report to this convention. [Italics added.]

Adverse Southern reaction, with particular, but by no means exclusive, reference to the italicized sentence, made it immediately apparent that the ADA had been misled as to the extent of agreement reached at the afternoon conference. Many Southern delegates, initially disinclined to support the Daniels resolution adopted by the National Committee, now reappraised their position in the light of this new assault by sectionalist liberals. Most important for an understanding of subsequent swift-moving and frequently confusing events, the statements of FDR, Jr. and the ADA draft served to fix much of the debate and attitudes on the problem in the terms of a "loyalty pledge" or a "loyalty oath" even though, as will be noted shortly, the revised resolution actually submitted for the convention's consideration included no such feature.

A Loyalty Resolution is Passed / At Monday evening's session, the keynote speaker, Paul A. Dever (governor of Massachusetts and temporary chairman), lambasted the Republicans as "the voice of the fossil." He called on Republicans to "form their battalions, captained by the lords of the press, the oil tycoons of Houston, and the money-changers of Wall Street."

The convention was recessed for several hours after Dever's speech to permit further negotiations behind the scenes on the loyalty issue. The efforts met with only limited success. Shortly after midnight, Governor Shivers of Texas and Tom Tubb, Mississippi's state Democratic chairman, acting in accordance with the agreements reached at the afternoon conference, announced to the reconvened delegates that in the "spirit of justice and fair play" neither delegation would vote on any question "that affects seating or its contest." This voluntary concession did not satisfy the sectionalist liberals.

One of these leaders, Senator Blair Moody of Michigan, chairman-designate of the rules committee, proposed a resolution on a temporary rule of order for the seating of all state delegations in the convention. (This tactic was necessary because the credentials committee was scheduled to report to the convention before the rules committee, and the sectionalist liberals wanted to impose new conditions that would have to be met before a delegate's credentials could be found acceptable by the credentials committee.) Moody's resolution was virtually identical with that portion of the ADA draft previously quoted, with the important exception that the italicized sentence (morally committing each delegate to personal support of the national ticket) was omitted.

After reading the text of his amendment, Moody explained that the last sentence ("and shall not be binding . . .") meant that any delegate who did not make such assurance would not be seated at the convention. Alluding to the afternoon conference, Moody said: "While . . . there was no complete agreement . . . a large majority of those present felt that there is nothing in this resolution . . . which should not be subscribed to by anyone who calls himself a delegate."

But the big question remained: what was it that each delegate was being asked to promise? The answers varied according to the interests represented by each speaker in the debate that followed. All the speakers against the Moody amendment were Southerners. Several of them voiced support for the Daniels resolution instead. Only two of the pro-amendment speakers were Southerners, and both were Kefauver supporters.

Some interpreted the proposed new rule as seeking only the inclusion of the national ticket on the ballot of every state, to prevent a repetition of the 1948 Alabama situation. Senator Moody himself, perhaps to attract the widest possible backing, said his resolution involved only one issue: "whether any delegate shall be entitled to . . . participate in [this convention] . . . and then return and do anything that would prevent the people of his State from casting their votes for the [Democratic presidential nominee]." (After the convention, in keeping with that interpretation, Senator Moody frequently referred to his rule as the "anti-disenfranchisement resolution.")

Texas' Governor Shivers, whose position was vulnerable because the Texas seating contest had yet to be determined by the convention, indicated that he could accept the Moody resolution because it required "nothing more than our State law requires, that is, that those in Texas who desire to vote for the nominees of this Convention shall have an opportunity to do so. . . ."

In general, the Southern delegations, including those of clearly loyalist sympathies that later filed assurances, confined the meaning of the rule in a similar manner, thereby bypassing the question of whether the national ticket would be located under the state party emblem. The North Carolina delegation, for example, informed the credentials committee simply that "under the laws of North Carolina the nominees for President and Vice President will go on the ballot in North Carolina."

The fears of other Southern speakers concerning their involvement in ambiguous commitments were confirmed when Governor Williams (Michigan) spoke in terms of Democratic delegates joining in convention "to elect our captain," and then added pointedly:

> I expect that not a single one of them [Democratic delegates] will go over and say to the other captain, "I want to play for you." I don't expect them to play for any other captain or any other general. . . . Under this resolution, we say we are Democrats, we will stay Democrats, we will fight shoulder to shoulder to elect our Democratic candidates . . . this year.

And Moody's second round of comment differed in implication from his own earlier observation:

> I personally cannot . . . see why the delegate who is a Democrat, who comes here to nominate a President and a Vice President, . . . should not be glad to say that when . . . our collective judgment has been exercised by a roll call of the States, that we are not any of us willing to stand up and fight for the nominees of this Convention.

Whether the Moody resolution was understood as seeking to commit the delegates to getting the national ticket on the state ballot, or on the state ballot under the state party label, or to their positive support of the national ticket, the Southerners wanted no part of it. They regarded the resolution as a calculated insult to the South, and as a major first step in a power play by arrogant Northern liberals to take over the convention and the party. Southern spokesmen launched a six-theme attack in hopes of defeating the proposed Moody rule:

(1) Adoption of the Moody rule would disrupt the convention and the party and, because of the bitter division within the Democrats thereby created, election defeat would be inevitable.

(2) The rule would endanger Stevenson's nomination, on the assumption that many Southern delegations would leave the convention if the rule were adopted. The total Kefauver and Harriman strength would be closer to majority proportions in a Southless convention.

(3) The rule was being pushed through under high pressure, without adequate opportunity for the delegates to consider its wording and implications.

(4) Regardless of its substance, the retroactive effect of the rule made it unfair and undemocratic, i.e., the conditions of eligibility for delegates were being added to well after the delegate-selection process had been completed.

(5) The rule would clash with the laws or party rules of several Southern states, thus precluding those state delegations from giving the assurances required under the rule.

(6) The rule would constitute a usurpation of power by the convention "to lecture duly elected delegates . . . as to how they should conduct themselves in the next election."

During the course of the discussion, Senator Spessard L. Holland (Florida) and Jonathan Daniels (North Carolina) proposed as a substitute motion the latter's resolution that had been adopted by the National Committee and was then in the process of being considered (favorably) by the convention's credentials committee. The Daniels resolution, it will be recalled, sought to handle the loyalty problem by having the convention endorse the moral principle of support by all delegates of the convention's decisions, but without requiring individual delegate assurances or calling for the denial of seating to any delegate. The Daniels amendment was seen as a compromise, one less extreme than Moody's proposal. (And so it was in terms of enforcement mechanisms, but not in terms of scope and nature of delegate commitment. In fact, the Daniels resolution closely resembled the italicized sentence in the ADA draft that had been later struck out as too extreme, with the consent even of the sectionalist liberals. The meaning attributed to both resolutions, in short, was more related to their auspices than to their contents.)

Two separate voice votes climaxed the extensive discussion of the Moody amendment. On both, the Southern delegates, in themselves comprising more than 20 per cent of the convention (the figure needed to sustain a demand for a roll call), voted solidly for a roll call. But Temporary Chairman Dever, displaying an arbitrariness that angered the South further, ruled each time that the demand for a roll call was insufficiently supported. On voice vote, then, the convention rejected the Daniels resolution and next passed the Moody amendment. The delegates took a well-earned recess shortly after 2 A.M.

The Tide Turns Against the Sectionalist Liberals /   On Tuesday, July 22, while the convention's standing committees were hard at work (having been officially constituted by the convention on Monday night), the convention proper relaxed by listening to a variety of speakers, including Mrs. Franklin D. Roosevelt (U.S. Delegate to the United Nations) and Perle Mesta (U.S. Minister to Luxembourg). Southern delegations caucused and gave vent to their anger over the Moody rule. They notified the credentials committee that several Southern states could not comply with the assurances demanded by the Moody resolution because of conflicting state law or party rules. During this same period the Draft Stevenson Committee, given a powerful assist by Barkley's withdrawal on Monday evening, no longer lacked for delegates, leaders, and delegations anxious to declare for Stevenson. On Wednesday, the convention acted on the reports of its standing committees and it became certain that Stevenson's name would be placed in nomination. The net effect of all these activities was to demonstrate that the compromise-oriented delegates, in loose alliance with a similarly motivated convention management, had displaced the sectionalist liberals as the commanding force in the convention.

The credentials committee, headed by the same man (Calvin Rawlings of Utah) who chaired the credentials subcommittee of the National Committee, accommodated National Chairman McKinney's request and Southern demands to modify the impact of the Moody amendment at the current convention. Senator Moody was induced to give his consent to the addition of the following language in the report of the credentials committee: "That for this Convention, only, such assurance shall not be in contravention of the existing law of the State, nor of the previous instructions of the State Democratic governing bodies." As this new exception lifted the requirements of the Moody rule from the very states against which the latter had been aimed, its acceptance was widely and accurately viewed as a major defeat for the sectionalist liberals. It seemed, at this juncture, that the controversy over the so-called loyalty pledge was over, for what state delegation could fail to comply with the amended Moody rule? But, as will be seen, the fight was far from over.

In probing the matter of the two contested delegations from Texas and

Mississippi, the credentials committee could not get the chairmen of the regular delegations to go beyond a commitment to work to secure a place on the ballot for the national ticket. Although the insurgent delegates eagerly pledged their personal support for the convention's nominees, the committee voted to seat Coleman's Mississippi delegation (33–17) and Shivers' Texas group (36–13). At the convention, William Proxmire of Wisconsin led a short-lived counterattack by liberals by means of a minority report signed by 13 members, which proposed to seat the insurgent Texans in place of the Shivers delegation. The Proxmire minority report was defeated, and shortly afterwards the majority report was adopted, both by voice vote.

Sectionalist liberals could take some solace from the fact that in an exchange between Orville L. Freeman, gubernatorial nominee and chairman of the Minnesota delegation, and Temporary Chairman Dever, it was determined that Virginia, South Carolina, and Louisiana were the only three states that had as yet failed to comply with the amended Moody resolution, and that they were not entitled, therefore, to vote on the then-pending question of the adoption of the majority report of the credentials committee. (There was considerable irony in the timing of this determination: three Southern states were being excluded from the permanent roll in connection with a vote that appeased the South by placing on the permanent roll two Southern delegations whose future party loyalty was most questionable.) Leaders of the three excluded states made no attempt to address the convention or to question Dever's ruling. It was a rebellion by silence, which made it all the clearer that they would continue their refusal to sign. The lengthy and uneasy quiet that followed Dever's statement was finally broken when the band struck up with George M. Cohan's "You're a Grand Old Flag."

Senator Moody next presented the report of the rules committee, of which he was chairman, which recommended adoption of the original (unamended) Moody resolution so that it would become part of the temporary rules governing the *next* convention. Before the convention unanimously passed the report by voice vote, Freeman again elicited from Dever the ruling that the same three delegations could not vote on that pending question either. Their discussion was interrupted by a half-hour demonstration that arose in the wake of Kefauver's violation of tradition by his appearance (along with his 81-year-old father) on the convention floor. Doubtless planned to offset Stevenson's presence on the opening day of the convention, the Senator's folksy explanation of his appearance merits inclusion in any collection of political humor: "My father and I wanted to sit in and listen to the proceedings. I didn't expect a demonstration. I was pleased, though, that so many people wanted to give me a hand."

Temporary Chairman Dever, restoring order after Kefauver had shaken the last hand and left the convention floor, responded negatively to Free-man's request that the Chair agree to recognize him at once for a point of order inquiry if at any time one of the three excluded states attempted to vote or otherwise participate. A curious situation was thus fixed: the three Southern states not entitled to participate were not asked to leave the floor and they did not leave, and at the same time Dever's rulings made it clear that those three states would have no right to vote in the future if their position remained unchanged. (One important clue in unraveling the situation related to the conference hurriedly called by National Chairman McKinney, after Dever's first ruling and during the Kefauver demonstration, attended by the leaders of the three excluded Southern delegations and several Northern moderates. No official word of what happened at that conference was ever revealed, but rumor has had it that McKinney promised the excluded delegates that their delegations would be seated. The Southerners agreed, according to the reports, on condition that their acceptance by the convention did not come about by back-door maneuvers and that they could have the opportunity to state their position publicly to the convention delegates.)

Late Wednesday evening, the delegates suffered through a reading of the lengthy party platform and then adopted it—without discussion—by voice vote. (Such an anticlimax to what was initially anticipated to be the chief bone of sectional contention should not obscure the fact that days of intense and sometimes frantic negotiations were necessary to produce compromises satisfactory to all factions and interests.) It was, broadly, a liberal platform—strong on foreign policy, for repeal of the Taft-Hartley labor law, for rigid agricultural price supports at not less than 90 per cent of parity—one that the CIO happily approved as "in the Roosevelt tradition."

The civil rights plank was forceful in its statement of objectives and of the type of federal implementing legislation called for; it deliberately omitted, however, mention of the specific terms so abhorrent to the South: "FEPC" and "closure." Although the civil rights plank was carefully worked out with party harmony as the goal—Senator John Sparkman of Alabama acted as the main mediator between the South and the North—the Georgia and Mississippi delegations asked the Chair to have the records show that they voted against the adoption of the platform. Any further Southern objections that might have arisen were gaveled away by Chairman Rayburn and by the standing threat of Senator Lehman (New York) that he would propose strengthening amendments to the civil rights plank if the South fought adoption of the compromise plank. The delegates adjourned at 1 A.M. Their thoughts turned to the presidential nominating contest that lay just ahead.

Should the Virginia Delegation Be Seated? / Thursday's session, which was to continue without a recess until 2 A.M., got underway shortly after noon with a roll call of the states to make nominations for the presidency. Late in the afternoon, Delaware's Governor Elbert N. Carvel yielded the floor (as prearranged) to Indiana's Governor Henry F. Schricker, who then placed before the convention the name of "the man we cannot permit to say no, Adlai E. Stevenson of Illinois." "It was then," reported Felix Belair, Jr. in the New York *Times,* "that the convention really went wild." Stevenson issued a statement that was immediately interpreted to mean that he would accept a draft nomination: "I had hoped they would not nominate me, but I am deeply affected by this expression of confidence and good will." In the midst of the mass demonstration for Stevenson the Missouri delegation caucused, and Thomas J. Gavin, the President's alternate, announced that he had been instructed by President Truman to cast his ballot for Stevenson. The Stevenson bandwagon was becoming a steamroller.

Nine candidates had been nominated, seconded, and demonstrated for and it was close to 7 P.M. (with many delegates out to dinner) when the reading clerk called the name of Louisiana. Louisiana promptly yielded to Governor John S. Battle of Virginia, while Chairman Rayburn admonished the Minnesota delegation, which was frantically seeking recognition to challenge Louisiana's right to be called, that "[they] will not get the floor until they are in order." Governor Battle phrased a parliamentary inquiry, on behalf of Louisiana and South Carolina as well as of his own Virginia. Governor Battle wanted to know "whether we are entitled to full participation in the deliberations and votes of this convention," because the names of the three states had not been removed from the permanent rolls, which, incidentally, explained why Louisiana's name had been called by the clerk. And thus the loyalty struggle flared up anew and headed into its last climactic phase. Before setting forth the close of that story, a brief look backward should be useful.

At the outset of the 1952 convention, the party loyalty of six Southern state party organizations was suspect and their delegations were expected to be the most intransigent on sectional issues at the convention. The freedom of action of three of those delegations became greatly restricted: in Texas and Mississippi because of the challenge of insurgent delegations, and in Georgia because of the effort to sustain the presidential candidacy of Senator Russell. Accordingly, these three states did attempt to comply with the Moody rule, although in as minimal and protesting a fashion as they could. Georgia, for example, filed a short statement that it could not give the assurances required because to do so would contravene existing laws and party regulations. Nothing was said about whether the national nominees would appear on the state ballot.

The Moody resolution, once amended, became meaningless verbiage as far as its ability to commit delegates at the 1952 convention to anything was concerned. The acceptance by the credentials committee of Georgia's statement proved that, and also testified to the convention management's desire *not* to have a sectional showdown on the issue. Why, then, were the three states of Virginia, Louisiana, and South Carolina still in a position of noncompliance with a "requirement" that no longer required anything?

The Southern recalcitrants had asserted in public so often and so vociferously that they would not make any attempt to comply with the Moody rule—an insulting attempt by young radicals to make the South bow down or be read out of the party—that they felt their action would be construed as a surrender if they voluntarily adhered to the Moody rule even after they had succeeded in emasculating it. In the light of the Southern dissidents' reiterated assertions of noncompliance, the convention managers, no matter how committed to party harmony, dared not presume to announce that they had complied.

Elements of strategy also entered the picture. Southern militants did not want to be put in a position of rejecting the convention, but rather of being rejected by the convention. By Thursday, it was probable that these dissidents no longer desired to be separated from the convention. For one thing, other no less regionally conscious Southern states had gained full participative rights at the convention. For another, the readmission of the three Southern states would complete the humiliation of the sectionalist liberals, whose influence obviously had been on the wane ever since their first success in getting convention adoption of the Moody rule. Finally, if the rumor was to be believed, the convention management had promised the Southern intransigents that they would be seated on honorable terms even without formal adherence to the amended Moody rule. If these considerations help to answer the question raised initially as to why the three states remained in a situation of noncompliance, then the narrative of events may now be resumed.

In response to Governor Battle's inquiry as to the status of the three Southern delegations, Rawlings, chairman of the credentials committee, said that as none of the members involved had conformed to the Moody rule, as amended, none was qualified to vote. Rayburn next recognized Senator Russell B. Long, Huey's son and Earl's nephew, who strode to the rostrum to declare emphatically and dramatically: "Mr. Chairman, the junior Senator from Louisiana does not propose to leave. If I am the only man who stays, I propose to stay here." He recounted the Dixiecrat takeover of the Louisiana Democratic label in 1948 and his own straddling of the issue at the time, and passed judgment that "it was not the correct thing to do." Long then went on to support the essential fairness, in terms of "the right of the people," of the requirement that the national ticket be located under the state party emblem. Long concluded that he was willing to "abide by the majority rule of this Convention," as long as that did not contravene any instructions imposed on the Louisiana delegates by the Louisiana Democratic party. Rawlings and Rayburn promptly responded that Long's statement constituted compliance with the Moody rule, and that he was therefore accepted as a fully accredited delegate.

Louisiana's Governor Robert K. Kennon secured the floor and he reiterated, in hostile fashion, his delegation's inability to conform to the amended Moody rule because of conflicting state party instructions and because it sought to commit him in advance, in his capacity as governor, to "act officially" in support of decisions made by a majority of the convention. Making no secret of his estimate of the situation, Kennon concluded, "So, I suppose that I should say good-bye and God bless you."

Governor Battle gained the floor again, and he re-explained Virginia's position in a sincere and conciliatory manner that had a visible effect on the delegates. He stated that because state law guaranteed that the national ticket would be on the Virginia ballot, that point was not at issue. But, he stated, "With us it is a matter of principle. . . . We are not going to sign any pledge . . . which will prevent that freedom which we claim for ourselves and believe you would like for yourselves."

After Battle completed his statement, Rayburn, expressing his personal regrets, held that the three Southern delegations had not complied with the rules adopted by the convention, and again encouraged any individual members who wished to comply to do so (in the manner of Senator Long) and thereby become entitled to vote.

The roll of the states was resumed. Maine passed. When Maryland was called Lansdale G. Sasscer, delegation chairman and senatorial nominee, promptly made a motion: "in view of the statement made by Governor Battle, that the delegation from Virginia be seated as acting and voting delegates of this Convention." Senator Willis Smith of North Carolina rose to support the motion, and reminded the convention that to deny seating the three states would adversely affect popular attitudes toward the Democratic national ticket in the entire South. Sasscer then further explained that as it had been made clear by Governor Battle that the national ticket would be on the Virginia ballot, and "as that is substantial compliance with the Moody resolution, and as all others here in this Convention are primarily interested not in technicalities but in winning a victory in November, I hope the motion will prevail."

Chairman Rayburn recognized, at long last, Orville Freeman of Minnesota. Freeman raised a point of order: that Sasscer's motion really was an attempt to amend the rules (i.e., the rule that compliance with the amended Moody resolution was required for the qualification of a delegate) and therefore it was out of order or, if in order, it required a two-thirds affirmative vote. Rayburn, however, chose to interpret Sasscer's motion as "tantamount to an appeal from the ruling of the Chair" (i.e., the ruling that Virginia had not complied with the convention's rules); it was in order, therefore, and was subject to the customary majority vote. (Freeman's view appeared to be sounder, because Sasscer had not labeled his motion an appeal nor had he made it before other business had followed the Chair's determination that Virginia had not complied with the convention's rules. Here was another of the many examples at the 1952 convention of the power of the convention managers, and of the direction in which they chose to exercise that power.) Determining that the demand for a roll-call vote had been supported, Rayburn, at a few minutes before 8 P.M., ordered a roll-call vote. The vote was on Sasscer's motion; the question before the delegates was: should the Virginia delegation be seated?

Even though the loyalty issue was by then a most familiar one to the delegates, the cues for voting on the seating of Virginia remained unclear to those who were not committed partisans of Kefauver, Harriman, or the South. Thus, on the first reading of the roll, 16 delegations passed, and at its completion, more than 100 delegates who had voted then changed the direction of their vote. There were two important delegations whose actions might be taken by the convention as indicative of Stevenson's position on the issue—Illinois and Pennsylvania (the latter delegation included the floor leader of the Stevenson forces, former Senator Francis J. Myers). But Illinois, temporarily led by Senator Paul H. Douglas, a Kefauver supporter, at first voted 45–15 against Virginia, while Pennsylvania voted 57–13 in favor of Virginia. This state of affairs did little to provide guideposts for other delegates. But what it did accomplish was the immediate recall of Jacob Arvey and other Illinois leaders from their dinners to the convention floor.

At the completion of the first reading of the roll, with about one-third of the 1,230 votes not cast, the forces opposed to the seating of Virginia had about a 110-vote lead; after all vote changes had apparently taken place, Sasscer's motion seemed to be defeated by about 175 votes. Then, in a shift that turned out to be critical for the balloting, Illinois rose and "having confidence in the Governor of Virginia, changes its vote to 8 noes and 52 yes." An additional hour of vote changing by many other delegations followed, since Arvey's switch of the Illinois vote was interpreted by many, accurately or not, as "Stevenson wants Virginia in." Two hours after it had started, the last vote was cast. Chairman Rayburn, who had held up his gavel to permit all these vote shifts, announced the final tally as 615 in favor of the seating of Virginia, 529 against, and 86 not voting.

The roll call of the states for the purpose of making presidential nominations then resumed. It had progressed as far as Nevada when Rayburn recognized Governor Battle again. Battle expressed his appreciation for the action of the convention in seating Virginia. He told the delegates: "I shall never betray your confidence." He then urged the admission of the other two Southern states as a "fair" and "reasonable" action that "would unite this party of ours." The Chair's attempt to call a vote on Battle's motion was interrupted by Senator Douglas, who made a motion to adjourn until the next day. Fearing that the motion was part of a "stop Stevenson" strategy, another Illinois delegate moved that it be tabled, and demanded a roll-call vote. The motion to table carried: 671 to 534, 25 not voting. A little later, a voice vote carried the motion to seat Louisiana and South Carolina delegations.

Senator Lehman then demanded a roll-call vote, and a New Jersey delegate, on a point of parliamentary inquiry, asked whether the delegation chairmen from the two states had "signed the pledge of loyalty." Senator Long then read a statement, on behalf of the entire Louisiana delegation, which committed Louisiana to the same position as that taken by Governor Battle of Virginia. Governor James F. Byrnes of South Carolina next took the floor and, in a rather testy manner, informed the delegates that under state law, action by Democratic national party officials would automatically place the Democratic national ticket on the South Carolina ballot, but that state party instructions prohibited the delegation from making any pledges. Byrnes refused to affirm that he would take the initiative in getting the national ticket on the state ballot, but he did emphasize that "I would regard it as indefensible if . . . the list of the Democratic national electors . . . would not be placed on the [South Carolina] ballot in a national Democratic election." Rawlings, chairman of the credentials committee, commented that Byrnes' statement was "practically identical" with that of Virginia, and should be submitted to the convention on the same basis. It was then determined that an insufficient number was in support of Lehman's demand for a roll call. The running fight over party loyalty thus was finally concluded. The weary delegates adjourned at two o'clock in the morning.

The alignments on the balloting were clearer in retrospect than during the event. The nine-state South voted 218–28 in favor of seating Virginia, and the ten-state South voted 229½–44½ to table Douglas' motion for adjournment. (Virginia was excluded from voting on the first item, South Carolina on both items. Senator Long and two other delegates who became qualified to vote were permitted to cast the entire 20 votes of the Louisiana delegation on the Chair's ruling that "unless some member of any delegation raises the point of no quorum, those remaining can cast the entire vote.") On both votes, the South provided about one-third of the deciding majority vote, and the minority votes within the region were cast almost entirely by Kefauver supporters. In the non-South delegations, the bulk of the anti-Virginia vote was cast by Harriman and Kefauver delegates, while most of the pro-Virginia vote came from those who subsequently supported Stevenson's candidacy.

The convention's decision to seat Virginia was interpreted, then and since, as a crushing blow to the candidacies of Kefauver and Harriman. In

Kefauver's case in particular, because he was a Tennessean, his commitment to a resolutely liberal line, including opposition to Virginia's seating, bitterly angered the South and offended the border states as well. (It was the chairman, Sasscer, of the Maryland delegation, which was pledged to Kefauver, who introduced the motion to seat Virginia.)

Stevenson's nomination chances were greatly enhanced by the convention's broad rejection of the sectionalist liberal strategy and specific repudiation of the Harriman-Kefauver attempt to bar Southern recalcitrants from taking their seats. The acceptance of Virginia was seen as a victory for the South made possible by the supporters of Stevenson. Yet it is clear that Stevenson himself had no hand in the seating controversy, that many of his backers, taken unawares by Virginia's bid to be seated, were confused as to its implications and therefore were neither well-coordinated nor unified in action, and that little pro-South sentiment was involved. The boost given to the Stevenson candidacy by the resolution of the sectional conflict over party loyalty was due as much to luck, therefore, as to the foresight and strategy of his supporters.

In an article in late 1953 in the *Reporter,* Colonel Arvey, boss of the Chicago Democratic organization, put into print his reasons for shifting the Illinois delegation vote in favor of seating Viriginia. His statement documented, among other things, the unpreparedness of the Stevenson leaders in dealing with that issue and the confusion that generally characterized the delegates' votes on Virginia.

> Cook County Chairman Joe Gill and I were having dinner in the Stockyards Inn when one of our ward committeemen came running over to tell us an important roll-call vote was under way on the seating of Virginia. . . . Gill and I hurried back to the hall. Illinois had already been recorded 45–15 against seating of Virginia. It suddenly dawned on us what was happening. The strategy of the Kefauver backers and the Northern liberal bloc was to try to make impossible demands on the Southern delegates so that they would walk out of the Convention. If the total Convention vote was thus cut down by the walkout of delegates who would never vote for Kefauver, then the Tennessee Senator would have a better chance of winning the nomination. Our Illinois delegation quickly huddled and then changed our vote to 52–8 in favor of seating Virginia. The eight opposed included Senator Douglas and other backers of Kefauver.

Adlai Stevenson, it is clear, personally offered no guidance to his convention supporters on the Virginia dispute. In seclusion and neither an active nor declared candidate, Stevenson was in an awkward position to intervene even if he had a mind to do so. (Indeed, in view of Stevenson's activity in the 1948 convention against the seating of the Mississippi delegation, it was entirely possible that his personal judgment in 1952 would have been that of opposition to the Southern dissidents. In this sense, Arvey and other major supporters of Stevenson retained a greater flexibility of action on his behalf *because* they had no way of consulting him in advance.)

Northern sectionalist liberals promptly undertook to reappraise their candidate commitments in the light of the new situation produced by the seating of the Southerners. In the knowledge that the Harriman bid had been stopped and the Kefauver candidacy effectively stalled, and on the conviction that Stevenson personally was a liberal, the new strategy became one of supporting Stevenson's nomination to head off any Stevenson debt to the South for his convention victory.

The Stevenson-Sparkman Ticket and Election Defeat / Harriman, after obtaining no more than 121 votes (out of 1,230) on the second ballot on Friday, withdrew and announced his support of Stevenson. Kefauver achieved his peak strength of 362½ votes on that second ballot. Stevenson captured the nomination on the third ballot. Of its total of 290 votes, the eleven-state South went from 75 to 82 per cent for Russell over the three ballots, 14 per cent (mostly Tennessee) for Kefauver, and from 2 to 10 per cent for Stevenson. Russell's highest convention vote was 294, reached on the second ballot, of which 81 per cent came from the South. The liberal factions of Governor Sid McMath (Arkansas) and Governor Kerr Scott (North Carolina) gave Stevenson virtually all his Southern vote support.

The final action of the convention was to endorse Stevenson's assignment of the vice-presidential post to loyalist and liberal Senator John Sparkman of Alabama, a move designed to placate the South—but one that probably miscalculated the mood of the South and underestimated the desirability of soothing the resentful followers of Kefauver. Many of the Kefauver partisans felt that their man "wuz robbed" of the nomination by a boss-created "synthetic draft" of Stevenson as well as by the biased actions of the convention managers.

The South emerged from the national convention in one sense triumphant —Governor Battle was given a hero's welcome upon his return to Richmond. But in another sense, the South was embittered by what it viewed as the ordeal by fire that it had been put through by much of the rest of the party. (That the South should have to affirm *its* loyalty to the Democratic party!) In addition, Stevenson's domestic policies, while less doctrinaire than those of the Fair Deal, fell far short of satisfying Southern economic conservatives. His position on federal ownership of tidelands oil, for example, notably alienated Texas and Louisiana leaders.

As the campaign progressed, it became apparent that the antipathy of Southern Democrats to the Democratic national ticket would be expressed in a form different from that of 1948. In every Southern state, the Stevenson-Sparkman slate was located on the ballot under the emblem of the state

Democratic party. Most state party organizations did not openly defect. Many, in fact, worked hard for the national ticket. But various influential Southern Democratic leaders defected on an individual basis, provoking Vice President Barkley's furious characterization of the defectors as being like "the woman who keeps her husband's name . . . but bestows her favors to the man across the street." For example, Governor Shivers of Texas and Governor Kennon of Louisiana led a "Democrats for Eisenhower" movement in support of presidential Republicanism, Governor Byrnes of South Carolina took the alternative route of leading an "Independents for Ike" group that had its own electors on the ballot, and Senator Byrd of Virginia broke his silence late in the campaign to declare that he could not support Stevenson but did not endorse Eisenhower. (Such party rebellion had been facilitated by changes in party rules and state law that permitted a Democrat to remain in good standing regardless of his expressed party or candidate preference in the presidential election.)

In his defeat in the November election, Stevenson carried only two border states and seven Southern states—two of the latter, Louisiana and South Carolina, by slim margins. Eisenhower won the four Southern states of Florida, Tennessee, Texas, and Virginia by from 50.1 to 56.3 per cent of the popular vote. The 1952 presidential election thus continued the Southern revolt and introduced the possibility, confirmed by subsequent events, that presidential Republicanism had become a respectable avenue of protest for Southern economic conservatives and others disaffected with the presidential wing of the Democratic party.

Aftermath: 1953–1960

Notwithstanding their almost continuous involvement with the party loyalty controversy at the 1952 convention, the delegates had not solved the problem—a situation underscored by subsequent Southern defection in the election. The loyalty problem remained a source of bitterness within the party, one that threatened to disrupt the 1956 convention and to handicap Democratic prospects for election victory. Under those conditions—and since a party in defeat has obvious incentives to minimize disunity within its ranks —an effort was mounted to settle the issue and to bind up the wounds. This effort, which was successful and resulted in the adoption of new party rules, constitutes the concluding section in this account of the party loyalty fight within the Democratic party.

National Chairman Stephen A. Mitchell, with the backing of Stevenson and of the successor National Chairman, Paul M. Butler (who took office in December 1954), gained the confidence and support of many Southern and Northern leaders in undertaking a good-will approach to resolve the party loyalty issue in advance of the 1956 national convention. In September 1953, the National Committee authorized Mitchell to appoint a special advisory committee to study the convention's rules, with emphasis on the Moody resolution. (It is suggestive of the powers that may be exercised by an aggressive national chairman and national committee to note that the national convention had not authorized either to undertake a settlement of the loyalty issue.)

One year later, after careful consultation, Mitchell had appointed 82 members to that advisory committee, adequately representing the power centers in the state parties, the congressional leadership, and the less extremist partisans on both sides of the 1952 loyalty conflict: the two vice-chairmen were former Governor Battle of Virginia and Senator Hubert H. Humphrey of Minnesota. (Battle, though unmistakably a Southern dissident at the 1952 convention, was more moderately disposed on the issue than Senator Byrd, Governor Kennon, or Governor Byrnes. Humphrey, an advocate of the minority report strengthening the civil rights plank in 1948, and a resolute liberal in the Senate, had not been an enthusiastic backer of the Moody amendment and had acted as a mediator between the sectionalist liberals and the Stevenson forces at the 1952 convention.) Mitchell assumed the chairmanship himself, thereby indicating the importance that he assigned to the committee's task.

At its third and final meeting as a committee in April 1955, the advisory committee proposed the adoption of three new rules, a recommendation that was subsequently supported without dissent by the National Committee, the convention's rules committee, and the 1956 convention itself. The new rules were included in the National Committee's official call for the convention, which was issued in December 1955, *before* the state parties had elected delegates, to avoid charges of a change of the rules in the middle of the game.

New Rule 1 read:

> That it is the understanding that a State Democratic Party, in selecting and certifying delegates to the Democratic National Convention, thereby undertakes to assure that voters in the State will have the opportunity to cast their election ballots for the Presidential and Vice Presidential nominees selected by said Convention, and for electors pledged formally or in good conscience to the election of these Presidential and Vice Presidential nominees under the Democratic Party label and designation.

In contrast to the Daniels resolution and the Moody amendment of 1952, Rule 1 focused on the state party organizations and not on the state delegations and individual delegates. Most of the protest within the special advisory committee against Rule 1 came from loyalist Southerners, on the grounds that the state parties remained unbound under the rule. But, as

Humphrey and others stressed, since the states controlled access to the ballot and the selection of electors, there was no way that the convention could legally bind the state parties on such matters, i.e., the national party had to depend on the cooperation of its state party affiliates to accomplish the objectives set forth in Rule 1.

The wording of Rule 1 repeated an unintentional ambiguity that had also been present in the Moody resolution of 1952: the omission of the word "State" before the closing words of the sentence, "Democratic Party label and designation." Read literally and technically, Rule 1 might permit the legalistic argument—and Southerners have demonstrated a developed capacity for legalistic argumentation—that the "understanding" was met if the Democratic national ticket was placed on the ballot under some such designation as "national Democratic party," while the state party emblem and label were assigned to another ticket. That is exactly what happened in Mississippi in 1948. A letter to this writer from Stephen A. Mitchell, chairman of the advisory committee, made clear the intent of Rule 1: "The purpose was to bring the national nominees and the state candidates under the same label and party name and ticket as the state candidates." Should this question arise in some future convention, then, presumably that clear intention would be controlling for the interpretation of Rule 1.

New Rule 2 read:

> That it is understood that the Delegates to the Democratic National Convention, when certified by the State Democratic Party, are bona fide Democrats *who have the interests, welfare and success of the Democratic Party at heart,* and will participate in the Convention in good faith, and therefore no *additional* assurances shall be required of Delegates to the Democratic National Convention in the absence of credentials contest or challenge. [Italics added.]

Rule 2 deliberately rejected test oaths, which were "repugnant and offensive to many sincere Democrats," and relied on a good-faith assumption that participating delegates would support the nominees and decisions of the convention. That assumption did not hold, however, and was replaced by a formal requirement of additional assurances in the case of a contested delegation or of a delegate challenged by reason of his past record or his anticipated actions in the immediate future. (The words set in italics in the text of Rule 2 above were those added by the special advisory committee to satisfy at least partially the desire of the loyalist Southerners for a stronger rule.)

In fulfillment of an additional commitment made to Southern loyalists, Mitchell served notice, in April 1955, that he would challenge (under the new rules) the seating of Governors Byrnes, Kennon, and Shivers if they came as delegates to the 1956 convention. He warned:

The delegates will not forget that these men participated in the 1952 convention as Democrats, and then went home and, as Democratic Party officials, supported the opposition. Ever since Roosevelt's first term, there have been people in the South who tried to be Democrats in the state and Republicans nationally. If those characters lived in Peoria, they'd be Republicans. That's what they ought to be. We've got rid of the shotgun [the Moody pledge]; now we're working with a rifle to pick off the worst ones.

Neither National Chairman Butler nor Governor Stevenson, the titular leader of the party, gave any strong support to Mitchell's challenge and no showdown occurred in the 1956 convention because the declared targets did not appear: the Kennon faction had been displaced by Earl Long, the Shivers group by the Rayburn-Johnson faction, and ex-Governor Byrnes chose not to be a delegate.

New Rule 3 read:

That it is the duty of every Member of the Democratic National Committee to declare affirmatively for the nominees of the Convention, and that his or her failure to do so shall be cause for the Democratic National Committee or its duly authorized subcommittee to declare his or her seat vacant after notice and opportunity for hearing.

(Each state is entitled to have one man and one woman on the National Committee. In practice, the designation is made at the state level, either by the state party, direct primary, or the state delegation to the national convention. In form, however—and this provided the solid basis for Rule 3— the national convention elects the members of the National Committee to serve for a four-year term beginning from the adjournment of the convention.)

In August 1949, the National Committee had dusted off its Rule 11— which empowered it "to expel members for cause"—and, operating under an 1898 precedent, had declared the seats vacant of six Southern members from the four states carried by Thurmond because of misfeasance—that is, the support of an opposition presidential ticket. (In 1898, the National Committee had expelled the Pennsylvania committeeman for his support of the Gold Democrats in the 1896 presidential election.) Prior to the 1952 election the National Committee had ousted the Florida and Texas committeemen for the same reason. These actions, and the assumed power underlying them, had never been officially sanctioned by the national convention.

Rule 3, therefore, formalized the Committee's power in this respect and extended the grounds for expunging a member's name to include nonfeasance. The implicit premise of Rule 3 was a flat rejection of the thesis that a national committee member was primarily an agent of the state party organization; rather, he or she was one appointed by the national convention who belonged to a national organization to which the appointee had certain obligations. National Chairman Butler applied that premise in 1958, when the Louisiana Democratic organization replaced National Committeeman Camille F. Gravel, Jr., partly on the grounds that he supported the civil rights position set forth in the national party platform. Butler refused to accept the legitimacy of the firing of Gravel; he successfully insisted that Gravel had been elected for a four-year term and only the National Committee could oust him from that office, and then only for cause.

The broad consent within the party to the adoption of new rules on party loyalty did not signify, of course, the end of sectional conflict. In the 1956 convention, Northern liberals failed in their bid to strengthen a weak civil rights plank, and the Southerners gave 75 per cent of their votes to a Massachusetts Catholic, Senator John F. Kennedy, in a vain effort to prevent the nomination of Kefauver in the open vice-presidential contest. (The extent of Southern antipathy to Kefauver may be gauged by the South Carolina governor's comment that the selection of Kefauver "was the most severe setback to the South" at the convention.) In 1960, much the reverse situation occurred: the South unsuccessfully protested the strongest civil rights plank ever endorsed by a Democratic (or Republican) national convention, and then was partially placated when Senator Kennedy, the presidential nominee, assigned the vice-presidential spot to the South's losing presidential aspirant, Senator Lyndon B. Johnson of Texas. In the 1956 election, Stevenson lost Louisiana, Texas, Florida, Tennessee, and Virginia to the Republicans. In 1960, the last three states again went Republican and, in addition, some of the electoral votes of Alabama and all of those of Mississippi were withheld from Kennedy.

Kennedy's loss of electoral votes in the latter two states was the end product of what had begun in 1958 as a major attempt by the six Deep South states to emulate the 1948 pattern of party revolt, an objective which necessarily involved a repudiation of the good-faith assumptions underlying the new rules. The sensitive nerve of the Deep South had been rubbed raw by the Court's education desegregation rulings in 1954–55 and by the passage of the Civil Rights Act of 1957 (and that of 1960), as well as by Chairman Butler's reiterated statements that the Democratic party did stand and must stand for an uncompromising position on the "moral issue of racial integration." The plan involved either the familiar technique of delaying the decision on the ballot location of the Democratic national ticket until after the national convention or the more novel device of "freeing" Democratic electors from any obligation to support the national ticket. If such "free electors," running under the state Democratic emblem, were elected in November, they could then vote for anyone they desired or that the state party governing body designated. By these means it was hoped that a bloc of at least 57 electoral votes from the six Deep South states (plus, perhaps, Virginia's 12) might comprise a balance of power between the two major-party candidates that could be exploited to the South's advantage.

Reacting to these threats, the National Committee in September 1959, at Butler's request, pointedly readopted the 1956 rules that would govern the 1960 convention. In the months before the convention, Butler and some Northern liberal spokesmen directed much tough talk to the Deep South on the possibility of their delegates being challenged or of rival delegations being formed, to the end that the regular delegations might be ejected from the convention. However, partly because the "free elector" movement had waned in several of the states and partly because the Kennedy forces had no desire to take action in addition to the strong civil rights plank that would further alienate the South, no Northern challenge of a Southern delegate or delegation was forthcoming at the convention. (The most likely targets of such a challenge, according to press accounts in the preconvention period, were delegates from Alabama and Louisiana.)

Judged by its intentions, the Southern plan was mostly a failure. The original plan was adhered to only in Alabama, in which unpledged electors and those pledged to the national ticket competed in the May primary, resulting in victory for six unpledged and five national-ticket electors. In Georgia, Governor Ernest S. Vandiver announced shortly before election day that the slate of unpledged Democratic electors, if elected, would vote for Kennedy. Elsewhere, as in Louisiana and Mississippi, anti-Kennedy unpledged electors ran on a separate ticket, leaving the state party emblem to the Kennedy-Johnson electors. (The Louisiana decision to locate the Kennedy ticket under the state party emblem was by 51–49 vote of the Democratic State Central Committee. At that same meeting, the Louisiana party disassociated itself from the national party platform.) The independent slate won Mississippi's eight electoral votes by attracting 39 per cent of the popular vote; that in Louisiana lost with only 21 per cent.

After the election, in which Kennedy secured only 34 electoral votes over the required majority of 269, attempts were made to persuade enough of the other Southern electors to deny their vote to Kennedy in order to deadlock the election. These attempts failed, and the "free" Alabama and Mississippi electors ultimately cast their total of 14 votes for Senator Harry F. Byrd of Virginia. Thus ended the most recent of the Southern attempts to become a balance of power between the major parties in presidential elections.

The South, Party Loyalty, and the Democratic Party

The extent of the unsolidness of the Solid South in recent national politics may be seen at a glance by noting which Southern states went for whom in the last four presidential elections and that of 1928. (It should also be kept in mind that Republican presidential strength has increased markedly in all states of the South, including those in which the electoral votes continued to go to the Democratic ticket.)

Non-Democrat Victories in Southern States, Presidential Elections of 1928, 1948–60.

STATES	1928	1948	1952	1956	1960
Georgia					
Arkansas					
South Carolina		SR			
Mississippi		SR			U
Alabama		SR			½U
Louisiana		SR		R	
North Carolina	R				
Texas	R		R	R	
Virginia	R		R	R	R
Tennessee	R		R	R	R
Florida	R		R	R	R

R = Republican.   SR = States' Rights (Dixiecrat).   U = Unpledged or "free electors," who voted for Senator Byrd (Va.).

Broadly speaking, Southern disaffection with Democratic presidential candidates stemmed primarily from conservative economic interests or from racial anxieties, or from a combination of both. While it would be misleading to attribute the rim-South's turn to the Republicans to economics and the Deep South's movement to third parties to race, the distinction between the two motives is a useful one in speculating about future Southern political behavior and the likely shape of the party loyalty problem.

It is difficult to predict the paths that Southern political action based on the racial fears of whites may take. (Parenthetically, it might be noted that the future of Southern politics will be all the more unpredictable if Southern Negro registration and voting rates continue to increase significantly.) It appears certain that neither major party will endorse the South's views on maintaining the subordination of the Negro through ingenious circumvention of the law. It seems equally clear that there is no long-range future to

Southern attempts to translate racial fears into regional third-party movements in presidential elections. Nonetheless, given the intensity of feelings
on the race problem in parts of the South, it would be rash to analyze
Southern politics by logic alone. Therefore it does not follow that because
separatist party activity by the South is futile, it will not recur.

On the other hand, shifts in party preference caused by economic considerations are more predictable. These shifts should continue and be intensified as the states of the South become more diversified both in economic
interests and peoples and as these states participate more in the "nationaliz-
ing" trends evident in American politics. The Eisenhower-Nixon period
helped establish for many economic conservatives in many areas of the
South not merely the respectability, but the habit of voting Republican
presidentially. That trend cannot help but be sustained as the South advances economically.

The continuing attractiveness of presidential Republicanism to many
Southern voters suggests that there will be no more Solid South in presidential politics. Viewed as an example of a deep-seated change in voter allegiance, this development is of high importance to the region and to the
nation, but by itself it raises no problem of party loyalty in terms of the
focus of this study. Large-scale shifts in the party attachment of voters
need not result in changed relationships of a fundamental sort between
state parties and national party. What accounts, then, for the eruption of
the party loyalty issue in the wake of the Southern change of heart on the
national Democratic party?

The party loyalty problem arose because Southern Democratic party and
public officials insisted, even as they defected from the national Democrats
in presidential elections, that they remained Democrats in good standing.
Dissident Democrats in the South took this position—rather than declaring
themselves Republicans—for obvious reasons, the most compelling of
which were their desire for political survival and their satisfaction with the
Democratic monopoly of state and local politics in the South. In rational-
ization of this position of being, at one and the same time, true Democrats
and defecting Democrats, Southern rebels emphasized that the state Democratic party was sovereign. Their argument justified more than the support
of non-Democratic presidential candidates by leading state Democrats. It
also defended the right of full participation in the Democratic national convention by state delegations that were not bound to respect the convention's
decisions and it permitted the assignment of the state Democratic label to
the electors of whatever presidential ticket the state party chose to support.
These Southern views and actions inevitably provoked a reconsideration
of the mutual ties and obligations of state and national party and gave rise
to a controversy that still remains to be effectively resolved by the national
Democratic party.

The uncompromising states' rights view of intraparty relationships is expressed well by Senator Harry F. Byrd of Virginia. In a recent letter to the writer discussing the 1952 convention, he reaffirmed his belief "that the National Convention is without power and authority to impose conditions of any sort on free and untrammeled delegates who are duly and regularly elected by their respective States in accordance with the laws and party rules obtaining in those States." He added that Virginia law lodged all authority over the nomination of candidates for all offices in the Democratic party of Virginia, although a 1948 amendment required the names of the nominees of all recognized national parties to appear on the state ballot. In Senator Byrd's view, then, the status of the national party is akin to that of a confederation. To the extent that this view presumes that a state party is entitled to participate on its own terms in the national convention, it grants to each state party the right of nullification of the convention's decisions.

An uncompromising centralist view of the party loyalty issue would argue that the state party and/or the convention delegates were basically agents of their principal, the national party. None of the major participants in the story here unfolded advanced such an extreme position, but several unsuccessful efforts, such as those of Congressman Roosevelt, the ADA, and the Daniels resolution, pushed mightily in that direction. Centralists do urge that the needs of the times call for a strengthened national party system, and that a national convention, by majority vote, should be able to impose whatever new conditions it wants on delegations and delegates.

A consideration in the abstract of the relative merits of the respective legal and theoretical positions on the loyalty issue would reopen a discussion of the federalistic bases of American politics and political institutions. The progress of the party loyalty controversy is more likely to be determined by the interaction of contending forces and interests within the party than by such an abstract discussion. It will proceed from political considerations, in both the best and worst senses of that term. Among the many examples of the interplay of politics and the loyalty conflict that could be drawn from this study, the following items are both representative and important and, therefore, merit some particular mention:

(1) Not even the most extreme Southerner cares to justify the Alabama situation of 1948, when the Democratic national ticket was excluded from the state ballot. Note, however, that the impropriety of denying the national party slate entrance to the state ballot is admitted to in terms that enhance the power of the national party not one bit: the "right of the people" is being violated thereby, and state law will see to it that said violation does not take place.

(2) Because Southern Republicrats conducted their defection in 1952,

1956, and 1960 without seeking the assignment of the state Democratic label to Republican presidential electors, it is not likely that such a maneuver will be attempted in the near future. It is more possible, though still unlikely, that the state Democratic emblem might be given over to a dissident third party, most especially if presidential electors are chosen (as in Alabama) by the primary and not directly by the state party organization.

(3) The new party rules of 1955–56 do involve the state parties and delegations in good-faith commitments that make of the national party something more than a confederation but something less than a centralized governing organization. The political capacity to enforce the new rules, however, remains a big question. Until these rules are enforced, their real meaning and their implications for intraparty relationships are less than clear. (It is probable, though hard to prove, that the ability of Southern dissidents to defy the national party with relative impunity after 1948 helped to stiffen the South's resistance to the new patterns of racial desegregation.)

(4) The new rules do appear to nail down the national party status and obligations of a member of the National Committee. Nonetheless, the ouster of disloyal Committee members is a political act, and the ways of politics favor the imposition of short-term penalties, not lifetime banishment. Politics often requires yesterday's enemies to be accepted as today's friends. Thus, for example, Fielding Wright, vice-presidential candidate of the Dixiecrats in 1948, turned up several years later as Mississippi's national committeeman.

(5) Quite apart from the nature of the contemporary party rules, the capacity of a Democratic president and of the national party to retaliate effectively against party bolters is pre-eminently a function of political considerations. None of the few Southern senators and representatives who had stumped for Thurmond in the 1948 election (or of the many who had remained neutral) was denied his regular committee assignment, chairmanships included. Presidential-controlled patronage was at first channeled through active Truman supporters, but gradually, due to Truman's need for legislative support, the overriding criterion came to be that of roll-call behavior during the session and not that of past behavior in the 1948 presidential election. Similarly, in 1960, the slimness of Kennedy's election victory and of his working majority in the Congress militated against punitive action directed at Southern Democrats who had supported the Republican candidate or "free electors." Southerners predisposed to party rebellion have not been unmindful, of course, of the practical difficulties that prevent the rest of the party from applying sanctions against them for their disloyalty.

The South and Aspects of the American Political System

South-North conflict is expressive of political sectionalism—the durable cleavage of interests along territorial lines—that provides much of the raw materials of national politics. Out of such intersectional tensions a national party forges a durable coalition of areas and interests that not only is capable of winning elections but that tries to govern effectively so as to minimize the potentialities for territorial disruption latent in pluralism and intersectional rivalry. The minority national party, through the years, attempts to dislodge important segments from the orbit of the majority party in order to transform itself into the new majority party of the day.

This picture conforms to the "sun-moon" view of national parties advanced by Samuel Lubell: "Our political solar system . . . has been characterized not by two equally competing suns, but by a sun and a moon. It is within the majority party that the issues of any particular period are fought out; while the minority party shines in reflected radiance of the heat thus generated." And the drift of Southerners away from the Democrats in presidential elections represents one of those political movements that, in Lubell's words, "shed such penetrating light on the inner torments of the majority party" (as well as of the protesting region itself).

The inhospitality of the American political system to national third parties that attempt to be both durable and significant (that is, that try to affect the course of the two-party sysem) suggests the futility of Southern reliance on more Dixiecrat and "free elector" movements. True, the Electoral College procedure permits sectionally based third parties to secure electoral votes, as did the Dixiecrats, who had about the same total popular vote as that of the Wallace Progressives, but got 38 electoral votes while the latter got none. But, by the same token, the capture of a few large Northern states by the Democrats more than counterbalances the loss of Southern electoral votes. Equally damaging to the punitive (or "blackmail") aims of this form of Southern defection from the national Democrats is the fact that, again in Lubell's words, "When any one element [of a party] becomes disaffected, the power of antagonistic elements is automatically enhanced—and so is their attachment to the party. . . . No third party . . . is ever a complete liability. If it diverts votes, it also adds votes in counterattraction." Thus, in the 1948 election, the Dixiecrat rebellion helped solidify the Negro vote for Truman in the same way that the Wallace revolt, by strengthening the anti-Communist image of the Democrats, contributed to a higher rate of Democratic support among Catholic voters.

Such handicaps to the successful operation of presidential third-partyism buttress the conclusion earlier arrived at that the strategy attractive to

Southern party revolt in the future will be that of presidential Republicanism. The appropriate question then becomes: can two-party presidential politics stably coexist with one-party state and local politics in the states of the South? If it be argued, for example, that the character of state politics ultimately will conform to that of presidential politics, then it would follow that the much-talked-about two-party South (in state politics) may be well on the way.

In suggesting answers to that question, it would be well to distinguish between two categories of Republicrats: rank-and-file Democrats who vote Republican presidentially, and Democratic party and governmental leaders who openly support the Republican presidential ticket. The appeal of presidential Republicanism in the South, being based solidly on the satisfaction of persistent economic and other interests, is only partly dependent on the willingness of Democratic leaders to take up the cause of the Republican national ticket. The leadership element, on the other hand, does occupy a crucial role in discouraging or hastening the development of state and local Republicanism in the South. At the same time, it is the Republicrat tendencies of the Democratic leaders that have brought about the conflict over party loyalty. For these reasons, the principal focus in answering the question raised at the outset will be on the likely actions of Southern Democratic leaders rather than on those of the mass electorate.

The development of presidential two-partyism in a state does not guarantee the subsequent development of an analogous two-party system in state politics. The former does give rise to pressures, however, which if capitalized on and manipulated skillfully, could push a state one-party system in that direction. The key problem in the South is how to alter current conditions so as to make it more advantageous for Southern Democratic leaders who are dissatisfied with the national Democratic party to declare themselves as Republicans rather than to remain as Republican-supporting Democrats. Extensive coercion doubtless would be required to "persuade" such Republicrat leaders to forego the advantages of their standing as Democrats. The conversion of Republicrats to Republicans, therefore, is a formidable undertaking that would involve certain actions of the President, the Congress, and both parties at state and national levels:

(1) Democratic presidential candidates and platforms would have to remain sufficiently liberal to encourage the Republicrat movement in the South.

(2) Liberal factions would have to secure more durable control of state politics in the South in order to heighten the incentives of Republicrats not to remain Democrats in state-local politics.

(3) Republicrat activity on the part of Democratic leaders would have to become an issue in state politics—and this has already occurred in

several Southern states—so that would-be Republicrats might then have to choose between being Republican or Democratic.

(4) The national Republican party, in periods when it controlled the White House, would have to encourage and nourish the growth of Republican organization in Southern states on a scale not even thought of, much less attempted, during the Eisenhower-Nixon period.

(5) The national Democratic party, when in control of the presidency and the Congress, would have to use the powers of those institutions together with majority action at the national convention to discourage and punish Republicrats, to the end that the latter would be forced to declare themselves as Republicans in name as well as fact.

Even assuming such a massive effort to establish a two-party system in the South could be mounted—and the practical obstacles to it are legion—it is probable that the result would be to transform Republicrat leaders not into Republicans but back into straight-line Democrats. Many Southern Democratic leaders who were not in sympathy with the national Democratic party placed such a high value on the important practical advantages involved in remaining Democrats that they refrained from participating even as Republicrats in any party revolt. Similarly, when Republicrat leaders determine that their pro-Republican activities will jeopardize their standing as Democratic leaders, many (if not nearly all) of them will return to the Democratic fold.

Essential to the possible success of any attempt to convert Republicrat leaders into Republicans, then, would be changes in current institutions and procedures which would deprive nominal Southern Democrats of those advantages that make them loathe to shed their Democratic label. And central to that strategy would be alterations in the power distribution of the Congress.

The Power Distribution of the Congress /   A striking facet of the 1960 presidential election in the South was that notwithstanding intense popular resentment against the civil rights plank and considerable concern about the religion of the Democratic nominee, most state and congressional political leaders came out actively for the Democratic national ticket. (One conspicuous exception was Virginia's Senator Byrd, who maintained a strict neutrality in 1960 as distinguished from his pro-Eisenhower neutrality in 1956.) The advocacy of party regularity by Southern Democratic leaders strongly opposed to Kennedy's policies may be considered, somewhat paradoxically, as not the latest but the most persistent of Southern techniques of party "revolt." The reasoning advanced by these Southern leaders in 1960 was similar to that set forth by former Governor Cameron Morrison of North Carolina, when he advised his state delegation in July

1952 how to react to that "political insult to the South," the Moody resolution:

> We've been Democrats too long to let any hotheads drive us out of the party. . . . We are probably going to get a terrible platform plank on civil rights. But we've had planks we didn't like before, and our representatives and senators have been able to beat them off in Congress. . . . After all, so long as we can hold powerful places in the Congress, the President can recommend all he wants to, but he still can't get his bills through if our fellows won't help him.

The 1960 application of this line of argument was that: (1) Kennedy was likely to win, with or without the support of the Deep South, and in any event, there was little point in aiding the Nixon-Lodge ticket because their view of the Negro problem was no more pro-Southern than Kennedy's; (2) if the Deep South denied its support to Kennedy, and he won, then the Northern liberals, supported by President Kennedy, would attempt to "purge" opposition Southerners from their strategic committee chairmanships and seats; and (3) therefore, the best protection for the South would be to vote for Kennedy and for anti-Kennedy Democratic legislators who would return to their positions of high influence within the Congress and prevent the passage of those parts of the Kennedy program (and of the Democratic platform) deemed obnoxious by the South.

How these Southern leaders felt when Kennedy won by only a very thin margin of popular and electoral votes can only be conjectured. More importantly, if this strategy of Southern resistance is followed exclusively in the future, it will put an end to the Republicrat problem and to the party loyalty issue as related to presidential politics. It may eventually raise, however, the even thornier problem of an issue-focused sectional conflict over party loyalty in the Congress—over "nominal" versus "real" party membership. The battlefields of confederationists and centralists within the party would shift from the national convention to that of presidential-congressional relationships, of legislative structure and procedure, and of party practices in each chamber.

Should such a struggle occur, and the outcome be the victory of the centralists, then the pressures on Southern Democratic party dissidents to switch over completely to the Republican party (state and national) would become notably intensified. The advantages to Republican-leaning Democratic leaders in remaining Democratic, in short, would have become seriously curtailed. Far more crucially, such an outcome would herald a radically revamped national party system and a set of intraparty relationships that, in turn, would bring about a differently functioning governmental system for the United States.

Sources

Official Proceedings of the Democratic National Convention of 1936, 1940, 1944, 1948, 1952, and 1956. Several of these volumes include the proceedings of some Democratic National Committee meetings as well.

The New York *Times* provided the main newspaper source, supplemented by such Southern papers as the New Orleans *Times-Picayune,* the Richmond *Times-Dispatch,* and the Raleigh *News and Observer.*

The following persons kindly responded to my letters of inquiry, and thereby helped to clarify one or another phase of this case study: Jacob M. Arvey (leader of the Chicago Democratic organization); Professor Samuel H. Beer (national chairman of Americans for Democratic Action); Senator Harry F. Byrd (Va.); former Governor James F. Byrnes (S.C.); Jonathan Daniels (loyalist North Carolinian and author of the Daniels resolution); Professor Paul T. David (analyst of national party conventions); Professor Leon D. Epstein (analyst of Wisconsin politics); Professor Ralph M. Goldman (analyst of national party conventions); Professor Abraham Holtzman (a participant in and an analyst of the making of the new party rules in 1955–56); Senator Hubert H. Humphrey (Minn.); Professor Walter Johnson (co-chairman of the Draft Stevenson Committee); Arthur Krock (political columnist of the New York *Times*); Stephen A. Mitchell (former National Chairman and chairman of the Special Advisory Committee on Rules); Senator William Proxmire (Wisc.); and Joseph L. Rauh, Jr. (a vice-chairman of Americans for Democratic Action). I am especially appreciative to Messrs. Byrd and Mitchell for permitting me to quote from their replies to me.

ARVEY, JACOB M. "The Reluctant Candidate—An Inside Story." *Reporter,* November 24, 1953, pp. 19–26.

BAIN, RICHARD C. *Convention Decisions and Voting Records.* Washington, D.C.: Brookings Institution, 1960.

DAVID, PAUL T., MALCOLM MOOS, and RALPH M. GOLDMAN. *Presidential Nominating Politics in 1952.* Baltimore: Johns Hopkins Press, 1954. 5 vols.

DAVID, PAUL T., RALPH M. GOLDMAN, and RICHARD C. BAIN. *The Politics of National Party Conventions.* Washington, D.C.: Brookings Institution, 1960.

DAVIS, KENNETH S. *A Prophet in His Own Country: The Triumphs and Defeats of Adlai E. Stevenson.* New York: Doubleday, 1957.

HEARD, ALEXANDER. *A Two-Party South?* Chapel Hill: Univ. of North Carolina Press, 1952.

HOLTZMAN, ABRAHAM. "Party Responsibility and Loyalty: New Rules in the Democratic Party." *The Journal of Politics,* August 1960, pp. 485–501.

JOHNSON, WALTER. *How We Drafted Adlai Stevenson.* New York: Knopf, 1955.

KEFAUVER, ESTES. "Why Not Let the *People* Elect Our President?" *Collier's,* January 31, 1953, pp. 34–35, 38–39. (Includes Kefauver's comments on the

1952 convention on "how easy it is for the faction that controls the convention machinery to operate unfairly against the candidates it opposes.")

KEY, V. O., JR. *Southern Politics.* New York: Knopf, 1949.

LEVENTHAL, HAROLD. "The Democratic Party's Approach to Its Convention Rules." *American Political Science Review,* June 1956, pp. 553–68.

LUBELL, SAMUEL. *The Future of American Politics.* New York: Harper, 1951.

STRONG, DONALD S. "The Presidential Election in the South, 1952." *The Journal of Politics,* August 1955, pp. 343–89.

TRUMAN, HARRY S. *Memoirs.* Vol. 2, *Years of Trial and Hope, 1946–1952.* New York: Doubleday, 1956.

The Tax that Beat a Governor:

The Ordeal of Massachusetts

John P. Mallan

SMITH COLLEGE

George Blackwood

BOSTON UNIVERSITY

"Massachusetts is like the Congo—a maximum of social and economic problems, and a minimum of effective political leadership."

O N JANUARY 1, 1961, a Boston newspaper reporter interviewed retiring Democratic Governor Foster Furcolo, who, after several years as a strong vote-getter in Massachusetts, had just suffered a shattering defeat in the 1960 Democratic primary. One of the reasons given by most observers for Furcolo's defeat—in which he received only about 40 per cent of the vote against a relative unknown—was his advocacy of a state sales tax.

Did Furcolo believe, the reporter asked, that this tax proposal had been an error of judgment?

"I would not characterize that as a mistake," he replied.

"I was fully aware of the political consequences. Before I sent it in, I had a meeting of 26 people at the University Club, members of my staff and others. Twenty-five were against it. They were thinking politically because 20 of the 26 agreed that the state should have a sales tax."

"Was it a politically wise thing to do?" he continued. "All 26, including me, agreed that it was not. You'd have to be a simpleton not to see that. I still feel that it was not only necessary but inevitable—and so do 90 per cent of all students of government who look into it."

At that same meeting, very early in the Furcolo administration, one of the most powerful and politically experienced Democrats in Massachusetts, after listening to the governor's presentation of the need for new taxes, had muttered, half under his breath, "Who does Furcolo think he is—that he can solve all the state's problems?"

These two contrasting attitudes—the governor who felt a major new tax was vital to meet *governmental* needs, as he saw them, and the shrewd politico, who felt that "solving problems" must come second to *political* necessities—symbolize in many ways the controversy that seemed to tear apart the state of Massachusetts in 1957.

In the years since World War II, every state and local government in the United States has had to face the same problems that confronted Massachusetts. Since 1945, state and local spending has tripled to nearly $50 billion a year; it may increase to $85 billion by 1970. Tax rates have gone up everywhere, and new taxes have been added. A great many states— New York, Pennsylvania, Michigan, California among them—have been sharply divided over taxation and spending. Tax questions create more political controversy than even rural-urban frictions or debates over the reapportionment of legislative districts. Taxes must fall on *some one*. Upper-income people, and lower-income people, city people, and small-towners are usually determined that they fall on someone else.

Men in positions of executive responsibility in governors' offices in every state have found it necessary to ask for increased government spending. But legislators, members of both political parties, pressure groups, and the public have often reacted differently and from a diversity of political motivations.

This is the story of one such controversy.

"The Governor Proposes . . ."

Governor Foster Furcolo: 1956 /   Foster Furcolo is a liberal strongly interested in social and economic problems. He had been a political lone wolf who had won high office without close association with other party leaders. He was somewhat of an impulsive maverick.

The son of an Italian immigrant father who became a successful physician, Furcolo was the first man of partially Italian ancestry—his mother was of Irish descent—to hold high office in a state previously dominated by Yankees and Irishmen. He was graduated from Yale and the Yale Law School, and then practiced law in Springfield, Massachusetts, where he ran unsuccessfully for district attorney in 1942. After serving in the Navy in World War II, he returned to run for Congress in 1946. Again his bid was unsuccessful. But his fortunes soon mended. In 1948 and again in 1950, he was elected to Congress as the second Democrat in history to carry his western Massachusetts district.

By early 1952, his name was being mentioned for state office. Democratic Governor Paul A. Dever liked Furcolo personally and felt that the party had too long run an "all green" (all-Irish) state ticket and that it would be desirable to have an Italian-American in high office. Dever therefore persuaded the incumbent state treasurer to resign, and named Furcolo to fill his unexpired term. Furcolo won election in his own right to the treasurer's office that fall, and in 1954 ran a close but unsuccessful campaign for the United States Senate against the popular Republican incumbent, Leverett Saltonstall. In 1956, many Democrats supported Furcolo for governor, and he was nominated and elected without great difficulty.

In eight years, Furcolo had risen to the highest office in the Commonwealth. However, he had never had to work closely with other party leaders. One reason for this was the nature of the Massachusetts Democratic party. In some states, political parties are based on an organization or machine that advances and develops candidates according to their party loyalty. This is not the case in Massachusetts. A candidate usually wins his first office by personal appeals to his friends and neighbors with no help from any party group. He advances to higher office by appealing to financial supporters who enable him to purchase enough commercial advertising to reach a broader electorate. Winning state-wide office may thus depend on a handful of "fat cats" (major financial backers), a good television personality, or simply a familiar name. There is no state-wide party organization that delivers the votes, but rather dozens of small squabbling factions built around individual candidates and colorful personalities like the late Governor James Michael Curley, immortalized in *The Last Hurrah*. So raucous is the in-fighting among this multitude of personal organizations that a former state chairman once boasted, "When cats howl in the middle of the night, they're not fighting; they're making more cats. Well, we're making more Democrats."

Thus, Furcolo did not owe his rise in politics to anyone except a small group of personal backers and the special interest of Governor Paul Dever. He was somewhat skeptical of many local political leaders and their factions, in part because he felt that they could not deliver the vote, and that a candidate must depend on his own direct appeals to the electorate.

Indeed, Furcolo was capable of viewing the machinations of local politics with considerable humor. Against the advice of some of his supporters, he published during his first year in office a satirical political novel called *Let George Do It!* This novel, a Damon Runyonesque portrayal of a campaign for state representative in an Irish district, was a semi-farce, but it was not too far removed from Massachusetts political reality. It caught some of the endless purposelessness and irrationality that can be found in state and local politics, as well as the petty attempts by some local candidates to hoodwink the voter—to use any appeal whatsoever to reach what seems to be a totally indifferent electorate.

In Congress, Furcolo had been marked by an enthusiasm for social and economic programs, notably education; as a freshman, he had not been deeply involved in the political counterplay of the legislative process, although he had managed to make an excellent impression on majority leader John W. McCormack, who also came from Massachusetts. As state treasurer, Furcolo had handled a specialized job that did not bring him into close contact with other party leaders, particularly in the legislature; above all, he had never been involved either in the interminable bargaining and the establishment of subtle personal relationships which took much of the time of members of the Massachusetts state legislature.

Furcolo was only 45 years old in 1957. He was a man of considerable energy and bounce who made a practice of working fourteen-hour days seven days a week and who often telephoned his staff advisors as early as six in the morning. He was a man of wide-ranging interests and enthusiasms who often began the preparation of a message by calling together his staff and saying in effect, "Give me all the hot ideas you've got." Between 1957 and 1960, a multitude of "hot ideas" poured out of his office, and quite a few were adopted into law: a large-scale new state scholarship program, a new state technological institute, a network of two-year community colleges, new psychiatric clinics in many parts of the state, an expanded housing-for-the-aged program, an Audit of State Needs that carried out research studies in many areas of government, proposals to reorganize state management agencies and to hold a state constitutional convention, plans for a state medical school, and so on—not to mention a more debatable proposal during the Little Rock desegregation crisis of 1957, calling for a group of northern and southern governors to mediate between President Eisenhower and Governor Orval Faubus of Arkansas.

It is fair to say that Furcolo has always been one of the more controversial figures of Massachusetts politics, a man who has seemed to have many different images. To his friends and supporters, he has seemed warm, intelligent, and articulate—with a far greater interest in programs and issues than most Massachusetts Democrats. But he has also appeared as a nonteam player who often leaps into a political situation without enough regard for political consequences. To his opponents, especially in the legislature, he had been criticized not only as a poor politician but as a man who "couldn't be worked with," who was not one of the boys. His background separated him from many of the Democratic legislators; he was urbane and well educated, with a broad interest in national and international issues, while many of them were self-made men—small businessmen, lawyers, or insurance salesmen—whose education had ended with high school or perhaps with night law school. But more essential was the fundamental interest Furcolo had in broad and sweeping programs, combined with a determined if not stubborn willingness to push for an idea he believed in against the political judgment of his own advisors.

The Governor Reviews the Need / Soon after his election in November 1956, Furcolo came to the State House to confer with the state budget commissioner and other officials who were preparing the budget recommendations for the coming fiscal year. As is the practice in almost all states, a governor is elected in November and takes office in January. In the interim, he must prepare complete budget recommendations for the fiscal year beginning the following July 1. He must also ready his recommendations for new legislation and prepare his inaugural message to the legislature. When a governor from a different party is elected—Furcolo succeeded Republican Christian Herter—he usually does not have access, until after his election, to the state records upon which his budget recommendations must be made.

When Furcolo met with the career officials of the budget and taxation departments, he discovered at once that he was faced with a staggering problem. The budget commissioner and other fiscal advisors told him that they anticipated a deficit for the coming fiscal year of more than $40 million. The reason for the deficit was that state expenditures were rising at a considerably greater rate than estimated state revenues. Massachusetts was committed, under existing laws, to provide for constantly increasing numbers of students at the state colleges, patients at the state hospitals and clinics, and people drawing relief assistance payments, and to provide also for many other groups. At the same time, the state had to deal with constantly rising prices for food, supplies, and equipment for all state services, and the state legislature in the previous administration had also authorized salary increases for most state employees. Further, interest payments on the state debt—already over $1 billion, the largest in the United States— were mounting rapidly.

In the successful political campaign that Foster Furcolo had just conducted, he had emphasized his promise that Massachusetts would go forward to provide better services for its people. Now, a few days after victory, he was faced with columns of cold, unpleasant statistics—statistics that told him that he would have to raise the budget from about $363 million in the fiscal year 1957 to $387 million for the following year, just to provide for existing programs. Further, he would have to raise new taxes to make up an enormous anticipated deficit.

Beyond the revenue-gap crisis was the painful question of additional state needs. During the 1956 campaign Furcolo had campaigned for new programs in many fields, notably in health, education, and welfare. He had also stressed that state salaries, especially for professional personnel such as teachers and physicians, were falling far below the rates in other states. He had especially emphasized education, pointing out that Massachusetts, despite its fine private college system, ranked lowest among the states in its per capita support of public higher education, having starved its state university and state colleges for many years.

During the campaign, Furcolo had become impressed with the social and economic problems that have threatened to overwhelm every state and local government since World War II. The major reason for the great pressure on government is our national population explosion: Americans have had more than 50 million babies since 1945. This has meant a tremendous expansion of our school systems and of health, welfare, and other services. At the same time, our aged population has increased greatly, along with the numbers of people in state hospitals and prisons. A growing population has meant twice as many automobiles and a fantastic expansion of our highway and other transportation facilities. Also, the movement of millions of people to the suburbs and the decay of our older "central cities" like Boston and New York have meant that additional funds are needed for housing, urban renewal, recreation, and a dozen other programs.

Thus, while Furcolo was told that he would need an additional $40 million simply to continue existing programs, he also believed with a passionate intensity that Massachusetts must do far more. This emphasis on new government services at all costs was a key to understanding many of the program-minded advisors of the Furcolo administration. Much later, when it appeared that Furcolo and other Democratic leaders might literally destroy each other over the sales tax, in what one observer called "an instinct for Götterdämmerung," one member of the administration mused,

> "You know, I'm completely aware of the political consequences of what we're trying to do. I know that every politician has been telling us for months that we are making a mistake. But every time I drive through the slum areas of Boston or Fall River, or visit a state mental hospital, or talk to the people in our public school systems, I believe that what we are doing is the right thing. It is a risk worth taking, even if we fail miserably."

To do justice to state needs, as Furcolo saw them, would cost a great deal of money. But Massachusetts faced another problem which was to some degree unique—the special needs of local government, particularly in education. During the 1956 campaign, Furcolo had made repeated use of a federal government survey that emphasized that many Massachusetts public schools, especially in the cities, were falling into physical decay, and that many were fire hazards; that Massachusetts teachers' pay scales were falling in relation to those in competing states; that school construction costs were mounting rapidly; and that the Commonwealth was already faced with the postwar tidal wave of students.

The state could provide only one major kind of assistance to the public schools: money. Like all states, Massachusetts collects certain tax revenues at the state level and distributes them to the cities and towns. However, in part because of the New England tradition of home rule, local governments receive an unusually low amount of financial aid from the states, compared to cities in most other states. In a recent year, for example, the Commonwealth ranked thirty-ninth in the nation in the proportion of local educational costs paid by the state.

This in turn—since education accounted for the larger part of local budgets—led to another great problem. The local property tax, which bears almost all of the local tax burden, is much higher in Massachusetts than elsewhere; indeed, Massachusetts cities have the highest average per capita property tax in the nation. An average family may pay only about $40 a year in state income taxes, but over $400 a year in local property taxes.

The local property tax is generally considered very undesirable from almost every viewpoint. Conservatives generally charge that it tends to drive away industry. Rising property taxes have made it uneconomical for many kinds of businesses to locate in major cities. Tax experts object to it because it does not place the tax burden directly on the ability to pay —that is, on income—but rather on the house and land a man happens to own. Further, it is difficult to administer and sometimes unfair to individual taxpayers.

Furcolo felt a definite responsibility to provide local property tax relief if possible, as many tax experts had urged for years. He had campaigned in 1956 on a program to bring new industry to the state, and his economic advisors, like the nationally known Professor Seymour Harris of Harvard, believed that high property taxes tended to discourage to some extent industrial growth. Furcolo was also conscious of the new, home-owning suburban middle class—a group that tended to shift politically from one party to the other but a group that nevertheless had given him the margin of victory in 1956. He believed that this group had become especially conscious of local property taxes inasmuch as many of them had been rent-payers rather than home-owners before 1945–1950. He believed they would appreciate a fiscal program that did not increase their local burden.

In November and December of 1956, Foster Furcolo thus faced a series of dilemmas. Unless he raised taxes to provide the needed millions, he would enter his second year, 1958, with a very large deficit. 1958, however, was an election year: the legislature would be especially reluctant to vote new taxes and he himself would have to stand for re-election. But merely raising taxes to meet the deficit would mean that he could carry out none of the new programs he believed in so strongly, and on which he had campaigned. Local property taxes would also mount—so that he would have done little to help provide the better climate for industrial expansion that he had promised in 1956.

It is difficult to convey the sense of real shock that surrounded the governor-elect and his advisors during the short period between election and inauguration—a period that was also filled with the usual political hurly-burly about appointments and patronage, the organization of a new state administration, and the drafting of new programs for the coming year.

Unless drastic action was taken, Furcolo came to believe, he would face in 1957 or 1958 a financial shambles—accompanied by charges that he had "accomplished nothing" as a governor.

Alternative Tax Strategies for Furcolo /   As Furcolo and his advisors wrestled with the fiscal problem, several strategies appeared to be open to them; each would require a different approach to different groups within the Massachusetts configuration of powers elite. One strategy would be to try to pass a "small tax" or taxes, providing perhaps $30–$40 million, which would take care of the expected deficit, although not of new state or local programs. Another alternative would be a major increase in the state income tax, which already served to bring in the largest part of state revenues. A third would be the introduction of a sales tax.

The "small tax" approach was rejected by Furcolo fairly early in the game. There were several reasons for this; the most important was his belief that a small tax would mean two years in which he would accomplish little or nothing to meet new social needs, that he might need another "small tax" in 1958 or in 1959–60—if he were re-elected in 1958—and that a series of battles over the years for such tax increases would not only fail to meet state needs but would also hurt his political future. One big tax fight, presumably quickly and cleanly over, and held as early as possible in his administration, seemed to him a better strategy.

An increase in the state income tax was the approach favored by leaders of organized labor and the liberal Americans for Democratic Action (ADA). In the fall of 1956, before the election was decided, Professor Arnold Soloway of Harvard University, an ADA leader, published a study called *A Balanced Fiscal Program for Massachusetts*. Soloway, like Furcolo, was very much impressed with the state's need for more money. He emphasized that state revenue needs were rising faster than state tax receipts, and believed that at least $26 million more would be needed for the coming fiscal year. He did not, of course, have access to the private budget figures showing an estimated decline in revenue; he believed that $26 million would be needed for *additional* state programs.

Soloway, who had made some surveys of the fiscal problems of Boston, also expressed concern for local needs, emphasizing that the cities of Massachusetts needed at least $55 million a year in additional state aid immediately to help cover the costs of local education, welfare, and other programs. This meant total additional revenues of at least $81 million for the following year—and Soloway stressed that these figures were minimal.

Soloway rejected a state sales tax. He disagreed with the conventional liberal argument that such a tax is always regressive—that is, that it falls on those least able to pay. If the tax were "limited" by exempting food, prescription medicine, children's clothing, rent, and utilities—as had been proposed in recent Massachusetts tax studies—it would fall to about the same extent on most families regardless of income; an average family would pay about 1 per cent of its annual income.

Soloway preferred an increase in the state income tax. This tax, which brings in about 60 per cent of Massachusetts state revenues, requires a word of explanation. It is not a graduated or progressive tax like the federal income tax. Under the Massachusetts constitution it is levied at the same rate: a little more than 3 per cent on annual income in excess of $2,000, with large exemptions for dependents. Because of the exemptions, some observers argue that the tax is graduated to a degree; that is, it falls to a greater extent on higher-income groups. To amend the constitution and permit a graduated tax would take at least four years; it would require favorable action by two successive legislatures and on a state popular referendum. This time barrier was a definite factor in the sales tax debate; Governor Furcolo felt that even if a graduated tax were desirable the state could not afford to wait four years.

Soloway recommended that the state begin the amendment process. Meanwhile, he urged that personal exemptions on the income tax be sharply lowered to bring in more money, and that smaller amounts be raised by other taxes. He did not give details on his income tax plan, but later ADA recommendations called for roughly doubling the average family's payment, from perhaps $30–$40 a year to $60–$80.

Soloway's arguments were a well-developed presentation of one view of the problem: raise at least $81 million immediately through a considerable increase in the income tax, give some badly needed help to local government, and make use of a tax system that would place a somewhat greater burden on upper-income taxpayers but also take considerably more from middle- and lower-income groups. Soloway also argued that the conservative argument that higher income taxes create a bad "business climate" and drive industry away from a state was being greatly exaggerated by businessmen for political reasons. He argued that since businessmen deducted state and local taxes from their federal income taxes, the tax burden tended to become equalized from state to state. He also emphasized that many other factors, such as job and profit opportunities and the level of public services, influence an industry's decision to locate in a given state.

Furcolo's advisers studied the Soloway plan, but they were unconvinced. One reaction was that the plan was politically unfeasible. Republicans and the business-conservative community were united in their opposition to increase the income tax; some of them, in fact, were hoping that it could be reduced. The long-term decline in textiles and some other industries had made Massachusetts businessmen especially sensitive to the "business climate" argument; and they were especially afraid of the political power of organized labor and the Democratic party. Later efforts by members of the

Furcolo administration to persuade them that Massachusetts actually has a favorable business climate—that it is a wealthy state in which new industries have more than compensated for the loss of textiles—fell on deaf ears. The fear that "industry will leave the state" is a frequent cry of conservative groups across the country, and it carries some weight, especially in the older states of the Northeast and urban Middle West that have not been growing as fast as parts of the South and West.

Baldly, it was also a political fact that higher income taxes would fall more heavily on upper-income groups, and this was a major reason for their opposition.

While Democrats controlled the state House of Representatives by a good margin, Republicans controlled the Senate, and there was a strong feeling that the GOP would never permit an increase in the income tax.

Further, a great many Democrats whom Furcolo consulted were opposed to any increase in the income tax. They pointed out that a rather small income tax increase in the previous Democratic administration of Governor Paul A. Dever had caused a great deal of political unrest and might well have resulted in Dever's defeat in 1952. They felt that any income tax increase would lead to great political controversy.

The income tax has always been a source of special taxpayer hostility, especially when it is collected all at once in the spring of each year, as was true in Massachusetts until 1959 when a withholding system was adopted. Payment of a lump sum of perhaps $30–$40 has seemed to anger the average taxpayer much more than paying an equivalent amount or more, pennies at a time, through his taxes on alcohol, tobacco, and gasoline—the other major sources of state revenue. To most Democrats, presenting the voters with a much larger tax bill in March or April of 1958 seemed a sure way to political suicide in November; and they tended to reject the Soloway plan.

As the governor moved toward a final decision in January 1957, he called the previously mentioned meeting of 26 top Democratic leaders, including legislators. He explained his financial predicament to them and asked their advice. The reaction of the Democrat who wanted to know why Furcolo thought he could "solve all the problems" was typical of their response. The great majority of those present believed strongly that any political compromise was preferable to new taxes of any kind. They urged, in effect, that he write off the problem of local needs as previous state administrations had always done. Massachusetts Democratic leaders had never been overly concerned with this problem. Most of them—except for some Boston mayors—simply did not believe that they had a responsibility to provide financial aid to the cities.

The position of these leaders was primarily a reaction to political realities as they viewed them. They argued that new taxes of any kind—small taxes, an income tax increase, or especially a sales tax—would mean political suicide. With one or two exceptions, they were not fiscal experts nor had they been primarily responsible for the preparation of previous state budgets; and they did not attempt to offer specific ways in which the budget could be balanced without new taxes.

The political nature of their reaction helped to encourage Furcolo, who was accustomed in any case to making his own decisions and who strongly felt that he bore the responsibility for fiscal stability, to move toward the sales tax.

The Sales Tax's Chances: A Preview of Political Strategy /   If the reaction from Democratic leaders indicated that any tax proposal would have rough going in the legislature, why did Furcolo believe that a sales tax might pass? Such a tax had been strongly opposed by many people in Massachusetts, on the grounds that it "soaked the poor." As an urban state, with a large number of lower-income people and a strong labor movement, the Commonwealth had preferred taxes on income. Both the Democratic party and the unions had opposed the tax in their state platforms for many years. In 1960 the same state convention that endorsed Furcolo reiterated its opposition.

Nevertheless, Furcolo believed that considerable support could be found for a sales tax. A number of Republican leaders had been friendly to the tax for years; former GOP Governor Robert Bradford had filed such a proposal, though unsuccessfully, in 1947, and Governor Christian Herter, whom Furcolo succeeded, had stressed many times that the state needed millions of dollars in additional funds and that he would sign a sales tax "if one were passed by the legislature." Herter, indeed, was one of the first to endorse the Furcolo sales tax, in a statement the day after the governor's message.

What was more, the business community and part of the press in Massachusetts had long been concerned about rising property, business, and income taxes, and had argued that other states had a competitive advantage over Massachusetts in obtaining new industry because they placed less of the tax burden on business. The powerful Massachusetts Federation of Taxpayers Association (FTA), which represented for the most part well-to-do owners of real estate as well as business groups, was also strongly in favor of the sales tax, and extremely concerned about the rising costs of local government. Then there was the new class of suburban home-owners, who for the first time in their lives were paying heavy property taxes and were very much aware of it; this group, as we have already mentioned, is the key to winning elections in Massachusetts, since it swings between the Republican and Democratic parties.

Furcolo, like most Democrats, had always been impressed by the very close working relationship between business groups and the Republican party. While the Democrats were a relatively disorganized group of "cats in the night," often unresponsive to any pressure-group appeals, Republican representatives from the suburbs and smaller towns tended to be members of the local community power structure who almost always voted for the economic position favored by business leaders. To business, a vote against their interests was literally a vote "to destroy the economic base of society" and to drive industry out of the state; and Furcolo did not believe that Republican legislators would oppose business- or property-owners on such a vital issue.

Furcolo believed, therefore, that the leaders of the more disciplined Republican party and the business community would swing substantial GOP support to his side in the legislature. He also believed that many Democrats could be won over, despite the hostility of party leaders. He was aware, for example, that Democratic mayors in several large cities, like John B. Hynes of Boston, were for the sales tax because of their desperate need for state financial aid. He was also aware that government employees, especially teachers, had already endorsed a tax; the state and local employees' union was one of the few labor unions that came out in favor of the tax, as did the influential Massachusetts Teachers Association.

Beyond the support of some mayors and city employees, Furcolo believed that he could win over many Democrats in the legislature. While most of these Democrats were unfriendly to the tax, many of them were not especially "ideological" in their views. Furcolo believed that personal appeals and the use of patronage could persuade many of them. The experience of the 34 states that had adopted sales taxes, including Democratically controlled urban states such as Rhode Island in 1947 and Pennsylvania in 1954, indicated that the people usually accepted a sales tax once passed; indeed, no state sales tax has ever been repealed once it has remained on the books as long as two years.

Furcolo was playing a risky political game. In his first month in office, he would abandon many of the leaders of his own party in order to try to build a new coalition of rank-and-file Democrats, Democratic mayors, educators, and government employees—and Republicans. He would—in effect—try to use a tax often thought of as "conservative" for "liberal" purposes, for new state and local programs. As he saw it, this new tax would benefit most groups in the Commonwealth, from local home-owners and property-owners to the lower-income groups who had the most to gain from increased government services.

Furcolo's Conception of the Governorship /   What led Furcolo to believe that he could sell such a controversial proposal to such a complex coalition of interest groups? The answer is probably to be found in his image of what a governor should be.

An American governor, as the President, or the mayor of a large city, must fill several different roles. He is first of all chief administrator; that is, he is responsible for supervising the work of a large number of departments and many state employees. As crises arise in any area, from transportation to juvenile delinquency to a forest fire or natural disaster, the governor must be in command.

A governor must also be chief legislator. Like the President, most governors today are responsible for the preparation not only of the annual budget—which usually is accepted in considerable part by the legislature—but also for most major state legislation. The governor in most states must devote much of his time to the preparation of messages and proposed legislation; and when the legislature is in session he must spend hours persuading and sometimes literally wheedling legislators to support his programs. In Massachusetts, this is an especially difficult job, because the state has one of the nation's largest legislatures—240 representatives and 40 senators—because the Democratic party is so undisciplined, and because the legislature is in session for much of every year. Many of the state's most successful governors have served in the state legislature and have developed a familiarity with its attitudes; Furcolo had not.

A governor must also be, or try to be, chief of party. Because he is elected as a Democrat or Republican and must depend on his own party for support in the legislature and at the next election, he must devote at least part of his time to maintaining his lines of communication and support with the party leaders and the rank and file. In Massachusetts, we have stressed the disorganization of the Democrats, and Furcolo's own relative independence from other party leaders in his rise to power. We have also said that he tended to view much of the ordinary process of state and local politics with a certain humor and skepticism, which at times gave way to distaste. To call a party leader into his office to discuss some problem in education or transportation, and to have the leader begin by asking about patronage or some minor job for a friend, was an experience to which Furcolo never quite became adjusted.

A governor is also tribune of the people. The President of the United States serves the American people as a whole, and in some ways must be "their" representative, a symbol of the united nation meeting its problems; the President can never be simply a party leader or an administrator of government departments. To a lesser degree, a governor must also represent and symbolize state interests as a whole; he owes his election to the whole people in a way that a legislator from a small district does not, and sitting in the governor's chair, he is likely to try to see problems from an over-all viewpoint, the viewpoint of "the general public interest." Many a conservative, once in the chief executive's chair, suddenly becomes an advocate of extended government spending to meet needs he had scarcely been aware of; many a liberal suddenly becomes conscious of fiscal responsibilities and the need to balance budgets.

Foster Furcolo saw himself above all as a tribune of the people. We have already given some of the reasons for his previous lack of contact with the legislature and the Democratic party. But his confidence in himself and his commitment to broad and sweeping solutions to over-all state problems—as he saw them—were also vital. As a congressman, Furcolo had been fascinated with his Congressional Council, a group of citizens representative of business, labor, civic groups, and other organizations that he had brought together in his district to discuss local problems. He felt that by dealing directly with these citizen organizations and their leaders he was getting their viewpoints, and also in a sense serving to educate them about the problems of government. That he was also bypassing the local Democratic leaders was not important in the congressional context.

As governor, Furcolo continued to see himself in this role. He made frequent appearances on television, and tried such innovations as having the members of his staff appear and explain the functions of the governor's office. He organized a series of so-called "Citizens Participation Programs," to which he invited civic leaders from all over the state, leaders who had never played a part in state government. He held a great many state conferences for civic leaders, on education, problems of the aged, and other subjects. He organized a privately endowed scholarship foundation during his first year in office, a foundation that raised and distributed several hundred thousand dollars to needy college students. Even during some of the most critical moments of trouble with the legislature or party leaders, Furcolo found time for such activities.

Above all, Furcolo, who prided himself on his ability to talk to people, believed that he could go before the public and sell a new program or idea. He believed that the public wanted better educational facilities, better hospitals, more homes for the aged; the favorable reactions he received from his many audiences encouraged him to believe so. To him, the support of groups like the Taxpayers Federation and the Teachers Association was valuable in selling the sales tax; but he really counted on his ability to persuade "the public" as a whole.

The Inaugural Message and the Sales Tax / On January 3, 1957, Foster Furcolo was inaugurated as governor. His address departed from the usual general summation of proposals for the coming year; he emphasized that "we are beginning our stewardship with a staggering deficit left us by the outgoing administration." He continued,

We have inherited the worst "financial mess" in the history of the Commonwealth. And with it we of necessity have inherited the greatest taxes. Our inheritance is taxes, more inherited taxes, and still more taxes.

The Commonwealth has been living high, not paying its bills, and putting up a good front on credit. The day of reckoning is here. The cold and harsh fact, which must be clearly recognized and appreciated, is that our financial situation is the worst it has ever been in the history of the Commonwealth.

The governor's intent here was clearly shock technique, an effort to show the voters that costs were mounting enormously, and that there was an automatic and built-in need for additional revenue because of commitments already made by the previous administration. It was an attempt both to build a groundwork for his own forthcoming tax proposals and to forestall criticism that "profligate Democrats" were suddenly in fiscal trouble while thrifty Republicans had not been. The overwhelmingly Republican press had said little during the previous four years about the sharply rising budgets and debts of the Herter administration, and Furcolo was especially anxious to explain that the need for new revenues was bipartisan.

Furcolo went on to suggest three possible alternative budgets: a "No Progress" budget of about $387 million, which could simply meet existing commitments and provide no additional programs; a "Slight Progress" budget of about $418 million, which would provide for some of the new programs he supported; and a "Fair Progress" budget of $450 million. He did not, however, indicate at the time a preference between the three budgets, nor did he indicate what kind of additional taxes he would request.

On January 23, the governor submitted his annual budget for the coming year, calling for a "Slight Progress" budget of $423 million, and asking for a "limited" sales tax to provide the necessary funds for both state and local needs. He did not, however, spell out the details of his sales tax plan, except to say that it would exclude many consumer items.

This tax, which was new to Massachusetts, is one of the most familiar in the United States; in 1961, it was used in 34 states. It was first adopted in the depression of the 1930's as a way to raise money when both incomes and the value of real estate were falling rapidly. Sales taxes have always been a source of controversy between liberals and conservatives, since liberals have charged that such taxes fall more heavily on lower-income groups when they include food and other consumer items, while conservatives believe that they are fairer than taxes on income and property. The tax, the source of several billion dollars a year throughout the nation, is generally accepted by taxpayers in many states. States not levying the tax include Vermont, New Hampshire, Massachusetts, New York, and New Jersey—states that have traditionally relied to a greater degree on local taxes and placed a greater burden on local government.

When Furcolo's plan was filed on April 23, after three months of research and discussion, it provided for a 3 per cent tax on consumer items other than food, children's clothing, prescription medicines, rent, insurance, utilities, fuel, and gasoline. (Some of the latter items, of course, already were subject to taxation.) It was anticipated, based on a similar tax in Connecticut, that about $112 million a year would be raised, of which one-third, or about $37 million, would go to the state, leaving about $75 million for local government.

A rather complex formula had been worked out to provide for a degree of local property tax relief. It was felt that the tax would never pass unless the conservatives felt that a good part of it went for an actual reduction of local taxes, and also that the state legislature would never support it unless they could go to their constituents and say, in effect, "Yes—we did pass a sales tax but we also gave you a property tax reduction." The decision in any case was for a plan in which a local government would receive state aid only by adopting a property tax ceiling for one year, a ceiling that would mean that in 1958 about three-fourths of the sales tax funds to localities would apply to tax reduction.

After the first year of operation, a city could vote to drop its tax ceiling by a fairly complicated procedure that included a popular referendum. This plan, which conservatives applauded, was by no means ideal from the viewpoint of helping to meet local needs. To critics, indeed, this plan was a subsidy for property-owners rather than a local aid program. However, sales tax supporters were quite certain that only this plan had a chance to pass the legislature. And some pro-sales tax liberals believed that within a year or two the pressure for spending for education and other programs would be so great that the state would drop the ceiling arrangement.

There was an interminable argument during the sales tax debate about how much the tax would cost the average person and the extent to which it would fall upon lower-income groups. While this argument was never really resolved to everyone's satisfaction, later computations showed somewhat ironically that the tax would have fallen to about the same degree on lower- and middle-income families as the Soloway income tax plan. Either tax would have taken about 1 per cent of the income of most people, or about $30 to $50 a year from those of moderate means. This fact, however, was lost in a flood of emotion-drenched oratory from all sides about the "rich" and the "poor."

Foster Furcolo had thus proposed a plan of some scope and breadth, a plan that undoubtedly appealed to his flair for sweeping action. He might almost have said, with the pioneering city planner, Daniel Burnham, "Make no little plans; they have no power to stir men's blood." In one sweep, he would wipe out a large anticipated deficit, find enough money for new programs, help the desperate cities and towns, and lower property taxes—

all through a tax that many other states had found politically acceptable.

This was the plan. But as Michael Skerry, Democratic Speaker of the House, said after the governor's presentation, "The Governor proposes, but the legislature disposes."

The Massachusetts Political Spectrum

The Shillelagh and the Cod /   Politics is related only in part to issues or government programs; most voters do not maintain allegiance to their party because of its stand on mental health or urban renewal. In Massachusetts, as in many industrial states, politics has long been dominated by the single event of immigration. Irish Catholic immigrants poured into the state in great numbers in the nineteenth century. Penniless and without special skills, they found themselves at the bottom of the social and economic ladder, looked down upon by the native Yankee Protestant population. In part because the Yankees were Republicans, the Irish became Democrats; by the 1930's, they controlled most of the larger cities in the Commonwealth and frequently carried state offices as well.

Words like "liberal" and "conservative" or even "Republican" and "Democrat" are less significant in Massachusetts politics than ethnic and religious background. Indeed, so pervasive is this Irish-Yankee dichotomy that a political history of the state could well be called "The Shillelagh and the Cod." As other nationalities—Italians, French-Canadians, Jews, and Poles—came into Massachusetts, they too organized along ethnic political lines, usually under the tutelage of the Irish Democrats. The election of "our own kind" was more important to many voters than the development of particular social and economic programs, although in general the Democrats have tended year after year to support increased social welfare and labor benefits, while the Republicans have usually been in opposition. But there is relatively little overt ideological commitment to programs for their own sake on the Massachusetts political scene.

Nevertheless, Foster Furcolo's case for the sales tax rested on his ability to persuade key political groups in Massachusetts of the importance of the social and economic problems—as he saw them—that confronted the state. His success would depend on the perception which each group had of these issues, and especially of the four great problems of the revenue gap, state needs, local needs, and the growing pressure on the local property tax.

The Republicans and the Business Community /   With few exceptions, the Republican party leadership and their business allies viewed the sales tax almost entirely as a way to cut back or limit other taxes on property and income. Few of them were impressed with the need for additional state or local services, even though Republican Governor Herter had talked repeatedly about the state's need for additional millions of dollars and Republican legislators, like Democrats, voted each year for increased state spending.

What is the ideological position of most Massachusetts Republicans? Nationally, the party often brings to mind names like Henry Cabot Lodge and Leverett Saltonstall. Massachusetts Republicanism is considered a "liberal" organization, and at national conventions most of the Massachusetts delegation is to be found on the side of candidates like Thomas E. Dewey and Dwight D. Eisenhower as opposed to Robert A. Taft and other GOP conservatives.

But on the state and local level the GOP often sounds more like the neighboring Republican organizations of New Hampshire or Vermont than the party of Nelson Rockefeller and Earl Warren. Perhaps the best explanation of this may be found in an essay on Massachusetts politics by William V. Shannon. Shannon argues that the party is "liberal" only at the top. Traditionally, the leadership has been "Brahmin"—old family, Harvard, and State Street (the Boston financial center). However, says Shannon:

> State Street furnishes the money, the brains, and the political generalship of the GOP, but Main Street furnishes the non-commissioned officers and the voting rank and file. The mass of Republicans are rural and small-town men. They inherit their conservatism, and years of Grange-going or Rotary Club attendance reinforces it . . . Like Calvin Coolidge, their perfect archetype, they deeply respect the almighty dollar and the almighty men who possess it.[1]

In the legislature, this conservative rank and file has been especially powerful in recent years, especially since frequent Democratic victories have driven many of the older Brahmins from state office. Men like Leverett Saltonstall and Christian Herter were once Speakers of the Massachusetts House, serving a long legislative apprenticeship before moving on to become governors and United States senators. But the more recent GOP legislative leadership has been made up of the "rural and small-town men," minor lawyers and businessmen of a rather conservative stripe, not especially oriented toward government programs.

This lower-rank GOP conservatism helps to explain why the Republicans saw the sales tax almost entirely as a way to lift some of the burden off other taxes. They were skeptical not only of state spending but in many cases of local educational needs; at the same time, many Republican repre-

---

[1] "Massachusetts: Prisoner of the Past," *Our Sovereign State,* Robert S. Allen, ed. (New York, 1949).

sentatives had served as selectmen in communities where the costs of education were skyrocketing and they were hostile to further increases that they believed unnecessary. When confronted with the estimated revenue gap, their usual answer was simply to assert "spending can always be cut to fit revenues."

The Regular Democrats / For the Democratic party, the situation was more complicated. Most Democrats, including the leadership, had always been "spenders" in a general way—men who believed that government exists to help those in need. Yet, as we have seen, the Democrats in Massachusetts have never been strongly or consistently ideological in their views. Because the party had grown out of the aspirations of the Irish and other ethnic minorities for political self-expression, its leaders believed in helping individuals who needed a job or some other temporary assistance, but often had relatively little interest in broad social programs as such. At Democratic rallies, one can get a big hand by talking in generalities about "the party of the people," but mention of specific government services is likely to draw blank faces.

Few Democrats, except candidates for governor, campaign for office on specific issues. This is especially true of legislators who, as in most states, campaign almost entirely on a personal basis and whose voting records are unknown to most of their constituents, many of whom have probably never used the expression "voting record" in their lives.

The most influential, and in many ways most representative, Democratic legislative leader in 1957 was State Senator John E. Powers, the very model of a legislative personality. John Powers, an extremely hard-driving and dynamic man, had risen out of poverty to devote almost his entire adult life to politics. Born in 1910 in South Boston, a heavily Irish district that has contributed more than its share of state and national political leaders, Powers grew up in hard work. His father, a streetcar motorman, died when Powers was eight, and Powers had to leave high school to help support his family. After holding various jobs, he joined the welfare department of the city of Boston; at 28, he was elected to the legislature. After eight years in the House, during which he became increasingly popular in the legislature and in his district, he was elected to the Senate. In 1949, he was chosen Democratic leader, the post he held in 1957–58. When the Democrats carried the Senate in 1958 for the first time in a century, he became Senate president.

In 1955 and again in 1959, Powers ran very strong but unsuccessful campaigns for mayor of Boston. In 1959, he was the overwhelming favorite, but was defeated in an exciting and somewhat bizarre campaign involving a last-minute federal raid on a bookie parlor operated by one of his own supporters. Powers was tarred with this incident by his opponent, who had charged during the campaign that he was a "power politician." He was defeated by a larger margin than in 1955, but retained his influence in the legislature.

Like Furcolo, Powers has always been a somewhat controversial figure. His supporters have seen him as a man who gets things done, like the earlier leader James Michael Curley—a practical man who cuts through red tape and knows how to deal with people in the corridors of power. In 1959 there was a great deal of talk in circles far removed from City Hall, among businessmen, newspaper editors, and intellectuals, that only Powers had the political know-how and even ruthlessness necessary to deal with the overwhelming problems faced by the old central city of Boston with its mounting governmental costs and its declining economy. On the other hand, Powers' critics have charged that he lacks interest in the problems of government, except as government may help some particular individual with whom he is concerned. A lifetime of political in-fighting, critics charge, has made Powers a man who literally lives for the political process rather than for the governmental product.

Powers, the political pro who had served almost twenty years in the legislature, was a striking contrast to the program-oriented Furcolo. From the first, the two men did not get along. Powers felt that he was not being consulted often enough by Furcolo, while the governor viewed Powers as a man not sufficiently interested in governmental needs. Powers in 1957 was already planning his second campaign for mayor of Boston; Furcolo felt that Powers should be interested in a tax plan to provide millions in state aid to the city, but Powers' view was that the political disadvantages of the tax outweighed any advantages.

"Why Should We Help Those Bums in City Hall?" / While Powers and other Democratic leaders had a commitment to state programs, this feeling was not strong enough to lead them to support new taxes at any cost. Like the Republicans, they had a general feeling that "state budgets can always be cut," and that governors and department heads had a tendency to overdramatize the state's needs. Furthermore, many Democrats were not especially interested in educational needs either at the state or local level.

The Democrats were also generally cool to local needs. In many states, there is a continuing conflict in the legislature over the local problem involving the proportion of state tax revenues that goes for local aid, and the share that remains for state purposes. At least part of the recent fiscal troubles of Michigan have been caused by the fact that the state constitution provides that five-sixths of all funds collected from the state sales tax must automatically be distributed to local governments, regardless of state needs. The state has thus appeared to some observers as "bankrupt" when in fact it simply could not make use of its own tax collections for state purposes.

While in most states local governments, especially in small towns and rural areas, have combined in the legislature to take a lion's share of state revenues, in Massachusetts the situation has been the reverse. One reason for this is the long New England tradition of home rule; until very recently local governments have simply taken it for granted that they must pay their own costs out of local taxes. In the larger cities, political apathy or ignorance seems to be the best explanation for a lack of interest in state financial aid; voters are simply not aware that this is a possible way to meet their needs.

While all Massachusetts legislators work to obtain funds for their districts for such projects as roads and public works, few seem to think of themselves as "ambassadors," like those in Congress and other state legislatures, dedicated to obtaining large-scale state aid for their districts or helping to keep down local taxes. Instead, the state legislature frequently votes to add to the costs of local government by such devices as raising the state minimums for salaries paid to local employees without providing state funds, or giving life tenure to particular local employees and groups of employees. This practice of what might be called "anti-aid"—adding to the costs of government in their own areas—is especially prevalent in legislation relating to Boston and other large cities. There is no apparent public awareness on the part of voters in these cities that this is happening, in part because few voters understand the relation between state aid and their local tax rates.

John E. Powers was not especially anxious to help the city of Boston meet its financial needs in 1957 simply because he felt that his political rival, the incumbent mayor John B. Hynes, would receive the credit. But Powers' attitude was typical of many Democratic legislators; they did not believe their responsibility included "bailing out" the local governments, especially in the field of education. What was more, the lack of Democratic party unity meant that many legislators viewed the mayors and city councillors in their own cities as rivals or potential opponents. "Why should I help those bums in City Hall?" was a frequent Democratic cry during the sales tax debate.

Besides Powers, the principal Democratic leaders in 1957 were Michael Skerry, Speaker of the House; John Thompson, House majority leader; and John Toomey, chairman of the powerful Ways and Means Committee, which would review the state budget. Of these men, Toomey, a conservative who especially disliked expenditures for education, was strongly opposed to a sales tax or any new taxes. Skerry, a dignified man who tried to avoid controversy, remained publicly neutral, although he later revealed that he had always been opposed to the tax, and would have voted against it on a tie vote.

Only Thompson was to support Furcolo. Thompson was a burly and extroverted man who came from Furcolo's own part of the state, and the two got along very well; late in 1957, Furcolo appointed Skerry to a lifetime job and Thompson became House Speaker. Thompson's support of Furcolo, however, was primarily because of personal loyalty to the governor; he was not especially favorable for the tax per se.

The Labor Movement and the Liberals /   In many states labor unions and liberal, program-oriented Democrats have worked very hard for the expansion of state and local services and have served as a counterbalance to conservative Republicans and stand-pat regular Democrats. But in Massachusetts this has never really been the case, except in the field of labor legislation. Massachusetts unions are for the most part led by men rather like the state and local leaders of the Democratic Party—men whose orientation toward social problems is "meat and potatoes," immediate short-run economic benefits rather than broad social programs. Labor unions have taken an active and effective part in the election of governors and legislatures sensitive to their interests, and as a result Massachusetts has some of the most pro-labor legislation in the country; its benefits in such programs as workmen's compensation and unemployment compensation are among the highest in the United States.

But, especially before the Furcolo administration, labor unions took relatively little interest in such programs as education or health. Furcolo changed this attitude to some extent; he was the first governor to appoint many labor leaders to state boards of education and other similar posts, and as a result several of them became interested in these problems. But they were not especially concerned in early 1957—and they had always been opposed to a sales tax.

In some states, liberal groups like the Americans for Democratic Action have also been effective in state and local affairs. But in Massachusetts, where the Democratic party itself is relatively nonideological, a rift has always existed between the regulars and the handful of liberals, many of them intellectuals and members of college faculties. Organizations like ADA are very small in Massachusetts, and many of their members have had little respect for the "Irish pols" of the Democratic Party. Liberal interests have been primarily in national and international affairs, not in state and local government.

The long debate in the 1950's over domestic Communism and McCarthyism also marred the relationship between liberal intellectuals and regular Democrats. Most liberals, like their counterparts in other states, believed firmly in the right of every group, no matter how unpopular or objectionable, to freedom of expression. Liberals also believed that the handful of domestic Communists in the United States did not represent a threat to American democracy, but that men like Senator McCarthy who used the Communist issue to attack liberal goals were a very great menace indeed. Many Irish Catholic Democrats, on the other hand, believed with equal conviction that domestic Communism was a very great menace. At the height of the furor over Senator McCarthy in the winter of 1953–54, a study of a fairly representative middle-class Boston ward, overwhelmingly Irish and Democratic, revealed that almost 90 per cent of the ward's residents were generally sympathetic to McCarthy and believed that internal Communism represented a great threat to America.

Most liberals split with Foster Furcolo over this same issue. Liberals had admired Furcolo's voting record in Congress, and some of them had worked in his congressional campaigns. In December 1953, Furcolo, then state treasurer, was asked to address the state convention of ADA in Boston. He agreed; then, without prior warning, he made a speech in which he stated that he believed that only the Democratic party was an effective instrument of social reform in Massachusetts, that ADA had "lost the confidence" of the people of Massachusetts, and that the organization should, in his opinion, disband.

To the liberals, this was an indication of Furcolo's unwillingness to stand up and be counted on the McCarthy issue, and many of them never supported him again. To Furcolo's supporters, this was primarily an example of his personal impulsiveness, his tendency to make a point by a dramatic political gesture. Furthermore, as one Furcolo supporter later said,

> While Furcolo should not have made such a speech, the real problem we faced in 1953 and 1954 was that a large majority of Massachusetts Democrats were convinced that McCarthy was right, that the federal government and the universities were full of Communists. John F. Kennedy had the same problem, and he never took a position on McCarthy in that period. Foster Furcolo wanted to go to the United States Senate to work for the same domestic and international programs he favored in Congress. Association with the ADA, at that time, meant that he would be "linked," to use a McCarthyite word, with an organization which believed in abolition of the House Un-American Activities Committee, repeal of the Smith Act under which Communist leaders were being sent to prison at the time, and recognition of Red China—all ADA positions. Furcolo would never have a chance to work for the social programs in which he believed if he was considered to be involved with a group which held these views—and we could spend the whole 1954 Senatorial campaign on the defensive, trying to explain away a lot of views which were not related to most of the things Furcolo was most concerned about. And we heard that McCarthy himself might come to Massachusetts to campaign in 1954.

Besides, the ADA was a very small and ineffectual organization. Most of its members had never worked in a state campaign and knew little about state politics. In fact, we found later that most liberal intellectuals were no help to us in the Furcolo administration; they simply knew nothing at all about state programs such as public higher education or mental health, and they seemed to take little interest in these programs. They never even appeared to testify at legislative hearings for the expansion of state services.

In any case, neither labor unions nor liberal organizations were especially sensitive toward the need that Furcolo saw for increased state and local spending in 1957. While Arnold Soloway of the ADA had published a research report urging an immediate expenditure of at least $81 million for additional government services, this part of his program received very little attention from liberals in the debate that followed. And neither the ADA nor organized labor ever filed legislation, in 1957 or later, for the Soloway plan for a drastic increase in the income tax and other taxes. Their original hostility to Furcolo seemed to lead many liberals to a lack of interest in most state problems.

The Public and the Press / We have already said that Foster Furcolo relied above all on his ability to reach the people themselves. However, like other political leaders, he was faced with a fundamental ambivalence on the part of the public: it is an old political saw that the way to be re-elected to office is to vote for every appropriation and against every tax. In Massachusetts, it is quite probable that the people "wanted"—in a vague sort of way—better education, hospitals, highways, parks, and beaches. However, it did not follow that they identified these wants with higher taxes.

Furthermore, Massachusetts voters have a special hostility to government and politics, in part because of a strong belief that state and local politics is corrupt. An extensive public opinion poll in the 1959 Boston mayoralty campaign revealed that a great many voters believed that city politics was hopelessly corrupt, controlled by a handful of special interests variously identified as politicians, businessmen holding city contracts, and racketeers. These beliefs were widespread not only among upper-income voters but also in the lower-income districts that have traditionally accepted corruption as part of the political game.

It is difficult to say whether corruption in Massachusetts is more widespread than in other urban-industrial states, but it is an important part of the state's political folklore because of the number of political leaders—congressmen, mayors, legislators—who have served jail sentences, and the frequent exposures and charges that fill the press. As in other states, political corruption was traditionally related in part to the problems of the immigrant, who gave his vote to the boss in return for an occasional government job or other favor. Today, corruption is related in part to the problem of financing campaigns, since large sums have to be raised, and the most available contributors are those who do business with government or seek special government favors. But it is true that many politicians appear to enter public life simply in order to make money or to obtain some lifetime political job.

In any case, corruption or the public image of corruption makes it difficult for any political leader to appeal for more taxes. Furcolo, for example, frequently made use of statistics showing that one-third of all state employees worked for the Department of Mental Health, and another one-third for Education, Public Health, and Correction—in order to show that most state funds went for essential government services. But his arguments often fell on deaf ears.

The Massachusetts press, which has a notoriously mediocre reputation in the nation, is in part responsible for this public image of government. Most of the press is conservative, more or less Republican, and not friendly to government spending. Furthermore, the typical newspaper reporter's idea of political news is a story headed, "Senator Blasts Mayor." Political name-calling and petty controversy make up most of the press coverage of state government, and most papers seldom if ever print stories about the state's higher educational system or its hospitals. The readers, therefore, seldom get the idea that taxes are going for useful or necessary services.

A number of influential newspapers were pro-sales tax during the debate, but they could not resist the opportunity to lambaste a Democratic governor at every opportunity. Furcolo himself on occasion tried to persuade some editors to soft-pedal partisanship until the sales tax fight was over; but the press did not go along. The result was that their editorial pages were urging new taxes of over $100 million, while at the same time their headlines screamed of political in-fighting and buffoonery.

This, then, was the spectrum of political and pressure groups that Furcolo confronted in 1957—a Republican party and business community devoted to cutting property taxes; regular Democrats who believed above all in "not stirring things up" by spending more than existing tax revenues provided; liberals and labor leaders without a special interest in government services and in some cases hostile because of Furcolo's anti-ADA speech; and a public with more than the usual American skepticism about politicians and politics.

". . . The Legislature Disposes"

Reactions to the Tax / Immediate reactions to the sales tax proposal in late January were strong and mixed. Business groups, the Taxpayers

Federation, and some newspapers responded with enthusiasm, as had been anticipated. Most Republican political leaders were much more cautious, despite the immediate endorsement of the tax by outgoing Governor Herter.

The Boston *Herald,* perhaps the most influential organ of GOP opinion, and a central participant in the whole debate, took what was to become one Republican line. This newspaper argued that a sales tax was badly needed, and that only a Democratic governor could get such a tax passed; a Republican would meet too much opposition from the Democrats in the legislature. However, the *Herald* also demonstrated the wide range of motivations of sales tax supporters. "We would wish," it stated editorially, "that Mr. Furcolo could for the moment restrain his fine and humane desire to help the underprivileged with new social welfare schemes."

Still, the *Herald* tried to take a relatively moderate view. The conservative House Republican leader, Frank Giles, a symbol of the "rural and small-town men" who dominated the GOP legislative wing, stated almost immediately that the Republicans would demand a substantial reduction in the state budget, plus the reduction or elimination of the state income tax, as a price for sales tax support. The *Herald* reprimanded him for "playing politics," and said on January 31, "replacement of the income tax is not feasible." Eliminating the personal income tax at that time would have deprived the state of about $100 million a year in revenue.

Many Democrats and labor leaders reacted with equal vigor to the tax; John E. Powers at once said that it would only "make the rich richer and the poor poorer." Powers was unimpressed with the argument that the tax would help the cities; noting that one-third would be kept by the state, he charged that this was a way of taking three dollars from the local taxpayer and giving him back two. Many of the rank-and-file Democrats in the House, however, did not immediately take a position.

Foster Furcolo had anticipated this reaction from his own party, and— true to his conception of the governor's office as spokesman for and educator of the people—he decided during the period between January 23 and April 16, when the tax message was filed, to make a speaking tour of most of the large Massachusetts cities. In this tour, Furcolo emphasized all of the state and local problems that had led him to support the tax; he emphasized particularly tax relief for the local home-owner. Even unfriendly newspapermen who accompanied him seemed to feel that he won support on this tour—but, one commentator wrote, he was gaining it everywhere but where it counted, in the legislature.

Furcolo's tour was met by a counter-tour, organized by groups that included Powers, Arnold Soloway, and Massachusetts AFL Secretary-Treasurer Kenneth Kelley. Powers placed most of his emphasis on the impact of the tax on lower-income people, and continued to assert that the state budget could be cut; Kelley called the tax a betrayal of the workingmen who had supported Furcolo, and Soloway repeated the arguments he had already made in his tax study.

The Massachusetts Inner Circle /   Books like *Advise and Consent* and *Citadel* have shown that even the United States Senate, which must be concerned with the most important national and international issues, is governed to a considerable extent by an "inner club," a small group of men who work together on a subtle personal basis and who may vote for or against a bill not on its merits alone but on the basis of their relationship to its sponsors. Such inner clubmanship is much more typical of state legislatures, where most members are less concerned with issues. In Massachusetts, clubmanship has been developed to a high art; someone once characterized the average legislator as having "a lust for lapels" because so many representatives seem to spend all of their time talking in the corridors of the State House, seizing other legislators who pass, and endlessly reestablishing personal relationships along lines that often baffle the outsider.

Legislators who "get along" with the leadership often find their bills rushed through the parliamentary process so rapidly that they may not even be able to follow their passage. Those who do not get along find their bills stalled and killed; sometimes they cannot even find whether a bill is still in committee, on the day's agenda, or in some special legislative limbo.

Given this club atmosphere, it is not surprising that one of the present authors, interviewing members of the legislature, found that the governor's speaking tour did not influence very many of them. Whatever popular support the governor generated was apparently not translated into pressure on the legislature, and in any case the inner club was not moved by this approach. Still, however, there appeared to be considerable wavering among influential Democrats and Republicans by April 16, when the governor filed his sales tax legislation.

Legislative Hearings and the Budget Fight /   The tax bill was referred to the joint House-Senate committee on taxation, and Furcolo began to work more directly on the legislature itself. He called small groups of legislators into his office and indicated that their future patronage could depend on their supporting the bill; he also began to call meetings of mayors and other local officials and of pressure groups like the Teachers Association, and urged them to bring pressure on their representatives.

However, before the committee hearings opened, the Massachusetts Federation of Taxpayers Associations hardened its position. The group now demanded that three-fourths rather than two-thirds of the sales tax revenues go to local government, which, of course, would mean further property tax relief and less money for state services. The FTA's position was to be the asking price from many conservatives in the weeks ahead. Furcolo, however, continued to insist that the state retain one-third of the money.

The public committee hearings which opened on April 30 were among the most heavily attended in recent Massachusetts history. A large audience heard Governor Furcolo, business representatives, spokesmen for local government, and others defend the tax, along with John Thompson and five House Democrats. Still, there were embarrassing fractures in the pro-tax coalition. The Associated Industries of Massachusetts, local affiliate of the National Association of Manufacturers, supported the tax strongly but protested the fact that industrial machinery was not exempted. Candy manufacturers insisted that a tax on candy would drive them out of business. And lobbyists for the Massachusetts Retail Druggists and Retail Grocers Association appeared with shopping bags full of items such as soap and paper towels, which would be taxed.

The anti-sales tax forces, headed by Powers, Soloway, and Kelley, also appeared to present their case, predicting that if the limited sales tax were enacted, exemptions on food and clothing would be stripped away within a few years, creating a tax that would be even more burdensome for lower-income groups.

The hearings were highly emotional and marked by much bitterness and recrimination; it was plain that the sales tax would have hard going. But this was only the beginning; Furcolo was soon to be hit from another direction. The House Ways and Means Committee was engaged in reviewing the governor's budget recommendations, and its chairman, like Senator Powers, had argued repeatedly that it was not necessary to raise the budget to $423 million, as Furcolo had asked.

On May 13, after many weeks of deliberation, the Ways and Means Committee announced that they had cut $43 million from the governor's budget and that, given more favorable estimates of revenue for the coming year, the $380 million budget could be balanced without new taxes. When House Speaker Skerry and Chairman John Toomey of the committee came to Furcolo's office to tell him of this large-scale budget reduction, Furcolo was so angry that he rose and stalked out of the office.

Just what had been cut from the budget? This question was central to an analysis of who was "right," i.e., whether the state actually needed the additional $43 million, yet no Massachusetts newspaper, to the present writers' knowledge, ever raised this point or attempted to answer it.

The politics of budget-making is usually one of the most mysterious parts of the entire governmental process. Even in the federal government, where a great deal more information is available about budgets and appropriations, the average congressman often has only the most general idea of why a given department is being given more or less this year than the previous year. Even those with a special interest in a particular program may have trouble in translating a given budget into actual services rendered, and sometimes the department itself must spend days or weeks estimating the effect of a given appropriation on its operation for the coming year.

In Massachusetts, only a handful of people have enough information to evaluate a particular appropriation—the budget commissioner, one or two people on the House and Senate Ways and Means Committees, and sometimes a member of the governor's staff. The annual budget recommendations are published in very general language; for example, a state mental hospital may be allowed $2,100,000 with no explanation of what this sum is for.

It was critical for Furcolo's strategy that he demonstrate that his budget could not be cut without damaging essential services; yet the committee moved so rapidly that he did not have this opportunity, and their published report gave no details on what had actually been cut. The committee had begun by eliminating a $12 million "reserve fund" that Furcolo had requested to cover additional recommendations that were to follow later in the year, of which he planned to recommend about $6 million for educational facilities, about $3 million for programs for retarded children, and the remainder for a variety of other programs. None of these had become law when the budget was reported out, although most of them were enacted in 1958 and later years.

Of the remaining $31 million, over a third was intended for the five major social service departments: Education, Mental Health, Public Health, Public Welfare, and Correction. The other two-thirds was to have gone for certain state financial aid payments to local government, certain debt payments, and an increase in the Department of Public Works budget. With the cut budget there would be no additional state aid for local government; the issue was not even raised in the committee report.

The report, in effect, called for what Furcolo had earlier described as a "No Progress" budget; but the news that the budget could be balanced without new taxes was a crippling blow to the sales tax.

Senator Powers at once called the new budget proposal "a courageous action which will be heralded by an overburdened citizenry." On the other hand, the conservative Taxpayers Federation, sharing Furcolo's concern, emphasized that the budget would not even pay for millions in existing state aid payments owed to local government, much less cover additional needs. Most newspapers praised the reduced budget, which was still about $17 million larger than that for the current year. The ambivalance of the press is well-shown in a Fall River *Herald-News* story, in which the reporter recognized that the reduced budget was a blow to the passage of the sales tax and yet wrote, "Nevertheless, no citizen can be anything but amazed and pleased that the House has seen fit to cut a budget."

Furcolo was now desperately seeking some way to dramatize that state services would be hamstrung. When the House met on May 16 to take up the budget, every legislator found in his box a message from the governor stating that he believed the additional $43 million was absolutely essential to the state's needs, and that he would submit another budget including all the cut items. Further, if necessary, he would force the legislature to stay in session until a vote had been taken on the entire program—presumably item by item. It was his apparent belief that legislators would not want to be placed on the spot by specific roll-call votes on each item that had been cut from the budget.

This strategy, however, was completely unsuccessful. Both Democrats and Republicans reacted violently against what they considered undue executive pressure, and whipped through the entire $380 million budget in twenty-five minutes with no discussion whatsoever. The Senate soon afterward took the same step.

Furcolo had lost a most important move. The public and the press had not reacted sufficiently to his arguments about needed services and the legislature had simply rebelled against his tactics. Still, enough support remained for local aid that the sales tax still appeared to have a chance.

D-Day for the Sales Tax /   Furcolo was still determined to work for the sales tax, and to offer additional recommendations for state services later in the session. But he was now much more dependent on the Republican party and the conservative community for support, since only the local aid argument appeared to carry much political weight. Frank Giles and other Republicans were more determined than ever to press their advantage, to push for a larger share of tax receipts for local government, and to try to reduce the state income tax, or perhaps the tax on dividends and interest that struck most directly at upper-income taxpayers. Some Republicans were demanding an income tax reduction of at least $30 million, and Giles predicted in early June that not more than thirteen House Republicans would support the sales tax plan as it stood.

On June 16, the joint House-Senate Committee on Taxation reported the tax to the House with an unfavorable vote of 7 to 5. Three Democrats had voted for the bill, and two against it, while Republicans, demanding greater concessions, had opposed it 5 to 2. Furcolo now conferred with the powerful Republican leader on the committee, Senator Edward Stone, whose support was critical. After a great deal of discussion, the governor made a substantial concession, shifting to the GOP plan to permit three-fourths of the revenues to go to local government. With this concession, the committee reviewed the bill once more, and this time reported it out with a favorable vote of 7 to 6, Stone and one Democrat changing their positions.

The new bill next went through the Ways and Means Committee, a necessary step before floor debate, but received an unfavorable 8 to 6 vote. All five Republicans opposed it. Despite Stone's shift, House Republicans simply felt, as one remarked, "It isn't enough. The governor doesn't give us enough." Since it appeared that the House would go along with the adverse committee report, the governor now decided to file a new message to keep the proposal alive while he talked to more representatives. The House voted 132 to 103 to admit the new proposal and send it to the Taxation Committee; most Republicans voted against admission. The Boston *Herald,* now convinced that further concessions were impossible, bitterly castigated the 69 Republicans who had opposed admitting the new proposal.

Once again—in this confusing series of moves that baffled even close observers—the Taxation Committee voted 7 to 6 for the bill, and the Ways and Means Committee opposed it, this time by the closer vote of 8 to 7. And so the sales tax at last came to the House floor—on July 17, a date when most state legislatures in the country had long since adjourned.

At this point, Furcolo and John Thompson had made a maximum effort to round up Democratic support through every conceivable appeal, and they felt that they had as many votes from their own party as was possible. As for the Republicans, Furcolo and his staff were relatively optimistic because most of the GOP power elite and their business allies were now actively and indeed frenetically working for the tax. Frank Giles, the influential Republican party chairman Charles Gibbons, many spokesmen for business- and property-owners, and the press were hard at work. Tempers were frayed on all sides, and both parties were seriously and bitterly divided; and yet the conservative leadership of Massachusetts had shown a remarkable ability to mobilize their votes on other occasions. Many of Furcolo's supporters felt that they had the votes, and that, once the tax passed the House, the Republican majority in the better-disciplined Senate would carry the ball.

The hot summer afternoon and evening of July 17 began with what was essentially a rehash of familiar arguments. Only when the legislators reconvened after supper was there a more dramatic interval. A Republican representative, Theodore J. Vaitses, took the floor to charge that, although he had been an advocate of the tax, he had seen "blackmail" and "threats" resorted to by interests lobbying for its passage. Reporters and editors for Massachusetts newspapers, he said, had approached legislators and "told them to vote for the tax or be destroyed," and GOP financial contributors were threatening to withdraw their support.

Then the House, which was in a commotion over these charges, suddenly subsided to almost perfect quiet. A woman representative, Irene K. Thresher, a respected member of the House, took the floor, and the whisper went around the chamber that it was she who had been "blackmailed" and "threatened" during the dinner hour. Mrs. Thresher, vice-chairman of the Republican State Committee and a long-time GOP worker, told the hushed audience:

> I have just been told by an eminent newspaperman that if I vote against this sales tax bill, I will be defeated for re-election. It could be that I will be defeated. I have enjoyed my several years of service in the House, and I have learned to respect my colleagues. I have also a profound respect for this institution and the democratic processes by which it operates. But if I have to vote in favor of something I find so distasteful to stay here, then I'm afraid I can't pay the price.

When Mrs. Thresher took her seat, the silence was broken and there was a rousing, stamping cheer from the floor and the gallery. She had not identified the newspaperman, but it was rumored to be someone from the Boston *Herald-Traveller* papers, the newspapers that had taken such an active part in the entire controversy and had attempted to act as major spokesman for the GOP. Most newspapers ignored this story the following day, but the liberal Democratic Pittsfield *Berkshire Eagle* stated that much of the intense pressure from newspapers came from Robert Choate, publisher of the *Herald,* and Hal Clancy, city editor of the Boston *Traveller.*

While dramatic, the Thresher episode probably had little effect on the outcome. The roll was called, and it was soon apparent that the vote would be very close. At the completion of the roll call, there were 93 votes for the tax and 95 against it. However, 57 members had not voted; under Massachusetts House rules, they were entitled to be recorded. At this strategic moment, a group of House Republicans caucused just outside the door; their leader was Representative J. Robert Ayers, who wanted a sales tax but had demanded more concessions than Furcolo was willing to make. As these men came in and were recorded, the anti-tax margin widened, and more and more members from both parties asked to be recorded against the bill.

The final vote was 130 to 105, all but 5 House members voting. The sales tax had been defeated.

And yet, despite perhaps the most bitter political controversy in twentieth-century Massachusetts history, the tax had come close to passage; a switch of 13 votes would have made the difference, and many Republicans and a few Democrats were on the fence until the last moment. What was more, a majority of Democrats, despite their distaste for the tax, had supported it while most Republicans had broken with their own leadership and strong conservative pressures to oppose it.

	DEMOCRATS	REPUBLICANS	TOTALS
For the Sales Tax	68	37	105
Opposed	61	69	130

The sales tax had been defeated in the final analysis by members of the very party that was supposedly ideologically committed to it, members who had not gone along with their leadership and some of whom, indeed, may have rebelled against what they considered undue pressure. But the final GOP opposition seems to have been due, in good part, to an effort to get even greater concessions from Furcolo, and also to a desire to administer a defeat to a Democratic governor. Off-the-record conversations with many Republican legislators indicated that this latter motive was one of the most important. The Boston *Herald,* in an editorial on July 19 entitled "The Republican Dishonor," argued that the tax had been defeated "by a Republican party that lacked the integrity to place the state's needs above narrow political ends."

Conclusions

Can State and Local Government Govern? /   There are several ways to view the Massachusetts sales tax controversy. To some observers, the state seemed at the time to be like a great prehistoric beast in agony, an aging organism faced with needs that its political processes did not permit it to meet. This was the view of many who agreed with the Furcolo position. As one of them said at the time, the state seemed to have many of the aspects of an underdeveloped area. "Massachusetts is like the Congo," went the quip, "—a maximum of social and economic problems, and a minimum of effective political leadership."

Many of our large cities, like Boston, New York, and Chicago, now seem to suffer similar problems. Some observers consider these cities to be almost ungovernable. These cities are faced with a massive concentration of lower-income and minority groups, urban blight, and crises in transportation, housing, and law enforcement at the very time that they lack adequate financial resources. Further, the political process in the cities often brings mediocre or corrupt men into governing positions. But even the most able men with the best intentions find that neither financial resources nor united community effort are available to meet their problems. As a result, the United States Conference of Mayors and other spokesmen for city government are turning increasingly to the federal government for help; at present, they are concentrating their attention on requests for a new federal Department of Urban Affairs, at the cabinet level.

Many of our states seem to be in the same dilemma, faced as they are by acute social problems. The present writers are inclined to agree that state and local governments will continue to look to Washington for help, given the political and economic situation that exists in many parts of the United States.

Other observers disagree with the pessimistic view that state and local government "cannot govern." They believe that a democracy must always reflect the multitude of voices with which the people speak. In a complex, urban-industrial society like Massachusetts, no one social or economic group can hope to command a firm majority. The older, Yankee-dominated Massachusetts was a quiet place, governed relatively well by a well-disciplined, but conservative, Republican party that had due respect for its leaders. This older Massachusetts did not have to wrestle with complex social issues, or at least it failed to do so.

Spokesmen for this latter view agree that a governor must accept that he can govern only with a coalition making up at least 51 per cent of the votes in the legislature. He must, therefore, compromise with what might be called "institutional conservatism"—the tendency of most elected political leaders to avoid or postpone controversial decisions. Most state and local leaders, sensitive to public opinion, are especially anxious to avoid new taxes as long as possible. The experience in most states and cities demonstrates that sales taxes and other major new taxes are usually voted only when the situation is really and obviously desperate.

Foster Furcolo did not accept this view of the governor's function—and he paid the price. A little more than three years after the defeat of the sales tax, on September 15, 1960, the price he had personally paid was dramatically illustrated when he broke down and cried in front of a large audience at the opening of the first two-year community college in Pittsfield, Massachusetts. He was unable to make his address.

To Furcolo, the opening of the first link in a new state-wide network of colleges was symbolic of the kind of programs for which he had risked his political life. Ironically and painfully for him, the opening of the college came on the very day after his overwhelming repudiation by the voters in the 1960 Democratic primary. He had, in his own view, sacrificed "politics" for "government"—he had accepted four years of endless political controversy to work for his programs, and he had lost.

Political Aftermath, 1957–1960 / How had the four problems that Furcolo faced in 1957 actually been resolved—the revenue gap, state needs, local needs, and the local property tax burden? The simplest answer is that Massachusetts state government had managed to muddle through because of a large and unexpected rise in the Gross National Product. The GNP, the total goods and services produced by the American people, rose to a record high in 1957—and in Massachusetts, which shared in the nation's prosperity, money flowed into the state's coffers at an unexpected rate. Long before the end of the year, it was apparent that there would be no deficit and that state revenues would reach a new high.

The state legislature, early in 1958, responded to the new revenue picture by voting substantial additional funds; the Democratic majority, true to its traditional behavior, was quite willing to vote the money as long as the books balanced. Total state appropriations for the fiscal year 1958 reached $401 million—not far from the original Furcolo request for $411 million, plus his $12 million reserve fund.

By 1960, most of the major state programs that Furcolo had requested in 1957 had become law, and Massachusetts was spending more than $100 million more per year than in 1957. This meant a considerable expansion of programs for health, welfare, and education. Higher education expenditures alone advanced 50 per cent in those four years. Further, the continuing rise in the Gross National Product and in resulting tax revenues meant that these new programs were achieved without major new taxes. The only taxes adopted were a minor increase in cigarette taxes and a new withholding system that brought in some revenue. Economic growth accounted for most of the increase in state funds.

When Furcolo left office in 1960, therefore, the state situation was "neither heaven nor hell" by his standard; state programs had been considerably expanded, although he still argued that, in his view, important social needs were not being met. Furthermore, population increases were rapidly "sopping up" the increased services being provided.

The local problem, however, the issue that legislators had refused to face in 1957, had not really been resolved. Property taxes continued to rise sharply from 1957 to 1960. When Furcolo left office, local taxpayers were paying $133 million more per year than in 1957—or about the same amount which would have been raised by the sales tax! In a sense, therefore, within three years the people of Massachusetts were actually paying the equivalent of a new tax in property taxes alone; but this was not all. When we add the more than $100 million in additional funds that the state was spending, and another $37 million the state was collecting and distributing as local aid, we find that the total cost of state and local government in 1960 was more than $270 million a year higher than in 1957. And further increases were on the way; the Republican governor who succeeded Furcolo, John A. Volpe, pushed through a still larger budget in 1961.

Furcolo had, therefore, been "correct" in a sense in predicting that taxes must rise to meet needs. But he had misestimated the kind of political process by which tax increases would be achieved. Rather than a single sweeping tax increase, the electorate or their representatives "preferred" a slow and somewhat confusing method, meeting needs through the subtle process of economic growth and the reluctant action of more than 300 separate local governments. More correctly, the public may not have "preferred" this method, but it was more acceptable; it seemed to hurt less, and political professionals knew it.

This was not Furcolo's conception of the nature of political leadership. Indeed, despite what had happened in 1957, he continued to advocate the sales tax; he was also influenced strongly by the continuing threat of a large state deficit. In 1958–59, an actual deficit loomed, which had to be made up not by economic growth alone but by the bookkeeping device of adopting a withholding system and collecting taxes six months earlier. After his re-election in 1958—in an election in which neither party made use of the sales tax issue, in part because it was quietly favored by the GOP candidate —Furcolo again offered a sales tax in 1959 and 1960. This, however, led only to further controversy, and this time the Republicans made no attempt to support the tax. In each year, again, economic growth provided the necessary revenues.

The Republicans and the business community, it appeared, might have special reason to regret their refusal to support a sales tax. Not only did the property tax continue to climb, but labor and the Democratic party took the first steps toward a constitutional amendment to permit a graduated income tax. This amendment was approved by the 1959 and 1961 legislative sessions over GOP opposition and will appear on the ballot as a referendum question in 1962. The debate of 1957–1961 appeared to foreclose the possibility of a sales tax for some years to come, which makes increases in the income tax more likely.

In one sense, Furcolo's experience differed from that of many other governors in the late 1950's. In many states, growth was not enough, and there were severe budgetary crises that were resolved only by substantial new taxes. In retrospect, one can say that Furcolo might have been proved "correct" if the GNP had not increased as it had; a real deficit would have helped to vindicate him, although even in that case the legislature would probably have adopted only a small tax to cover state needs.

Furcolo's tactics were also a source of great controversy. Many observers felt that a man who had more sympathy for the legislative mind, who spent more time with legislators and tried harder to win them over on a personal basis, might have been more successful. However, it is doubtful that this approach—helpful as it may have been—would have given Furcolo a major new tax. The legislature was simply not willing—and the price of "better legislative relations" would have been giving up the sales tax before he had begun. Since this also seemed to Furcolo at the time to mean giving up new state and local programs, he refused to accept this approach. In hindsight, we have seen that many new services were provided without new taxes; but this circumstance was not plain in 1957 nor has it been the pattern in many other states.

"Government" and "politics" will undoubtedly continue to be at opposite poles in the years ahead. Our population statistics indicate clearly enough that we face ever-increasing demands for government services, but our political experience indicates that we are unlikely to see sweeping solutions. State and local politics, as in Massachusetts, is likely to mean less "solving" problems than living with them year after year. Given many competing powers elite, we can expect to see either political stalemates or a clumsy and painful inching forward, meeting needs only on a short-term basis and under great pressure.

Sources

MUCH of the information in this case study came from interviews with members of the Furcolo administration, the state Department of Corporations and Taxation, the legislature, pressure groups, and political parties. The Boston *Herald-Traveller,* Boston *Globe,* Boston *Record-American,* and *Christian Science Monitor* were used, as were several newspapers published in other cities.

DUE, JOHN F. *Sales Taxation.* Urbana: Univ. of Illinois Press, 1957.

LATHAM, EARL, and GEORGE GOODWIN. *Massachusetts Politics.* Medford, Mass.: Tufts Univ. Civic Education Center, 1960.

LEAGUE OF WOMEN VOTERS OF MASSACHUSETTS. *Massachusetts State Government.* Cambridge: Harvard Univ. Press, 1956.

LEVIN, MURRAY. *The Alienated Voter: The Politics of Boston.* New York: Holt, Rinehart, and Winston, 1960.

LOCKARD, DUANE. *New England State Politics.* Princeton: Princeton Univ. Press, 1959.

MCCLAIN, ROBERT H., JR. "Taxes, Services, and the Massachusetts Economy." *State Government and Public Responsibility,* ed. by Robert R. Robbins. Medford, Mass.: Tufts Univ. Civic Education Center, 1959.

RANSONE, COLEMAN B., JR. *The Office of Governor in the United States.* University: Univ. of Alabama Press, 1956.

SHANNON, WILLIAM V. "Massachusetts: Prisoner of the Past." *Our Sovereign State,* ed. by Robert S. Allen. New York: Vanguard, 1949.

SOLOWAY, ARNOLD M. *A Balanced Fiscal Program for Massachusetts.* Boston: Americans for Democratic Action, 1956.

Pressure Politics in Pennsylvania:

The Truckers vs. The Railroads

Andrew Hacker

CORNELL UNIVERSITY

"I am again a candidate
for the legislature.
What if any assistance
can I expect from your
Association? I can
assure you I do not
forget my friends."
—A PENNSYLVANIA
LEGISLATOR

A MERICAN society is composed of many groups, and many
of these groups seek to promote their interests by means of political action.
Public officials are responsive to group pressures; lobbying is regarded
as a legitimate means of political expression. Members of groups are also
voters, and there is a presumption that they will support friendly office-
holders on Election Day—or will punish those who are unfriendly. Groups
are also able to help sympathetic legislators by contributing to campaign
funds, for there is a tacit understanding that bread cast upon the waters in
this way will be returned. On occasion, groups will seek to influence
public opinion so that it appears that "grass-roots" sentiment favors a particular course of legislation.

The truckers and the railroads operating in Pennsylvania are two groups
with a vital interest in the state laws regulating long-haul transportation.
The organizations representing the two industries sought to influence the
decisions of both state legislators and the governor in a heated campaign in
1949–1952. One of the two took the ambitious step of retaining a professional public relations firm to create popular feeling in support of its side.
The other group retaliated by taking the case to the courts in the hope that
the judicial branch would declare against the methods used by their opponents. In this case, therefore, pressure politics are seen to affect legislators,
administrators, judges, and members of the general public. The specific issues involved in the case are now closed, but the major questions of pressure politics that were raised remain open and recurring questions.

In a free society the right of citizens to petition their rulers is an incon-
testable one. And when these rulers are elected officials, it behooves them
to give respectful attention to those with the power to keep them in office.
The days of the formal petition, embellished with flowery prose and replete
with the signatures of an aggrieved citizenry, are all but gone. There are,
nowadays, other and—it is thought—better ways to express popular sentiment. With the growth of government and the widened scope of political
activity, more and more groups within the population are affected by legislation. To ensure that laws and regulations do not harm their interests, individuals join together in associations to pool their power and maximize

their effectiveness. In the twentieth century, therefore, the chief petitioning agency has become the pressure group. Until a few decades ago pressure groups confined themselves, for the most part, to lobbying: direct contact with legislators and, on occasion, administrators. It was felt that if a case were stated privately and persuasively, a lawmaker would listen to reason and would give his support to one or another side of an issue. More recently, however, pressure politics have taken a more ambitious turn. Working on the assumption that elected officials are responsive to public opinion, groups now seek to arouse favorable sentiment to their cause among the electorate at large with the thought that this grass-roots feeling will be conveyed upward to the politicians. The consequence is that old-style lobbying is supplemented by new-style public relations. The intimate contacts of the capitol cloakroom are bolstered by the practiced techniques of Madison Avenue. These themes are well illustrated by an episode in Pennsylvania politics that took place more than a decade ago.

Trucks and Railroads: Economics and Politics

For a period of two and a half years—from mid-1949 to early 1952—the railroads and the trucking firms of the Commonwealth of Pennsylvania were embroiled in a fierce political struggle. The prize was legislation that would give one kind of transportation an important cost advantage over the other in the competition for freight traffic. The targets of the campaign were not only the members of the legislature and the state's governor, but also the ordinary men and women whose individual attitudes and sentiments go to make up what is called public opinion.

The weight load a truck may carry is a matter for state legislation. A weight limit is set for obvious reasons: highway safety and the prevention of road damage. But such limits also serve a less obvious purpose: weight restrictions can drive up the costs of truck shipments and therefore impel shippers to use alternative means of transport. It is clearly in the interests of railroads, therefore, to have the weight limits on trucks set as low as possible. The economics of this are quite simple. Suppose that a state law sets the legal total weight limit at 45,000 pounds. The truck and tractor weigh 20,000 pounds, meaning that a "payload" of 25,000 pounds is permitted. On an interstate run from Pittsburgh to Cincinnati, a trip of 293 miles, the trucker will charge at the rate of 41.2 cents per hundredweight of freight, or a total cost of $103 for the truckload. If the weight limit is raised to 60,000 pounds he can then add 15,000 pounds to his payload and still keep constant his outlays for drivers and fuel. This means that the truck-owner will be able to make $61.80 more on a Pittsburgh-Cincinnati haul. Even assuming that all his trucks returned empty from Cincinnati, he would gain $9,270 additional revenue per truck per year. In this position he would be able to lower his per hundredweight rate on shipments and would be in a better position to compete with rival means of transportation, such as railroads.

In 1943 the over-all weight limit for trucks in Pennsylvania was fixed at 45,000 pounds. This figure (along with Kentucky's) was the lowest in the country. Furthermore, immediately neighboring states permitted anywhere from 60,000- to 67,000-pound loads. This meant that an interstate truck originating in New York or Ohio or West Virginia might have to stop before entering Pennsylvania territory and transfer its excess weight to another carrier. Similarly, trucks leaving Pennsylvania would have what amounted to waste space the minute they left their home state and were traveling in a new and more liberal jurisdiction. One truck operator summarized the kinds of problems he encountered:

> Generally there were many instances of additional costs of operation of the business due to the restricted weight limits permitted on vehicles. There was the business that could not be solicited because of the weight limitation, which also limited the rate that could be applied to the commodity. There were many times that four trucks had to be used to haul commodities that could have been handled with three trucks if the increased weight had been available. There was a general overall cost of working under a hampered condition between movements for the commerce of Pennsylvania from the manufacturing point within the State of Pennsylvania out to places beyond the borders of Pennsylvania. Also there was the additional costs of moving of the commodities necessary to industry in Pennsylvania from points beyond the border into the manufacturer and user of these various commodities.

How had this state of affairs come about? The answer is that for three-quarters of a century the railroads of Pennsylvania had had virtually undisputed power in the Commonwealth. Legislatures and governors might be attentive to other interests, but they would always take careful heed of the railroads' suggestions concerning public policy. This was not so much the result of bribery or overt pressure as it was the result of an implicit feeling that "what's good for the railroads is good for Pennsylvania." It is not surprising, therefore, that weight restrictions on trucks remained on the statute books year after year.

But times were changing. Whereas in 1930 there were only 28,000 large trucks in the United States, by 1950 the total had risen to almost 450,000. (While the figure of 450,000 seems impressive, it should be pointed out that it constituted only 1 per cent of all the vehicles on the roads and only 5 per cent of all the trucks in operation in 1950.) The accelerated growth of the trucking industry over this twenty-year period made it a serious

competitor to the railroads. While in the 1930's it was not difficult for the
railroads to keep legislative restrictions on truck weights, by the end of
World War II the truckers were a sizable political force in their own
right. In the period immediately following the end of the war, they set as
their goal the repeal of the 45,000-pound weight limit. A partial victory was
scored in the 1949 session of the state legislature. A bill to raise the weight
limit from 45,000 to 60,000 pounds passed in the House of Representatives
by a comfortable margin of 114 to 86. However the Senate was less
sympathetic and referred the bill to a committee, where it languished for
the rest of the session and subsequently died. The truckers, accustomed by
past experience to a total rebuff, were heartened by having won over half
the legislature. They began to prepare themselves for the 1951 session.

Legislative Oratory and Organized Lobbying /   By 1951 the truckers'
bill, now called S. 615, was a familiar story to the lawmakers of Pennsylvania. Senator John H. Dent, a Democrat from Westmoreland County, put
the matter quite frankly. "We are all set," he told his colleagues. "Every
man has been talked to either by one interest or the other because, basically, it is an interest fight. It is the fight of one means of transportation as
against another, and seriously and honestly I say to the Members of this
Senate, this bill has been a long time coming." But familiar or not, legislators like to make speeches, and in both chambers the debate was a rousing one. While ostensibly much of the talk had to do with the merits and
demerits of S. 615, never far from the surface were the competing interests that sought its passage or defeat.

The opponents of the bill stressed the dangers inherent in large trucks.
Not only might the state's road system be pounded to pieces if truck
weights were allowed to be raised, but the lives and limbs of the Commonwealth's citizens would be put in further jeopardy. To underscore this
point, Representative Louis Leonard, a Democrat from Pittsburgh, alerted
his colleagues by reading aloud from his collection of newspaper clippings:

CRASH KILLS PITTSBURGHER

Two men died today from injuries suffered when a tractor-trailer plunged
down a 100-foot embankment four miles west of Fulton County community.

THREE DRIVING FROM HERE TO WEDDING
KILLED IN CRASH

A Pittsburgh family of seven Detroit-bound to attend a wedding of rela-
tives met a nightmare of death instead. Three were killed near Akron and
four others injured when a trailer truck crushed their two cars. All three
occupants of one car were killed.

16-VEHICLE PILE-UP KILLS FOUR, INJURES 20

Four killed, 20 hospitalized is the total of this sixteen-vehicle smash-up on crowded Highway 17, near Huntsboro, N.Y. Here is what happened. Big trailer truck crashed out of control into rear of New York-bound taxi while going down a four-mile grade. The truck's gasoline tank exploded. The taxi, with seven occupants, three of them were killed, plowed into car ahead and resulting "chain reaction" piled up 15 autos, resulting in a fourth death. The truck carried propane gas, which did not explode. Driver Marsdon Reese, Jr., Bayonne, N.J., said truck's air brakes suddenly gave out.

Senator T. Newell Wood, a Republican from Luzerne County, echoed this theme in the upper chamber when he spoke of the "big, over-the-road box cars—the huge monsters that destroy our pavements, wreck our bridges, clog our streets, crawl up one side of the hill and roar recklessly down the other." To his mind it was unnecessary to underline this point in any detail: "Everyone knows that our highways are being pounded to pieces by these huge highway trailers." However, just to make sure that no one forgot what everyone knew, Senator Wood referred to a highway test that was being conducted in Maryland. One of the preliminary conclusions of the test, quoted by the senator, was that "increased frequencies of heavy loadings on paving surfaces will seriously disrupt the functioning of highly essential highways." The Maryland road test, which imparted scientific authority to everyday knowledge, was to figure heavily in the debate. In the lower chamber, Representative Robert F. Kent, a Republican from Meadville, cited a report by a T. J. Kauer, director of the Ohio Department of Highways and a member of the committee supervising the Maryland test. The early results of the test, Representative Kent quoted Kauer as saying, "already indicate conclusively that further weight increases in legal weights of commercial vehicles should be halted." He went on to add, however, that the Kauer report was neither final nor official. But this did not seem to deter Representative Kent. So far as the Maryland test was concerned, he said, "there are no reports available which contain the conclusions which I presume will be drawn from the facts that have been gathered to date. . . ." What were available were nine highly technical preliminary reports, the last one dated May 1951. The opponents of S. 615 had all of these printed in the appendix of the Legislative Journal, and they ran to 46 large double-columned pages.

The defenders of the bill could not come out in favor of highway accidents or breaking up the state's roads, but they saw the possibility of grave economic damage to the Commonwealth were the trucking industry to be stifled by outdated weight limits. In the upper chamber, Senator G. Robert Watkins, a Republican from Delaware County, was willing to take certain risks in the cause of progress:

When you create business, when you bring business into your State, when you allow trucks from other states all around us to move across our State, like they do in every other state without being stopped and blocked by policemen and fined, then we can make some headway with the laws that we have in this State. Gentlemen, I know there are two sides to this question, naturally, but at the same time I feel that it could be a curse to this State of Pennsylvania to build a wall around us and stop the movement of goods in and out of our State.

His sentiments were repeated in the lower house by Representative Albert S. Readinger, a Democrat from Reading. "I say when it boils down to a question of whether we are going to try to impede progress or whether we are going to stand aside and let progress roll on, we should have enough facts today on which to make this decision." But what of the findings of the Maryland road test that had been quoted so freely in the debate? Representative Readinger was not a little skeptical about those reports, and he wondered aloud to his colleagues whether they might not be an excuse for yet another postponement of the truckers' case.

How long are we going to delay? Suppose two years from now we have the result of the Maryland road tests! How conclusive are they going to be? Are we going to argue for another two or four or six years as to whether or not it was the weather conditions which caused the damage to the Maryland Road Tests or whether it was the weight of the trucks?

Indeed, that it might be the weather rather than the trucks that was threatening Pennsylvania roads was a point that had been raised earlier by Senator Dent in the upper chamber debate.

I will tell you what wrecked the roads in my County if you want to know— old man Winter. Now, if you can legislate against old man Winter, then you can have pretty good roads in Pennsylvania. Where the roads are not properly drained and where the base of the road is not properly put in, you get a road failure. . . . The big trucks have not done it.

Another issue in the debate was the ultraconservative position of Pennsylvania compared with nearby states. Whereas Pennsylvania held its trucks to a 45,000-pound limit, surrounding states were far more generous. Representative Hiram G. Andrews, a Democrat from Cambria County, raised this point as a simple matter of equity and intelligence. If S. 615 were passed, he said, it would put Pennsylvania truckers on a more equal footing:

It is interesting to compare Pennsylvania with some of the neighboring states. The increases in weights on the various combinations are designed

to bring Pennsylvania more nearly in line with surrounding states. . . .
On the tandem axle on the trailer, the weights permitted in surrounding
states read as follows: Ohio, 67,000; New York, 61,500; West Virginia,
60,000; District of Columbia, 65,400; Maryland, 65,000; Delaware, 60,-
000; New Jersey 60,000. The average being 65,000. Are the eminent highway authorities in those states clearly crazy? Have they no roads? Are
they all negligent of their highways? What is so special about the Pennsylvania highway situation that it is not found in neighboring states?

But these questions were not new ones. They had been raised in the debate
on the weight limit bill in the House of Representatives two years earlier,
and at that time answers had been given. Representative J. P. Moran, a
Democrat from Turtle Creek, had agreed that both equity and intelligence
were issues; but he wondered whether it was the Pennsylvania legislature
or the other lawmaking bodies that should be faulted. For one thing the
liberal weights allowed in surrounding states had in each case been passed
over the strenuous objections of experts in the respective highway departments. And so far as equal treatment for truckers was in question, having
Pennsylvania raise its 45,000-pound limit was not the only solution. "If
Ohio, New Jersey, and several of the other states have made a mistake in
permitting greater weights," Moran said, "let us ask them to come down to
our weights rather than we go up to theirs."

"Basically, it is an interest fight," Senator Dent had told his colleagues;
and this fact was not far from the minds of members of both houses of the
legislature. Nor were the lawmakers reticent about naming the various
groups lined up on one side or the other. The opponents of S. 615, in
particular, had collected a glittering array of organizations ranged against
the bill. Representative Moran read into the record letters and telegrams
from various groups that wished to retain the prevailing weight limit on
trucks. These were: the Pennsylvania State Association of Township
Supervisors, the Pennsylvania State Grange, the Pennsylvania Motor Federation, the Rural Letter Carriers Association, the Pennsylvania Federation of Women's Clubs, the Keystone Auto Club, the Pittsburgh Auto
Club, the Pennsylvania State Association of Boroughs, the Brotherhood of
Railway and Steamship Clerks, the Brotherhood of Railway Trainmen,
the Brotherhood of Locomotive Firemen and Enginemen, the Brotherhood
of Railroad Conductors, the United Mine Workers of America, the Pennsylvania CIO Council, the Brotherhood of Railway Carmen of America,
and the United Steelworkers of America.

Not all of the communications received by Representative Moran were
from established organizations like the Pennsylvania State Grange or the
Pennsylvania State Association of Township Supervisors. Some of the
letters came from ordinary citizens, such as one Pittsburgh resident who
wrote from his convalescent bed:

I came home from the hospital a few days ago, a victim of an auto carrier crashing into my car. I am fortunate to be here to tell about it, as my car was completely demolished. I believe every person on our highways today fears these monsters. They are killing ever so many people, and yet they want to increase their loads. The number of these road monsters is increasing daily. They defy the laws by overloading, and their mechanical condition, brakes, etc., are reported frequently as failing. This all requires the careful attention of our lawmakers. . . . The public needs protection against these road monsters!

Another constituent was aroused by reading a magazine article, and he conveyed his feeling to his representative in the legislature:

I want to register my opposition to that portion of the truck bill which will permit the increase of weights of trucks. In my conversation with neighbors and acquaintances on this bill, there is not one in ten that is in favor of the increase of weight of trucks. A recent article in the *Reader's Digest* claims that it would require thirty-five billion dollars to restore our present highways for passenger travel. The present condition of the highways, it is alleged, is due to the overweight of trucks.

Yet it was not simply the Federation of Women's Clubs and the United Steelworkers, coupled with ordinary citizens, that opposed S. 615 as a matter of public safety and convenience. If there were many interests at work, the defenders of the bill thought that some of them were behaving with rather extraordinary vigor on behalf of a cause that affected them only remotely. Why, Senator Dent wanted to know, was the Grange so concerned to defeat the bill? "When you speak about the Grange opposing this bill, how many Grange roads or farm roads are subjected to the traffic of this kind of truck?" he asked. "It does not pay to take these trucks over back roads because they are, in the main, used for hauling between the ports or main industrial centers." A similar question was raised in the House by Representative James J. Gleason, a Republican from Muncy:

Another thing I would like to bring out is that the State Grange has been flooding us with mail and mail, and I cannot understand the members of the State Grange standing back and having all this money spent when it is not so much of their business, because a farmer depends on the trucks just as much as they do the railroad. But I understand that the State Grange and the railroad are in the same office and I was always told that politics makes strange bedfellows.

Representative Andrews also wondered what was going on. He was puzzled about the role of the Pennsylvania State Association of Township Supervisors as well as about that of the Grange:

I know that an unusually clever advertising agency is responsible for much of the propaganda against this bill. It is an advertising agency that was retained by the American Association of Railroads. I am wondering whether the expense of the Grange in fighting this bill was financed out of Grange money or financed from some other source. I am wondering whether the Association of Township Supervisors are, out of their own funds, responsible for the campaign they have waged or whether they have been financed from other sources.

The debates in both the Senate and the House of Representatives were spirited, but everyone knew that the rhetoric was for the record more than anything else. The last, and mercifully brief, speaker in the lower chamber was Representative Samuel B. Dennison, a Republican from Reynoldsville, who said what was probably on everyone's mind: "I do not believe that anything that I could say or anything that anybody else has said here this afternoon has changed a single vote in this House. I will, therefore, ask that the debate be terminated and a vote be taken."

And the votes were taken. In the Senate, S. 615 passed by a comfortable margin of 31 to 18, and in the House it won by a vote of 112 to 79. In both chambers party considerations were completely irrelevant. In the Senate, 17 Republicans voted for the bill and 12 against, with 14 Democrats for and 6 against. In the House, 66 Republicans voted for the bill and 44 against, with 46 Democrats for and 35 against. The slight differences between the Senate and House versions were ironed out and on December 20, 1951, S. 615 was passed by both chambers in its final form and sent to the governor for his signature.

Why had S. 615 passed so easily? The opponents of the bill had more speakers on their side. They had lined up a wide assortment of groups to support their cause. They had a bulging file of letters, resolutions, and newspaper clippings. They had advance information on the Maryland road test that they cited in speeches and read into the record. Indeed, the supporters of S. 615 seemed extremely casual, if not confident, during the debate; and they appeared to have made no effort to secure technical information or the sympathy of various organizations in the state. Yet they scored a victory after a dozen or more years of defeat.

A partial answer was that the truckers decided to engage in behind-the-scenes lobbying in a serious way, and the agency they employed was the Pennsylvania Motor Truck Association—the PMTA.

The PMTA is a trade association, and in this respect it is like the tens of thousands of organized groups that characterize the American business scene. Its members consist of the various trucking companies doing business in Pennsylvania. While the official "members" are companies rather than individuals, a large proportion of the trucking firms are small businesses owned by a single man. Thus while one PMTA "member" might, for example, be the Noerr Motor Freight Company, the real member was Floyd B. Noerr, the president and principal owner of the company. The individualistic character of the PMTA membership is important to note here. An association composed of small businessmen situated in local communities has, for that very reason, a potential array of groundtroops for a political battle.

Between 1945 and 1951 the PMTA was hard at work. First of all, it set up an impressive lobbying establishment in Harrisburg, the state capital. Experienced and well-financed representatives of the trucking industry made it their business to get to know the legislators and to impress upon them the need for repeal of the old 45,000-pound weight limit. Yet it is not sufficient for a lobbyist to buttonhole a lawmaker and to engage him in conversation. For politicians have many—and often conflicting—pressures operating on them. The politician asks a lobbyist: "Why *should* I listen to you?" And here it is up to the lobbyist to demonstrate that he is speaking for a group that can affect the electoral fortunes of that lawmaker. At the same time, therefore, the PMTA's officials were mobilizing the rank-and-file truckers of the state.

In 1950 the Treasurer of the PMTA had collected a total of $76,000 from more than 600 truckers as a political war chest. These funds were then handed over to the parties: $37,000 to the Republicans and $39,000 to the Democrats. Like many groups, the PMTA was nonpartisan: it was willing to cultivate the votes of both major parties and it sensed that both Democrats and Republicans would support its cause. Campaign contributions are one of the great lubricants of pressure politics. No candidate for public office ever has sufficient funds for his campaigns, and the best way to earn a politician's gratitude is to help him defray his electioneering expenses. Even small investments sometimes pay large dividends. Nor was the initiative wholly on the part of the truckers. One state legislator, in March 1950, wrote to the PMTA: "I am again a candidate for the legislature. What if any assistance can I expect from your Association? I can assure you I do not forget my friends." The PMTA replied that, as an association, it could not contribute to his campaign fund. However it got in touch with its local members in that legislator's district and advised them to open their checkbooks. This policy was followed over the length of the state. By 1951 the truckers had, in one way or another, the majority of the state's senators and representatives in their debt. Six years of patient lobbying, six years of local participation by members of the trucking industry, had paid off. Much time, energy, and money had been invested. But these expenditures would be more than recouped by the new profits available to the trucking industry as a result of increasing the weight limit from 45,000 to 60,000 pounds.

What the truckers had not reckoned with, however, was a counterattack by the railroads, which had been gaining momentum for two years, and which, by 1951, was a powerful force indeed.

The Experts Arrive: Public Relations and Politics

As far back as the spring of 1949 the railroads were becoming seriously concerned about the rising economic and political power of the truckers. It was plain that even with the 45,000-pound limit the trucking industry was making inroads on their business. Trucks could offer a door-to-door service that was often speedier and more efficient than that which the railroads were able to provide. This was true even though, at the time, trucking rates—figured on a ton-mile basis—were appreciably higher than those charged by the railroads. In political terms it was clear that the railroads no longer had a hegemony at Harrisburg. One by one the legislators were forgetting their historic fealty to the railroads and were succumbing to the blandishments of the truckers. If these developments were to be checkmated, then strong and swift measures were called for.

Under the leadership of the Pennsylvania Railroad, the railroads' own trade association met to consider the matter. This group is known as the Eastern Railroads Presidents Conference (ERPC), and it embraces not only Pennsylvania but all the other eastern states as well. In May 1949 the ERPC appointed a "Competitive Transportation Committee" and it in turn set up a public relations subcommittee. This group considered the resources at its disposal. Compared with the truckers, and figured in terms of personnel, they were comparatively meager. The PMTA had members in every Pennsylvania county, and these owners or operators of trucking firms were relatively wealthy men who were often leading lights in their local communities. As was seen, these men were in a good position to exert influence on the various legislators throughout the state. The ERPC, on the other hand, had as its "members" various railroads: the men who sat on the ERPC's committees at any given time were not the owners of railroads but salaried executives. The typical railroad is a large corporate enterprise, owned by thousands of stockholders over the country. As far as the application of political pressure is concerned, this kind of structure is disadvantageous. The Pennsylvania Railroad, for example, might try to deploy its local stationmasters and freight agents in a legislative campaign. But it is not easy for a corporation to use its employees in this way, and it is illegal for corporations to hand over money to their employees for them to pass on to politicians. These deficiencies were pointed out later by the people in charge of the railroads' political efforts:

> Generally speaking, the entire campaign . . . has been badly handicapped because the railroads themselves have not been organized properly to ex-

ploit their many contacts. . . . The more railroad people whose contacts can be utilized, the more people you involve on your side. The more people on your side, the greater the publicity and the greater the public pressure.

Mobilizing great numbers of people, however, is difficult work. The stark fact was that the truckers had more "contacts" because of the character of their business, and on that basis the railroads could not hope to compete.

But what the railroads did have was money, which they were prepared to use on a generous scale.

In the summer of 1949, therefore, the public relations subcommittee of the ERPC let it be known that it would retain a professional public relations firm to plan and execute the countercampaign against the truckers. This decision was not an unusual one. For many years public relations firms have been doing political work, especially on the state level. Their services are particularly suited to business corporations, which are not set up for the specialized activity of applying legislative pressure. These public relations firms undertake to ensure—or block—the passage of certain bills by creating among the general public a climate of opinion that is favorable to the objectives of their clients. It is strictly a payment-for-services-rendered business, and public relations practitioners concentrate on technical means rather than on philosophical ends. Furthermore, when a group such as the railroad association indicates that it is in the market for public relations help, it is normal to allow several firms to make presentations. In this way the group can assess the experience and qualifications of various firms before it makes its choice.

During that summer a number of public relations firms made proposals. Selvage and Lee, for example, said: "We know how to put on a hard-hitting campaign and have done so many times." They cited their success in getting discriminatory legislation against oleomargarine repealed. Hill and Knowlton stressed its "extensive experience in dealing with similar public relations and legislative problems both on national and state levels." It mentioned its campaigns against price controls, government fertilizer plants, and gasoline taxes. The Fred Eldean Organization said: "We like the direct-action drive to get a result." And among their past results were the elimination of real estate taxes and restricting new companies from entering the international air travel field. But the most impressive presentation was made by Carl Byoir & Associates, Inc. In 1936 they had, on behalf of their client, the Freeport Sulphur Company, got the Louisiana legislature to reduce a tax on sulphur by almost 50 per cent. In the 1930's they worked for the A&P Company and were successful in thwarting chain-store taxes on both state and national levels. They had also served the tile and distilling industries with signal results. But perhaps the most persuasive campaign of the Byoir organization was its work for the A&P.

In 1937 there was a bill pending in the New York legislature that would have levied an annual tax of $1,000 on each chain store in the state. As A&P had 2,000 stores, the passage of that bill would have cost the company $2,000,000 per year. Byoir was retained and his firm set out to arouse public opinion against the bill. "We went out to farmer organizations, co-operatives, and labor organizations, and civic groups, women's clubs, consumer organizations . . . and preached the distributive method of the chain store. . . ." The gospel was transmitted so effectively that the bill never got out of committee. A&P then had Byoir turn to the national level, where Congress was considering a similar bill. Not only did Byoir induce hundreds of labor, agricultural, industrial, and consumer groups to pass resolutions against such legislation, but the firm also helped to stage-manage the open hearings on the bill that took place in 1940. Whereas the proponents of the bill could only muster twenty witnesses, Byoir arranged that the A&P side would have almost eight times that number. These spokesmen, including farmers and labor leaders, gave the impression that vast sectors of the public would be harmed if the bill were passed. The apparent voice of the people prevailed, and the bill never reached the floor of Congress. Since that time Byoir opposed 247 anti-chain-store bills in state legislatures. Of these, only six passed.

The railroads were clearly impressed with the Byoir record: they engaged the firm's services in August 1949. Byoir agreed to put his staff of 160 employees at the disposal of the railroads. The annual fee was $75,000, but this did not include operating expenses. That is, the ERPC was to be billed for the actual salaries of the Byoir staff people who worked on the account and for the costs of using various departmental services such as research and writing. Furthermore, the railroads would pay for all advertising and publishing expenses. The total bill for the first year—over and above the $75,000 fee—was estimated at $274,190. Within a few years it rose to almost $1,000,000.[1] The railroads had financial resources of this order to spend, and they felt that the Byoir firm's services would be a worthwhile investment in their struggle against the truckers.

The scene now shifts to the offices of Carl Byoir & Associates, Inc. in Manhattan, which at that time were on 40th Street, just off Madison Avenue. (The firm later moved to new offices on New York's fashionable East Side near the United Nations.) Byoir's offices were not (and are not) what Hollywood might expect. There are few platinum blondes, modest use of carpeting (only in executive offices: other floors are resounding asphalt tile), and a certain air of newsroom informality about the place. To be

---

[1] The ERPC is a regional group and Byoir was retained to work on the anti-truck campaign in New York and New Jersey as well as in Pennsylvania. But the most important activities that were political in character took place in Pennsylvania, and those are the ones that will be described here.

sure there are some dramatic touches: the bronze bust of Byoir himself
in the paneled reception room, and a large portrait of him in the photo-
graphic department. (Near this portrait is a novelty sign with letters shaded
in such a way that they jump before your eyes. The letters spell out the
word TENSION.) The informal air apparently begins with the chairman
himself, who moves about the offices in suspenders and shirt sleeves, visiting account executives in offices with signs reading: "Bulova Is On The
Move," or "Let RR's GO! GO! GO!"

This was the firm that the railroads decided to put completely in charge
of their campaign against the truckers. Indeed, except for writing out the
monthly checks, it may be said that the ERPC bowed out of the picture
to all intents and purposes. To understand how a public relations campaign
operates in the political sphere it is necessary to appreciate its basic approach to the structure of society. The public relations practitioner sees
society as a congeries of groups. While it is possible to regard society as a
mass of millions of isolated and autonomous individuals, such a view carries with it the tenuous assumption that "the public" has political power.
In fact real power lies with organized and articulate groups that have
discernible interests to pursue and the will to promote those interests. The
Pennsylvania truckers, organized into the PMTA, had such power. To
counteract them, countervailing groups would have to appear on the scene.
This analysis was spelled out in the Byoir "Campaign Plan," circulated in
the New York office.

> The public is only a collective name for countless groups of people, many
> of whom have bonds of common interest. In terms of our objectives, our
> subsidiary goals include informing, organizing and activating as many
> legitimate, strong and politically aggressive groups as already exist or that
> can be brought into existence for their own self-interest.
>
> The public and its separate parts must be informed by a purposeful bar-
> rage of continuing publicity. Our men in the field must organize the in-
> dividual groups. Together, the publicity given the subject and the actions
> of the groups must be directed toward the legislators so that they will act
> in accordance with the demands of the voters.
>
> As we see it, the whole program must have a basic appeal so broad that
> it will enlist the active support not only of the direct friends of the rail-
> roads, but, for example, a group of motorists conscious of the shocking
> hazards prevailing on our now inadequate and damaged highways, or tax-
> payers' organizations up and down the several states, or a group of tax
> authorities interested in improving state revenues, or the state grange and
> all others who can be shown where their own self-interests parallel those
> of the railroads.
>
> In other words, the railroads are simply identifying themselves with a
> program in the public interest.

What emerges here is that the emphasis is to be on the "public interest." Little attempt would be made to persuade the public that the railroads had a legitimate case to press. On the contrary, groups in the public would be approached in their role as motorists or taxpayers. While within the inner sanctums of the Byoir office it would be known that it was a railroad campaign, the public would be led to see the matter in an altogether different light. Indeed, the strategy that was finally adopted was to have the railroads excluded from the picture entirely. This was to be, purely and simply, an anti-truck campaign. In public relations, as in war, the best defensive is to take the offensive. This was spelled out more concretely in another Byoir memo:

> Specifically, we must write all publicity in terms of the self-interest of certain groups. This publicity must be aimed at Motor Groups, Real Estate Boards and individual owners, Economy Groups, Service Clubs, Safety Groups, City and County Officials, Rural Road Improvement Groups, and all others *who have something to gain if the burden of financing the highways can be transferred from the individual citizen and the individual motorist to those who alone profit by it—the heavy trucks.*
>
> You can see from the foregoing that this account is utterly unlike the conventional one. Here we do not have a client for attribution. Of course, we will release some stories under client attribution, but they will be of lesser propaganda importance than those we can generate from motorists, property owners, taxpayer, farmer or women's groups. In sum, we not only have to create publicity ideas; we also have to go out in the field and create the groups and occasions so that those publicity ideas will become realities.

Several points are interesting here. First of all, suspicion and resentment are to be raised against the heavy trucks that travel the roads. The latent hostility of motorists towards road-hogs is to be brought into the open. And the theme that trucks are destroying the roads, and that taxpayers then pick up the tab for these damages, is to be emphasized. Second, if various groups in society cannot be mustered to the anti-truck cause, then Byoir people will have to create organizations that will take an anti-truck position. Third, "we do not have a client for attribution." This means that the railroads did not want their names appended to publicity or their support for the anti-truck campaign made public. If it was necessary to present a source for the information that was to be distributed, then either existing groups of motorists or taxpayers should be used, or new groups should be brought into existence. Generally speaking it is the task of public relations firms to give extensive publicity to their clients. After all, what they are paying for is to get their names known as widely as possible. But the ERPC account was an unconventional one: the client wished to remain carefully shrouded in the background. The Byoir organization did not mind this at all: it gave these public relations experts all the more leeway in which to exercise their talents. For, as will be seen, it is far easier to spread information harmful to the truckers than it would be to arouse public sympathy in favor of the railroads. In other words, the average citizen has no particular reason to be "pro-railroad"; but reasons can be found to make him an "anti-truck" partisan.

The Group Process: Cultivation of the "Grass Roots" /   As has been indicated, public relations men prefer to look on the public as a composite of groups. A message can best be presented if it is communicated to a group. For if such a group can be enlisted on your side, then you have a strong piece of evidence that at least one section of the public is sympathetic to your aims. Illustrative of this approach is the way in which the Byoir organization worked with the Pennsylvania State Grange and the Pennsylvania State Association of Township Supervisors. Both of these were established groups in the state and both had extensive memberships. Neither one had any direct connection with the railroads of Pennsylvania, but both were capable of being enlisted to the side of the anti-truck campaign. A public relations practitioner, furthermore, does not simply assume that if virtue (or even self-interest) is on his client's side a host of groups will flock to support him. On the contrary, matters such as these cannot be left to chance. The good public relations man will go out into the field and enlist his allies. That is what the Byoir organization did.

It first contacted Joab K. Mahood, Secretary of the Pennsylvania State Grange and editor of the *Grange News*. The Grange had long had an interest in the state's road system, and it was entirely natural that its activities be dovetailed into the Byoir campaign. Mahood, like all salaried and full-time officials of associations, had great discretion in deciding which legislative issues his organization would support. In 1949, 1950, and 1951 the Grange's annual meeting passed resolutions asking that weight limits on trucks be retained. The 1951 resolution, adopted in October when S. 615 was being considered in the legislature, contained the following provisions: "There is pending before the State Senate . . . a measure, S. 615, commonly known as the Big Truck Bill, which we consider contrary to the public interest. Therefore, be it resolved, that we respectfully ask Governor Fine to veto this bill . . . if or when it reaches his desk." Once the Grange had gone on record as being opposed to any change in the law, the Byoir organization moved in to give them aid and assistance. Whenever a Grange resolution was passed or a Grange statement was made Byoir's staff members would arrange to have it given as wide distribution as possible. In these instances the extra printing and postage costs were put on the ERPC expense account. In July 1951, for example, Byoir's

office staff actually wrote a letter, attacking S. 615, which was sent to the
editors of Pennsylvania newspapers for publication. The letter, however,
was signed by J. K. Mahood and his title as Secretary of the Grange was
appended. For an extended period a member of Byoir's staff set up his
office in the Grange headquarters. From that location he sent out letters
and press releases on Grange stationery, and generally acted as if he were
a Grange spokesman. Any bills that were incurred for these "Grange"
activities were forwarded to Byoir's New York office, which paid them and
charged the sums to the railroad account. All in all it can be said that the
Grange would probably have been anti-truck in any event. But it is also
clear that its anti-truck activities became more energetic and that these
efforts received wider publicity once the Byoir organization supplied additional help and, acting for the railroads, subsidized the additional costs.

Much the same tactics were followed with respect to the Pennsylvania
State Association of Township Supervisors. This organization, unlike the
Grange, was quasi-public in that it was created by statute and public funds
were used to underwrite its operations. Nevertheless its Secretary, Harold
A. Thomson, was also amenable to accepting Byoir help. Indeed, as early
as 1949 Thomson and his Association of Township Supervisors had shown
an affinity for the railroads' cause. In that year there was also a bill before
the Pennsylvania legislature that would have raised the truck weight limits.
This bill, known as House Bill 560, was substantially the same as the
Senate Bill 615 to be introduced two years later. The Association of Township Supervisors worked closely with the Associated Railroads of Pennsylvania in opposing this bill. Appearing in 135 Pennsylvania newspapers was
an advertisement showing a large truck (decorated with the features of a
greedy pig) stuffing itself at a trough marked "House Bill 560." The
message opened:

> You can't satisfy a road hog!
>
> Big tractor-semi-trailer trucks are the hogs of the highways. They've been
> getting *bigger* and *heavier* year by year.
>
> They'll be still heavier if House Bill 560, now before the Pennsylvania
> State Senate, becomes law.
>
> BIG-truck operators behind this bill want to add another 7½ tons to the
> weight of these monster vehicles . . . the old story . . . a few more tons
> every year.
>
> You are the victim.
>
> You pay the taxes to fix the roads that are broken by these terrifying loads.

At the bottom of the page, the advertisement was signed "Pennsylvania
State Association of Township Supervisors, H. A. Thomson, Secretary."

Yet it is highly doubtful that the Association of Township Supervisors paid the cost of running this advertisement in 135 newspapers. While the Association supplied its name as sponsor, all indications are that the railroads supplied the money.

In 1951, therefore, Thomson and the Association of Township Supervisors were willing to receive assistance from the Byoir organization. An experienced member of Byoir's staff, for example, spoke against the passage of S. 615 on the radio. While the program was announced as being sponsored by the Association, the bill for the time was sent to Byoir and then charged to the railroads. In addition, tens of thousands of anti-truck postcards were mailed out to Pennsylvania motorists. These, too, were signed by the association even though they had been written, printed, and mailed by Byoir. It must be emphasized that the association was historically predisposed against the trucks. As early as 1933 it had prepared a resolution asking that weight limits on trucks be held down. This is altogether understandable, for a large part of the budget of any township involves road construction and repairs. If big trucks break up these roads, then local authorities will clearly resent having to pick up (and replace) the pieces after them. What must be added is that after Byoir entered the picture the anti-truck activities of the Association received measurably greater publicity throughout the state. At the 1951 convention in Pittsburgh the Association voted unanimously:

> Whereas the huge freight trucks traveling the highways of Pennsylvania continue to cause excessive damage to our roads and streets, therefore be it resolved that we continue our opposition to any increase in existing weight limits of trucks and demand a decrease in the present excessive weights when and where such trucks are to be used on township roads.

Whereas in the past such a resolution might have lain moribund in the official minutes of the association convention, in 1951 Byoir's public relations men saw that the story was reprinted and broadcast throughout the state.

This, then, is what is meant by "working through existing groups in the community." Byoir discovered organizations that were already predisposed against the trucks, and it offered to supply them with money and expert help so that the anti-truck message might be disseminated more widely and more effectively. In much the same way resolutions opposing S. 615 were obtained from the Pennsylvania Federation of Women's Clubs, the Pennsylvania Motor Federation, and other organizations having no discernible connection with railroads. Necessary, of course, were cooperative officials such as Mr. Mahood of the Grange and Mr. Thomson of the Township Supervisors. In one sense they were allowing the names of their organizations to be used by Byoir and the railroads. In another sense, however, the railroads' fight had always been their fight—so it cannot be said that these organizations entered the struggle against their will or for ulterior motives. At the same time, it should be pointed out that the rank and file of the Grange and the Township Supervisors Association did not know that railroad money and talent were behind the advertisements, broadcasts, and mailings distributed by their groups in the anti-truck campaign. Such arrangements were made quietly between Byoir and Messrs. Mahood and Thomson: these "treaties" were not discussed or voted on at annual meetings of the members, nor were the alliances disclosed in the groups' publications.

The Uses of Mass Media /   One of the points that the Byoir firm had emphasized in its presentation to the railroads was the work done by the magazine department of his organization. While a good public relations campaign centers much of its attention on groups, an effort must also be made to create a general climate of opinion in the community favorable to the client's objectives. One way to achieve this is through the mass media. Public relations firms specialize in placing articles in newspapers and magazines that present—in the form of news stories or feature articles— their client's message. This, in a word, is what distinguishes public relations from advertising. Advertising agencies *buy* space in periodicals and then prepare the copy to fill it. Public relations firms have a harder job: they must *persuade* newspaper and magazine editors to run certain stories or to give free coverage to certain events. Whereas the advertiser is cast in the role of the buyer with money to spend, the public relations man must all too frequently act as a supplicant asking for favors.

Yet the relationship is not entirely a one-sided one. Byoir's magazine department realized that magazine editors are continually searching for interesting articles. They will be receptive to suggestions by public relations firms, for they know that a good public relations firm will be aware of the particular needs of their magazine. The Byoir people saw it as their job to place as many articles as possible that would take the anti-truck campaign themes to the magazine-reading public. One way to solicit the interest of editors is to show them that they have been neglecting an important subject. A standard reference work, as one Byoir employee pointed out, can be valuable in this approach:

> The *Readers' Guide to Periodical Literature* is a volume which is put out monthly and then again put out annually, which lists, under certain classifications, everything that has been written on a given subject. It is useful in helping you not to miss anything that is coming out, and it is also useful for you to see. You can check the *Guide,* and if you see that Magazine X hasn't published something on the subject of roads for five years, you think, well, perhaps the editor might then be interested because he hadn't covered the subject.

At the same time Byoir's magazine department was building up a file of information on trucks and road problems. This became an ambitious project, and the people who put it together were quite proud of it: "We had almost, I would say, a duplicate of anything that you would find in either the New York Public Library or perhaps the *New York Times* morgue." Among their prized possessions were photographs of sensational truck accidents, featuring smashed bridges and mangled passenger cars. These were on hand to provide graphic illustrations for magazine articles yet to be written. In addition, a list was compiled of experienced magazine writers. These writers were offered access to the Byoir files if they would do an article with an anti-truck theme. A Byoir representative would then approach a magazine editor saying that a particular writer was available to produce an article on the subject of roads and trucks. If the editor liked the idea and commissioned the article, then the Byoir magazine department was prepared to give all possible help to the writer. What this usually amounted to was giving him their file materials on trucks: in effect, doing his "research" for him. The magazine editors were willing to publish the articles, and the freelance writers were willing to write them. What Byoir did was to bring the editors and the writers together and to supply the writers with materials for their articles.

The process of acting as a go-between is well summarized in an inter-office memorandum coming out of the Byoir magazine department. A writer had been obtained, an anti-truck article had been written and had been approved by the ERPC, and the next step was to get it placed in a magazine. ("Coly" was the Byoir executive in charge of the ERPC account.)

> The enclosed opus has passed the board of censors of ERPC and now we are ready to decide which magazine should perpetrate it upon the defenseless public. Coly is convinced it can be slicked into a slick mag, advertisers be damned, since it really doesn't take any roundhouse swipe at the truckers. I'm inclined to agree that it could hit a good general circulation magazine. If you could get a nibble from some such I could, I think, convert it to the appropriate style or get sex into the lead or whatever is needed. But, then, you get paid to worry about these things so I will accept your decision in good grace. Then you can convince Coly.

This memorandum is valuable as much for its tone as for its content. The air of casual cynicism displayed by the public relations man suggests a wholly disrespectful outlook. Not only is the "defenseless public" patronized, but so are the magazine editors who print the articles and the clients who pay the bills.

During 1950 and 1951, Byoir's magazine department was responsible for various articles in national magazines.

TRUCKS: help or headache?

You Can't Satisfy a Road Hog

BIG tractor-semi-trailer trucks are the ho— the highways. They've been getting bi— heavier year by year.

They'll be still heavier if Hou— fore Pennsylvania's Stat—

BIG-truck operato— add another — monster — tons —

JUNE 1950

The Reader's Digest

29TH YEAR

An article a day of enduring significance, in condensed permanent booklet form

Overloaded trucks are breaking up our highways faster than we can find the money to replace them

the roads. YOU have to drag along behind hese iron curtains on hills.

idents of Townships are now over-burdened real estate taxes to repair bridges and vs. Increased BIG-truck weights will reased repair costs for YOU.

OUR roads! YOUR bridges! And something about it. YOU can enate know that YOU oppose ouse Bill 560. DO IT NOW.

THE RAPE OF OUR ROADS

Condensed from Buffalo Evening News

Frederick G. Brownell

AMERICA FACES a transportation crisis of the first magnitude. Under the relentless battering of outsize and overloaded trucks, the three million miles of roads that comprise this nation's arteries are going to pieces faster than we can find the money to replace them.

Of the 37,800 miles of interstate trunk highway in the country, 35,500 miles need immediate improvement at a cost of 11 billion dollars. It would cost another 49 billion dollars to bring all our roads up to traffic requirements. Even the famed Pennsylvania Turnpike is,

Ou

THE GIANTS
THAT WRECK OUR
HIGHWAYS

BERTRAM VOGEL

WHEN, on May 13, 1949, a heavy truck carrying carbon disulphide exploded in the Holland Tunnel, an aroused group of highway officials got out their note books, jotted down the facts, and clamored for a Federal grand jury.

To Joe Public, however, it was just another big headline. It happened to be a spectacular explosion in a spectacular place, a tunnel under the

this was no isolated case—that it was a lot more than a sensational headline in a daily newspaper. What Joe failed to realize was that the heavy truc~ operators had played him for ~ er—and would continue for an even bigge~ got hep.

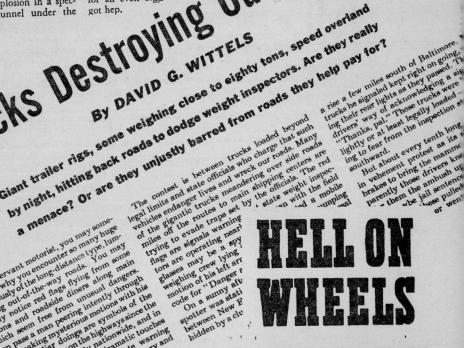

Are Trucks Destroying Our Highways?

By DAVID G. WITTELS

Giant trailer rigs, some weighing close to eighty tons, speed overland by night, hitting back roads to dodge weight inspectors. Are they really a menace? Or are they unjustly barred from roads they help pay for?

IF you're an observant motorist, you may sometimes wonder why you encounter so many huge trucks, obviously of the long-distance type, lumbering along out-of-the-way roads. You may also occasionally notice red flags flying from some gasoline stations and roadside diners along main highways which seem free from unusual dangers. You may even pass a man peering intently through field glasses and making mysterious motions with his left arm. These peculiar doings are symbols of the most fantastic battle of wits on the highways since the rumrunning era. It is practically nationwide, and in some sections it includes such melodramatic touches as spies and counterespionage, elaborate warning networks, high-speed chases, ambushes, bribery and even hints of sudden death.

The contest is between trucks loaded beyond legal limits and state officials who charge that such vehicles endanger lives and wreck our roads. Many of the gigantic trucks meandering over side roads miles off the routes to main shipping centers are trying to evade traps set by the officials. The red flags are signals warning ~ tors are operating near~ state weight inspec-
glasses may be a spy ~ ~n with the field motion of his left arm ~ ~d a mobile
code for "Danger a ~ ~umping
On a sunny afte ~ ~al
spotter was stati ~
between New F ~
hidden by a clu ~

a rise a few miles south of Baltimore. trucks he signaled kept right on going, ing their rear lights as they passed. T~ drivers' way of acknowledging a sig "Thanks, pal." Those trucks were~ lightly or at least legally loaded~ ing to fear from the inspection s~ southward.
But about every tenth long in vehement protest as its ~ brakes to bring the mamm~ parently those drivers kne~ ~ them the ambush up~ ~be jail sentence ~these pulled~ or wen~

HELL ON
WHEELS

by HARRY HENDERSON

Roads Are Going to Pot

Public Relations at Work: The Anti-Truck Campaign

Among the articles appearing were these:

Everybody's Digest for April 1950 contained an article entitled "The Giants that Wreck our Highways" by Bertram Vogel. The message: "Heavy trucks are making their runs on your tax dollars."

(CIRCULATION: about 280,000)

The *Reader's Digest* for June 1950 contained an article entitled "The Rape of Our Roads" by Frederick G. Brownell. The message: "Overloaded trucks are breaking up our highways faster than we can find the money to replace them."   (CIRCULATION: about 9 million)

Harper's for September 1950 contained an article entitled "Our Roads are Going to Pot" by Myron Stearns. The message: "Trucks have apparently been a large factor in hastening highway destruction."

(CIRCULATION: about 150,000)

The *Saturday Evening Post* for September 16, 1950 contained an article entitled "Are Trucks Destroying Our Highways?" by David G. Wittels. The message: "Giant trailer rigs, some weighing close to 80 tons, speed overland by night hitting back roads to dodge weight inspectors."

(CIRCULATION: about 4 million)

Argosy for July 1951 contained an article entitled "Hell on Wheels" by Harry Henderson. The message: "Gunning his big trailer truck up to 60, often driving 24 hours without a rest, breaking the law and risking his life, Butch Watson is typical of the tough breed of gypsy truckers."

(CIRCULATION: about 1 million)

Parade for August 1951 contained an article entitled "Trucks: Help or Headache?" by Karl Kohrs and Edward Fales. The message: "Owners and road experts alike look for the answer as eight million crowd our inadequate highways."   (CIRCULATION: about 5 million)

These magazines had a combined nation-wide circulation of almost 20 million in this period, and it is clear that the articles were read by many tens of thousands of Pennsylvanians during the time the legislature was considering S. 615. The Byoir organization, in its reports to the railroads, took complete credit for sponsoring, writing, and securing the publication of these anti-truck messages. The public relations firm was charging its client at the rate of $50 per day for the services of the magazine department alone, and it presumably wanted to show that it was earning its fee.[2]

---

2 One of the first tasks of a public relations firm, it should be noted, is to do a public relations job *on its own clients*. Much time, money, and energy is spent in persuading the client that his money is being well spent, that the firm is being effective in getting the message across. Thus all public relations firms take a great deal of trouble to put together huge scrapbooks of clippings that show the client all the newspapers and magazines that have run stories on his product or idea. The theory seems to be that if the client *thinks* the word is being spread on his behalf three-quarters of the job has been done—even if the general public is oblivious of the campaign.

It is possible that some of the articles might have been printed anyway without Byoir intervention, but the contents of most of them indicate that the authors drew on the Byoir files. It is hardly necessary to say that none of the articles give any indication to the reading public that they were sponsored by Byoir on behalf of the railroads. The reader is led to believe that it is the view of authoritative magazines such as the *Reader's Digest,* the *Saturday Evening Post,* and *Harper's* that big trucks are responsible for road damage and highway accidents. It is here that public relations, when successful, pays higher dividends than straight advertising. For a regular advertisement, no matter how public-spirited its message, is signed by the advertiser. The reader, in consequence, may suspect that the advertiser has some self-serving ax to grind. But if a public relations firm succeeds in placing its client's message as a news story or feature article, then the reader will—it is assumed—accept the ideas on their own merit because he has faith in the integrity of the magazine.

The Maryland Road Test: Science and Strategy / As the citizens of Pennsylvania read these magazine articles in 1950 and 1951 they must have been struck with one item of information that presented a most compelling case against the truckers: in a number of these articles were reports on what came to be known as the "Maryland road test." Among laymen, opinions might differ on the extent of damage done by trucks to roads. But the Byoir writers were able to cite scientific evidence to the effect that controlled tests demonstrated that heavy trucks were indeed the culprits. Behind this charge lies an involved and controversial story.

In 1949 the Conference of Governors, all naturally concerned with the question of roads, decided to sponsor a test so that once and for all they would know how much highway damage the trucks were causing. Connecticut, Delaware, Illinois, Kentucky, Maryland, Michigan, New Jersey, Ohio, Pennsylvania, Virginia, Wisconsin, and the District of Columbia agreed to share the costs of the experiment. A contract was signed with the highway research board of the National Academy of Sciences, and a stretch of road in Maryland was picked as the test site. The study, which began in June 1950, was intended to be an exhaustive one. Trucks carrying various weight loads were observed, and the road itself was carefully checked before the test started. A round-the-clock schedule was carried out for several months, with the loaded trucks thundering back and forth on the section of highway. In all, the experimental trucks traveled a total of 389,605 miles on the 1.1 mile strip of U.S. 301 in Maryland. At the end of this time the piece of road was thoroughly broken up: it was clear that the trucks had more than worn out the lanes on which they had been traveling. The engineers who had been conducting the test, however, were interested in the reasons rather than in recriminations. The chairman of the highway research board had two explanations for why the road had fallen apart. The first was that 389,605 miles of truck traffic on a 1.1 mile section is the equivalent of the burden a road might receive in 40 years of normal use. No one expects any road to last forever, and 40 years is not a bad lifespan. The second reason was that, upon further investigation, it was discovered that the most damaged sections of the road actually had a subgrade of fine grain soil, which hastened the deterioration. What the engineers seemed to have concluded was that road damage is more to be attributed to the quality of the highways than it is to the weight of the traffic carried by them. If an investment is made in good materials and if an adequate subgrade is provided, then heavy trucks should not be a threat to roads. This, at least, was the interpretation of the test results made by the highway research board.

But it was not the only possible interpretation. After all, the facts of the case were visible to the naked eye. Heavy trucks had been traveling back and forth on a stretch of highway, and within a matter of months that once excellent road was pock-marked with holes and cracked like the riverbed of a dried-up stream. The chief agent for this interpretation was one Clinton Johnson, director of publicity for the Maryland Roads Commission. It is not clear how he came in contact with Byoir, but soon after the commencement of the road test he was a frequent visitor at the New York office of the public relations firm. He would make periodic personal reports on the fate of the experimental section, and Byoir paid all the expenses for these trips. One of these junkets, billed of course to the railroads, cost $190.38 as it included theatre tickets and meals for Mr. and Mrs. Johnson over a Labor Day weekend. Through Johnson's good offices Byoir's magazine department was able to amass both information and photographs on what it liked to call the "Crackathon" in Maryland. This view of the road test as being wholly the fault of the trucks found its way into David G. Wittels' *Saturday Evening Post* article and the piece by Karl Kohrs and Edward Fales in *Parade*. In January 1951 a tentative report on the Maryland road test results was sent to representatives of the states that had sponsored the experiment. Even though this report was supposed to be confidential, a copy was soon in the hands of the Byoir organization and Byoir's interpretative summary of its contents was shortly thereafter put in the hands of *Newsweek* magazine. The Byoir version, which was featured as a specially boxed-off item, claimed that all the damage to the road could be laid at the door of the truckers. Once again, the presumed authority for this was the highway research board of the National Academy of Sciences—vouched for by *Newsweek*.

The Maryland road test was set up as a scientific experiment conducted by engineers for the information of experts in state highway departments.

Its conclusions were tentative and some degree of technical knowledge was needed to understand them. If there was any inference to be drawn, it was that attention must be fixed on the quality of subgrade that underlies a road's surface. However the strategic importance of the test lay not in its technical application but in the use that Byoir made of it. All the magazine articles he placed were made more persuasive because they could cite the purported "findings" of a reputable experiment. And this information came to him, it should be added, because he was able to persuade someone intimately connected with the test to divulge selected facts while the test was still underway.

The Governor Decides: Arguments and Access

All the time that the Byoir organization was working in Pennsylvania through groups such as the Grange and the Association of Township Supervisors, and all the time it was placing articles and stories attacking the truckers, the Pennsylvania legislature was considering S. 615. The Pennsylvania Motor Truck Association, as has been pointed out, had done an effective lobbying job. Despite the opposition of organized groups and the climate of opinion created by the anti-truck messages, the legislators paid back their campaign debt to the truckers by voting through S. 615. Both houses of the legislature gave large majorities to the bill in the winter of 1951. The scene—and many eyes—therefore shifted to the office of Governor John S. Fine. He had the power to veto the bill and in Pennsylvania the legislature almost never overrides a governor's rejection.

It was clear to the governor that this was no ordinary dispute between two interested parties, the railroads and the truckers. For a far wider segment of the Pennsylvania public had been roused on the subject at issue. It appeared as if important groups in the state had strong opinions on S. 615, and there was also an intimation that ordinary citizens throughout the community were thinking about the role of trucks in their lives. In consequence the governor took the unusual step of holding a public hearing at which citizens or groups could present their views on the bill. The hearing was scheduled for January 17, 1952, and the governor gave notice that written statements as well as personal appearances would be welcomed.

The hearing proved to be yet another battleground in the war between the railroads and the truckers. The latter hoped to sustain their legislative victory; the former hoped to kill the bill by persuading the governor to veto it. Approximately 100 individuals from 94 organizations attended the hearing. But their presence there was not altogether a spontaneous matter. One of Byoir's staff claimed that the public relations firm "went out and organized 21 witnesses from 21 organizations against the bill." The Pennsylvania Motor Truck Association solicited 30 witnesses in favor of the bill, and PMTA even went so far as to charter plane transportation to bring some of them to Harrisburg. Speaking against the bill were some 15 persons representing women's clubs, automobile associations, railroad labor unions, the Grange, the Association of Township Supervisors, the State CIO, and the Associated Railroads of Pennsylvania. Speaking for the bill were 24 persons representing the teamsters' union, the state AFL, the food, chemical, oil, steel, glass, and automotive industries, and the Pennsylvania Motor Truck Association. The hearing was an all-day affair, and the governor was presented with a variety of viewpoints. On the surface, he acted as if he did not know that the various witnesses had been organized and transported by the chief contending parties. What he heard looked like the independent views of Pennsylvania groups, and their opinions could be taken on their merits. A few days later he wrote: "A hearing was held in the Executive office at the State Capitol on Thursday, January 17th, 1952. A myriad of views were presented by representatives of various civic, municipal, labor, industrial, and railway organizations, and the trucking industry of Pennsylvania itself." What went on in the governor's mind as he listened to his fellow citizens is a question that only he can answer. But it was his responsibility to come down on one side or another.

And on January 21—four days after the hearing—he vetoed the bill.

The truckers were dismayed. They believed that they had capped an effective lobbying campaign on the legislature with a persuasive presentation of their case to the governor. The railroads appeared to have kept a satisfied silence, but a memorandum circulated in the Byoir office was less constrained. "Veto of this bill meant that some $5,000,000 worth of freight was retained on the Pennsylvania Railroad, because the trucking limit was not raised," a Byoir executive reported. "This represented one of the most dramatic illustrations of the power of organized public opinion that anybody could hope to find." It was assumed, in this instance, that the Byoir firm could take the credit for organizing the anti-truck public—and for giving this public its opinion.

But this was not the entire story. In his veto message Governor Fine gave his principal reason for rejecting a bill that would aid the trucking industry. He began by saying, "I am fully mindful that the trucking industry plays a significant and important role in the economic and community affairs not only of this Commonwealth, but also in the entire Nation." He continued:

> I am also mindful of the possible destructive effect which, as demonstrated by the tentative findings of the highway research board of the National

Academy of Sciences, based on actual tests during the last year and a half on a section of highway built by the State of Maryland in 1941, may result from the increase of permissible gross and axle loads. I should point out, however, that all of the information available to me was *not* available to the Legislature when this bill was being considered.

Ordinarily, in such a matter as this I would feel constrained to accept the legislative views, but after careful and thorough consideration, . . . I am convinced that the wisdom of subjecting our highway system . . . to additional burdens should be carefully considered by the Legislature in the light of the final findings and recommendations of the highway research board, which unfortunately will be published too late for me to consider.

On its face this is a rather puzzling statement. Governor Fine underlined the fact that the results of the Maryland road test were not available to the members of the legislature when they considered S. 615. Yet even a cursory reading of the debates would have shown him that the test was mentioned on several occasions, and it is hard to see how he missed the nine reports covering 46 double-columned pages that were read into the official *Legislative Journal*. It was true that the reports on the Maryland test available to the lawmakers were unofficial and incomplete, but the governor himself conceded in his veto message that all he had were the "tentative findings." In other words, it was never established that the facts he had on truck weights and road damage were any more up-to-date or authoritative than those known to the legislature. The preliminary results of the Maryland test, at least as quoted by the opponents of S. 615 in the Senate and the House, indicted the trucks in an unqualified way. It is difficult to imagine what new information the governor might have had that would have made the anti-truck case even more persuasive.

It should be mentioned at this point that the transmission of an early Maryland road test report to the legislative opponents of S. 615 was not entirely a disinterested or accidental matter. Representative J. P. Moran, one of the chief spokesmen against the bill in the House, got his information on the test from Joab K. Mahood, secretary of the Pennsylvania State Grange. The report which Mr. Mahood transmitted was written by T. J. Kauer, the director of the Ohio Department of Highways. What was not known to the legislators was that both Mahood and Kauer were in close liaison with the Byoir organization, and their sole intention was to distribute a report that would so interpret the Maryland test that trucks would be seen as the chief cause of road damage. Their aim was to release their report with such a bias before the official findings of the highway research board came out. However, as was seen, even though they had that document in their possession, the lawmakers went ahead and passed S. 615.

The next question, quite clearly, is to ask where Governor Fine got his information on the Maryland road test. Subsequent developments brought out that the Pennsylvania secretary of highways was personally opposed to S. 615, and it was his department that provided the governor with a version of the Maryland road test report infused with an anti-truck bias. It was also revealed that the chief engineer and the assistant chief engineer of the highway department drew on materials emanating from the Byoir firm, and these they passed on to the secretary who passed them on to the governor. The secretary later claimed that he never knew that the report he transmitted to the governor had its origins in the Byoir office. If he had unwittingly served as an instrument of the anti-truck campaign, he acted in all innocence. "Well, it seems to have the style of my subordinate," he said. "I assumed . . . it was prepared by my people in my department." Governor Fine was a layman and he had no specialized or expert information on truck weights or road engineering. As a layman he had to rely on the advice of the secretary, the chief engineer, and the assistant chief engineer of his highway department. The governor, like the citizens who read the *Saturday Evening Post,* was obviously impressed with the ring of authority of a body like the highway research board of the National Academy of Sciences. He was able to contend that he had scientific evidence linking road damage to truck weights—evidence apparently more compelling than that presented to the legislature—and on this basis he exercised his prerogative under the Pennsylvania constitution and vetoed the bill.

Why did Governor Fine refuse to sign S. 615? The chief reason he gave in his veto message was that the legislature had been unaware of the latest findings of the Maryland road test and that no attempt to raise the 45,000-pound weight limit should be made until that test was completed. Yet the lawmakers were very much aware of the test reports but they nevertheless felt compelled to pass the bill. At all events, the Byoir firm was sure that its efforts had been responsible for the veto. Whether it was due to their public relations campaign or to placing a biased version of the Maryland test report before the governor, Byoir had secured a last-minute victory for the railroads.

During the winter of 1952 and into the spring, the truckers smarted under the governor's veto. They, too, conjectured as to what had motivated the eleventh-hour rejection of S. 615. One memorandum circulated among Pennsylvania Motor Truck Association officials expressed their perplexity:

It is of the utmost importance that we ascertain the reasons or motives for the Governor's veto. At present the evidence leads to a wide range of conjecture. It is possible (a) that he acted out of purely conscientious convic-

tions based upon the preponderance of evidence adduced at the hearing; or
(b) that whatever his personal convictions might have been he acted from
practical political considerations based on indications of a substantial, organized "grass-roots" protest against the bill adduced at the hearing; or
(c) that for this same reason Duff urged him, directly or indirectly to veto
the bill. [Both (b) and (c) suppose that national convention strategy
primarily dictated the move—to conserve internal state power which might
be jeopardized by a strong issue split.]

The first two hypotheses are straightforward. Governor Fine may have been
persuaded, from what he heard at the hearing and elsewhere, that the
passage of S. 615 would inflict further damage on the state's highways.
Or, on the other hand, he may have been persuaded that there was great
public sentiment against the bill and that he had better veto it no matter
how he felt about its intrinsic merits. The third hypothesis demonstrates
that state policy decisions can be influenced by national political considerations. James Duff, a former Republican governor of Pennsylvania and in
1951 a United States senator, may have induced Governor Fine to veto
the bill as a means of holding the state Republican party together. If the
Pennsylvania delegation to the 1952 Republican convention wanted to
maximize its effectiveness, so the thinking ran, then it could not afford to
be internally split on the railroad-truck issue. The best way to secure this
cohesion, it appeared, was through a veto because, although a majority of
the Republicans in the state legislature favored S. 615, it seemed that many
influential outside party supporters were strongly opposed. By withholding
his signature, the theory ran, Governor Fine might restore equilibrium
within the party.

But all three of these theories were only theories, and the truckers were
mainly interested in action.

The Truckers Counterattack / Fire has to be fought with fire. The
truckers decided that their next step was to stimulate a pro-truck ferment
at the grass roots as a means of counteracting the railroad victory. In
April 1952, therefore, officials of the PMTA contacted David Charnay, the
president of Allied Public Relations Associates of New York City.

Charnay's firm had neither the reputation nor the resources of Byoir's.
Indeed, he asked only a $36,000 annual fee of the truckers for his services.
Nor could the firm boast much experience with legislative and political
campaigns. However he had as clients the United Mine Workers of America and the Nationalist Bank of China, and his commercial accounts
included Eversharp and Ballantine Beer. At the outset the Charnay firm
showed as much zeal as the Byoir. One of its projects was to create a
letterhead organization known as the "Pennsylvania Motor Safety League."

The already existing automobile clubs in the state were predisposed against the truckers, and it was felt that a new pro-truck auto group would give the impression of public support. Charnay went so far as to hire an executive secretary for the Pennsylvania Motor Safety League and to rent office space for it—all with the truckers' money. The secretary, furthermore, was given elaborate instructions about how he should cash the truckers' checks at one bank and then deposit the money in his personal account at another. The ostensible purpose of the league would be to promote highway safety: its real reason for being was to arouse public sentiment for raising the weight limits on trucks. The Charnay firm spent $10,000 organizing the Pennsylvania Motor Safety League and a successor project, the Citizens' Committee for Highway Safety. Neither of these groups, however, ever got off the ground. For one thing, they were unable to obtain a membership of any significant proportion. For another, the truckers were in close contact with Charnay's activities and the idea of a "letterhead" ally was distasteful to many of them.

At the same time, Charnay was attempting to spread the truckers' message among the public. Like Byoir, it concluded that the best defense was to take the offensive, hence it began to map out an anti-railroad campaign. To obtain materials, a letter was sent to the office of the American Trucking Associations in Washington, D.C.:

> I would appreciate your sending me along at your earliest convenience any material you may have on the subject of railroad nuisances. . . . We can use, if your office can supply them, the following photographs, preferably the usual 8″ x 10″ glossies: (1) a good juicy train wreck with bodies if possible. . . .

Again, however, the puritanical instincts of the truckers were wont to check these exuberant tendencies. They preferred to accentuate the positive side of the pro-truck case. To this end a film entitled "Knights of the Highway" was distributed throughout the state, and trucks were donated—with much fanfare—for the purpose of distributing the polio vaccine.

The truckers did not stint on money. Even if Charnay's fee was comparatively low, the PMTA handed over $139,347.87 to cover expenses during the first thirteen months of his operation. These outlays were not covered solely by the trucking firms. An alliance was struck with the large oil companies, and they were willing to make common cause with the truckers. During 1952, the Sun Oil Company contributed $2,500 to the war chest, Esso gave $3,500, Gulf gave $2,500, and Atlantic Refining came through with $5,000. The picture of small and defenseless trucking firms being victimized by the powerful railroads therefore needs some revision: any group fortunate enough to have oil-company help loses its underdog status. Charnay's efforts were beginning to pay off. That year the Grange abandoned its traditional anti-truck position, and while it did not adopt a resolution favoring weight increases, it was willing to take a neutral stance on the issue. In addition, the United Rubber Workers, a CIO union, joined the truckers' side. And a persuasive case was made to the United Mine Workers, stressing that the railroads were turning to diesel engines and were no longer consumers of coal. But Charnay's greatest accomplishment, as is so often the case in public relations, took place behind the scenes.

Back in July 1951, seven months before Governor Fine's veto of S. 615, a disgruntled employee walked out of the Byoir office in New York. Not only did Miss Sonya Saroyan empty out her own desk drawers on leaving, but she also took with her a wide assortment of letters and memorandums dealing with the anti-truck campaign, on which she happened to have been working in a subordinate capacity. Armed with these documents, many of them revealing the intentions and methods of the Byoir firm, and all intended to be confidential, she contacted the Washington office of the American Trucking Associations. There she was at first given a suspicious welcome, the kind usually accorded someone from the enemy's camp. But once it was established that Miss Saroyan was a genuine defector, her loot was given careful inspection and she spent two days at the ATA office making recordings about Byoir activities. For this she was paid $50 a day plus expenses.

Soon thereafter an ATA staff member passed on to the PMTA, their Pennsylvania affiliate, the word that the Washington office had some information on the sources of the anti-truck campaign. However, for reasons that are not entirely clear, PMTA officials showed little inclination to delve into the Saroyan papers that the ATA offered them and no inclination to put them to use. It was not until almost a year had passed that the PMTA and Miss Saroyan got together. During that year Governor Fine had vetoed S. 615 and the PMTA had made the decision to retain Charnay's firm. Charnay was not long in realizing the value of Miss Saroyan and her revelations for his client's cause. But even though the truckers had suffered a defeat in Pennsylvania, their parent ATA would not turn over the Saroyan documents to Charnay without her permission. Miss Saroyan had been having some trouble finding new employment in the public relations field and she had also changed her residence several times in a relatively brief period. Charnay finally tracked her down in New York City, however, and asked her to help out again. It seems to have taken this persuasive public relations man the whole summer and fall of 1952 to induce Miss Saroyan to release the papers. She finally did, after having given 21 more days of her time (at $50 a day) filling in further details. Charnay now had in its hands a day-by-day and blow-by-blow account of the anti-truck campaign as it was conceived and carried out by the Byoir office. Letters, memos, reports, instructions on the placement of magazine articles, accounts of working through organized groups, the Maryland road test—everything was there. Charnay's big decision was what to do with this haul.

Its advice, which was accepted by the truckers, was to carry the fight to the courts.

Legal Logistics: the Battle in the Courts / On January 17, 1953 the Pennsylvania Motor Truck Association and thirty-seven trucking firms sued the Eastern Railroad Presidents Conference, thirty-one railroads, and Carl Byoir & Associates for the sum of $250 million—a quarter of a billion dollars.

The launching of the suit had several consequences. The most immediate was that the federal district court in Philadelphia issued an injunction enjoining Byoir from any further activities on behalf of the railroads. In other words, the public relations firm was told that it must cease its lobbying efforts and its appeals to public opinion. For this reason—and several others having to do with the changing complexion of Pennsylvania politics —within a matter of eighteen months after the initiation of the lawsuit a successor bill to S. 615 was again passed by the Pennsylvania legislature. And this time the governor, now George M. Leader, signed it into law. The reconsideration of truck weight limits by the legislators was a relatively placid affair when compared to the tension and acrimony that marked the debates on S. 615. The House of Representatives passed the new bill, H. 1288, by the comfortable margin of 138 to 62 on June 7, 1955; and the Senate was almost unanimous in its judgment, voting 40 to 5 two weeks later. As had happened in the 1951 session, party lines were broken on the truck-weight issue. In the House, 73 Democrats voted for the bill and 33 voted against it, with 63 Republicans for and 29 against. In the Senate, 18 Democrats voted for the bill and 2 voted against it, with 22 Republicans for and 3 against. Governor Leader, a newly elected Democrat, had supported S. 615 when he was a member of the state Senate four years earlier, and there was no doubt that he would sign H. 1288 once it reached his desk. Among other considerations, the railroads had not supported him in his campaign for the governorship and he certainly was not going to veto the bill for their sake. With the affixing of his signature on June 30, 1955 the legislative side of the railroad-trucker struggle came to an end. Henceforward trucks of up to 60,000 pounds could travel the roads of Pennsylvania.

No less important from a public relations standpoint was the fact that the truckers could utilize the federal courts as a forum for reinforcing their position in the eyes of the public. The announcement of a $250 million suit for damages made the front pages of the newspapers, and the truckers were sure that the revelations during the trial would receive like publicity for, with the Saroyan papers, they could paint a picture of dishonest means being used to achieve illegal ends. "I have every reason to believe," Miss Saroyan said, "that the suit is based, in great part, on my testimony." There is great truth in this, not because Miss Saroyan became a star witness at the trial but because the Byoir employees named by her were subjected to penetrating cross-examination by the lawyers for the truckers. The case opened in the federal district court in Philadelphia in October 1956. It lasted for almost four months, with the trial transcript running to 6,000 pages and with 1,000 exhibits being offered in evidence. Called as witnesses were not only Byoir employees, but railroad and trucking association officials, secretaries of organizations such as the Grange and the Association of Township Supervisors, individuals connected with the Maryland road test, and countless others. About the only participant not called to give evidence was Governor Fine.

Counsel for the truckers decided to sue under the Sherman and Clayton antitrust laws. They claimed that the railroads, in alliance with Byoir, had conspired to put the truckers out of long-haul freight business. By means of a public relations campaign and the corruption of public officials, it was contended the railroads had caused the truckers to lose the good will of their customers on the one hand and of the general public on the other. The whole record of Byoir's activities was laid out on the table. It was further suggested that the railroads and Byoir had tried to damage the truckers by securing, through illegitimate means, statutory restrictions that would do economic harm to their competitors. The truckers did not contest the Pennsylvania legislature's right to set weight limits or the governor's right to sign or veto a bill. However, the railroads were accused of using unfair techniques as political pressure. The underhandedness of these methods cast a shadow over what would have otherwise been a legitimate political objective.

The truckers' emphasis was on the violation of the Sherman and Clayton Acts. The aim and intended result of the anti-truck campaign, they said, was to throttle competition in the long-haul freight business by giving the railroads a monopoly in the field. It is worth noting that in antitrust suits it is not necessary to *prove* that you have suffered actual loss of business as a result of the tactics used against you by a competitor. It would have been extremely difficult to show such damage, as the trucking industry in the entire region had been making steady economic progress despite the unfavorable public relations campaign being leveled against it.[3] All the

---

[3] According to statistics gathered by the Interstate Commerce Commission it is apparent that the total number of carriers (trucking companies) and total freight

truckers legally had to demonstrate was that the railroads had engaged in a conspiracy the intention of which was to put their long-haul freight competitors out of business. Armed with the "Saroyan Papers" and prepared to summon Byoir's public relations men to the witness stand, they were sure they could make the charge stick.

The railroads, for their part, contended that they had retained Byoir to give them expert assistance in more effectively exercising their rights under the First Amendment: An association of railroads, just like any other group, has the constitutional rights of free speech and petition. While the emphasis in the campaign may have been on pointing out the shortcomings of the trucking industry, there is no law that says free speech must accentuate the positive and cannot stress the negative. As for working through other groups instead of conducting the anti-truck campaign in the name of the railroads, it was contended that these organizations agreed with the railroad position of their own free will and they would have voiced anti-truck sentiments even had they not been approached by Byoir. Railroad money and Byoir talent, in short, subsidized groups that coincidentally were favorable to the railroad cause.

This viewpoint was expressed by David Mackie, the president of the Eastern Railroad Presidents Conference, on the witness stand. He was being questioned by Harold Kohn, counsel for the truckers:

KOHN: Do you believe generally that when people express a view on a matter of this kind, that the person responsible for the expression should make himself known?

MACKIE: I think the whole test in this is, what do the people who are running the organization at the time the advertisement is published or the

---

revenues increased year by year during the period of the Byoir anti-truck campaign. The following figures apply to Class I common carriers of general commodities in the business of intercity trucking in the Middle Atlantic region:

YEAR	NUMBER OF CARRIERS	FREIGHT REVENUES	AVERAGE REVENUE PER CARRIER
1949	211	$238,127,581	$1,128,567
1950	219	310,559,361	1,418,079
1951	232	345,350,164	1,488,578
1952	245	384,409,832	1,569,061
1953	261	438,313,657	1,679,018

Carrier and revenue figures are, unfortunately, available only for the region taken as a whole (New York, New Jersey, Pennsylvania, Delaware, Maryland, West Virginia, and the District of Columbia). However during this period Byoir was also conducting anti-truck campaigns in the states of New York and New Jersey as well as in Pennsylvania. And these three states would account for the great bulk of intercity motor freight business in the Middle Atlantic region.

pronouncement is made, what do they believe? . . . Because if they don't believe in what we suggest to them that they put out, they don't have to put it out. But if they do believe in it, I don't think there is any reason why they shouldn't put it out in their own name.

KOHN: Suppose the people who are in control and running it are not the people who are ostensibly the members of the organization? . . . Does that make a difference?

MACKIE: I think the whole key to it is simply whether or not the people, whoever they may be, who are responsible for and in control of the organization honestly believe in the veracity of what they put out. If they do, I think they are entitled to put it out. . . . I feel they are completely entitled both legally and morally to publish that material over their name.

KOHN: In your opinion, in disseminating facts to the public is it of importance that the public know who is disseminating what information?

MACKIE: I think that so long as the person disseminating the information believes in it and is willing to put his name to it, he is entitled to do that, and I think that is true of just as many people, members of the public, who feel that way.

KOHN: Can you tell me why it was decided that the railroads were not to appear as the sponsors of the factual discussion for which the railroads actually paid over a million dollars?

MACKIE: The Byoir people went out and told the story to the public. They went to various elements of the public, told them the story, asked them if they agreed with us. If they did, would they be our allies and would they in turn pick up and carry along with us in telling this story? Now, everybody knew when they were approached by the Byoir people in the first instance that the Byoir people were working for us. All of the organizations, all of the allies, that we obtained from the public knew who Byoir was, knew whom they worked for. All that Byoir did was to help in the gathering together of factual, basic, underlying data which, so far as I know, has never been demonstrated to be untrue or inaccurate, and to take that data to these segments of the people, and if they agreed with us, to ask them to say the same story to the people in the public whom they knew.

The contention of the railroads, therefore, was that even if the anti-truck message was distributed over the name of the Grange or the Association of Township Supervisors, those organizations agreed with the sentiments being expressed. Furthermore, the facts in that message were accurate and so long as the public is given information that is factually correct, the identification of the original source is not needed. Indeed, if an anti-truck pamphlet were to be labeled "Distributed by the Railroads" then there is good reason to believe that the public would not take the factual arguments on their own merits. On the contrary they would assume that the railroads had a special ax to grind and readers would throw away the pamphlet without reading it. By having "third-party" organizations present their case for them, the railroads avoided any prejudgments on the part of the public that they might have encountered had they spoken in their own name.

Finally, the railroads claimed that it was not their intention to put the truckers out of business. The whole controversy was a political rather than an economic one. The entire campaign was one of political persuasion: to rally and arouse public support for legislation that was beneficial to Pennsylvania and, as it happened, also favorable to their own interests. The use of a public relations firm might be an innovation, but bringing one's case to the general public is a legitimate and time-honored practice. The application of pressure on lawmakers and executive officials is, furthermore, a necessary and desirable component of the democratic process. And just as the Pennsylvania legislature's passage of S. 615 was a legal act, so was the governor's veto. If one is to inquire into what motivates public officials to act as they do in the performance of their constitutional duties, then the campaign contributions of the truckers to the state legislators were just as suspect as was the railroads' supplying of information to the governor. And if it is suggested that Byoir organized public sentiment to give the governor the impression of "grass-roots" opinion unfavorable to the truckers, the answer is that the governor was an experienced politician and ought not to have been so easily deceived.

The Judges Decide—and Disagree

United States District Court Judge Thomas Clary was not impressed by the arguments presented by the railroads. Eight months after the close of the trial he handed down a 73-page opinion in favor of the truckers. He granted the truckers damages of approximately $200,000, which when trebled under the provision of the Sherman Act, came to about $600,000. He also required the railroads to pay the legal costs, an amount of $200,000, that the truckers had incurred in fighting the suit. Judge Clary's characterization of the Byoir operation was that it was a "campaign of vilification." He found the techniques to rouse public resentment against the truckers distasteful and, on some occasions, illegal. And he concluded that the intentions of the railroads were, indeed, economic: to render irreparable harm to the competitive position of the truckers. His summary was:

> The entire campaign and its objectives did not constitute a mere appeal to the legislators; nor was it a large scale lobbying campaign. True, one phase of the activities was of a legislative nature—but a rather new approach to legislation, to say the least. The other phase, and the more important one of the campaign, was one of vilification designed to destroy the good will of the long-haul trucking industry.

The employment of the antitrust laws in the case is of interest. Counsel for the truckers decided to sue under the Sherman and Clayton Acts, and the court based its decision on these statutes. Yet if there had been a "campaign of vilification" conducted against them, the truckers could only contend that its results had been to lose them "good will." For there was no evidence that the trucking industry had lost money or that individual firms had lost so many customers that they were forced into bankruptcy. They might claim that *if* the weight limit had been raised to 60,000 pounds then they would have been able to make more money than they were previously earning. But to say that money *not earned* because a particular law was on the statute books is the same thing as money *lost* is an arguable proposition and one not easily substantiated: you cannot "lose" something you have never had. At all events, the law of the case was founded on the loss of that intangible phantom, "good will." Why was this approach taken?

The answer is that the only other alternative would be to claim that the railroads, through Byoir, had been abusing their right of free speech. The constitutional guarantees of the First Amendment, it might have been argued, provide for liberty but they do not protect license. On this ground the truckers could have contended that Byoir's presentation of the anti-truck story was an altogether distorted one; that biased selection of facts amounted to a deliberate dissemination of half-truths. This was the case with the magazine articles it placed, and was particularly in evidence in the exploitation of the Maryland road test. Furthermore it was possible to claim that the use of nonrailroad organizations to make the railroad case could not have the status of free speech because the true "speaker" preferred to remain undercover and mask himself from public view. A voice from behind the scenes, it might be said, cannot legitimately claim the protection of the constitution.

But the lawyers for the truckers stuck to the antitrust laws, and with good reason. An "abuse" of free speech is very difficult to demonstrate to a court. Were this not the case, legislatures and other agencies in society would have a field day curbing the expressions of individuals with whom they did not agree or who damaged their sensibilities. Speech is only considered abusive, then, if the words are slanderous and if their written counterparts are libelous, or if the utterances will clearly serve to corrupt some portion of the population. Speech can be curtailed, in addition, if its exhortations lead to a "clear and present danger" that acts of violence will be immediately following. But the activities of Byoir came under none of these heads. No individual truck operators were libeled or slandered by name; and no mobs of angry Pennsylvanians were stirred to such a degree of wrath that they overturned trucks in the streets. The railroad campaign may not have been conducted according to a gentlemanly code, but there is nothing in the statute book that says that the game of politics must be played according to the rules of chivalry.

Counsel for the truckers, therefore, did not feel justified in claiming that the railroads had abused the right of free speech. But their pleas that the railroads had violated the antitrust laws were recognized by the district court. There was evidence, the judge said, that the railroads had conspired to restrain trade, that they purposefully sought to put the long-haul truckers out of business. In spite of the facts that the Pennsylvania legislature has every right to enact weight limitations for trucks traveling on public roads, and that the railroads have every right to support the passage and retention of such legislation, the court was convinced that the means used by Byoir and the ERPC transcended the limits of fair competition. A conspiracy to destroy one's competitors, the judge asserted, cannot be excused simply because the constitutional rights of petition and free speech are elements of that conspiracy.

The railroads appealed the decision. As so often happens, the case took three years to reach the United States Court of Appeals. But when it did, in December 1959, the three-judge tribunal voted 2–1 to uphold the judgment of the district court. The two-man majority, in a brief opinion, contented itself with echoing the sentiments of the judge in the lower court. However their dissenting colleague was not impressed with the truckers' argument that the political activities of the rairoads were in violation of the antitrust laws: his conclusion was

(1) that the Sherman Act was not intended by Congress to be applicable to governmental restraints by way of legislation whether or not induced by private activity and (2) that private activities such as those conducted by the Railroads and Byoir under the circumstances presented here cannot be deemed to constitute unreasonable restraints or monopoly under the Act.

This judge, at least, was not prepared to use an act of Congress intended to control economic activity as a means of stopping political activity. He did not necessarily approve of the political techniques used in the Pennsylvania affair, but he could find nothing in the law that forbade such behavior. "The methods employed by the public relations agencies of both the railroads and the truckers left much to be desired in respect to moral consciousness," he said. "It was a no-holds-barred fight by both sides." Heartened by this view, even though it was outvoted at the appeals level, the railroads carried their case to the Supreme Court of the United States.

Counsel for both railroads and the truckers were given the opportunity to argue their cases before the Supreme Court in December 1960. Each side, as is the custom, was allowed not only to submit written briefs but also to make an oral presentation lasting one hour. Garbed in morning coats, striped trousers, and winged collars, Mr. Philip Price approached the bar for the railroads, and his fellow Philadelphian, Mr. Harold Kohn, joined him for the truckers. The proceedings were not as formal as the dress and demeanor might suggest, for the nine Justices all had the right to interrupt counsels' arguments and to ask questions on matters of fact, law, or opinion. Indeed, it is frequently in these questions, and the answers given to them, that some illuminating sidelights of a case are brought to view.

It thus became apparent, for example, that the railroads had no intention of denying that they had used underhanded methods in their anti-truck campaign. At one point Justice Felix Frankfurter interrupted: "I happen to open to this article in *Harper's,* 'Our Roads Are Going to Pot.' Was there a disclosure in the publication that these represented the views of the railroads, rather than some disinterested expert?" To this Mr. Price answered: "No, it was not. . . . The District Court called it 'the big lie' technique. . . . Often materials were supplied to authors for the preparation of articles they wanted to write." Justice Hugo Black then joined in and referred to a newspaper editorial opposing S. 615 that appeared in a Pennsylvania paper but that had actually been written by the Byoir organization. "Was it shown that the railroads had anything to do with this editorial?" he asked Mr. Price. Counsel for the railroads again admitted that his clients remained behind the scenes. This prompted Chief Justice Earl Warren to inquire: "Was there any evidence that the railroads had paid for the editorials?" Here Mr. Price answered:

No, sir. . . . But a great majority of the newspaper and magazine articles presented in evidence were initiated by some activity on the part of Byoir. The writers were given an opportunity to examine statistics collected by Byoir and sometimes the articles were written by Byoir itself. The bulk of these articles were the result of Byoir's activity in publicizing the railroads' argument that the truckers were damaging the highways and were not paying their share of the costs.

In a similar vein the railroads' counsel was willing to admit that his clients had used existing organizations in order to put across the anti-truck message in a more persuasive way. Justice William Brennan interrupted to ask about the origins and financing of a newspaper advertisement that attacked the truckers:

JUSTICE BRENNAN: There appears to be an advertisement by the Pennsylvania Association of Township Supervisors. Was that organization inspired by Byoir?

MR. PRICE: Yes, sir. That was paid for by the railroads.

BRENNAN: But it nowhere appears, that fact doesn't appear.

PRICE: That is right. The Pennsylvania State Association of Township

Supervisors was an organization of supervisors in Pennsylvania which for a long time had been fighting increased weights in trucks because of the damage they did.

BRENNAN: It was an existing organization?

PRICE: Oh, yes. It is an association of the supervisors of the townships of Pennsylvania who had a direct interest in the cost of maintaining roads and the cost of maintaining bridges, and therefore for a number of years they had been opposed to increased truck weights and decreased truck fees.

BRENNAN: My question was whether the organization itself—its creation had been inspired by them.

PRICE: No, not at all, no, sir. That has been in existence for a long time. And if your Honors will turn back one page, you will see another advertisement—"You Can't Satisfy a Road Hog." That likewise was paid for by the railroads, but put out in the name of the township supervisors, which asked for the opportunity to publish that information.

The Justices then turned to hear the arguments of Mr. Kohn, the counsel for the truckers who had been successful in persuading the district and appeals courts to rule in favor of his clients. While Mr. Kohn repeated his charge that the railroads had violated the antitrust laws, he also emphasized that the public relations techniques employed by Byoir added to the gravity of the case. Justice Black wondered how far the truckers were alleging that the railroads had violated the right to free speech. He referred to the use of "third-party" organizations such as the Pennsylvania State Association of Township Supervisors and the "big lie" technique in placing magazine articles which were not attributed to the railroads. "Does it make any difference," Justice Black asked, "whether they do it openly or not?" Mr. Kohn replied:

I think that it is a very important element which cannot be divorced from this case. . . . You can have a pure legislative campaign, honestly and openly putting forth only truth to an appropriate legislative body. But as the findings of fact in this case made clear, you do not have such a legislative campaign in this case. You first of all, quite clearly, have a public relations campaign which was intended to injure us in every possible and conceivable way, whether or not there would be legislation.

In other words, the truckers were contending that the veto of S. 615 was not the only aim of the railroads. Had their campaign been solely political in character, then some First Amendment questions would be central to the case. But in this instance the railroads were seeking to put the truckers out of business, and that was an economic objective; the political activities were supplementary. Yet if this was the truckers' approach to the case, then Justice Frankfurter wanted to know why they were so anxious to show that the railroads had concealed their participation in the anti-truck campaign. Mr. Kohn seemed to be suggesting that had the railroads spoken in their own name, they would have diminished their chances of success. "Does that mean," Justice Frankfurter asked, "that the railroads are so discredited in the legislative eyes, that if they candidly did this, rather than Madison Avenue, that the problem wouldn't be as serious to you as this?" Mr. Kohn answered:

> As this Court said, I think, in the Hazel-Atlas Glass case, truth needs no disguise. Everybody is influenced by the source of the material. If you know that I have a frankly antagonistic competitive position, you weigh differently what I say than if it comes from an ostensible third party who has no motive whatsoever, no axe to grind. The first thing they ask any witness in any case is who he is, what is his bias, what is his motive. And the railroads themselves, I mean anybody would react that way. And time and again we see throughout all of the legislative patterns of Congress and elsewhere that it is important, in matters of this kind, where you have economic struggle, economic content, to reveal who was the source of the information.

And to this Justice Frankfurter was moved to inquire: "Do you reject the notion that the public relations counsel is part of our American way of life?" Mr. Kohn rejoined: "He is definitely a part of our way of life, but he must conduct himself under the same rules as the rest of us."

The Supreme Court then retired to make its decision. On February 20, 1961, it announced its unanimous judgment: the verdict of the two lower courts was overturned and the case was decided for the railroads.

Justice Hugo Black, speaking for himself and his eight colleagues, stated that the Sherman Act could not be applied to the struggles of the political arena. Were the antitrust laws to be extended to this sphere, then the very workings of democracy itself would be impaired:

> Such a holding would substantially impair the power of government to take actions through its legislature and executive. . . . In a representative democracy such as this, these branches of government act on behalf of the people and, to a very large extent, the whole concept of representation depends upon the ability of the people to make their wishes known to their representatives. To hold that the government retains the power to act in this representative capacity and yet hold, at the same time, that the people cannot freely inform the government of their wishes would impute to the Sherman Act a purpose to regulate, not business activity, but political activity. . . .
>
> Secondly, and of at least equal significance, such a construction of the Sherman Act would raise important constitutional questions. The right to petition is one of the freedoms protected by the Bill of Rights, and we cannot, of course, lightly impute to Congress an intent to invade these freedoms. Indeed, such an imputation would be particularly unjustified in this case. . . .

The fact that the intention of the railroads was to keep on the books legislation that would help them and harm the truckers is, Justice Black went on, no ground for a lawsuit. There is no requirement that lobbying or public relations campaigns must have altruistic motives or be in the general interest. "It is neither unusual nor illegal for people to seek action on laws in the hope that they may bring about an advantage to themselves and a disadvantage to their competitors . . . ," he wrote. "Indeed it is quite probably people with just such a hope of personal advantage who provide much of the information upon which governments must act." The Supreme Court noted that both parties to this contest were well supplied with money, talent, and energy. It did not overlook the fact that if Byoir used nonrailroad groups in his efforts, Charnay was quite prepared to set up a "Pennsylvania Motor Safety League" for the truckers. While the trucking firms may have felt unfairly constricted by a 45,000-pound weight limit, the railroads had economic problems that admitted of no easy solution. Whereas Judge Clary, at the District Court level, had painted a picture of truckers as underdogs suffering from unfair attack by a powerful competitor, Justice Black wished to restore the picture to what he considered was its proper perspective:

> We have restored what appears to be the true nature of the case—a "no-holds-barred fight" between two industries both of which are seeking control of a profitable source of income. Inherent in such fights, which are commonplace in the halls of legislative bodies, is the possibility, and in many instances even the probability, that one group or the other will get hurt by the arguments that are made. In this particular instance, each group appears to have utilized all the political powers it could muster in an attempt to bring about the passage of laws that would help it or injure the other. But the contest itself appears to have been conducted along lines normally accepted in our political system, except to the extent that each group has deliberately deceived the public and public officials.

In a final note, Justice Black took his place in the grandstand and indicated that he was rather enjoying the contest before him: "Since the commencement of this litigation, a new bill increasing truck weight limits has passed the Pennsylvania Legislature and has become law by virtue of the Governor's approval. Thus, the fight goes on."

Some Unanswered Questions

The fight goes on, not only between the truckers and the railroads, but between the many thousands of competing groups that dot the American political scene. The Pennsylvania episode, however, highlights a number of questions that are bound to recur again and again in the political process. Some of these are worth raising, however briefly, for pressure politics provide one of the most controversial arenas in the entire study of government.

(1) *Public Relations and the Political Process* /   The railroads found it desirable to retain Byoir; the truckers, in turn, called on Charnay. The chief question has to do with what a professional public relations expert can accomplish for his clients in a political campaign. It may readily be granted that the officials of both the ERPC and the PMTA were not politicians. Their main tasks normally involved coordinating information on the economic problems of their respective industries. While they had some experience in lobbying and the direct contact with legislators, they felt inadequate to the job of rousing widespread sentiment to their respective causes. It is therefore understandable that they approached firms that would bring their messages to the general public.

The prime difficulty here is that the world of public relations is largely a world of appearances. Byoir was retained to work up anti-truck feelings among the residents of Pennsylvania. Did the firm accomplish this objective? It is impossible to say. There are no precampaign and subsequent postcampaign public opinion surveys to tell us whether there was a discernible shift in attitudes toward trucks on the part of Pennsylvanians over the years. Consequently it was Byoir's job to persuade its clients—the railroads—that the public *was* being persuaded to the anti-truck views. The organization did this by showing the ERPC officials all the anti-truck articles the firm had placed in magazines. The presumption, and it could only be a presumption, was that these articles reached many people and that they caused these people to respond negatively to trucks. The firm also pointed to the anti-truck resolutions it had got various organizations to pass. The presumption, and again it could only be a presumption, was that the members of these groups throughout the state then spread the anti-truck message to their friends and neighbors in local communities. Indeed in the world of public relations the suspicion arises that so long as the client who pays the bills *believes* that his message is reaching and persuading the public, it does not really matter whether the public is actually reached or persuaded at all. For example, although there were specific and organized letter-writing campaigns by those who were affected directly, we have no way of knowing whether or not a ferment was created in the minds of the millions of citizens of the state who were supposed to be persuaded by the anti-truck campaign. This is not to say that public relations is a gigantic fraud. But it does suggest that the reports made to clients may exaggerate the extent of the accomplishments made by the presumed experts in this field.

Indeed, the tangible results were in the field of lobbying. One particular

instance was the ability of the truckers, through the PMTA, to secure legislative majorities for S. 615. Here the chief means seems to have been
generous campaign contributions. Another instance was the lobbying of
Governor Fine by the railroads, not so much through the open hearing as
by getting an abbreviated and one-sided version of the Maryland road test
report to him. The Byoir organization demonstrated its adeptness at working behind the scenes, and this is what appears to have ultimately paid off.
If this is so, then the question arises as to whether the expertise of public
relations men lies more in old-style contacts with officials than it does with
the new-style "engineering of consent" campaign at the grass roots of the
community.

(2) *Free Speech and the Right of Petition* / The First Amendment
to the Constitution was originally intended to protect the rights of individual citizens. If free speech was to be guaranteed, then the speaker was
thought of as a citizen who might wish to climb up on a soapbox or a platform and express his views to his neighbors. And the right of petition would
similarly apply to any group of citizens who either in person or through
representatives might wish to lay demands before their lawmakers. Free
speech implied that the speaker was visible and that he could be readily
identified. Petition implied that the interested parties would make themselves known and that they would not cavil at asking for legislation that
would frankly benefit their own interests.

The Pennsylvania case indicates that things are no longer so simple. It is
now necessary to ask whether a party that wishes to enjoy the rights of free
speech and petition may work through other organizations. The railroads
did not disclose to the public that the messages emanating from such groups
as the Grange and the Association of Township Supervisors were actually
prepared by railroad experts and paid for by the railroad association. There
is no law saying that the "real source" of messages addressed to the public
must be identified, and it is not clear that there should be such a law at all.
For if the merits of an argument are sound, then the public ought to consider that argument on its merits. To require the labeling of sources would
lead the public to turn its attention away from the merits of the argument
and to decide on the basis of its predisposition towards the sponsoring
group. For example, if an advertisement advocating the fluoridation of a
city water supply is required to state that it was paid for by the American
Legion, then readers will make up their minds on the basis of whether or not
they like the Legion rather than on the merits of fluoridation as a policy.

The question of disclosure has another side to it. The rank and file of
the Grange and the Association of Township Supervisors apparently were
not told that the officials of their organizations were getting help from Byoir
in promoting the anti-truck viewpoint. The Pennsylvania Railroad gave

$300,000 to the Eastern Railroad Presidents Conference to help pay Byoir's expenses, but the stockholders of the Pennsylvania Railroad were not told that their money was used in this way. It may be presumed that most of the people who belonged to the Grange or the Association of Township Supervisors or who owned Pennsylvania Railroad stock were not particularly friendly to the truckers to begin with. Nevertheless they were not asked for their explicit consent when their names or their money were used to aid the Byoir campaign. The question, then, is whether someone can speak "for" individuals without having received their specific permission to do so.

The Byoir operation was, according to the district court judge, a "campaign of vilification" directed against the truckers. Yet no matter how ungentlemanly it might have been, it was clear to the lawyers on both sides that there was not such a flagrant abuse of free speech that activities such as Byoir's ought to be prevented by some agency of the government. The whole doctrine of "prior censorship"—of establishing a government bureau that must give its approval to a political utterance before it can be released to the public—is repugnant to American principles of constitutional law. Nor have appeals to the courts for such preventive action proved effective, even if they are masked as suits under the antitrust laws. As matters now stand the right to free speech is virtually an absolute one when it is exercised in connection with an appeal to the legislature. Indeed, the Supeme Court even acknowledged that such campaigns would very frequently be negative in character, consisting more of tearing down one's opponent rather than building up one's own side. It would seem that in this area there can be no middle ground: the choice is between a free market in political expression on the one hand, and some form of government censorship on the other.

One more question has to do with the constitutional protections for free speech. The "members" of the Eastern Railroad Presidents Conference were, in fact, not individuals. They were approximately twenty-five *corporations* in the railroad industry. Does a *railroad* have the right of free speech and the right to petition? Under the Fourteenth Amendment a corporation is defined as a "person," but this is usually construed as meaning that it can make contracts and sue and be sued. A corporation cannot vote nor can it contribute to election campaigns. In short, a corporation may be an "economic person," but it is not at all clear whether it is a "political person." The men who sat on the ERPC committees and who planned its policies were not there as individuals. They filled these positions in their roles as salaried executives representing the railroads who employed them. In this sense, again, the ERPC is different from associations like the American Legion or the Farmers' Union which have individual *citizens* as their members. It may be argued that a railroad corporation is owned by stockholders and that the ERPC represents the interests of these stockholders in the political process. But this claim is not as persuasive as it might at first seem. For one thing, stockholders participate in the policy-making of a corporation in proportion to the number of shares they own: one share, one vote. In most other associations the principle is one vote per member. In addition, the important stockholders in a corporation are not widows and orphans, but rather investing institutions. Thus the large blocks of stock (and the significant voting power) will be held by insurance companies, banks, and investment houses. Furthermore there are no mechanisms, other than the annual cut-and-dried stockholders' meetings, where owners of shares have a chance to consent to the political activities carried out by a corporation. Votes are not taken on matters such as these, however, and the fact that they are going on at all is seldom even disclosed.

Nevertheless a railroad corporation can be helped or harmed by acts of legislation just as a real person can. For this reason corporations have always felt it legitimate to protect their interest through political means. In a very real sense lobbying and public relations are simply an extension of the business of selling goods and making profits. At the same time, however, the question of whether a railroad has the right of free speech remains unanswered.

(3) *Power Over the Minds of Men* /   One of the classical philosophical problems is that of "freedom of the will." How far, it has been asked since time immemorial, is man free to act as he pleases? We are all aware of the limitations placed on human freedom. On the one hand the forces of culture, of national heritage, of social environment throw up barriers that limit the behavior of individuals. On the other, centers of power and authority make rules that limit personal freedom. Various theorists, notably Jean-Jacques Rousseau and Alexis de Tocqueville, have distinguished between overt and covert sanctions. The former type of limitations are open and aboveboard; they are known to the individual and they frequently seem to him not a little oppressive. In this category might fall imprisonment by the state or the threat of imprisonment, dismissal by an employer or the threat of dismissal, social ostracism by one's neighbors or the threat of such ostracism. These overt limitations on freedom are usually easy enough to recognize and there is no difficulty in labeling many of them as tyrannical. But covert sanctions, on the other hand, are hard to detect. All of us are subject to forces that we neither perceive nor understand, and yet limit our freedom of action. Some of these forces are buried deep in our unconscious, others are the work of powerful agencies that have set out deliberately to shape our minds. Large numbers of people can believe that they are free, can think that they are at liberty to do whatever they want to do, can go through life never desiring to choose from other than the

alternatives open to them. Yet it is altogether possible to suggest that such people, despite their vociferous protestations that they are free men, are actually limited in their action by powers outside themselves.

How does such speculation on "freedom of the will" apply to politics? A few references to the railroad-truck case should make this clear. Take, first of all, the freedom of the members of the Pennsylvania state legislature. A majority of these lawmakers voted for the passage of S. 615, which was what the truckers wanted them to do. It may be assumed that many of them would have favored the bill even if the truckers had not conducted their lobbying campaign. And there would, in addition, have been some members of the legislature who were indifferent to the fate of the bill and therefore willing to be persuaded by one side or another. However, it is highly probable that there were also some who were predisposed to oppose S. 615 but who voted for it anyway because they wanted to continue receiving financial help from the truckers in their constituency. This last group, in particular, could be said to have acted contrary to the way it would have acted had it been able to exercise its free will. In one way or another the truckers secured the power to create a legislative majority for their bill. If they placed restraints on the freedom of action of some lawmakers, they were overt restraints. Many of the men who voted for S. 615 knew that they were doing so to repay a campaign debt or in anticipation of future contributions. They may not have liked voting for a bill that was personally distasteful to them, but they consciously made a bargain to limit their freedom in return for a payment.

The story is not nearly so simple in the case of Governor Fine. He vetoed S. 615, which was what the railroads wanted him to do. Was this act of his an act of his own free will? It might be said that it was if he felt that the consequences of the bill would do further damage to the highways of Pennsylvania. Or it might be said that it was if he felt, as an elected officeholder, that he was so representing the views of the ordinary citizens of Pennsylvania. But one would have to add that Governor Fine would have been a free agent only if it could be shown that he had reliable knowledge about truck damage to roads or about the true state of public sentiment—only, that is, if he had all the pertinent facts germane to his decision. There is good reason to believe that his knowledge was both incomplete and distorted. That is, the information that came to him was information that the Byoir organization had screened, shaped, and selected. If the governor supposed that trucks were the chief culprits in the matter of highway damage, that view of his may have stemmed from his reading a report on the Maryland road test. But the report he read was an abbreviated version—abbreviated by Byoir so as to put the blame squarely on the truckers. If the governor supposed that the citizens of Pennsylvania wanted him to veto S. 615, that view of his may have come from listening to the anti-truck opinions voiced at the public hearing—opinions organized and stage-managed by Byoir. Or if he felt that a groundswell of anti-truck sentiment was abroad in the state, this belief of his may have been engendered by the vigorous activities of groups like the Grange and the Pennsylvania State Association of Township Supervisors—activities spurred on by Byoir. Or, finally, if he sensed that criticism of trucks was at a high pitch at that particular time, he may have picked up this idea by reading anti-truck articles in the *Reader's Digest* or the *Saturday Evening Post*—articles inspired and placed by Byoir. In short, there is some ground for suggesting that the governor was not wholly a free agent when he vetoed the bill. The Byoir organization was able to create covert limitations to his freedom of action, was able to shape his perception of reality so that he saw things as the railroads wished him to see them. This is not to say that Governor Fine, a seasoned politician, was an utter dupe. But it must be remembered that he was a layman and had to rely on technical advisers for information, that he spent his time in the Capitol at Harrisburg and had to rely on secondary sources for his impression of public sentiment. What can certainly be said is that those who had access to the governor's eyes and ears were bound to be instrumental in helping him to make up his mind. In this endeavor Byoir and the railroads could legitimately claim success.

Furthermore, it must be asked whether the public is prey to the kind of forces that beset the governor. Public relations men claim that they can form opinions, shape attitudes, and generally mold the sentiments of the man-in-the-street. (Byoir's magazine department, it will be recalled, spoke of the "defenseless public.") They also claim that, given the resources, they can reach the ordinary citizen and motivate him to think and act in ways he would not have considered had he been left to his own devices. The truckers paid out more than $200,000 to Charnay for this purpose and the railroads gave Byoir more than four times that amount. This raises the question of what public relations campaigns are able to accomplish. First of all, it should be noted that there are many competitors for the attention of the average man. His eyes and ears, let alone his mind, are beleaguered with the demands of advertisers, politicians, friends, neighbors, and family. In order to get his attention, any message must have an extremely striking and personal appeal to him. It is open to question, for example, whether reading half-a-dozen magazine articles are sufficient to stir his mind. It must be remembered that most people do not read that many magazines regularly, and almost no one reads all the articles in any magazine anyway. Second, it is not easy to change people's minds. The technique of public relations is to take the latent predispositions of individuals and to direct them into particular channels. That is, if you wish to defeat a government health insurance program, you take the latent predisposition against "socialism" that exists in the minds of most Americans and channel it into opposition to "socialized medicine." It is true that few people are latently predisposed in favor of railroads, yet Byoir was able to play on the widespread mistrust of large trucks. Therefore the campaign stressed those things—accidents, pot-holes, road-hogging—that would strike home personally to the average automobile driver and taxpayer. But it is one thing to arouse latent anti-truck sentiment; it is quite another to play on that feeling so that individuals will become so aroused that they will go out and fight a bill like S. 615. Everyone has his own share of worries, but for most people, a dislike of trucks comes very far down on their list of grievances. Once again, public apathy presents itself as an obstacle that is tremendously difficult to overcome. People suffer not so much from indifference as from inertia; the average citizen is not easily stirred into action. It may be noted that despite Byoir's extensive and expensive campaign there was no indication that ordinary Pennsylvanians became so worked up against trucks that they deluged their lawmakers with letters or telegrams expressing anti-truck opinions.

Before concluding that there is a need to protect the public from biased and one-sided public relations campaigns, it should be recalled that the public already possesses its own built-in defenses: its inpenetrability, its unwillingness to change its mind, and its disinclination to become involved in other people's problems. A far more important question has to do with the power of well-organized and well-financed groups such as the railroads and the truckers. For if public policy is to be the end result of the conflicts and compromises among powerful groups with direct interests in legislation, it remains to ask whether policies that are battled out in this way promote that objective that Americans so frequently exalt: the public interest.

(4) *Pressure Groups and American Government* /

The legislature referees the group struggle, ratifies the victories of the successful coalitions, and records the terms of the surrenders, compromises, and conquests in the form of statutes. Every statute tends to represent compromise because the process of accommodating conflicts of group interests is one of deliberation and consent. The legislative vote on any issue tends to represent the composition of strength, i.e., the balance of power, among the contending groups at the moment of voting. What may be called public policy is the equilibrium reached in this struggle at any given moment, and it represents a balance which the contending factions of groups constantly strive to weight in their favor.

With these unequivocal words, Professor Earl Latham of Amherst College has laid the groundwork for a theory of American politics based on the interplay of pressure groups. While Latham goes on to say that "the legislature does not play the inert part of cash register, ringing up the additions and withdrawals of strength," he does suggest that the making of public policy may best be understood by focusing attention on the activities of groups pursuing their political interests.

This has been the emphasis in this case study. Public policy on matters of freight transportation, road construction, and highway safety appears to have been decided on the basis of the relative power of groups operating in the state of Pennsylvania. The two major participants, the truckers and the railroads, not only drew on their own human and financial resources but struck up alliances with other organizations. At various stages in the contest legislators, administrators, judges, and the general public were all subjected to the persuasive tactics of the contending parties. The lawmakers were offered campaign contributions, and the governor was tendered technical information on a specialized subject. But in both cases the intention was the same: to help individuals make up their minds. The judges were regaled with elaborate briefs and oral arguments, and the general public was showered with articles and advertisements. And in these instances, too, the purpose was to influence the thinking of those who participated in the policy-making process. The truckers were the victors at the legislative stage, but they lost an important round with the governor's veto. The railroads tasted the final fruits of conquest when they reached the highest court, but that victory was a formality as a new governor had signed the truckers' bill into law.

Who, then, succeeded in winning over the public? The railroads clearly made the most strenuous efforts to sway the public, but in the final analysis there is no way of knowing how far the sentiments of the average citizen were aroused or changed.

Any group theory is bound to be a simplification of reality. Individuals like Governor John Fine and Justice Hugo Black are personalities in their own right, and as public office-holders they have power that they exercise according to their own predispositions. Groups may influence most office-holders some of the time and a few office-holders all of the time, but they cannot and do not determine the actions of all office-holders all of the time.

And just as any theory must admit of exceptions, so must it be understood that a single case study cannot be representative of a diversified political process. The activities of pressure groups take many forms and not all the varieties can be observed in a particular episode. Several brief warnings are therefore in order. The Eastern Railroad Presidents Conference and the Pennsylvania Motor Truck Association, for example, are business groups and in this they represent only part of the political spectrum. American legislation is by no means wholly economic in its content and consequences, and a wide variety of noneconomic groups promote their interests in the fifty-one capitals of the nation. Racial groups like the National Association for the Advancement of Colored People and the Congress on Racial Equality, veterans' groups like the American Legion and the Veterans of Foreign Wars, religious groups like the National Catholic Welfare Conference and the National Council of Churches of Christ in America, national groups like the Japanese American Citizens League and moralistic groups like the Woman's Christian Temperance Union—each of these will have its own style of operations, its own source of power, and its own conception of the role of government. To generalize about group activities from the experience of the truckers and railroads in Pennsylvania would be a mistake. Economic motives constitute but one segment of the varied forces at work in the group arena.

There are differences, too, between pressure politics as they operate at the national and state levels. The Senate and House of Representatives of the United States are, for obvious reasons, less susceptible to group influence than are those chambers in a single state. And the American President will behave differently in the face of group pressure than will a chief executive at the state level. Furthermore, the use of professional public relations assistance is less common than a study of Byoir's campaign in Pennsylvania might suggest. The flamboyant, not to say expensive, method used by the railroads is not suited to all political campaigns; and at this point in our history it must be admitted that such techniques tend to be the exception rather than the rule. There are persuasive indications that employing public relations firms will become a more widespread practice in the years to come. But only the future will tell if the growth of "engineered consent" will actually continue. Finally, information on pressure group activities is not usually so readily available as it has been for the trucker-railroad contest. The facts and figures were made public in this instance because one of the parties took the whole affair into the courts and subsequently both sides had the other's records subpoenaed for the trial. But only on a rare occasion such as this, or when a legislative committee conducts an investigation into lobbying activities, can the public learn what has been going on behind the scenes.

While one case study will never be typical in all respects, in major outlines the Pennsylvania episode describes how public policy is made and how private groups interact with the official agencies of government. And as long as America is characterized by competing groups with conflicting interests, American politics will be the arena where power is organized and prizes are sought. But as to which methods of persuasion are to be deemed legitimate and whether the whole conception of pressure politics is salutary in its consequences—these are questions that each student of the subject must answer for himself.

Sources

MOST of the information in the case study was obtained from the trial testimony and the exhibits introduced in the case of *Noerr Motor Freight vs. Eastern Railroad Presidents Conference*. The trial transcript runs to about 17,000 pages and almost 900 exhibits were introduced by the railroads and the truckers.

Additional facts were taken from Judge Thomas J. Clary's lengthy judgment at the district court level, which is to be found in *Federal Supplement*, Vol. 155, at pp. 768–841. The opinions quoted from the court of appeals are in *Federal Reporter*, Vol. 273 (Second Series), at pp. 218–31. Justice Hugo Black's opinion, representing his own views and those of his eight colleagues on the Supreme Court, is in *The Supreme Court Reporter*, Vol. 81, at pp. 523–33. Quotations from the oral argument before the Supreme Court were secured from *The United States Law Week,* Vol. 29, at pp. 3,185–87.

The debates on S. 615 in the Pennsylvania state Senate and House of Representatives are transcribed in the *Legislative Journal* for the 1951 session, at pp. 3,759–69, 4,639–69.

Background material on the personalities figuring in the case can be found in Robert Bendiner, "The 'Engineering of Consent'—A Case Study," *Reporter,* August 11, 1955, pp. 14–23. An instructive portrait of a leading figure in the case is contained in Spencer Klaw, "Carl Byoir: Opinion Engineering in the Big Time," *Reporter,* June 10, 1952.